THE DIARIES OF
SARAH HURST

1759-1762

THE DIARIES OF SARAH HURST

1759-1762

LIFE AND LOVE IN 18th CENTURY HORSHAM

Transcribed by Barbara Hurst

Edited by Susan C. Djabri

AMBERLEY

First published 2003 by Horsham Museum Society
Copyright © in this edition 2009
Amberley Publishing

Amberley Publishing
Cirencester Road, Chalford, Stroud, Gloucestershire, GL6 8PE
www.amberley-publishing.com

Sarah Hurst's diaries are held by Horsham Museum
(HM MSS Cat. Nos. 3542-5)

The transcription by Barbara Hurst on which this edition is based is also held by Horsham
Museum (HM MSS Cat. No. 3541) and is published here with the Museum's permission

Diary text copyright © Horsham Museum 2009
Editing and editorial matter copyright © Susan C. Djabri 2009

ISBN 978-1-84868-353-2

A CIP Catalogue record for this book is available from the British Library

Typesetting and origination by Amberley Publishing
Printed in Great Britain

Preface and Acknowledgements

It is entirely due to the late Miss Barbara Hurst, a direct descendant of Sarah's brother, Robert Hurst, that we have the chance to read Sarah's diaries now. We can hardly overestimate our debt to her. She spent years transcribing the crabbed and sometimes faded handwriting in the tiny pocketbooks in which the diaries were written, which are in many places very difficult to decipher. It is a mark of her achievement that so few words were marked as illegible or questionable in the text she has given to us. As a former President of Horsham Museum Society, she most generously gave the diaries and a copy of the transcript to the Museum, shortly before her death in January 1999. She wanted the diaries to remain in Horsham, as they are such an important part of the history of the town. She also wanted Sarah's story to be told, and the diaries recognised as the important historical document that they are.

I am personally indebted to other members of the Hurst family for a great deal of help in bringing Sarah's diaries to publication. Sir Jeremy and Lady Morse generously arranged for the text to be put on to computer by Mrs. Caroline Dudley. Lady Morse and her nephew, Robert Mills, allowed me to include the letters written by Sarah towards the end of her life, and gave me access to Sarah's account books for her last ten years at Causeway House in Horsham. Lady Morse also made detailed notes and transcripts of the Hurst papers owned by her family, which she has most kindly allowed me to use. The bulk of these papers, which contain many documents of great significance in the history of Horsham, have now been lodged in the West Sussex Record Office, and will be made available to the general public as the Hurst-Mills MSS. Miss Barbara Hurst had already given other papers, relating to properties in Rusper and Horsham, and the life of her great-grandfather, Robert Henry Hurst junior, to the West Sussex Record Office, so now the Hurst family papers relating to their Sussex estates are reunited in one repository. The Rev. Antony Hurst kindly allowed me to photograph the silhouettes of Sarah Hurst and Henry Smith for the original edition, and has been another constant source of assistance and encouragement. In February 2009 he loaned the silhouettes to Horsham Museum, where they will feature in an exhibition on Sarah's life and then be put on permanent public display in the house that was Sarah's last home.

I have also received much help from other people in studying the period and writing the notes which accompany the text. Sheila O'Connell,

Assistant Keeper of the Department of Prints and Drawings at the British Museum, and her colleagues, Marjorie Caygill and Christopher Date, have made expert comments on the question of Sarah's visit to the British Museum, Dr. Annabelle Hughes has been a constant source of help on a wide variety of questions; Moira Bonnington, Frank Chasemore, A. J. Cragg, John Caffyn, Mrs. Jane Hurst, Miranda O'Connell, Alan Siney, and Claire Wickens, all gave me information from their own research which has illuminated various points at issue. I would also like to thank Alan Siney for redrawing the map of Horsham as Sarah would have known it. Finally, I am also most grateful to Jeremy Knight, Curator of Horsham Museum, for all his help and constructive criticism, and to the committee of Horsham Museum Society for their support in publishing the original edition, especially to John Baugh, Hon. Treasurer, who was also of great assistance with detailed checking.

Following the publication of the original edition of the diaries by Horsham Museum Society in 2003, John Farrant found Sarah's poem about the Sussex militia and most kindly sent me a transcript of that, together with further information about Francis Grose and some of the books that Sarah read. Mary Day kindly corrected some inaccuracies about Dorking history and topography. A chance discovery of the will of Mrs. Bridger has led to a different identification of her husband from that in the original edition, and more information about the Tudor/Nelthorpe family became available in a new publication on the history of Sedgwick Park. In her post-graduate research, Elizabeth Edwards came across the Chancery cases fought by Sir Charles Eversfield, and these records cast a revealing light on his character and personality. I have had the opportunity to do further research into the books and magazines that Sarah read; Google Books now gives direct online access to some of these publications.

I am now most grateful to Alan Sutton, of Amberley Publishing, for undertaking the publication of this new revised edition, which it is hoped will bring Sarah to the attention of a wider public, in this 250th anniversary year of the first of her diaries. This edition has new illustrations, expanded footnotes and an index that now includes authors, plays and publications, as well as the people and places that Sarah mentioned in her diaries and letters.

Susan C. Djabri

How the diaries were written and edited

The diaries were written in a series of printed almanacs, called *The Ladies' Complete Pocket-book*, published by John Newbery, a well-known bookseller of the time, of St. Paul's Churchyard. The pages on which Sarah wrote measure 3 inches by 5 inches (or about 8 cm by 13 cm). The pocket-books were bound in soft brown leather, in what was later called a Yapp binding, with a flap to cover the book and protect it if taken outside. They are the equivalent of today's Filofax, in that they contained useful printed information to help women organise their lives, as well as empty pages to be used as an appointments calendar, a notebook and an account book.

The four pocket-books used by Sarah were all basically the same, with some minor variations. In the opening pages, they all contained *"an explanation of the use of this necessary Pocket Companion"*, an *"Index to the year"*, giving anniversaries, feast days and saints' days, and a *"Chronicle of Remarkable Events"*, relating to the previous year, but additional items varied. The 1759 pocket-book contained an illustration of a lady in the dress of 1758, and a poem called *The Ladies' Advocate*, written by "*a Gentleman*". In 1760, there was a poem called *"Advice for the year 1760"* (quoted in the *Introduction*) and *"an explanation of the use of Stocks, for the use of Ladies who may have occasion, or are desirous of understanding the prices of stocks"*. (Sarah certainly would have been interested in this subject, but this table did not reappear in the following years). The 1761 pocket-book had a *"Marketing Table"* giving the price of beef, mutton, veal, lamb and pork, per lb. or stone (up to 4 stone). In 1762, there was a table to help cast up expenses, or wages, by the day, week, month or year, and another poem, *"To the Ladies"*. At the back, the pocket-books contained further information, such as *"some useful receipts"* (recipes) or *"ideas for suppers"*.

The diary pages were pre-printed with the days of the week down the left-hand margin of two facing pages. The date of the month was generally only given on the first day (Monday) and last (Sunday), though there were variations in the way the date was written in the different pocket-books. The left-hand page was divided into two columns, one for appointments and the other for *"memorandums or observations"*. The right-hand page was intended for accounts, as there were columns for monies received and monies paid. Sarah took no notice of these restrictions; she tried to compress each day's diary entry into the two main sections on the first page, but it usually spread on to the second page also. Sometimes she wrote in the separate sections; sometimes she wrote right across the page. Occasionally the entry for the day did not conform exactly to the space allotted for it, and the text continued into the next space. In some cases, Sarah ran out of space at the bottom of the page and there are words missing.

In her transcription, Miss Hurst reproduced as far as possible the arrangement of the page as Sarah wrote it, but in editing the diaries, I have related the text as far as possible to the day to which it refers, though in some cases an especially long entry will be spread over two or three days, as it appears in the diary. I have given the day of the week and month in full throughout, for ease of reference. Sarah wrote rather breathlessly, with very few full stops or capital letters to mark the beginning of sentences - punctuation has therefore been added where necessary to make the text easier to read. Abbreviations such as *"Cn Smith"* or *"C S"*, referring to Henry, have been silently expanded to *"Captain Smith"*. In respect of the many references to *"Dr Smith"*, it was necessary to differentiate between *"dear Smith"* and Doctor Smith, who is also frequently mentioned. Otherwise, spelling and capitalisation are generally left as written in order to convey the flavour of the original diary. Round brackets are given when used by the author; but other uncertainties, editorial additions or suggestions are in square brackets, and italics, so that they are easily distinguishable from the original text. The names of poems, plays, books and journals mentioned by Sarah have been put into italics, and the names of inns or ships have also been treated in the same way.

Some references to particular sources are given in the footnotes, but standard works of reference have not been specifically quoted. Information from parish records relating to individuals has not been detailed either, in order to avoid tiresome repetition. A short bibliography of the main sources of background information used for the footnotes has been added below.

Select Bibliography

Albery, William, *A Millennium of Facts in the History of Horsham and Sussex 947-1947*, Horsham Museum Society, 1947.

Albery, William, *A Parliamentary History of Horsham 1295-1885*, Longmans Green, 1927.

André, J. Lewis, article on Slinfold in *Sussex Archaeological Collections*, Vol. XL.

Brent, Colin, *Georgian Lewes 1714-1830*, Colin Brent Books, 1993.

Caffyn, John, *Sussex Schools in the 18th Century*, Sussex Record Society, Vol. 81, 1998.

Caygill, Marjorie, *The Story of the British Museum*, British Museum Press, 2nd edition, 1992.

Chatwin, Diana, *Slinfold Street*, The Slinfold Society, 2000.

Coomber, G.H.W. *Bygone Corn Mills in the Horsham Area*, Horsham Museum Society, 1996.

Corbett, Julian S., *The Seven Years' War*, first published in 1907, republished by The Folio Society, 2001.

Djabri, S.C., Knight, J. and Hughes, A.F., *The Shelleys of Field Place*, Horsham Museum Society, 2000.

Djabri, S.C. and Knight. J., *The Letters of Bysshe and Timothy Shelley*, Horsham Museum Society, 2000.

Farrant, John (edited), *Sussex Depicted*, Sussex Record Society, Vol. 85, 2001.

Foster, Joseph, *Alumni Oxonienses 1715-1886*, Archive CD Books.

Ham, Joan, *Storrington in Georgian and Victorian Times*, privately published, 1991.

Hughes, Dr. Annabelle F., *The King's Head* (1998) and *Chesworth*, Horsham Museum Society, 1998.

Hurst, Dorothea, *Horsham; Its History and Antiquities*, first published anonymously in 1868, second edition, 1889.

Kingsley, David, *Printed Maps of Sussex 1575-1900*, Sussex Record Society, Vol. 72, 1982.

Knight, Jeremy, *Horsham's History*, Vol. I, Horsham District Council, 2006.

Jackson, A.A. (edited), *Dorking, a Surrey Market Town through twenty centuries*, Dorking Local History Group, 1991.

Pottle, Frederick A.(edited), *Boswell's London Journal 1762-1763*, Folio Society, 1985.

Robinson, John Martin, *Arundel Castle*, Phillimore, 1994.

Slyfield, Brian and Turner, Tony, *The Story of Sedgwick*, privately published, 2006.

Steer, F.W.(edited), *The members of James Spershott, The Chichester Papers*, No. 30, Chichester City Council, 1962.

Trail, R.R. and Steer, F.W., *Dr. John Bayly of Chichester, The Chichester Papers*, No. 34, Chichester City Council, 1963.

Willson, A.N., *A History of Collyer's School 1532-1964*, Edward Arnold, 1965.

Land Tax records that have been used and frequently quoted are those of the Borough of Horsham and North Heath in 1758 (HM MSS Cat. No. 2542-2543), and in 1763 (HM MSS Cat. No. 2547-9). References to Land Tax records elsewhere, such as Goring and Eastbourne, have been taken from the 1785 Land Tax records for Sussex published by the Sussex Record Society as Vol. 77, *The East Sussex Land Tax 1785*, edited by Roger Davey, 1991, and Volume 82, *The West Sussex Land Tax 1785*, edited by Alan Readman, Lionel Falkner, Rosie Ritchie and Peter Wilkinson, 2000.

Abbreviations used in the footnotes

ESRO – East Sussex Record Office
HM or HORSM – Horsham Museum
HMS – Horsham Museum Society
PRO – Public Record Office
SAC – Sussex Archaeological Collections
SNQ – Sussex Notes and Queries
SRS – Sussex Record Society
TNA - The National Archives
WSRO – West Sussex Record Office

Table of contents

Notes on the illustrations and maps

The portraits of Sarah Hurst and Henry Smith are reproduced by kind permission of the Rev. Antony Hurst, and they and the diary were photographed especially for this book. The map of Horsham as it was when Sarah was living there was specially redrawn by Alan Siney, from the Enclosure Map of 1813 (HM MSS Cat. No. 4574). This is the earliest known map to give a detailed layout of the central part of the town. The map of Sussex by Richard Budgen, first published in 1723, was the first large-scale map of the county, based on his original surveys. It remained in use for the next thirty years.

The only known painting of Horsham in the 1760s is "A View of a Bridge near Horsham", a watercolour by George Robertson (1742-1788), purchased in 2006 by Horsham Museum, with the help of a generous grant from the National Art Collections Fund and a donation from Horsham Museum Society. It shows the turnpike road to London crossing the Red River near Warnham Mill, with the floodgates of the mill in the background. (Sarah often visited the miller's family). The Museum also possesses three watercolours of Horsham by Sarah's great-nieces, Dorothea and Maria Hurst, dating from the 1830s, which it seems very fitting to use as illustrations of Sarah's diaries. (Dorothea Hurst later wrote the first proper history of Horsham, first published in 1868 as *Horsham; its History and Antiquities).* Other early Victorian paintings of old buildings or views that Sarah would have known well have also been included, as the town did not change much until the 1860s or later. The engraving of Hastings Castle is from Francis Grose's *Antiquities of England and Wales,* published between 1773 and 1787. (Sarah met him in Eastbourne in August 1762 while he was serving in Sussex with the Surrey Militia). Other illustrations relating to the people Sarah knew, the places that she visited, the war in Canada, or the plays and books that Sarah read, are taken from the Horsham Museum collections and Library, or from prints or books in the author's possession.

List of Illustrations

27. Chesworth — artist unknown (HORSM X1996.1928).

28. Old cottages by St. Mary's churchyard — painting by Edith Harms (HORSM 1976.55).

29. Horsham from Denne Hill — artist unknown (HORSM X1996.1999).

30. Park House — painting by W. S. Syms c.1865 (HORSM X1997.620).

31. The old church at Slinfold - photograph before rebuilding c.1860 (HORSM 1996.1150).

32. The final page of the 1762 diary (HM MSS Cat. No. 3545).

33. London Bridge before 1760 — contemporary engraving.

34. Whitehall — engraving by J. Kip (private collection).

35. The Rev. Lawrence Sterne — frontispiece from *The Works of Lawrence Sterne, Vol. I*, 1793.

36. *The Way to Keep Him* by Arthur Murphy — titlepage from Bell's *British Theatre*, 1792.

37. *Tamerlane*, by Nicholas Rowe — titlepage from Bell's *British Theatre*, 1792.

38. Panoramic view of Palmyra — engraving from *The Grand Magazine*.

39. View of Eastbourne — engraving by J. and J. Brydell, published 1789.

40. The village of Upperton, near Eastbourne, — painting by unknown artist.

41. Hastings Castle — engraving by Richard Bernard Godfrey from Francis Grose's *Antiquities of England and Wales*, published 1773-1787.

42. Winchelsea — engraving from F. W. L. Stockdale's *Sketch of Hastings, Winchelsea and Rye*, 1817.

43. Chichester Cross — engraving by N. Whittock, 1829.

44. Chichester Cathedral — engraving by N. Whittock, 1831.

45. Robert Hurst in later life — from a miniature (HORSM 1996.752).

46. Bysshe Shelley — from a painting by Sir William Beechey in Roger Inkpen's *Shelley in England*, 1917 (Horsham Museum).

47. The memorial to Henry Smith — photograph taken by Henry Padwick jr. c.1862 (HORSM 1996.7271).

48. The interior of St. Mary's church — photograph taken by Henry Padwick jr. c.1862 (HORSM 1999.1401).

Illustrations 10 to 14 and 33 are from J. R. Green's *A Short History of the English People, Vol. IV*, Macmillan, 1894. Illustrations 15, 16, 41, 43 and 44 are from Frank Graham's collection of old Sussex prints, privately published under the title *Sussex One Hundred Years Ago*. Illustrations 39 and 40 are from J. C. Wright's *Bygone Eastbourne*, Spottiswoode, 1902.

Horsham as it was in Sarah's lifetime

1 - Daniels (Hurst's)
2 - Causeway House (Parham's)
3 - The Vicarage
4 - Collyer's School
5 - The Chantry (Smith's)
6 - The Manor House (Tredcroft's)
7 - Half Moon (Sheppard's)
8 - The Market House
9 - The King's Head Inn
10 - Park House (Wicker's)
    (bought by Robert Hurst in 1799)

1. Frontispiece – Horsham as it was in Sarah's lifetime.

Introduction

The diaries of Sarah Hurst are among the most important documents in the archives of Horsham Museum.[1] They were given to the Museum by the late Miss Barbara Hurst, whose transcript of them is the basis of this book. Few 18th century diaries, written by women, appear to have survived, and it is even more rare to find a diary written by a tradesman's daughter, rather than by a gentlewoman, with time on her hands.

The diaries record the day to day life of a young woman who lived in Horsham, Sussex, between 1759 and 1762, and are one of the most significant sources of information on the town in the mid-18th century. They throw a clear light on the society in which Sarah lived, and help us understand what life in Horsham was really like at that time. Sarah gives a telling portrait of many of the leading townspeople of the day; her bad-tempered father, the cynical Sir Charles Eversfield, the peevish Edward Tredcroft and the domineering John Shelley are all brought vividly to life. The diaries are a real treasure trove for the local historian, as the only other surviving documents of this period are mainly dry and dusty tax records or legal papers. Sarah's diaries are perhaps even more fascinating for anyone interested in the social history of women, since they contain the most intimate thoughts and feelings of a young girl living two hundred and fifty years ago, and describe her life in detail.

Sarah's diaries have the added excitement of a touching love story running through them, and read rather like an old-fashioned romantic novel, in which the happy ending is long in doubt. Sarah and Henry Smith fell in love when she was only sixteen — he was thirteen years older than her, with a military career that took him away from Horsham through much of their courtship. He served in the newly formed Marine Corps during the Seven Years' War with France, much of which was fought in Canada. Sarah suffered constant anguish waiting for his letters and praying to see her beloved Henry return safely from the perils of the sea and the war; "*My Heart dies within me when I reflect that my dear Harry is expos'd to this dreadfull storm, oh preserve him Heav'n*".

But there were also problems to be faced about their relationship, as well as worries about Henry's constancy and survival. Some members of the Smith family opposed the marriage on the grounds that Sarah's father was a local tradesman (while they were London merchants), and Sarah was uncertain whether Henry would be able to defy them and marry her. Also she did not know whether her father would be able to give her an adequate dowry, which would be sufficient to overcome the objections of Henry's family, and ensure them a sufficient income, if Henry were to be retired on half pay when the war was over. At the end of the Seven Years' War, there was no guarantee that the Marine Corps would be retained in peacetime.

Sarah's family background

Sarah Hurst (1736-1808) was the eldest child of Richard Hurst, tailor of Horsham, and his wife Mary, née Tasker. She had two younger sisters, Elizabeth (Bet) and Mary (Molly), and a much younger brother, Robert (Bob). Sarah was actually baptised on 4 May 1736, as *"the base-born daughter of Mary Tasker"*, some six months before her parents' marriage on 29 November 1736. There seems to be absolutely no doubt that Sarah was Richard Hurst's eldest child, and indeed they had a very close relationship. It is not clear whether it was the fact of her illegitimacy that lay behind the opposition to her marriage to Henry Smith by some members of his family, but it could have been a contributing factor. It is also not known why her parents did not marry before she was born, but possibly her father was working in London, where his brothers were both in business, and was unaware of Mary Tasker's pregnancy.

Richard Hurst, Sarah's father, bought Daniels, a house on the east side of Market Square, in 1746, when Sarah would have been ten years old.[2] This appears to have been the Hurst family home and shop at the time Sarah was writing her diaries, though he may also have had a workshop elsewhere. (It seems very likely that he employed journeymen tailors to do the work of his considerable business, although this is not actually mentioned in the diaries). Daniels lay on the east side of Market Square, at the north end of the Causeway, which leads down to the St. Mary's Church — the building is still there. Richard Hurst also leased Highlands Farm, a small farm on the east side of the town, from Guildford Hospital, presumably as a source of food for his family at a time when most people had to be self-sufficient. Living in the very centre of the town, he did not have any land attached to his house where he could keep a pig and chickens, and grow vegetables, as the great majority of townspeople did. Sarah frequently walked out to the farm, and on two occasions she collected some honey, which she divided with *"Dame White"*, who was presumably the wife of the man who looked after the farm for the Hursts.

In 1764, two years after the diaries come to an end, Richard Hurst bought Causeway House and moved there — a significant step for him up the social ladder. Causeway House had been owned successively by professional men, the lawyers Matthew White, George Arnold, Thomas and John Parham, since the previous century.[3] (It is now the home of Horsham Museum). Richard Hurst also acquired the copyhold of Northlands Farm in 1768,[4] and there is one reference in the diaries to land that he owned in Nuthurst, which had been planted with timber. By the time that he wrote his will, in 1778, Richard Hurst was a property owner — albeit on a modest scale — and able to style himself *"gentleman"*.

Richard's upward mobility provided a good starting point for the phenomenal career of his son, Robert Hurst, who became a barrister, a trustee of the Shelley and Sidney estates, steward of the Norfolk and Suffolk manors for the 11th Duke of Norfolk, M.P. for Steyning 1802-1807, and M.P. for Horsham 1812-1829. After the enclosure of Horsham Common by the 11th Duke of Norfolk in 1811-1812, Robert Hurst purchased a large bloc of land and became the largest landowner in the parish of Horsham. He eventually became *"Father of the House of Commons"* — the longest-serving member — but agreed to step down in 1829 to make it possible for the 12th Duke of Norfolk's heir, the Earl of Surrey, to take his seat, after the passing of the Catholic Emancipation Act. In the diaries, Sarah is seen to be very fond of her little brother Robert, who was fourteen years her junior. She seems to have found great delight in his company, though the age difference meant that in his childhood she must have been more of a mother than a sister to him. They clearly had a very close relationship throughout their lives, as is evidenced by some later letters that have survived, which are also published in this book. Sarah's devotion to her brother Robert was second only to her love for Henry.

Other members of the Hurst family also figure in Sarah's diaries. Sarah's widowed grandmother, Elizabeth Hurst, née Osmer, was still alive, living in a large house in the Causeway (now nos. 15 and 16), which seems to have been mainly let out to other tenants. Her husband Robert Hurst (1670-1729) had also been a tailor, and served as Surveyor of the Highways in 1700, overseer of the poor in 1706, and churchwarden in 1712. Sarah had two uncles who are mentioned in the diaries, and two aunts, on her father's side of the family. Robert Hurst of Salisbury Court, Fleet Street, in London, was a tailor, like his father, and had a business partnership with his younger brother Richard, about which they seem to have constantly quarrelled. The other brother, George Hurst, was *"for many years an eminent apothecary in Devonshire Street, Holborn"*, according to his obituary in the *Gentleman's Magazine.*[5] He married Isabella Lee, daughter of Eldred Lancelot Lee, of Coton Hall, Shropshire. He seems to have been a pleasant person and less bad-tempered than Robert and Richard. Of Sarah's two aunts, *"Aunt Smith"*, her father's elder sister Elizabeth, had married William Smith, an upholsterer, and lived in Fleet Street. *"Aunt Smith"* was sometimes disapproving; but Sarah was very friendly with her eldest daughter, Elizabeth (Bet) Smith, with whom she kept up a correspondence. *"Aunt Sally"*, her father's younger sister, was at this time unmarried and kept house for her brother Robert. After Robert's death in 1763, she married his journeyman Will Moore, who is mentioned in the diaries. Sarah was sometimes irritated by Aunt Sally's prejudiced or uninformed opinions.

The Hursts of Eastbourne, with whom Sarah went to stay in 1762, were descended from her great-grandfather, Thomas Hurst, who had married Elizabeth Roseham, a widow with some property in Eastbourne, in 1682, after the death of his first wife. His son Edward married the heiress of a well-known Eastbourne family — Ann Herriott of Upperton House. (Upperton was at that time a small hamlet lying between East Bourne, which was the main part of the parish, and South Bourne, both of which were at some distance from the Sea Houses on the beach). Edward was almost certainly in business as a brewer — his grandson founded the Old Town or Star brewery, in 1777, but the family is known to have been in the trade for some time before that. The *"Cousin Edward"*, who was Sarah's host, was the son of Edward and Ann Herriott, and married twice. Sarah knew his second wife, Mary, who bore him ten children in the 1750s and 1760s.

On her mother's side of the family, Sarah had three aunts and one uncle, all of whom lived in Horsham. Sarah's favourite aunt seems to have been Mrs. Wicker, born in 1723, a young and quite merry widow who owned her own house. Elizabeth Tasker, a younger sister of Sarah's mother, had married William Wicker, a younger son of John Wicker of Park House in Horsham, in the 1740s. He had died at the age of thirty-one in 1751. The eldest sister, Ann Tasker, born in 1716, and described by Sarah as an *"ill-natured woman"*, married Thomas Waller in 1751, as his second wife. They appear to have lived in part of the old burgage property, the Talbot and Wonder, and Thomas Waller leased land off Denne Road where he kept his stock for his butchery business. It is possible that his wife ran some sort of hotel or public house, as Sarah said that she went twice to *"Aunt Waller's"* to see the mountebank. The youngest sister Priscilla (born in 1727), had married the currier, Robert Grace junior, in 1755. While his father, Robert Grace senior, lived in Bishop's burgage house, it is not quite clear where the younger Graces lived. Sarah's uncle, Ellman Tasker, was in business as a tallow-chandler in Market Square. He was the baby of the Tasker family, and only surviving son, born only six years before Sarah, in 1730, and he married one of her closest friends, Elizabeth (Betsy) Sheppard, in February 1759. Betsy thus became Sarah's *"Aunt Tasker"*, but this appears to have taken some toll on their friendship. Betsy had to take into consideration her duties as a married woman and formal position as Sarah's aunt, but Sarah missed her companionship.

The Taskers originally came to Horsham from Balcombe, where their father, William Tasker, was baptised in 1691 and married Ann Middleton in 1715; his parents were William Tasker and Elizabeth Wood, who were married in Lewes in 1687. The younger William Tasker was usually referred to as a *"gentleman"*, and probably worked as a clerk for the Horsham lawyer, John Linfield. His wife, Anne Middleton, was a great-granddaughter of John Middleton, the ironmaster, who built the great mansion called Hill's Place and served as M.P. for Horsham from 1623 to 1628.[6] Anne's father, Richard Middleton, was a gentleman farmer, who lived at Whitesbridge, just outside Horsham on the road to Brighton. The most important consequence of her Middleton ancestry was that it made Mary Tasker first cousin to Mary Tredcroft (née Michell) of the Manor House. Mary Middleton, sister to Anne, had married the wealthy Henry Michell of North Heath, from a junior branch of the Michells of Stammerham, a family of great importance in Horsham in the 17th century. Their daughter, Mary Michell, brought the North Heath estates and a moiety of Whitesbridge into the Tredcroft family as her dowry.[7] Though Mary Tredcroft appears in Sarah's diaries as an extremely snobbish and silly woman, the relationship between the two families was of considerable social advantage to the Hursts in the context of Horsham society in the middle of the 18th century.

Sarah's relationship with her immediate family

Since his only son was still a schoolboy, it is clear that Richard Hurst treated his eldest daughter far more like a junior partner in his tailoring business. However, the close relationship between them was often marred by quarrels and upsets, and Sarah's discomfort with being a dependent (a surprisingly modern attitude). *"My father very much out of temper with us all, he is happy in a gainfull business & has a good income, & sure I, by keeping the Books, etc, contribute to his advantage, & yet I fear am thought to be an incumbrance. How painfull is dependence."* It is quite clear that Sarah played a very important part in her father's business, and he relied on her a great deal. She served in the shop, cut out *"round frocks"* (smocks) for farm labourers, and sailors' jackets, kept the accounts and wrote letters for her father to his suppliers or clients. She went up to London to buy stock at the London warehouses, and tried to smooth over the disagreements that occurred between her father and his brother Robert in their partnership. On a visit to London in November 1761, Sarah was entrusted with a large sum of money to invest in *"the Stocks"* (Consolidated Bank Stocks, or "Consols"). The money was sewn into her stays for safe keeping, but it was heavy and uncomfortable to carry. Nevertheless, Sarah made the journey without complaint and invested the money successfully.

But although her father's bad temper often caused her pain and led to tears, in moments of crisis - such as when Sarah mislaid her pocket-book and the silhouettes of herself and Henry on a trip to Cuckfield in July 1759 — it was her father who came to her rescue, getting up at four o'clock in the morning to go back and retrieve her treasures. When he fell ill with smallpox, Sarah's distress revealed her very deep affection for him. Sarah's relationship with her mother seems to have been rather more distant, although she said that she was a very good parent. Mary Hurst seems to have been much closer to her younger daughter Bet, and she and Sarah had little in common intellectually, though Sarah did read some of Shakespeare's plays to her, which her mother enjoyed. Sarah took a somewhat cool view of her parents' marriage, and in September 1759 went so far as to say that she was *"weak & ill in health and spirits, much disturb'd at the animosities of my father & mother"*. Sarah clearly thought that her parents were mismatched, but managed to retain her faith in marriage as an institution; *"t'is a most astonishing thing there is so little happiness in families, it must be want of care in the choice of a partner for life."*

Though Sarah constantly complained of having to work in the shop, she was able to make several trips to London, Arundel or Eastbourne, where she had an active social life, and seems to have been much admired. She felt that her father should allow her at least one week's holiday a year and, in fact, she seems to have taken rather more than that. She managed to persuade him to let her pay an extended visit to her cousins in Eastbourne in 1762 for nearly two months. She was also permitted to visit Arundel for about a month to recover her health after being very ill in 1761. So although Sarah did not have the freedom that she would have enjoyed if she had been of independent means, yet she was generally able to persuade her father to let her do what she wanted. There was only one occasion, in January 1760, when she was not allowed to go and meet Henry, that she complained that her parents were unreasonable and had forgotten what it was like to be in love.

The family of Henry Smith

Who was the man with whom Sarah fell so deeply in love at the age of sixteen? Henry Smith (1723-1794), was the third son of John Smith, a London merchant, and his wife Elizabeth, née Griffith. John Smith died in 1758, so he does not figure in Sarah's diaries, but his wife was a somewhat baleful presence, who apparently did not think that Sarah would make her son a good wife; "*Madam Smith says, what shou'd the Captain do with such a wife as me who can only sit with a book in her hand?*". Elizabeth Smith was the daughter of the Rev. William Griffith of West Hoathly, and Anne Nye, of a Sussex gentry family, related to another branch of the Tredcroft family, who had held the *Red Lion* and the *Anchor*, two of the principal inns in Horsham, in the 17th century. Elizabeth's brother Thomas was the "*Dr. Griffith*" of the diaries, and her sister Gainor was the second wife of Robert Grace, senior.

The Smith family probably considered themselves superior to the Hursts because their various businesses were in London, and because of their connection with the Lords Irwin, whose complete control of the "*rotten*" Parliamentary Borough of Horsham gave them the power of patronage in both military and political appointments. Henry's father, John Smith, had been appointed as a quarter-master in the Army by Rich, 5th Viscount Irwin, shortly before the 1715 election, and doubtless profited from the resulting military contracts. Henry owed his commission in the Marines to the support and patronage of Henry, 7th Viscount Irwin.

Henry was actually thirteen years older than Sarah, but she seems to have been exceptionally mature for her years. While the age difference does not appear to have troubled them, it may have been another reason why the Smith family opposed the match. The strong opposition of Henry's eldest brother, Griffith Smith, to the marriage, and his unpleasant remarks, made before it was realised that he was descending into lunacy, deeply affected Sarah and at times made her ill. Henry's other brothers, John and Charles, though initially opposed to the marriage, seem to have become much more sympathetic to the lovers during the period covered by the diaries; on one occasion when Sarah tried to avoid Charles, he teased her and said that he would not bite. In May 1761, John Smith took Sarah and her aunt, Mrs. Wicker, to visit the theatre in London. On this visit Sarah also had the opportunity of getting to know the wife of Adam Smith, whom she found charming and sympathetic. Her little daughter Maria, born in 1757, was mentioned as a loveable child in Sarah's diary for 1762, though at this point no one could have foreseen that she would become the wife of Sarah's brother Robert in 1784.

Sarah worked hard to improve her relationship with Henry's mother, often visiting her to share news of Henry when she received a letter from him, and by 1761 they seem to have established quite a warm relationship. But it was made painfully clear to her that Mrs. Smith still did not welcome the prospect of Sarah's marriage to her son, when the matter was raised in October 1762. Clearly, only time and patience would resolve this particular difficulty, and remove a deep-seated prejudice.

Sarah's friends

In Henry Smith's absence, Sarah spent most of her time with her family or with young women of her own age and similar social background, in Horsham and elsewhere. Sarah's closest woman friend and *confidante* during the period covered by her diary was Sarah (Sally) Sheppard, the younger sister of Betsy (Sarah's *"Aunt Tasker"*). Sally and Betsy were the daughters of Stringer Sheppard, a Horsham butcher, and his wife, Magdalen Denis, who were married in Bolney in 1728. While it is likely that Sarah first became friendly with the Sheppards because they were such near neighbours — the *Half Moon* faced Daniels across Market Square — they seem to have been intelligent and cultured girls, whose company Sarah enjoyed. Perhaps this was due to the fact that their mother was the daughter of two Huguenot refugees, Pierre Denis and Madeleine Ribotteau, who came to England following the revocation of the Edict of Nantes in 1685, which led to renewed persecution of French and Dutch Protestants. Pierre, who is thought to have come from Namur in the Low Countries, was a barber by trade. He married Madeleine Ribotteau in 1702, and they established themselves in Horsham. Their only child, Magdalen, was baptised there on 17 June 1703. She is known to have inherited money from her father's sister, Marie Denis Boutofflères, who was a silk mercer in Rotterdam.[8] It was perhaps because of her mother's little windfall that Sally appears to have been well educated and to have spent some time in London (she was either living or working in

London at the beginning of 1759, because Sarah went to Whitehall to visit her). Sarah frequently mentioned Sally's sweet singing voice, so perhaps she had received some sort of musical training.

Stringer and Magdalen Sheppard also had two sons; the elder, John Sheppard, was already married and living in West Street. He is not actually mentioned in Sarah's diary, although Sarah and he acted as the two witnesses at his sister Betsy's wedding to Ellman Tasker on 11 February 1759. The younger son, Stringer, was mentioned and played a part in events. Unfortunately, while Sarah was away in Eastbourne in September 1762, Richard Hurst quarrelled with young Stringer, and Sarah was forbidden to maintain contact with his sister. Although Sarah protested that only death should part her from her *"dearest Sally"*, and she did manage to meet her secretly after his edict, their relationship does seem to have been seriously affected. Probably the main reason for this was that Sarah did not wish to be at odds with her father just at the moment when she had to break the news to him that she and Henry were already married. Sarah did not attend Sally's wedding to Drew Michell on 19 October 1762, and it seems likely that she arranged to go away to Slinfold for a few days at this time, to avoid embarrassment. But no proper explanation of the quarrel was ever vouchsafed, and it seems a pity that such a close friendship was disrupted in this way.

Another valued friend was Miss Gittins, with whom Sarah corresponded, and with whom she went to stay in Arundel in 1759, and again in 1761. Ann Gittins (1738-1800) was the daughter of the Rev. Daniel Gittins, LLD, Rector of South Stoke, near Arundel, and Vicar of Leominster (as Lyminster was then called), and she later became quite well-known as a scholar-poetess. Her father had taught her classical languages and Hebrew, in which she became *"a great proficient"*, though it was probably after her marriage in 1764, to the Rev. Robert Bransby Francis, Rector of Edgefield in Norfolk, that she resumed her studies in earnest. One of her best known and most daring works was *A Poetical Translation of the Song of Solomon, from the original Hebrew*, published in 1781. This work was dedicated to John Parkhouse, author of a Hebrew lexicon, who was *"one of many very eminent and learned men"* with whom she was said to have corresponded. It defied the conventional belief that a woman lacked the learning for such a translation, and that the erotic material was not suitable *"for the exercise of a* female *pen"*. Other poetical works published were *The Obsequies of Demetrius Poliorcetes*, in 1785, *A Poetical Epistle from Charlotte to Werther*, in 1788, and *Miscellaneous Poems, by a Lady*, in 1790.[9]

In Sarah's diaries, Ann Gittins appears as a very lively and intelligent girl, sometimes given to indiscretion. Sarah learned that she was previously involved with a Captain Vaughan, for which she came under some censure from the Horsham gossips. At the time that Sarah knew her, Ann was expecting to marry her *"lover"* Mr. Turnpenny, but he behaved badly and eventually abandoned her. In 1762, Sarah was delighted to hear that she was going to marry a clergyman in Norfolk, but feared that it would be more difficult for them to remain in close touch. The marriage took place in 1764. Ann died on 7 November 1800 at the age of 62, and was buried in her husband's church at Edgefield where there is also a memorial to her mother, Jane Gittins, who had been Sarah's hostess when she stayed with the family.[10] Ann was highly praised in an obituary not merely for her *"mental acquirements"*, but as a daughter, wife and mother.

Sarah's education

One intriguing question — not properly answered by the diaries — is how and where Sarah obtained her own education. Clearly she had received a good grounding, and this sowed the desire to continue reading, writing and improving herself, but it is not really clear whether this had been obtained in Horsham or whether she had attended a boarding school elsewhere. There are some indications in the 1759 diary that Sarah had gone to school in Brighton or Lewes, or maybe both. She said that she had lived in Brighton some eight years previously, when she would have been only fifteen, and this suggests that she must have been at school there at the time, or continuing her education in some way. She also spoke of her *"acquaintance"* in Lewes, which included her friend, Miss Woodhams, and made a direct reference to Stephen Philpot, who ran a girls' school at Lewes at St. Anne's Rectory from 1733 to 1770, with the help of his wife. (Sarah also had a long acquaintance with the family of his landlord, the Rev. John Bristed, whom she visited at his other rectory in Slaugham). Philpot had studied with the best London dancing masters and published an essay in 1747 on the role of dance in women's education. Sarah mentioned this essay, and there is ample evidence in the diaries that she loved to dance. While these few allusions are not really enough to prove that Sarah was a pupil at the Philpots' school in Lewes, one can perhaps say that Sarah's attendance at a school like that would have fitted in very well with her good general education, her poise and apparent self-confidence.

Sarah - her looks, character and personality

From her silhouette one can see that Sarah had an aquiline profile and an elegant figure, and in her letters she talks of her *"small circumference"*. It is not surprising that Henry Smith fell in love with this slim, attractive and intelligent girl, since she clearly had something rather special to offer, in terms of character and personality. Sarah's capacity for hard work, her organising ability and her talent for writing letters and keeping accounts made her the ideal wife for an aspiring Marine officer, despite his mother's misgivings. She seems to have been perfectly at ease with any members of the nobility or gentry whom she met; she was not at all overawed by the Duke and Duchess of Richmond when she encountered them on two occasions, whilst visiting Goodwood with her friend Miss Gittins. This seems to indicate solid confidence in her manners and upbringing, which enabled her to face any social situation without qualms. She also seems to have been on friendly and familiar terms with Lord Irwin and Sir Charles Eversfield in Horsham, and John Shelley of Field Place, the three main local landowners, who generally appear to have treated her with consideration. It was the more snobbish, but less well educated, of her friends and relations, like Mrs. Tredcroft, who criticised her aspirations, and opposed her marriage to Henry on the grounds that she was a tradesman's daughter. Sarah was not surprisingly upset by such attitudes.

The diaries show quite clearly that the unkind remarks of other people caused Sarah headaches and depression, though it was perceptively remarked by her cousin Bet Smith that her more serious illness in 1761 was probably caused by Henry's absence. But Sarah was also resilient, and countered lassitude by fierce bursts of activity, in the shop or the house. She appreciated the value of physical exercise; even sawing wood or *"rubbing"* a room on occasion, and going for long walks to Slinfold and other places. After bouts of illness, she found horse-riding and cold baths, or sea-bathing, beneficial. The very practice of writing her diary may have begun as a literary discipline, but it may have continued because she found it to be a valuable emotional support during the long years of Henry's absence on active service.

It is clear that Sarah's life in Horsham was restricted, not only by the demands of her family and the shop but by her situation; an unmarried girl pledged to a lover who was far away with no certainty of marriage. At times she fretted against these constraints but she knew that it was essential that she should abide by convention and not be involved in any sort of scandal.

The fate of Miss Hutchinson, the Vicar's daughter, sent away from home because she pursued young men rather too openly, was an awful warning. With a reputation to safeguard, Sarah had to spend her free time almost entirely with girls of her own age, or visiting her relations. This necessarily gave her a rather narrow view of life, but she was also still very young and inexperienced in the ways of the world. She was completely taken in by a clever con-man posing as a old sailor, who pretended to have suffered in his country's service, and was deeply mortified when she learnt the truth about him a few days later.

Sometimes Sarah was delightfully inconsistent as she struggled to make sense of other people's behaviour — after whole-heartedly abusing Drew Michell for allegedly ruining Molly Luttman, she found him a very *"sensible"* and *"clever young fellow"* when she actually got to know him. Similarly, though frequently rhapsodising about the pleasures of a simple life in a village like Slinfold, after spending a couple of days there with her friends the Pigotts, in 1759, she actually found it rather boring. Later she came to appreciate life in Slinfold much better, as she found herself away from the back-biting of her Horsham neighbours, and she took every opportunity to go there. Sarah was always decrying vanity, and yet she could be very susceptible to a little judicious flattery, about her person or her poetry, as she was honest enough to admit herself. Her attitude to her own poetry was ambivalent – at one moment, when reading the poems of Mrs. Carter of Kent, she threatened to burn her all own works because they were not of the same standard; but only a few days later she sent four of them off to *The Monthly Review!*

As to her own personal behaviour, Sarah was quite capable of flirting and *"romping"* with other young men, despite her love for Henry. John Ellis called to see her in September 1760, on a visit from Chichester, and she recorded that he had flattered her *"sufficiently"* and kissed her *"enough"*. Younge Willes of Goring fell in love with her in July 1761, and spent an evening hugging her, but she dismissed him lightly, though his esteem was clearly quite a balm to her spirits, at a time when she was rather doubtful that Henry would ever be able to marry her. His brother, Captain Willes, with whom she said she *"romped"* wildly on one occasion, later told her how deeply his brother Younge felt for her, and this made her feel somewhat remorseful. Sarah was very angry with John Shelley when he suddenly *"tumbled her"* on to a bed, but she remained friends with him, because she realised that he had simply acted on impulse. The only occasion when Sarah seems to have flirted with danger was when she did little to discourage the attentions of Sir Charles Eversfield of Denne Park, even though she knew of his bad reputation where women were concerned, and deplored his cynical opinions about life. Perhaps she was flattered by his interest in her, or felt that she was safe because he was old enough to be her father, and knew and esteemed Henry. To do Sir Charles justice, he always seems to have behaved perfectly well with Sarah, whom he clearly admired and respected. But she reported that he made *"very indecent"* remarks to one of her friends, and hinted that he had some sort of relationship with Nany Cook before her marriage. Eventually she tried to avoid meeting him in order not to compromise her own reputation.

There were some intriguing aspects about Sarah's own relationship with Henry. When he was at home, Sarah sometimes entertained him late at night. On one occasion, Sarah spoke of waiting for him to come to see her at eleven at night, when her *"perverse"* mother had not gone to bed. She said that she *"sat up"* with him until three in the morning — and that he was *"all modesty, love and tenderness"*. However, this seems to be very understandable behaviour by lovers who had been parted for such long periods of time. Indeed, it is these intimate glimpses of real life and emotion that make Sarah's diaries so endearing, and allow us to see through the highly moralistic — even priggish — tone, which she felt that she had to adopt most of the time.

Sarah's attitude to religion

Sarah was a good practising Christian, often attending church twice on a Sunday, and the strength of her faith was clearly visible in much that she did or said. This was not just a case of uttering the conventional pieties, or doing what was socially acceptable. Sarah took herself to task for her bad temper and struggled hard to curb her sharp tongue. But while Sarah may have suffered from the unkindness of others, at times she seems to have been somewhat intolerant of other people, especially those who held different religious views, like the Quakers. This was probably not surprising in view of the narrow-minded and censorious attitude of many of the people among whom she lived. Sarah regarded the unmannerly and uneducated with distaste, perhaps with good reason; there was an incident on 30 January 1762 when she noted, *"some country people came in & are extremely vulgar in their behaviour, good God who can imagine we were all of the same species; what an amazing difference does education make"*.

Many of Sarah's male friends were clergymen, though it seems likely that she sought their company because they were among the best educated members of the community. They were among the few people who owned their own books, which she was able to borrow or read when staying with them. Sarah was particularly friendly with Mr. Pigott, curate of Slinfold, Mr. Manningham, Vicar of Wisborough Green, Mr. Bristed, Rector of Slaugham, and Mr. Jones, who married Miss Pigott and succeeded her brother as curate of Slinfold. She also knew Dr. Thomas Hutchinson, Vicar of Horsham, and the Mr. Turner, Vicar of Dorking, and esteemed them for their *"superior"* powers of reasoning and expression. She made a point of listening to their sermons with great interest and attention, but she was not afraid to criticise them, on occasion. Even though she greatly admired the sermons of Dr. Hutchinson, a renowned classical scholar, she said that one of his sermons was *"too political for a country Congregation"*, and on another occasion *"I thought he greatly wander'd from his text & drew conclusions no way deducible from it"*.

Sarah and domesticity

One very surprising feature of Sarah's diaries is that she said relatively little about food or domestic matters, seeing that women were certainly expected at this time to be good cooks and housekeepers. She did sometimes mention doing the ironing, and on a few occasions said she had done some pickling or baking, but otherwise these topics were scarcely touched on. However, Sarah does explain this by saying that she was not much interested in such matters, although she knew that she should be; *"Help pick & chop Raisins for Wine till I am exceedingly tir'd, t'is with reluctance I assist in any of these domestick affairs, but since my situation in Life renders it necessary am determin'd to overcome this reluctance"*. It should perhaps be noted that Sarah wrote this after two days spent washing and ironing; clearly the Hurst household was in the middle of the dreaded *"great Spring wash"*! Sarah's most significant comment on food was a passionate preference for plain food — she expressed a vehement dislike of anything with sauces or *"made dishes"*, such as those reportedly served at a dinner at Lord Irwin's house, and said that she would probably starve in such a family. But she enjoyed occasional treats, such as a venison dinner with the Curtis family or the lobsters provided by Mr. Mortimer at Eastbourne. She relished traditional delicacies such as Easter cakes at the Tredcrofts, or a plum cake at a celebration. She also enjoyed eating fresh fruit, such as the apricots given to her by Sir Charles and old Mr. Shelley, and hazelnuts (filberds) when in season.

Sarah was a very accomplished needlewoman, and made a highly wrought and elaborate gauze (cat-gut) apron that was very much admired, as well as a set of ruffles for her beloved Henry, and handkerchiefs for other people. This was work which she could probably do while serving in the shop, in the intervals between customers. She also helped Miss Tredcroft with *"work"* (needlework) given her to do by Miss Ingram of Hill's Place, and herself did *"work"* for Mrs. Turner of Dorking, probably in the way of business. She said little about her own dress, although she did mention the white linen negligée (informal dress) which she wore to Vauxhall (which her aunt said made her look like a woman of the town), and a dress that she made up from some Indian muslin that Henry had given her, which she said was *"much admir'd"*. It is clear that she took a great interest in her appearance and worked hard at it; *"Oh dress, thou enchanting thing, how much doth thou engross of most females' time & thoughts"*. She recorded the purchase of a new silk gown for £8, which she claimed was a *"necessary extravagance"* once every five years or so, and her acquisition of a sable tippet, made from furs that Henry had given her. She justified the secret purchase of a new silk dress and petticoat, bought for her visit to Eastbourne in 1762, by saying that she needed to do Henry credit!

Sarah's literary interests

Sarah's main interests were reading and writing poetry, and although her verses were belittled by some people in Horsham, it is worth noting that both Lord Irwin and Sir Charles Eversfield appear to have praised her work sincerely. They were almost certainly among the best-read people in Horsham, and would have had the opportunity to compare Sarah's poems with those of other poets of the day, so their opinion must be considered significant. Rather surprisingly, when the Bailiffs and Burgesses wished to send an address to the young King George III soon after his accession in December 1760, Dr. Smith, a previous critic of her literary pretensions, called on Sarah and asked her to draw it up. However, Sarah demurred on this occasion; *"No, Sir, I will not interfere with business that belongs to men of learning and genius"*. But she noted rather tartly next day that the address composed by William White, the lawyer, was *"neither English nor grammar"*.

It is difficult for us to assess the worth of Sarah's poetry because very little has survived — there are a couple of quatrains in the diaries, and two published poems that have been found. The poem on friendship, called *The Consolation*, published in *The Lady's Magazine* under Sarah's pseudonym, *"Amanda Rustick"*,[11] and Sarah's burlesque poem on the militia, published anonymously by *the Sussex Weekly Advertiser* in August 1762,[12] can both be found in Appendix I. It is also possible that Sarah wrote the poetic epitaph to the Rev. Thomas White in St. Mary's Church, as the style is somewhat similar.[13] However, it seems unlikely that Sarah would ever have made a great mark in literary circles - the poems that she is known to have written are rather derivative. Sarah gave details of about thirty poems that she had written in her diaries, and at other times mentioned that she had written a few verses. Some of these poems were merely word games — acrostic poems based on the letters in the name of the person concerned — while others were impromptu verses written about her friends or a particular incident, which she usually gave to the person concerned. Sarah clearly found it quite easy to write verse and find rhymes, and these poems were generally dashed off on the spur of the moment. But some poems, notably *The Consolation, the Elegy on Mrs. Shelley, Soliloquy by Moonlight* and the *Vision on the death of Admiral Boscawen,* seem to have been rather more serious and carefully worked, and she sent out copies of these to her friends, for their criticism and approval.

The writing of poetry was quite widely practised by educated and leisured women in the 18th century, but it was still quite unusual for a girl of Sarah's background to find enough time to do it. English women poets of this period have been shamefully neglected in the past, and it is only now, with the recent development of women's studies, that the works of many previously little known 18th century women writers have been brought to light. One of the poems of Miss Gittins, Sarah's friend, has now been published in an anthology of 18th century poetry by women.[14] But it is not surprising that Sarah's work does not appear in this collection, because the two poems of hers that are known to have been published did not appear under her name. It is only the references to them in the diaries that has enabled us to identify them positively as her work.

Sarah, like most other educated women of her generation, was also a good letter writer, and it is clear that in her letters to Miss Gittins, she was not only keeping in touch but was flexing her literary muscles. Amanda Vickery has noted that *"the well-turned letter became an unavoidable performance of the long-standing female work of kin, but in addition it enabled unprecedented numbers of women to participate in worldly exchange and debate. It was in their tireless writing no less than their ravenous reading that genteel women embraced a world far beyond the boundaries of their parish".*[15] This is particularly true of Sarah. Her correspondence with Henry, which was of course the essential lifeline of their relationship, enabled her to share his experiences. She also corresponded enthusiastically with some of his friends and messmates.

Sarah's choice of reading is of almost as much interest as her writing, though this was clearly dictated by what was available to her. There were, of course, no public libraries, and Horsham is not known to have had a bookshop at this time. (There was one in the 1780s, run by a lady bookseller).[16] Sarah bought herself the works of William Shakespeare and a *History of Russia* when she was in London in November 1761, but otherwise she had to depend on friends to lend her books, like Mr. Pigott of Slinfold, Mr. Bristed of Slaugham, John Shelley or Sir Charles Eversfield. The poems and letters of Alexander Pope, which she mentioned more than once, would have been found on the bookshelves of most educated men at that time, so it is no surprise that Sarah rated him highly, and seems to have modelled her style on his. Sarah probably had some knowledge of French, because she mentioned reading her French grammar, but generally she read translations of French authors. She also read Horace (translated from Latin by Dunster) and found his poems much superior to Pope's *Imitations* of Horace's satires. Altogether, the works of some 60 authors were mentioned in Sarah's diaries. Over 100 plays, novels, poems, articles and publications were recorded as having been seen or read.

Many of the books that she read had been written years earlier — even in the previous century — like the writings of the Duke of Buckingham, and this perhaps meant that her taste was necessarily a little old-fashioned. But there is evidence of Sarah reading quite recent works, such as the pamphlet about the trial of Earl Ferrers and the first two volumes of *Tristram Shandy*, which were lent to her by Sir Charles Eversfield very soon after their publication in 1760. Not surprisingly, she found the unconventional and risqué humour of the Rev. Lawrence Sterne difficult to comprehend and not at all to her liking. She also completely failed to appreciate George Colman's new comedy, *The Jealous Wife*, which she read in April 1761 and saw in London a month later. But she did like Arthur Murphy's plays, *The Way to Keep Him* and *The Orphan of China*, which she read very soon after they were published in 1759, and then read again in 1762. She also appears to have read Lord George Lyttelton's recent *Dialogues of the Dead* in 1760 and Dr. Johnson's *Rasselas* (though, when she read this, Sarah did not know who was its author). Henry gave her two new and controversial pamphlets by Charles Churchill when they were in London in May 1761.

A large part of Sarah's reading came from magazines, of a literary bent, of which there were several available to her and her friends, and it was through them that she appears to have managed to read something by several major 18th century poets and writers, both French and English, such as Pascal, Voltaire, Montaigne, Smollett, Richardson, and Goldsmith. *The Grand Magazine* in particular seems to have provided her with a wide range of articles, poems and other information, including a life of Voltaire and extracts from his work, and she was dismayed when it ceased publication at the end of 1760. Some of the novels she read were serialised in magazines — Smollett's *The Life and Adventures of Sir Launcelot Greaves,* first appeared in *The British Magazine.* Sarah organised a rota for sharing these magazines among her group of friends with similar interests. They were clearly a very important source of information in a country town, and widened the horizons of those who, like Sarah, did not have other resources or opportunities to obtain easy access to books. It is interesting that the publisher of some of these popular magazines, John Coote, was actually born in Horsham in 1733 (and probably came from the family that gave their name to Coote's Farm). In 1759, he started to publish *The Royal Magazine,* and during the next ten years he published several more. He concealed his proprietorship so that his readers would not think that the same material was used in more than one of his magazines, but this eventually led to a court case in 1771, and his bankruptcy in 1772. Sarah does not ever mention John Coote by name, so we cannot say whether this local connection was a factor in the availability of his magazines in Horsham.

It is difficult to find copies of any of these monthly magazines now — a few bound collections of a year's issues have survived in academic libraries, and fortunately some of these are now being made available to read on the internet. Sometimes the prints from individual copies have been extracted as collector's items, and ended up far away — the engraving of Palmyra, from *The Grand Magazine,* used as an illustration in this edition, was found in an antiquarian print shop in Beirut. At the time, most magazines would probably have been thrown away after reading or used for domestic purposes, to light fires or line drawers.

The historical and social background of Sarah's diaries

Horsham was a busy market town in a rural area; there were few industries other than tanning and brick-making at the time when Sarah was writing, and the majority of people worked on the land or had associated pursuits, like milling or butchery. In the past, Horsham had been a centre of the Wealden iron industry, but that had died out in the previous century. The town was however important in Sussex as one of the towns where the Assizes and Quarter Sessions were held regularly, and it was also the home of the County Gaol. It was a Parliamentary Borough where originally fifty-two burgesses, who owned and occupied their burgage properties, had the right to vote. The town was run by two Bailiffs, who were elected annually, and had mayoral powers. But by the middle of the 18th century, the ancient democratic institutions of the manorial courts, which elected the Bailiffs, had largely fallen into disuse.The burgage system had been corrupted by the splitting of burgages to create additional voters, and Horsham was now a *"pocket borough"* in the hands of the Lords Irwin, from Temple Newsam, near Leeds. Even the markets were said to be failing in 1756, undercut by *"higlers"* who bought up poultry beforehand, and by the diversion of fat beef cattle to the London market.[17]

The Irwins had taken over from the Eversfields as the most important land-owners in the town, mainly due to the irresponsibility of Charles Eversfield, the father of Sir Charles Eversfield, who figures in Sarah's diaries. Charles Eversfield died in 1749, leaving a will that left all his *"real and personal estate"* to the two daughters of his mistress, Mary Forman, despite the fact that most of his estates in Horsham and near Hastings were already entailed on his only son. This led to much litigation in the 1750s which seems to have left his legitimate heir, Sir Charles, the deeply embittered and cynical man described by Sarah in her diaries.[18] The other major landowner, John Shelley, also had a somewhat troubled personal history. Born and brought up in America, he had come to England at the age of fourteen, unprepared for the responsibilities thrust upon him as the prospective heir (after his father's death) to the estates of his great-uncle Edward Shelley, and his grandfather, John Shelley of Fen Place, near East Grinstead. He had been criticised for his lack of education and for wishing to marry Mary White, the daughter of the lawyer, William White, as she was said to be a woman *"of low degree..by no means suitable to his rank and fortune"* during the Chancery case fought to establish the provisions of Edward Shelley's will in 1752. As soon as he came of age later that year, he married Mary White, whose death in January 1759 was the first significant local event mentioned in Sarah's diaries.[19]

By the time Sarah was writing, the markets in Horsham seem to have revived, and she complained of the number of people who crowded into the shop on fair days, when cattle, sheep or horses were sold and there were entertainers and other attractions. On such occasions, the town was crowded with people come to trade and to enjoy themselves. They would take the opportunity to visit a tailor or a shoemaker, most of whom were situated around Market Square or in West Street. There were bakers, grocers and tallow-chandlers to supply the essentials, and cutlers, gunsmiths and clock-makers to provide luxury goods, for those who could afford them.

The people among whom Sarah lived were educated and aspiring tradesmen, clerics, doctors, lawyers and schoolteachers, and the minor gentry, like Edward Tredcroft and Samuel Blunt, who served as magistrates. Her father, Richard Hurst, and her uncle, Thomas Waller, were among the few remaining independent burgesses, whose votes were not subject to control by Lord Irwin. They were generally speaking sober and hard-working — Sarah always referred to drunkenness as a beastly vice, and it was only people like John Shelley and Nathaniel Tredcroft, younger brother of Edward, who were actually mentioned as being drunk on one or two occasions. But although they worked hard, there also seems to have been plenty of time for tea-drinking, card-play, dancing and dinner parties within their small circle, though these were also the occasion for a great deal of gossip. Sarah observed that *"the malice & envy of a country town is endless"*.

The more substantial tradesmen, like Robert Hurst, lived comfortably and employed servants; Sarah spoke of their maid and *"the boy"*, Richard Hurst's little apprentice, both of whom brought letters and newspapers to her when she was staying in Slinfold. Though Horsham was a small country town, people seem to have been remarkably well informed about what was happening elsewhere, as events which took place in London were often mentioned within the next day or two in Sarah's diary. Sarah said that she was accustomed to read a daily newspaper and missed seeing it when she was staying at Slinfold.

It is clear that the wealthier Horsham townsfolk aspired to the social life of the larger cities; *"balls"* took place at the various coaching inns, like the *Anchor* and the *King's Head,* and by the time John Baker was writing in the 1770s, there were regular *"assemblies"* attended by the local gentry. Sarah often spoke of going *"dancing"*, so it is clear that dances were already being held on a fairly regular basis by 1760, either in private homes or in public places. The town was also visited occasionally by entertainers; Sarah mentions two companies of strolling players, who performed a variety of plays with varying competence, a puppet show and a mountebank.

There is little in Sarah's diaries to indicate that there was much political activity in Horsham at this time, with only a passing mention of an uncontested Parliamentary election, and a sinecure held by Edward Tredcroft as a reward for political support. But this was not a period in which revolt or dissent were much in the air. It was perhaps too soon after the 1745 Jacobite uprising; the advance of Prince Charles Stuart as far as Derby had awakened deep fears of instability and civil war, which were still too fresh in people's minds to be forgotten. Besides, there were far more pressing concerns abroad which had united the country behind the Government.

In 1756, Frederick the Great, King of Prussia, invaded Saxony, and this provoked the outbreak of the Seven Years War. The War was, in fact, two separate wars, one fought in Europe between Frederick the Great and the combined armies of France, Austria and Russia, and the other a colonial war between Britain and France, fought largely in India, in North America, and at sea. To begin with, things went badly, and Admiral John Byng was executed in Portsmouth in March 1758 for failing to relieve the British garrison on Minorca, but then the fortunes of war turned. In 1758 the French fortress of Louisbourg in Canada was captured, and 1759 became known as *"annus mirabilis"*, the year of wonders, with British victories at Plassey in India, and at Quiberon Bay where Admiral Sir Edward Hawke destroyed an entire French fleet, thus putting paid to any risk of a French invasion of England. Finally, in North America, General James Wolfe became a national hero when he died while taking Quebec. The news from Canada was of especial interest to Sarah, since Henry Smith was involved in the taking of Louisburg, and the Quebec campaign. Her diary is an invaluable record of how the news of the fall of Quebec finally became known after rumour and false report had kept people in suspense for weeks. Meanwhile in Europe, the victory of Prince Ferdinand of Brunswick over French forces at Minden in August 1759 saved Hanover, and was celebrated in England. The battles fought by Frederick the Great also caught the public imagination — it is perhaps significant that there was a property in the Carfax in Horsham called *The King of Prussia*, almost certainly an inn named after him. The Peace of Paris, which concluded the War in 1763, ended the French presence in India and in continental North America, and left Britain undisputed master of the seas — Sarah recorded something of alternate hopes and fears felt by ordinary people during the long-drawn out negotiations in 1762.

Women's place in 18th century society

There is little doubt that Sarah will be chiefly remembered for the unique contribution that her diaries have made to our knowledge of life in mid-18th century Horsham. But her diaries also have a much wider significance in that they afford us a valuable insight into the mind of a young woman of that time. They prove — if proof were needed — that women of this period had aspirations to live a fuller, richer life than that usually considered to be their lot, when legally stripped by marriage of a separate identity and the right to own property, and formally excluded from any political activity. Sarah longed to excel and achieve something worthwhile in her life; at times she expressed her intense frustration with her circumstances and her sex; *"How trifling, how unimportantly, does my time pass away, I wish I had been a man; I might then have signalis'd myself in the service of my Country, but now I must live & die in a wretched obscurity"*.

There are many examples of the force of prejudice against women straying into fields at that time normally reserved for men, which clever, well-read, and aspiring young woman like Sarah would have had to encounter. Linda Colley has noted that *"male anxieties about female pretensions became mark-edly sharper in the second half of the eighteenth century"*. In 1762, while Sarah was writing the last of her diaries, Jean-Jacques Rousseau claimed in *Emile* that women were born to obey, and that, even if they possessed genuine talents, any *"pretension"* on their part would *"degrade"* them. He added the dictum that *"girls must be thwarted early in life"*.[20] While such theories appealed to those who held traditional ideas about a woman's place in society, an increasing number of women, like Sarah, who were actually leading useful, active and productive lives, effectively undermined them. By the end of the century, the French Revolution and the war against France led to a rise in patriotic activism among women as well as men, and this was recognised in a cartoon by James Gillray called *"Flannel-Armour — Female Patriotism"*, drawn in 1793.[21] In 1792, Mary Wollstonecraft was able to pub-lish *A Vindication of the Rights of Woman*, in a brief moment of opportunity, before the excesses of the Reign of Terror set back the cause of revolution and women's liberation for about another century.

Sarah herself was no revolutionary feminist, although she may sound like one in her burlesque poem on the men of Sussex, but this was clearly written with her tongue in her cheek. She was annoyed when she read that Montaigne considered that women should not have a *"learned education"*, and was moved to say *"are our minds then not worth improving, these Lordly men will have it so"*. On a personal level, she longed to escape from dependency on her often bad-tempered father, but she was quite prepared to defer to Henry, as her husband, out of the love and respect which she had for him. The *"passion for Fame"* of which she spoke once does not really seem to have been an overmastering aim. Her chief desire was to marry Henry and live with him for the rest of her life.

To appreciate the very real difficulties under which intelligent women like Sarah laboured in the 18th century, all one has to do is consider the anony-mous poem that was published in her *Ladies' Pocket-book* for 1760. Called *"Advice for the Year 1760"*, the writer instructed his readers in the use of their pocket-book in a most patronising manner, urging them to *"quench each spark of rising Pride"* and forego any intellectual activity, which he seems to have regarded as lacking *"virtue"*.

> *Ladies, for you, I now draw forth my Quill,*
> *From which replenish'd Fount these words distill,*
> *Survey this Diary — confess its Use,*
> *Nor turn its wholesome Dictates to Abuse.*
> *For this, if duly cherish'd by your Love,*
> *The parent of Oeconomy will prove.*
> *Here note your Payments — here too your Receipts*
> *But where your wanton Airs, and dear Deceits?*
> *Hold, there a vacant margin I espy,*
> *That looks unruffled to the gazing Eye,*
> *White and unsullied may it still remain,*
> *Nor shew th'Inscription of one Female Stain,*
> *Be't yours to quench each spark of rising Pride,*
> *And let firm Virtue be your constant Guide*
> *Then shall ye flourish and the World outvie,*
> *Shining the comet of the British sky.*
> *Yet mean I not to banish you from Tea,*
> *From cards — or such amusements of the Day,*
> *No, no, - sweet souls, that would indeed be wrong,*
> *Indulge your Taste, oft chaunt the lively song,*
> *And let kind Pleasure lead the dance along,*
> *In Time the Visit pay, in Time receive —*
> *For this at least, my Dears, you have my Leave ...,*
> *Let every wish be form'd with nicest care,*
> *Be chaste, discreet and virtuous, as Fair".*

Sarah took no notice of these precepts — the pages of her pocketbooks were anything but *"white and unsullied"* — but clearly she suffered similar remarks from those who disapproved of her writing or envied her intelligence. It is not surprising that she found this irritating.

Sarah's literary style

It does not seem likely that Sarah ever realised that her diaries would be of value to posterity; they were almost certainly written as a private source of comfort and interest during the long, lonely years when Henry was away, and not intended for publication. If she did seek recognition, it would have been as a poet, not a diarist. Yet it was in the diaries and letters that Sarah found her distinctive *"voice"* and personal style, while her poetry seems to have been rather more derivative. In general, Sarah wrote simply and naturally, with great freshness and spontaneity, about people and events. A typical entry is that of 17 January 1759, in which Sarah describes the events of the day in a straightforward manner, with underlying humour and feeling; *"At home. Work afternoon, drink tea at Aunt Grace's, just removed to their new house. Plan many subjects for poems but fear I shall never have time to finish them. Call on Betsy Sheppard, laugh at her going to be married but am really much concerned about losing my dear companion"*. Occasionally Sarah introduced a rather more literary note, when she reflected on her situation or her philosophy of life in rather self-conscious, elevated terms; *"Walk about the Forest & observe on the beautifull scenes around & admire the bountifull goodness of our all wise Creator, who has plac'd us here in a Paradise, as our little Island may be justly term'd, free from the severe cold of the North Pole, nor yet fainting under the excessive heat of the torrid zone, were our passions as moderate as our climate we might be term'd the happiest of nations, but alas we are made miserable by our own bad conduct"*. Such passages were probably inspired by the *"sentimental"* style which was becoming popular, and were written as a form of exercise to hone her writing skills. A rather more pithy, epigrammatic style, which she also used on occasion to some effect, probably reflected the influence of Alexander Pope, whom we know she admired, or his contemporaries. She used this style to write a crisp appraisal of a character; for example, her devastating comment on Arthur Bridger, who died in July 1759; *"he liv'd unregarded & dyed unlamented, has lost his fortune to those he never cared for, & disinherited a son who had a natural tho' not a lawful right to his possessions."*

Sarah as a historian

Sarah was a sharp-eyed and candid observer of life in Horsham and elsewhere between 1759 and 1762, and managed to capture atmosphere as well as relating events in her diaries. However, she was only able to write about what she saw or experienced; there were many things that went on in the town to which she had no access, as a woman. It should be borne in mind that Sarah never aspired to be a town chronicler, and her diaries were not written as a historical record. Nevertheless, that is what they have become. As such, we should perhaps consider the question of their historical accuracy, as well as style and content. It may be noted that the existence of nearly all the people mentioned by Sarah can be confirmed by reference to the Land Tax or other records, and her opinion of them also seems to tie in with other diaries or letters, where these exist. Thus we can be reasonably certain that when Sarah mentions a matter of historical importance — such as the celebrations for the various victories of 1759, or her visit to Portsmouth where she saw naval ships waiting to go to war — her account was truthful and accurate. Matters of interpretation are of course more dependent on hindsight. Sarah did not seem to be particularly concerned about the danger of a French invasion of England in 1759, beyond mentioning the rumours about it on 29 June of that year. It was only with the convincing defeat of the French fleet at Quiberon Bay in November 1759 that England was saved from this threat. Later historians writing about the war have seen the possibility of invasion as a very real and present danger, but this was probably not quite so obvious at the time. Sarah's fears for Henry's personal safety at this point in the war were understandably all-consuming, and of far more importance to her personally.

However, there are some events on which she might have been expected to report, and people who are omitted, and these should perhaps be mentioned in passing. Surprisingly there is no reference to one of the most significant occurrences in the affairs of the town during the period that she was writing her diaries; the death of Henry, Lord Irwin, at Hill's Place on 4 April 1761, an event for which unfortunately we do not have a detailed local account. His body was sent to Temple Newsam, his principal seat, for burial, doubtless with due solemnity and a proper escort of his tenants and dependants. It is hardly likely that Sarah did not know about this event, but she probably did not see it as being of any great significance to her personally. She gave a much fuller report of the death and burial of Isabella Ramsden, Lord Irwin's niece, in childbirth a few months later, because this tragedy was something that had an especial significance for her. Isabella Ramsden was a girl of about her own age, recently married to a soldier (Lt. Colonel Fretchville Ramsden). Sarah herself mentioned the similarity of their circumstances, which clearly inspired her interest in this particular event.

There were also other people living in the town whom one might have expected her to mention - for example, the Pilfolds were wealthy mercers living next door to Causeway House, who later married into the Shelley family. They would certainly have moved in similar circles to their near neighbours, the Parhams, the Powells, the Curtises and the Tredcrofts. Yet the Pilfolds never figure in the diaries — even though John Pilfold was one of the witnesses of Richard Hurst's will. Sarah probably did not mention the Pilfolds because there were no young people of her own age with whom she would have been well acquainted. But these few small omissions do not affect the overall value of her diaries. In other ways, Sarah seems to have been a fortunate witness of some significant events. She was lucky enough to be in London when the new King George III first went to Parliament, and she saw his Queen at the Palace window; but was not impressed — *"she is a very little plain woman, nor can I think her agreable"*. During this same visit to London in November 1761, she also saw David Garrick and Mrs. Cibber, the greatest actors of their age, play *Romeo and Juliet,* and watched the whole Royal family go to dine at Guildhall

Sarah and other diarists

In their Sussex context, Sarah's diaries were written during the same period as the diaries of Thomas Turner of East Hoathly, which date from 1754 to 1765, and make a very interesting comparison with them. Turner is generally considered to be the most important Sussex diarist of this period, with his detailed portrait of rural village life in East Hoathly, of which he was very much the pivot. Sarah was obviously not able to play the same sort of rôle in the affairs of Horsham that Thomas Turner played in those of East Hoathly, but her diaries throw important new light on to the life of the aspiring middle class in one of the main towns in Sussex. Although such people were still relatively few in number, they probably had a greater impact on their town and the county as a whole than their more rural neighbours.

It is also interesting to compare Sarah's diaries with those of John Baker, a lawyer who lived in Horsham Park House from 1771 to 1777, and wrote about his life in the town during that period. Though the two sets of diaries do not overlap, some of the same people appear in both diaries, but there are clear differences in the way in which they are depicted. Sarah was perceptive and revealed far more of the interior lives of the people that she encountered, than John Baker did, although he had all the advantages of education and experience of life. For example, as regards John Shelley of Field Place, Sarah sympathetically considered the effect that the loss of his wife must have had on him, and observed his unenthusiastic courtship of Phoebe Tredcroft with some amusement, although she also deplored his frequent rudeness, volatility and drunkenness. John Baker, on the other hand, only related what John Shelley said and did when in his company, or the gossip about him, and did not probe any deeper. It is perhaps surprising that John Baker spent far more time writing about the trivia of his existence - what he had for dinner, or what he wore on a particular occasion - than Sarah did. She was far more concerned with her longings and aspirations, the difficulties that she laboured under, and her passion for self-improvement. She had to fight for her right to read books and write poetry, since these activities came under censure from some of her neighbours and relations. John Baker had no such problems, as a man in a man's world.

Sarah's account of Isabella Ramsden's death, mentioned above, is a good example of Sarah's feminine perspective, as a diarist. It was the third such death of Sarah's contemporaries given special prominence in her diaries. The loss of Mrs. Shelley, wife of John Shelley of Field Place, in 1759, inspired Sarah to write an elegy, while the burial of her first really close friend, Mary Catherine Michell, who had secretly married Bysshe Shelley in the Fleet Chapel in 1752, caused her to reflect on the dangers of a hasty marriage. The early death of many of her contemporaries in childbirth or related causes — however wealthy or well looked after they were — must have created considerable disquiet in the minds of young women like Sarah, when they contemplated marriage. Sarah made quite frequent references to the possibility of her own early death, though generally she predicted that this would be the result of Henry's failure to return from the war. In fact, the possibility of mother or child dying in childbirth does seem to have been rather greater in the middle of the 18th century than it was either earlier or later, due to the lack of proper training of midwives, unhygienic practice and the controversial use of forceps.[22] It is therefore not surprising that some young women, who had the financial means to do so, chose to remain unmarried at this time. In Sarah's diaries, Phoebe Tredcroft, Henrietta Ellis and the young widow, Mrs. Wicker, are all recorded as turning down a proposal of marriage, though Phoebe did marry later. Even though Sarah longed above all else to be married to her beloved Henry, a sense of the danger and uncertainty of life was almost bound to colour her diaries, and this perhaps makes them rather different to those of a contemporary male writer.

The particular value of Sarah's diaries is that they give us a clear insight into what it was really like to be a young woman living in a small country town two hundred and fifty years ago — her thoughts and feelings, as well as her activities. In the final analysis, Sarah's diaries are about much more than her actual life in Horsham. They deal with some of the most fundamental concerns of human life — the pursuit of happiness in an imperfect world, the need for faith and courage to endure and surmount difficulties, and the sustaining power of love. In all that, they may still be an inspiration for us today.

The marriage of Sarah and Henry

There are several interesting points raised by the marriage of Henry and Sarah, in April 1762, which are not entirely resolved by the diaries. Despite the fact that Sarah always condemned those who married *"imprudently"*, and without proper provision for a future together, their marriage was a classic case of heart winning over head. Sarah married Henry at Slinfold on 28 April 1762, by special licence, with all the questions of his future and her dowry still unresolved, and knowing full well that their secret marriage would be controversial. This perhaps indicates that she was far more of a creature of passion and impulse than she would have liked to admit. Six or more pages of the diary were torn out in the month of the marriage, perhaps to obliterate the way in which it had been planned. This must have involved some measure of deception, where her parents were concerned.

It was Sarah, rather than Henry, who realised that, under Lord Hardwicke's new Marriage Act of 1754, she and Henry could marry privately, by Bishop's licence. Sarah was of age, and did not need her parents' permission, provided that she could establish residence in Slinfold for a sufficient period, and find a clergyman who would be willing to marry them. With the aid of Sarah's friend, the Rev. John Jones, curate of Slinfold, Sarah and Henry were married on 28 April 1762, in secret. Sarah and Henry chose not to disclose that they were married until Henry's future career in the Marine Corps was more certain. They still faced opposition from both families — Henry's mother, though more friendly to Sarah than she had been, was still unreconciled to her as a prospective daughter-in-law. Sarah's parents were well aware of her relationship with Henry Smith, and their intention to marry, but her father also seems to have had some reservations. Sarah felt that these were more concerned with his unwillingness to lose her help in his business than anything else.

The main point at issue seems to have been the financial arrangements that her father was expected to make on her behalf. After Sarah finally broached this matter to her father in September 1762, though still concealing the fact that the marriage had already taken place, Richard Hurst agreed to give her £300 on her marriage, plus another £300 in his will. Sarah felt that this was not enough, in the event that she and Henry might have to subsist on his half-pay. She was also upset when her father said, on hearing a rumour that Sarah was already married, that this would be a good thing because he could then make his own terms. But at the same time she may well have begun to feel guilty about having married in secret, since she said on 27 September *"I wish it* (the marriage) *was publick, I detest the artfull part I am oblig'd to act"*.

When the diary ends on 31 December 1762, it is not entirely clear that Sarah's parents knew of her marriage, as she does not actually say that she has told them. But in the entry for 30 December, Sarah said that she had received a letter summoning her to join Henry in Plymouth, and was preparing to do so, so one can only suppose that by now the fact of the marriage must have become known. Reading between the lines, it seems very likely that it was during the week of 24 November to 2 December, which was left blank for no apparent reason, that Sarah confessed to her parents that she and Henry were actually married. It seems very unlikely that she would have been able to keep it secret much longer, given the highly charged state of her emotions, at the time of her sister Bet's marriage to Will James on 14 November. On this day Sarah made an extraordinary entry in her diary, *"Bet Hurst married to young James, I cannot call her my sister; a dismal wedding day, many such I fear would kill me"*. She was also missing Henry quite desperately *"Think on & sigh for my dearest Husband, his absence grows every day more insupportable, when oh when shall I be forever with him"*.

However, when it did come to the point, the actual disclosure of her marriage to her parents must have been very difficult, and it may have provoked such an intemperate reaction by her father that Sarah could not even bring herself to write about it in her diary. This might also explain her rather bitter remark on 3 December *"Tell my mother she behaves exactly the same to Bet as tho' her conduct had been ever so good"*, and the heartfelt cry two days later, *"I wish, oh how much I wish to be with my dearest Harry, far away from all these turbulent folks who wanting Reason for their guide are perpetually driving Headlong down the stream of indiscretion"*. Most of the remaining entries for this month seem somewhat curt and guarded, and there are two more unexplained gaps between 8 and 16 December and 24 and 30 December, before Sarah received the letter from Henry for which she had been waiting.

Sarah's reaction to Bet's wedding was, perhaps understandably, a complex mix of jealousy, bitterness and frustration. Sarah had always had a difficult relationship with Bet, but her distress at Bet's hastily arranged marriage seems to have been out of all proportion, and indicates a much deeper feeling than mere disapproval of the way it took place. Bet had clearly been caught misbehaving with Will James, and her wedding was apparently rushed through to save her reputation. It seems very likely that Bet was feared to be pregnant, though the James' first child was not in fact baptised until January 1764. But Sarah must have felt that Bet at least had the substance of a marriage, while she had only the shadow, and this must have been very hard for her to accept. There was also the question of how much disgrace Bet's shotgun wedding would have on the reputation of her whole family. Perhaps the hardest thing of all for her to bear was that Bet apparently still retained her mother's preference and approval, while Sarah, who had loved Henry for so long and suffered so much while he was away, had been forced to marry in secret and was not yet able to acknowledge her husband. On 8 October, Sarah had equivocated about the marriage to Henry's mother, who exhibited signs of *"agitation"* at the possibility that it had taken place. When the disclosure did finally take place, it would have been very clear that Sarah had effectively told a lie on this occasion.

Was the shame and distress that Sarah clearly felt about Bet's marriage magnified by the realisation that her own behaviour had not entirely conformed to the highest moral standards? Were her parents deeply hurt and angered by the clandestine way in which her marriage had taken place? There is little doubt that Sarah had to confront these issues, during the last weeks of 1762. But the closing entry of the diary shows that Sarah was looking forward to the future with calm happiness. *"Memorandum: One more year is gone & I am thank God infinitely happier than I have been for many preceding ones"*. Surely this indicates that everything was now resolved and forgiven, perhaps with the help of other members of the family, after a difficult few weeks in which Sarah clearly found it very hard to write her diary at all. On 19 December she said that she had drunk tea with *"my dear Harry's mother"* at her Aunt Waller's house, in company with her ever-supportive Aunt Wicker. The turn of the year marked the start of her new life as Henry's acknowledged wife.

Henry's career

Unfortunately, we do not have any written record of what Sarah's life was like in the early years of her marriage, or indeed for the next twenty years. No further diaries have come to light, so we do not know whether Sarah continued to keep a diary, or whether, in the excitement and fulfilment of her new life, she no longer felt the need, or had the time, to commit her innermost thoughts to paper. There is one brief glimpse of Henry and Sarah in John Baker's diary, on 28 August 1773, the only time that the two Horsham diarists are known to have met. *"To Mr. Tredcroft's où Col. Smith (of Marines) and his wife, daughter Mr. Hurst, drinking tea as I did — went in just after 6 and stayed an hour".*[23] But there are other sources that can help us build up a picture of this period. It is clear from the Marine records that Henry proved his worth as an administrator, and reached the summit of his profession as a Marine officer. He was appointed Colonel Commandant of the Portsmouth Division of the Marines in 1772, one of the four most senior officers of the Corps, only ten years after he had married Sarah. The only officer of higher rank was the Commanding Marine Officer in London (later called the Colonel Commandant in Town) who answered directly to the Admiralty. From October 1777, the Colonel Commandant of each Division invariably held the rank of Major-General or Lieutenant-General in the Army.

A few extracts from the published records of the Portsmouth Division of Marines show how Henry imposed discipline, duty, order and a respect for proper appearance on the officers and men of the Portsmouth Division, who were described by General James Wolfe as *"dirty, drunken, insolent rascals"* in the early days of their formation. It is clear that Henry had an eye for detail and a shrewd appreciation of the foibles of human nature and, despite the courtesy and patience with which his orders were expressed, he was determined to enforce higher standards of behaviour.

"30 October 1772 Colonel Smith expects that the Officers of the Division will attend the Review of Arms & Necessaries & he likewise desires they will be very particular in giving directions that the Mens Linnen is well washed & proper Care taken of it....
21 March 1773 Colonel Smith observing the Officers do not appear when on duty in Uniformity of Dress thinks it necessary to give the following

Directions which he trusts will be strictly adhered to. When the Division is order'd under Arms the Officers will wear a plain Hat with a Uniform Button, and Loop, black Velvet Stock, Gorget, The Sword Slung over the Shoulder Short Spatterdashes and their Skirts tuck'd up, the Pouch & Laced Hatt to be added to the officers who parade for Guard …

13 November 1774 Colonel Smith thinks it is Necessary that every man at the Division whose Debts do not exceed ten Shillings shall in future have 4 Shirts & 4 pair of Stockings and they are immediately to be supplied by the Squad Officer with those articles to make up that Number.…

20 January 1775 It is Colonel Smiths directions that the Non Commissioned Officers, Drummers and Private Men, who are not in debt to the Division, shall for the future receive their full Pay…

23 July 1776 It appearing to Colonel Smith that the Serjeant & Corporal of the Barrack Guard have been very remiss in not keeping the Key of the Wicket agreeable to the Standing Orders of the division any of them who shall so neglect so essential a part of their duty, in future will be reduced for it – And it is the Colonel's further orders that no marine shall be suffer'd to go out of the Barrack before 6 o Clock in the Morning

25 July 1776 Colonel Smith observing two very dirty disorderly women coming from Lieut Moriarty's room this morning, thinks it necessary to order the Serjeant of the Guard to prevent in future, any of these loose common Creatures from coming in at the Barrack Gate —

28 December 1779 It is Genl Smith's positive orders that no Subaltern Officer is on any account to pass a Non-Commissioned Officer or Private man out of the Wicket after Retreat Beating…

17 April 1780 Genl Smith thinks it necessary to repeat in publick orders, his wishes that the young Officers at the division and those who shall hereafter join will make themselves perfectly acquainted with the Standing orders of the division, and their Military duty — And those who shall neglect attending any part of it, are to be reported to the Captain of the Week or Senior Officer of the Parade to the Commanding Officer of the division".[24]

Henry officially retired as Colonel Commandant of the Portsmouth Division on 24 December 1791, at the age of 68. He was appointed Colonel Commandant in Town, on the same day, though by now this was probably more of an honorary, rather than an active, post, as several other former Commandants of other Divisions had been promoted in this way. He held this post until he died in 1794, at the age of 71. Sarah's reference to Osborne's Hotel, Adelphi, as her *"former lodgings"*, suggests that this was where she and Henry stayed when he needed to be in London. Sarah said in her 1759 diary that Henry became an officer in the Marine Corps in 1755, when it was first set up, so it would appear that, at the time of his death, he had served for nearly forty years. However, the inscription on Henry's memorial states that he had served in the Marines for fifty-five years, but this was probably his entire military service.

The Smith memorial

While we can only speculate about the ways in which Sarah might have assisted her husband in his successful career, it is certain that they remained devoted to each other throughout life. Sarah rejoiced in the title of *"Mrs. General Smith"* and used it proudly to refer to herself. The epitaph which she wrote for his memorial in St. Mary's Church is beautifully crafted and perfectly expresses her feelings about him and their marriage.

Sacred to the Memory of Lieutenant General HENRY SMITH, Colonel Commandant and Adjutant General of the Marine Forces in which Corps He serv'd his King and Country Fifty five Years. He was Belov'd of all those He was destin'd to Command And Honor'd with the Confidence and esteem of all who Commanded him. He was a Soldier and a Christian who died the 29th of September 1794, Aged 71 years. This monument was erected by his disconsolate Widow SARAH who hopes soon to be united in a blissful Eternity to the Man who made it the study of his Life to Render hers happy.

Sarah was later buried beside him, very simply commemorated in the following words; *"His wife Sarah, daughter of Richard and Mary Hurst, died 1808, aged 73"*

In James Edwards' *A Companion from London to Brighthelmston*, published in parts from 1796 onwards, it was remarked in the section on Horsham parish church that *"a very magnificent monument has been lately erected to the memory of General Smith, of the Portsmouth Division of Marines, who was a native of this town"*. An early photograph, taken by Henry Padwick jr., of the chancel of St. Mary's Church, before its extensive restoration in 1864-5, shows a large memorial above the tomb of Sir Thomas de Braose that includes a weeping female figure and an anchor, with an inscription in the shape of a rhomboid below. All the available evidence suggests that this was indeed the *"magnificent"* memorial to Henry Smith. The rhomboidal inscription still survives today, along with other Smith memorials on the north wall of the tower, but it seems likely that the rest of the memorial was lost or discarded when the restoration of the church took place.

Sarah's Letters

Six letters have survived from Sarah's later years, written to her brother or his wife, which give us some indication of how the young woman of the diaries developed as a wife and as a widow. Though few in number, the letters are full of interest and round off the portrait of Sarah's remarkable personality very satisfactorily. The same unmistakable voice and style of her diaries is heard in the letters, which shine with wit, humour and depth of experience, and show that the older woman fulfilled all the promise of the young girl, in terms of character and personality.

One letter survives from 1785, and is the only one to give us any idea of Sarah's married life with Henry. It was written after Sarah and Henry had been staying in Horsham with Robert and his wife Maria (who was Henry's niece), and describes their journey home to Portsmouth, as well as conveying their thanks for the visit. It seems that Henry and Sarah were living in an outlying village, near the sea, rather than in the town, near the Marine barracks, as one might have expected. Sarah described the effects of a storm on their small and obviously rural community, but there is no clue as to where it was exactly. Portsmouth harbour is large, and there are many places where it could have been.

The other letters all date from the period of Sarah's widowhood, when she was living in Chichester, and before her return to Horsham to live in Causeway House. As the widow of a General, she was a woman of high social status, and she rose to the challenge of finding a new purpose in life, proving to be as good an aunt and sister as she had been a devoted wife. The letters mainly concern the early schooldays of Sarah's niece, Isabella Maria and nephew Robert Henry - the eldest daughter and son of Robert and Maria — who had been sent to school in Chichester, where their aunt could keep an eye on them and they could spend their weekends with her. (These letters were probably treasured by the children's mother as they include Robert Henry's and Isabella Maria's early attempts to write to their parents). Sarah was clearly a wonderful aunt, deeply interested in the children, and beloved by them — Robert Henry Hurst said in a letter shortly after her death in 1808 that he regarded her in the light of a second mother. The great sadness of her life must have been that she and Henry had no children of their own, but clearly she did not let this grief, and the loss of Henry, embitter her. There is talk of going to concerts and of a lively social life, with visitors and card-parties. Sarah was an efficient manager of her household, and a keen gardener.

Sarah's last known letter to Robert, in May 1797, shows that she still took a deep interest in everything he did, but it is significant because in it Sarah accepted Robert's offer of Causeway House as her future home. It is also interesting because it makes it clear that Sarah still felt that she had the right to advise and warn Robert if she thought he was being unwise, even though he was by now a respected lawyer and man of property. She took him severely to task for threatening to leave Horsham, because he did not like the presence of a military barracks in the town. This had been built in September 1796, when there were fears of a French invasion, with Sussex in the front line. Though she made her points with some diffidence and much humour, Sarah's was clearly very concerned to prevent Robert making what she perceived to be a grave mistake. She also expressed some doubt about the influence on him of his rather overbearing employer and friend, Bysshe Shelley. In the event, her advice seems to have been taken - Robert did not desert Horsham and his relationship with Bysshe Shelley cooled somewhat in later years. He gave up being a trustee of the Shelley estates around 1802, when he became a Member of Parliament for Steyning.

Sarah's last years in Horsham

Though one would expect that Sarah would have enjoyed life in Chichester, a city of fine houses and good society in the 1790s, it is obvious from the alacrity with which she accepted Robert's offer of Causeway House for her home that she missed her family and pined to return to Horsham. Causeway House (Mr. Parham's house in the diaries) was bought by her father in 1764 and was her brother's home in Horsham until he moved to Park House. (The purchase of Park House appears to have been finalised in 1799, but Sarah's account books show that she was installed at Causeway House by late 1798). It was a most suitable abode for Sarah's final years. The account books that survive from this period show that Sarah remained as active and self-sufficient as ever, keeping a cow (or cows) and a pig in the field which she rented across the lane at the back of her house, and allowing other people to keep their sheep there (for a charge). These *"farming"* activities, for which she had a separate account book, are the perfect expression of Sarah's common sense and down to earth attitude, which was evident throughout her life. The money she made — or saved — from these activities was added year by year to her investments in the 3 per cent Consols or the slightly riskier 5 per cent funds, and gradually accumulated during the years that she lived in Horsham at the end of her life.

Sarah died after what seems to have been a short final illness in March 1808, since her accounts were kept up until just a few days before her death. But Mrs. Bayley, one of her legatees, said in a letter to Robert Hurst that Sarah had suffered much ill health towards the end of her life and, in one of her letters to Robert, Sarah wrote amusingly of rheumatism making a tour of her whole body. It seems likely, from one of the references in her diary, referring to swelling as well as pain, that she suffered from rheumatoid arthritis.[25]

Sarah's legacy

The basis of Sarah's personal fortune appears, from her account books and the record made by her brother after her death, to have been her sale of Yewood Farm in Newdigate to the Duke of Norfolk in 1796, for £3,000. There is a reference in the Arundel Castle MSS to Robert Hurst as the owner of this farm in 1783;[26] whether he sold it to Sarah and her husband or whether he gave the farm or the proceeds of the sale to his widowed sister is not clear, as no other record of the transaction has yet been found. But, even if Robert did own the farm originally, it was Sarah who tripled the capital in the space of twelve years.

The bulk of Sarah's fortune was left to her brother Robert as the residue of her estate, but one does not realise at first how much this would be when reading her will, which details a long list of small bequests to her friends and relations. However, close study of the account books reveal that after Robert, as her executor, had paid out all the legacies, which amounted to some £1,260.15s. in all, he was left with £10,014.10s.9d for himself. Sarah's assets consisted of £4,700 in the 5 per cent fund, plus £5,500 in 3 per cent Consols, which was her own money, not Henry's, plus another £1,075.5s.9d. from cash left in the house, money in the bank, pension arrears, and the sale of furniture, plate, linen and other goods, including Sarah's carriage and three cows. £1,000 from Henry Smith's trust now went to Robert's wife Maria, and their children benefited from a further £1,000 which was to be divided between them when they reached the age of 21. So it is now quite obvious where Robert obtained the money he used to buy land on Horsham Common, when it was sold off in parcels after enclosure in 1812. Strangely enough, the capital sum that Robert laid out on these purchases was almost exactly the same as that he inherited from his sister's estate. In total he spent £10,005.16s.3d on his purchases in the sales of land in Horsham and Roffey in October 1812 and January 1813.[27]

Thus it only seems fair to recognise that it was largely due to Sarah that her brother was able to become the chief landowner in Horsham Parish, a fact of considerable significance in the development of the town throughout the 19th century. It is improbable that, without the legacy he received from his sister, Robert would have been able to raise enough capital to take advantage of this unparalleled opportunity. Even though he was a successful barrister, a trusted employee of the Duke of Norfolk and a paid trustee of the Shelley estates, it is unlikely that, with a family of seven children to support, he would have been able to put aside enough money to buy land on such a scale. He must already have dug deep into his savings, or any money left to him by his father, to finance the purchase of Horsham Park in 1799. As far as is known he received no other large-scale accretion of wealth between 1799 and 1812, other than the money he received from Sarah on her death. The extent of this legacy from his sister was previously unrecorded, but now that it is known, Sarah should surely be given the credit that she deserves for her thrift and her generosity. Indeed, it is perhaps not too much to say that, without Sarah's money, it would have been impossible for Robert to buy up so much of the Common. Had this been the case, the history of Horsham might well have taken another course, and the development of the town been quite different. Thus Sarah's importance in the history of Horsham is not confined to the existence of her diaries — in a very real sense, she played a part in shaping the town as it is today.

1   HM MSS Cat. No. 3542-3545; diaries. HM MSS Cat. No. 3541; transcript.

2   WSRO Hurst MSS (Acc. 3296) 25 and 26 March 1746 — conveyance by Lease and Release, Tapsfield and wife (formerly Martha Briggs) to Richard Hurst.

3   HM MSS Cat. No. 346, 13 February 1789. Robert Hurst to Thomas Charles Medwin — note; *"In my garret at Horsham are a prodigious number of papers which were left in my house by Mr. White, Mr. Arnold and Mr. Parham, all attornies and the former owners of it".*

4   WSRO Hurst MSS (Acc. 2271) 14 November 1767 — Worsfold to Hurst, surrender.

5   *The Gentleman's Magazine*, Vol. 53, December 1783.

6   John Middleton (d. 1636) had considerable business interests in forges in Sussex and Staffordshire. His son Thomas inherited Hill's Place and was M.P. for Horsham in the Long Parliament, but had his estates sequestrated after the Horsham rising in 1648. His grandson and namesake sold Hill's Place to John Machell in 1664, and moved to Hangleton. John Machell's daughter Isabella married Arthur Ingram, 3rd Viscount Irwin, of Temple Newsam in Yorkshire, and their second son, Rich, inherited the Hill's estate. This was the start of the Irwin connection with Horsham.

7   ESRO Drake and Lee papers, SAS-DD/362 — marriage settlement of Edward Tredcroft and Mary Michell, dated 24 June 1735.

8   Will of Marie Boutofflères - in author's possession.

9   Note on Ann Francis (née Gittins) in *Eighteenth Century Women Poets — an Oxford Anthology*, edited by Roger Lonsdale, Oxford University Press, 1989.

10   SNQ, Vol. XVII, No. 2, November 1968 — note on the memorial to Jane Gittins and Anne Francis.

11   British Library shelf mark PP 51240. The poem was found and identified by Lady Morse.

12   ESRO microfilm XA 46/7. The poem was found and identified by John Farrant.

13   *Horsham Heritage*, Issue No. 3, Spring 2001, *"A lost poem by Sarah Hurst?"*.

14   Lines from *An Elegy on a Favourite Cat*, in *Eighteenth Century Women Poets — an Oxford Anthology*, edited by Roger Lonsdale, Oxford University Press, 1989.

15   Amanda Vickery, *The Gentleman's Daughter: Women's Lives in Georgian England*, Yale University Press, 1998.

16   Anthony Highmore, *A Ramble on the Coast of Sussex*, written in 1782, reprinted in *The Horsham Companion*, Horsham Museum Society, 1995. The lady bookseller who is mentioned by Anthony Highmore was almost certainly Elizabeth Griffith, daughter of Thomas Griffith, the carpenter.

17   HM MSS Cat. No. 205, The Borough of Horsham Market Deed of 15 November 1756, drawn up after a public meeting on 1 October, and signed and sealed by 80 inhabitants of Horsham.

18   *Horsham Heritage*, Issue No. 17, Autumn 2008, *"The Eversfields of Denne House"*.

19   Djabri, Hughes and Knight, *The Shelleys of Field Place*, Horsham Museum Society, 2000, p. 46.

20   Linda Colley, *Britons; Forging the Nation 1707-1837*, Pimlico, 1994, p. 239-240.

21   Linda Colley, *op.cit*, p. 260.

22   In 1760, Elizabeth Nihell, a self-taught midwife, published a *Treatise on the Art of Midwifery*, in which she attacked the celebrated gynaecologist Dr. William Smellie for his use of forceps during childbirth. Ultimately, the use of forceps saved lives, but their use at this period was dangerous, as the need for sterilisation and hand-washing was not yet understood. The fall in the birth rate in the late 17th and early 18th centuries, and the rise in the death rate around 1720 have been charted by Peter Laslett in *The World We Have Lost further explored* , Routledge, 1983.

23   Philip C. Yorke, *The Diary of John Baker*, Hutchinson & Co., 1931, p. 266.

24   J.A. Lowe, ed., *Portsmouth Record Series; Records of the Portsmouth Division of Marines 1764-1800*, City of Portsmouth, 1990. pp. xv, 17, 20 and 22.

25   I am indebted to Lady Morse for interpreting the symptoms of this disease.

26   Francis Steer, *Arundel Castle Archives Vol. I*, (catalogue), p. 85. AC MSS 2/26, plan of Yewood Farm, Newdigate, Surrey, belonging to Robert Hurst Esq.

27   Albery, *Millennium*, pp. 195-196.

2. Horsham Market House *c*.1800. The house on the far right is Daniels, where Sarah lived. Sally Sheppard lived in the house behind the one shown on the far left.   The Market House was used for the Assizes and staging plays when the strolling players came to town.

3. Ashley's burgage house, in East Street, where Mrs. Bridger lived.

4. View over Horsham from Denne Hill.

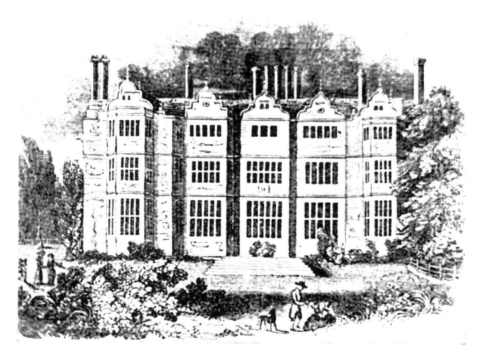

5. Hill's Place, Horsham — the home of Lord Irwin and his family.

6. John Shelley of Field Place.

7. Samuel Blunt and Winifred Blunt of Springfield Place.

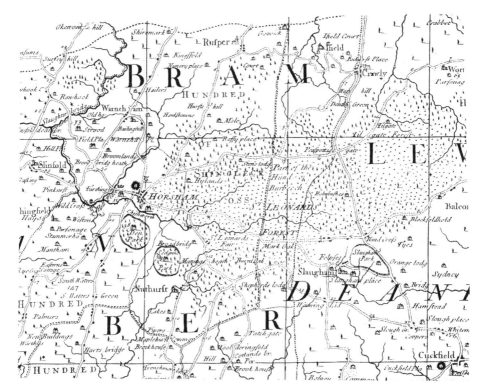

8.   Richard Budgen's map (1724) of the countryside around Horsham, showing Slinfold, Warnham, St. Leonard's Forest, Slaugham and Cuckfield. Among the houses marked are Strood, Field Place, Hill's Place, Chesworth, Denne Park, Sedgwick Park, and Hylands (Highlands) Farm.

9.   Farthing Bridge, on the road to Slinfold.

10. Medals celebrating the victories of 1758 and 1759.

11. General Wolfe, on whom Sarah wrote an *"Elegaic Acrostic"* and *"Epitaph"*.

12. The attack on Quebec on 12 September 1769.

Il fait vaincre a la fois et chante ses Victoires.

Fridericus II Rex Borufforum 1776.
a Londres chez Rob.t Sayer N.º 33 in fleet Street

13. Frederick II, King of Prussia ("Frederick the Great").

14. William Pitt the elder, Paymaster of the Forces, who directed the British war effort.

15. Arundel Castle, which Sarah visited with Miss Gittins.

16. Lewes, where Sarah may have been at school.

THE DIARY FOR 1759

(The diary is written in a printed almanack, The Ladies Complete Pocket-book, *a small leather bound book. Printed at the beginning is a* "Chronicle of Remarkable Events of 1758" *and a picture of* "A Lady in the Dress of the Year 1758". *On the blank sheets at the beginning of the Diary Sarah has written* "brief histories" *of previous years).*

A brief history of the year 1755

I had now carried on my affair with Lieutenant Smith[28] for 3 years unknown to my friends tho' not without great compunction of mind and several efforts to break with him, which however prove ineffectual. His regard for me was certainly real, tho' his slender circumstances render it improper to declare it to my friends.[29] In February there is a talk of the War breaking out with the French. This occasions an augmentation of the forces by sea & land & calls him to London. He first has a Lieutenancy in a marching regiment & soon after *[in]* a Company of Marines, by Lord Irwin's interest.[30] About this time I go to London, on a visit to my Uncles,[31] he calls on me several times, & I have no reason to be dissatisfied with his behaviour, but my relations *[illegible word]* all disapprove his visits & prevent my seeing him. This gives us both great uneasiness, & makes me reflect on the unhappy situation I have drawn myself into. *[I]* fondly love this Dear man, yet think it very improbable I can ever be his. I write to him, & tell him I now see the time approaching that I shall be forgot, & everything that has passed between us buried in oblivion. He assures me to the contrary, & that his love shall last as long as Life. We find means to meet at Kensington Gardens. He returns to Horsham & I soon after. I now

28 Henry Smith, then a Lieutenant in the Royal Marines.
29 "*My friends*", used in this context throughout the diaries, means Sarah's family.
30 Henry Ingram, 7th Viscount Irwin, of Temple Newsam, Yorkshire, and Hill's Place in Horsham. From the evidence of this diary entry, it appears that Henry Smith was one of the very first serving officers of the newly established Marines. Though there had been earlier Marine regiments, a permanent Marine establishment of 5,700 officers and men was set up in April 1755, with three "*Grand Divisions*" based on Chatham, Portsmouth and Plymouth.
31 Robert and George Hurst.

(as he is going abroad) determine to break with him & avoid him several days, but this scheme proves abortive. We meet & are reconciled, agree on a correspondence, & exchange mutual protestations of everlasting Love. We part, he goes, but little did either of us think it wou'd be for so long a time. He writes to me & the Dear consolation of receiving his letters & answering them is all my consolation.

The history of 1756

I've now enter'd my twentieth year, & consequently had more serious thoughts in regard to my affair with Captain Smith, I tell Betsy & Sally Sheppard that I fear absence will lessen his regard for me, but both those Dear Girls, ever my comforters in affliction, tell me it can never be eras'd,[32] but I, thinking it wou'd be better to conquer my passion, (which, alas, I found unconquerable) neglected writing to him, so of course did not hear from him for some months; this drove me to my wits' end. I severely repent my folly & find the continuance of his regard is absolutely necessary to my repose. *[On the]* 16 of May in this distraction of mind I go to London with my Papa, see War declared the 18, return home the 20 and find a letter from my Dear Smith, which I certainly do not deserve; this dissipates my fears. He makes several cruises in the Channel. In August I go to Lewes on a visit to Miss Woodhams; stay a month, commence an acquaintance with Miss Gittins,[33] a Clergyman's daughter of Arundel, a young lady whose personal & Intellectual accomplishments exceed most of her sex. We agree on a correspondence, & vow a friendship that I hope will never terminate but with our lives. I endeavour in the course of our acquaintance to rectify some little levities this Dear girl was apt to run into from too great liveliness of her disposition. My remonstrances have the desir'd effect, & she is all I can wish. Nothing more remarkable this year.

1757

Receive in January a letter from my Dear Smith acquainting me he will be soon at Portsmouth from whence he expects to visit Horsham, but this hope proves fallacious. I send him some verses I wrote; he returns me an

32 Elizabeth and Sarah Sheppard were the daughters of Stringer Sheppard, butcher, and his wife Magdalen.
33 Ann Gittins, daughter of the Rev. Daniel Gittins, Ll. B., Rector of South Stoke and Vicar of Leominster in Sussex.

Acrostick on my name. My friends often tax me with corresponding with him, to which I give evasive answers, & as all my letters are directed to Mrs Luttman's[34] their suspicions cannot be confirm'd. Captain Smith is now ordered on board a fleet going to North America; they sail to Cork in Ireland. I write to him there & receive an answer; they leave Cork in May, & I hear no more the whole summer & suffer inexpressible uneasiness. In September the long wish'd for packet arrives, gives me an account of a violent Storm; the fleet was near all disaster, & but for the providential turning of the wind wou'd have been all lost on the rocks of Louisbourgh.[35] Receive another letter in December.

1758

Pass my time as agreeably as possible, (with Betsy & Sally Sheppard) in the dreadful uncertainty I am under of not hearing from my Dear Smith. My sister Bet is Innoculated in April;[36] we go to London in May to buy goods for the Shop. In August news arrives that Louisbourgh is taken by the fleet Captain Smith is with.[37] His mother has a letter but I have not one, now is my grief inexpressible. I conclude he has forgot his Sally, which plunges me in the deepest distress, my appetite & sleep forsakes me but for the company of my Dear Miss Gittins, who happened to be with me, this stroke wou'd inevitably have depriv'd me of my senses. I summon pride & reason to my aid but both are ineffective. I then, as he was daily expected in England, determine to go for a visit to Eastbourn & avoid the sight of a man who no longer thought on me, but this scheme Betsy Sheppard pursuaded *(sic)* me to lay aside, & the very evening I did so I received a letter from him, he was in Camp when the last ship came, which prevented his writing before. In October I receive another, acquainting me of his arrival in England & expectations of soon coming to Horsham. This causes an unusual palpitation in my heart; I wish to see him but dread his coming,

---

34 Mary Luttman (née Butterly), wife of Robert Luttman, who was described as *"a poor man"* when he died in 1773.

35 Louisburg, on Cape Breton Island, was the French naval station in Canada, which the British were about to attack in September 1757 when a fierce hurricane blew up. There was great danger that the entire fleet would have been wrecked, but fortunately there was a change in the direction of the wind that enabled them to escape. Six ships were dismasted, and the attack had to be abandoned.

36 Inoculation for smallpox was now becoming more common, and treatment of the disease more successful.

37 The capture of Louisburg, under Admiral Edward Boscawen and Brigadier (later Major-General) James Wolfe, in July 1758, was a turning point in the war against the French in Canada.

fearing my friends & his will again be enrag'd. I now determine to acquaint my Mama with the whole Affair, & then write to him & absolutely declare that I will no longer carry on a Clandestine Correspondence. He arrives; we meet; I give him the letter, & the time he must return to Portsmouth to consider of it, which I pass in the utmost anxiety. At last we compromise. I tell my father; he gives a re1uctant consent. Captain Smith vows an eternal fidelity, & we pass our time tolerably Happy, till on the 17th December he goes to London & thence to Plymouth.

JANUARY 1759

Monday, 1 January

Received a letter from Captain Smith, the contents agreeable and disagreeable. I am now entered on a New Year; may I dayly improve in virtue & entertain a just abhorrence of vice however alluring.

Tuesday, 2 January

Spent the afternoon at Mrs. Wicker's.[38] Read Captain Smith's letter to her.

Wednesday, 3 January

Spent the whole day at home. Wrote to Captain Smith in the evening. Express'd in this letter all the regard I have so long felt & have no doubt but it is most sincerely return'd.

Thursday, 4 January

Spent at home. Drank tea at Mrs. Lutman's, talk chiefly of Captain Smith. Mrs. Luttman expresses great affection to us both.

Friday, 5 January

Heard of Mrs. Shelley's death;[39] extremely concern'd for this amiable Lady, began an elegy on her Death, in the afternoon at Mrs. Tredcroft's[40] & evening at [?cards] & Picquet.

Saturday, 6 January

At home, finish the Elegy and read it to Mrs. Wicker [who] desires a copy & promise her one. Wrote to Sally & Betsy Sheppard sent a copy of the Elegy. Call on [illegible].

---

38 Elizabeth Wicker née Tasker (1723-1802) was Sarah's maternal aunt.
39 Mrs. Mary Shelley, the wife of John Shelley of Field Place, was buried at Warnham on 10 January 1759. She was the eldest daughter of William White, lawyer and steward to Lord Irwin. He and his wife Bathia (née Waller) had ten children, of whom four died young. Their four surviving daughters were all said to be remarkably handsome.
40 Mrs. Mary Tredcroft (née Michell), wife of Edward Tredcroft of the Manor House in the South Street, now the Causeway. He owned the Manors of Hewells and Hawkesbourne in Horsham, and was a Justice of the Peace.

Sunday, 7 January

Spent agreably at Slinfold. Mr. Pigott[41] say[...*page torn...*] consequently he must think meanly of all he bestows them on, reflect on this. Read my Elegy and give a copy.

Monday, 8 January

Slinfold, write an Ode on Miss Pigott's [*and*] Mr. Donall's birthday; they give it undue praises. Mr. Pigott wavering in regard to Miss Godfrey;[42] unhappy Lady, I pity her, & think him a little ungenerous.

Tuesday, 9 January

Do tell Mr. Pigott of his behaviour to Miss Godfrey — conjure him to act justly or entirely break it off. He gives me unsatisfactory answers & says he has neither resolution for one nor t'other. Agreable conversation on many improving subjects.

Wednesday, 10 January

Mr. Pigott very cool to Miss Godfrey. I renew my remonstrances but fear that they will have no effect – fatal inconstancy. Miss Pigott & I are in great concern for her Plan — a watch paper for Captain Smith[43] The device; Cupid cronning (sic) him with a Chaplet of Roses & Mars with a Laurel Wreath: the motto; "*Love and Glory both Assail, Glory must O'er Love prevail*".

Thursday, 11 January

Left Slinfold with regret. Mr. Pigott walks with me & says how unhappy he is & thinks he must ever be. I can give him no consolation; he thinks I unjustly blame him for an inconstancy which he cannot help. At Mrs. Wicker's in the evening — [*?Faro*] trifling conversation. Read my Elegy [*illegible phrase*] the Prussian exercise.[44]

Friday, 12 January

Send Miss Pigott a copy of the letter I wrote to Captain Smith in October desiring him to break with me. Betsy Sheppard returns,[45] tells me that Captain Smith did not go to Plymouth until Sunday last. I am dissatisfied, yet I cannot tell with what, unless it be thinking that as Captain Smith staid so long in London he might have found time to have seen me. Oh this fatal passion, it devours my quiet.

Saturday, 13 January

A very restless night; reflect on my affair with Captain Smith, doubt his love, yet have no reason, wish I had never shewn my regard for him, yet sure he can never be ungratefull, but t'is Inclination not faith ties hearts. Receive a letter from my Dear

---

41   Mr. Pigott was living at Slinfold, as the curate of the parish.

42   Miss Pigott was the sister of Mr. Pigott. Miss Godfrey is mentioned several times, but does not appear to have lived locally. Mr. Donall was probably just a visitor, as he is not mentioned again.

43   Watch papers were small round pieces of paper bearing a design and a motto, slipped into the cover of a watch, usually by the maker or repairer.

44   The "*Prussian exercise*" was a form of military drill that Henry's Marines would have practised. Sarah had probably written some verses about it.

45   Presumably from London, since she had news of Captain Smith leaving from there.

Miss Gittins & 3 pieces of poetry. She returns my sermon & the 2 letters which contain'd the account of my affair with Captain Smith. Work all day on his ruffles.

Sunday, 14 January

Betsy Sheppard says Captain Smith was in expectation of leaving London every day so could not come to Horsham, besides he dreaded parting again. I am glad he had some reason to give, a drowning wretch will clutch at a straw. Spend the day in the Duties of it. Violent Headache, reflect on the uncertainty and vicissitudes of everything in this Life, pine to see Captain Smith yet asham'd of my weakness. Can't expect to hear from him before next week, t'is a long time.

Monday, 15 January

Receive a letter from Miss Woodhams.[46] Begin some verses — title *"A Ladder to Preferment"*. Evening at Mrs. Tredcroft's, play quadrille. Reflect on the trifling conversations generally found in mix'd company that never tends to improve and seldom to divert the mind.

Tuesday, 16 January

Work and write. Afternoon at Mrs. Wicker's, hear great commendation of my Elegy, can't help being pleased at it, tho' endeavour to suppress my rising vanity. Think often of Captain Smith, begin reading Ma…[?*Maximes*] from the French).[47]

Wednesday, 17 January

At home. Work afternoon, drink tea at Aunt Grace's,[48] just remov'd to their new house.[49] Plan many subjects for poems but fear I shall never have time to finish them. Call on Betsy Sheppard, laugh at her going to be married but am really much concerned about losing my dear companion.

Thursday, 18 January

Work all day on Captain Smith's ruffles. See the post, puts my heart in a palpitation thinking he has a letter for me. Finish my *"Ladder of Preferment"*, various moral reflections in it.

Friday, 19 January

Nothing worth recording. Chat with Jenny Hunt[50] and Betsy Sheppard. Hope I shall

---

46   Miss Woodhams was the friend Sarah visited in Lewes in 1756.

47   Probably the *Réflexions, ou Sentences et Maximes Morales* of the French writer, François de La Rochefoucauld (1613-1680), first published in 1665. The *Maximes* became very popular; they were epigrams expressing a harsh or paradoxical truth in the briefest manner possible, reflecting the pessimism of the disillusioned French nobility during the reign of King Louis XIV.

48   *"Aunt Grace"* was Sarah's mother's youngest sister, Priscilla Tasker (1727-1802).

49   The only entry for the Graces in the 1758, 1762 and 1763 Land tax lists for the Borough and North Heath is for Robert Grace senior, in East Street, and it is known that he lived in the burgage house called *"Bishop's"*. His son Robert is mentioned in other records as a tenant of part of *"The Chequer"* or *"Blake's and Booker's"* burgage on the east side of the Carfax, but it is not known exactly when he was living there.

50   Jenny (Jane) Hunt was one of the daughters of Charles Hunt, the Usher (or second master) at Collyer's School. Her name appears in the Horsham Parish Register as a witness at practically every wedding from 1754 to 1762, which suggests that she was acting as a parish clerk during this period.

have a letter from Captain Smith tomorrow, yet hardly expect it. Read my magazine, *The Life of Madame Pompadour* in it, can greatness compensate for the loss of Honour? Not in my opinion. Begin some verses to Betsy Sheppard on her marriage.

Saturday, 20 January

No letter from Captain Smith, well, I cannot help it. Mary tells me he underwent great uneasiness from his Mother while in Horsham, ill behaviour to him on my account. Received note from Miss Pigott, her brother in the same fluctuating disposition, cruel man.

Sunday, 21 January

At Church, then walk in the Croft[51] Chat with Betsy Sheppard on the inveteracy of Captain Smith's relations; she advises me not to regard it. Go to Mrs. Lutman's. My dear Captain sure I shall hear tomorrow. Am unjustly accus'd of borrowing Mrs. Shelley's Elegy from Mrs. Moore; write some verses on hearing it.

Monday, 22 January

Receive a letter from my dear Captain Smith. He has been in great concern; will be at Portsmouth in a fortnight; wishes I cou'd go to Arundel that he might see me once more. Wou'd to Heaven I cou'd but Oh it is impossible. A Bonfire & rejoicing made by Doctor Smith[52] & the Millers[53] on old Shelley's[54] losing his Chancery suit.

Tuesday, 23 January

Finish the verses to Betsy Sheppard, finish Captain Smith's ruffle. Spend the afternoon at Mrs. Wicker's. Read in Ma.. [*Maximes*] to her. Send a droll packet to Jenny Hunt; occasions great laughter. Lay a scheme to see Captain Smith but fear it will prove abortive; wish ardently to see him.

Wednesday, 24 January

Write to Captain Smith; propose a scheme to see him; send his ruffles and Mrs. Shelley's Elegy. Give Betsy Sheppard the verses; she promises never to part with

---

51 The Croft, where Sarah often walked, lay to the south-east of the parish church.
52 Dr. John Smith was a surgeon-apothecary, who in 1758 was living in part of the old Red Lion, a former inn, on the corner of West Street and the Carfax.
53 The Millers were related to "old" Timothy Shelley - his niece Helen Catherine Michell had married John Miller, a widower from Dorking, in 1758. There were legal disputes about the will of Edward Shelley (Timothy's uncle), of which the Michells were legatees.
54 Timothy Shelley was the father of John Shelley of Field Place and Bysshe Shelley (grandfather of the poet, Percy Bysshe Shelley). As a younger man, Timothy Shelley had gone to America, where he had married Joanna Plum from a leading family in Newark. Their two sons were both born in America, but John remained there with his parents while Bysshe was sent back to England in 1735, at four years old, to be brought up by his grandparents, John and Hellen Shelley of Fen Place, near East Grinstead. Timothy returned to England after his father's death in 1740, and became the chief heir of his uncle, Edward Shelley of Field Place, who died in 1747. A Chancery case was fought in 1752 which successfully established the trust set up by Edward Shelley's will. Although Timothy then inherited Field Place and Warnham Place, he preferred to live at *The Old Crown*, next door to the Manor House in the Causeway. He leased Field Place to his son John on his marriage to Mary White, in December 1752, and allowed Bysshe, who was working as an attorney in Steyning, to build a new mansion at Warnham Place for his bride, Mary Catherine Michell, the heiress to the Stammerham estates. This project was abandoned after her death in November 1760.

them. Drink tea at Mrs. Grace's. Thus my days roll on; hope I do no injury to any person, nor is it in my power to do much good.

Thursday, 25 January

Work on Miss Seawell's handkerchief.[55] Evening at my Aunt Waller's; am told that the "Merchant" says that Captain Smith shou'd pay his Debts to him before he thought of marrying me.[56] This at first makes me excessively uneasy, but I submit all events to the disposal of the all Just, all wise being who best knows what is proper for us.

Friday, 26 January

Find the "Merchant" certainly says what I was told. Determine to write to Captain Smith about it if I do not see him. Afternoon and evening at Mrs. Wicker's; read in *The Universal Medley* to her,[57] some of it very well & some of it an outrage to Modesty. Infamous wretches, what does that person deserve who prostitutes their pen in such a shameful manner? To be banish'd as a pest to Society.

Saturday, 27 January

Troublesome dreams, fancy I am in London, in great perplexity, then think I am on board ship with Captain Smith. We are in great danger but he is exceedingly kind; sleeping or waking he alone employs my thoughts. Evening at Bet Hunt's.[58] I & Bet play at cards with Bet Sheppard & Jenny Hunt. In whatever situation of Life I may be hereafter plac'd in, the many happy hours I have pass'd with those two dear Girls will be allways precious to my remembrance.

Sunday, 28 January

At Church twice. Bet Hunt more inveterate against me than ever; what can be the meaning of it? I never injur'd her; she gives Captain Smith a bad character but I despise her impotent malice.

Monday, 29 January

See Betsy Sheppard's new lace & bridal ornaments.[59] Dear girl, may she ever be happy. Go to dancing, no rational company, a disagreeable evening; believe I shall go no more. Tell Mrs. Wicker I fear Captain Smith is indebted to his brother. She thinks t'is true but Heaven avert it.

Tuesday, 30 January

Very busy making mourning for the Princess of Orange.[60] Begin some verses on her

---

55 Miss Seawell lived in London.
56 Griffith *"Merchant"* Smith, elder brother of Henry.
57 *The Diverting Muse or The Universal Medley* is mentioned as a monthly magazine in an advertisement quoted by John Ashton in *Social Life in the Reign of Queen Anne, from Original Sources*, Chatto and Windus, 1883, now available as an Elibron Classics facsimile online.
58 Bet Hunt was the eldest daughter of Charles Hunt, the Usher of Collyer's School, and his wife Mary. She had two younger sisters, Jenny and Sally, both mentioned in Sarah's diaries. Their brother Charles was born in Horsham in 1738, but the baptism of the girls is not recorded there. The Usher's House was in the north wing of Collyer's School.
59 In preparation for her wedding to Ellman Tasker, Sarah's uncle.
60 The Princess of Orange was the wife of the Dutch sovereign, and closely related to the British royal family, so people in society would be expected to wear mourning for her.

death. Bet Phillips drinks tea here; we play at cards.[61] Write in the evening, but am Ill and go to bed. Will embitter the repose of my whole future Life, fatal effect of Girlish indiscretion.[62] Reflect on business, its difficulties & disquiets very numerous, but what situation is exempt?

Wednesday, 31 January

Betsy Sheppard & I all day at Mrs. Wicker's a quitting *[quilting]*.[63] We are merry, who can be otherwise in company with Mrs. Wicker. Uneasy reflections on my unfortunate affair with Captain Smith. I fear   *[words omitted]* consent of my parents. Captain Smith has my letter this evening. How I wish to know if my seeing him is possible, but I cannot expect to hear before Saturday evening.

FEBRUARY 1759

Thursday, 1 February

Go down to Mrs. Wicker's to help her quilt but am sent for home to Mr. Piggot who dines with us. Ask him concerning his affair with Miss Godfrey, he says they shall part by consent, but I am certain it will not be with hers. Miss Piggot has begun 3 watch papers, hopes this last will be compleat. Return to Mrs. Wicker's, begin reading *The Invisible Ship* to her, a true picture of the world.

Friday, 2 February

At home, violent headache. Miss Powell[64] sends for *[words omitted]* to wishing I send her that, with my Poem to Betsy Sheppard & on the Princess of Orange, Mr. Maningham[65] likes my *Elegy on Mrs. Shelley*. Read the supplement to my magazines, finish the *Life of Madam Pompadour*.[66] Heaven preserve me from greatness on such shocking terms & keep me mean.

Saturday, 3 February

Receive this morning, quite unexpected, a letter from my dear Captain Smith containing

---

61 Elizabeth (Bet) Phillips was probably related to the Tredcrofts, as Edward Tredcroft's grandmother was a Phillips.
62 It is not clear what Sarah means by a *"girlish indiscretion"* - probably she fears that she has been indiscreet in pursuing her relationship with Henry without the consent of her parents.
63 It seems likely from this and later entries that Sarah and Betsy were helping Mrs. Wicker make a patchwork quilt - this was often done as a communal activity in the 18th century.
64 Miss (Amie) Powell was the eldest daughter of the Rev. Thomas Powell, the previous Vicar of Horsham, who had died in 1742, and his wife Anne Seymour. They were married in Bath Abbey in 1728, and Amie was baptised there in 1729.
65 Mr. Manningham was the son of a previous Vicar of Slinfold, and was himself the Vicar of Wisborough Green.
66 The Marquise de Pompadour captivated the French King, Louis XV, and was installed at Versailles as his mistress. For twenty years she was immensely powerful, appointing her favorites as Ministers. Ultimately her influence on the policy of the French state was disastrous, but the arts flowered under her bountiful patronage, and it was she who founded the *Ecole Militaire*.

some small hopes of his being prefer'd & not going this voyage. This gave me infinite pleasure, may it so happen, if for the best, & grant Oh Divine father that I may for this & all thy mercies be unfeignedly thankfull. Taste Betsy Sheppard's Wedding cake.

Sunday, 4 February

Receive the most holy Sacrament, Oh may this heavenly Mistery imprint on my Mind a most gratefull sense of the opportunities given to me to obtain ever-lasting Happiness, & may I deserve this Blessing by a strict adherence to Thy commands, Oh thou Almighty Ruler of the Universe. Dine at Mrs. Wicker's, hear that Thyer White is elop'd.[67] Strange inhuman girl to leave her mother already involved in so much trouble for the death of Mrs [*Shelley*].

Monday, 5 February

Hear that Thyer White is found at a little Alehouse, Oh may I by observing the faults of others learn to regulate my own conduct.[68] Go to meet Miss Pigott & Miss Godfrey, who come & lay one night with us on their road to London, poor Miss Godfrey excessively unhappy, ungenerous Mr. Pigott. Receive Captain Smith's watch paper, vastly pretty. Make a motto for Mr. Harbroe of Ryegate [*Reigate*].[69]

Tuesday, 6 February

Sit up all night, stay at Tanbridge till 3 in the morn. Miss Pigott goes at six, at seven I write to Miss Gittins, make some verses on the fine morning. Talk to Betsy Sheppard concerning her wedding, it is to be next Sunday. The afternoon at Mrs. Wicker's, begin Miss Seawell's handkerchief & read in *The Invisible Ship*.

Wednesday, 7 February

Company at home, play quadrille & picquet, hear that Doctor Hutchinson's family make a great joke of my *Elegy on Mrs. Shelley*, they are prejudic'd, consequently their opinion is not to be regarded.[70] Poor Lady, if Malice can reach her who shall be safe from censure, may I never do wrong & then be quite indifferent what construction the World puts on my Actions.

---

67 Thyer, Bathia or Bethia White, second daughter of William White, the lawyer, was nineteen years old at the time of this escapade. "*Eloped*" is probably used here in the sense "*to run away*" rather than to run off with a lover, as no one else is specifically mentioned. She married Charles Pilfold in May 1762, and her eldest daughter, Elizabeth, married Timothy Shelley, son of Bysshe Shelley and his first wife, Mary Catherine Michell. Percy Bysshe Shelley, the son of Timothy and Elizabeth, perhaps inherited something of his grandmother's rebellious nature!

68 There were a number of alehouses in the Bishopric, where troops passing through Horsham or camped on Horsham Common would go to drink. Some are known to have had special "*Soldiers' Rooms*". The Whites lived in a house called Badmerings in the Bishopric, so Bathia would not have had to go far to find an alehouse.

69 Mr. Harbroe was a foppish young man (from Reigate) who visited Horsham on 27 May and again at the beginning of July.

70 The Rev. Thomas Hutchinson, D.D.(1698-1769), was Vicar of Horsham from 1742 until his death. He was a renowned classical scholar, known best for his two translations from Xenophon, the *Cyropaedia* (the education of Cyrus), first published in 1727, and the *Anabasis* (the Persian Expedition), first published in 1735.

Thursday, 8 February

The Post puts my Heart in a tumult, tho' I cannot expect a letter from Captain Smith before Saturday, if then, may Heaven preserve & return him safe to bless his faithfull Sally. Mrs. Wicker, Jenny Hunt & Betsy Sheppard spent the evening here, we play at cards. Tell my sister Bet of her ill behaviour but is has no effect on her, sad girl.

Friday, 9 February

Great sinking in my spirits, fear I shall hear some bad news, but believe it is weak nerves, so will not be superstitious. A great dispute with Bet, she keeps Will James[71] company, & intends to persist in it in spite of opposition, Mama uneasy that she is thus running headlong into ruin. Go to Dame Reynolds' with Betsy Sheppard, a charming pleasant walk.[72]

Saturday, 10 February

Receive a letter from Smith, he is [to] sail from Plymouth, no mention of preferment, nor any certainty that he can meet me before he goes to America. Pray Heaven I may see him, but if I do not may I be all patience & resignation, write to him, appoint to meet him at Chiltington if he can come. Send him the watch paper.

Sunday, 11 February

Go & attend Betsy Sheppard to be married to my Uncle Tasker. We breakfast & dine at Mrs. Wicker's. At Church in the afternoon, drink tea & spend the evening with the new married couple, may happiness be their lot. Papa does not approve the Match [and] says I made it up, I am angry at the unjust accusation & we dispute about it but I am determined to have no [word omitted].

Monday, 12 February

Receive a letter from my Dear Smith, he is on board the *Orford*, at Spitthead. [He]expects to sail for North America in 3 or 4 days, so all my hopes of seeing him are over, Oh may I with patience bear this disappointment. Go up to Mrs. Lutman's, mention Drew Michell's name,[73] Molly bursts into tears & says she fears he will use her ill; pity the poor girl, oh these vile men. Go to dancing; eleven couples.

Tuesday, 13 February

Go again to Mrs. Lutman's, comfort her on Molly's account, tell her Michell is not worth regarding. A great dispute with Papa but we make it up, very uneasy on Smith's account, exert my reason but in vain, his lov'd Idea is ever in my mind &

---

71   Will James was a butcher, who appears to have had a bad reputation where women were concerned.

72   Dame Reynolds was probably the widow of John Reynolds, barber and peruke maker, who died in 1740.

73   Drew Michell was a tanner and cordwainer, the son of John Michell of Horsham, turner, originally descended from the Michells of North Heath. He and his brother, John Michell, benefited from the will of a great-uncle who left them money and property. Drew served as a Bailiff of Horsham in 1780 and 1790, and died in 1800.

the danger he is now going to be expos'd to shocking, I write to him but doubt he will not receive it before he sails.[74]

Wednesday, 14 February

Receive a letter from my cousin Bet Smith,[75] she says all my relations disapprove my writing poetry, I am sorry for it but must & will persist. Am determined in my answer to say something in defence of this, my favourite amusement. Hope for a letter from Captain Smith tho' have but little reason; am disappointed, as all ought to be who depend on impossibilities.

Thursday, 15 February

Papa blames me for not mentioning who was Sheriff, it was certainly wrong but he tells me of it with too much asperity for my impatient temper to bear. How trifling, how unimportantly, does my time pass away, I wish I had been a man I might then have signalis'd myself in the service of my Country, but now I must live & die in a wretched obscurity.

Friday, 16 February

A solemn fast for the War. At Church twice, Doctor Hutchinson makes an excellent discourse but rather too political for a Country Congregation; it would have been better adapted if it had been preach'd before the House of Commons. A charming pleasant day, walk in the Croft; miss Betsy Sheppard. Go a walking with my Mama & Aunt Waller[76] to 'Dales'.[77]

Saturday, 17 February

Another letter from Smith sends me 3 more franks, says nothing shou'd have prevented his meeting me but the certainty of being left behind if he had attempted it. [He] expected to sail yesterday so he is now gone. Oh thou Almighty power return him safe & well to his native country, & the arms of his Sally, who in his absence cannot be happy.

Sunday, 18 February

At Church twice, with Betsy Sheppard that was, now my Aunt Tasker, am at a great loss for my Walking companion, wish her sister Sally wou'd come home. Go to Mrs. Lutman's; read part of Captain Smith's letter to her. More chat about Drew & poor Molly, comfort her. Miss Hutchinson very unhappy on Bill White's account.[78]

---

74 The *Orford* sailed from Spithead in 14 February, as part of a well-equipped convoy under Admiral Holmes for the Quebec campaign.

75 Bet (or Elizabeth) Smith was Sarah's first cousin. Elizabeth Hurst, Richard Hurst's elder sister, had married William Smith, an upholsterer in London, and lived in Fleet Street.

76 *"Aunt Waller"* was Sally's mother's eldest sister, Anne, married to Thomas Waller.

77 Thomas Dale was the miller at Warnham Mill. His father had bought the mill in 1700, with the help of a mortgage of £150, advanced by William Ansell. The younger Thomas had been unable to keep up the mortgage repayments and in 1744 the mill was sold to Thomas Nye, knacker. His widow owned it at the time that Sarah was writing her diaries. It was probably the nearby miller's house that was called *"Dales"*.

78 Bill White was the eldest son of the lawyer William White and the brother of Thyer (Bathia), Mary and Elizabeth.

Oh fatal love, what misery dost thou occasion.

Monday, 19 February

A letter from my Dear Smith, he is on board the *Orford* just sailing to America, he is extremely concern'd that we cou'd not meet, tells me I shou'd direct my letters to Mr. Masterman who now lives at Plymouth. I walk to Mr. Bristed's[79] at Slaugham, with Miss Curtis[80] & my Sister Bet, they receive us very kindly.

Tuesday, 20 February

Write to Captain Smith & to Mr. Masterman desiring he wou'd give me a fortnight's notice when any ship goes to America. Walk to Cuckfield,[81] send a man to Horsham with my letters & come late to stay at Slaugham, till Friday. Mr. Bristed does not approve of Hutchinson's works & says it is a system of absurdity, I had thoughts of reading them.[82]

Wednesday, 21 February

Chat with Mr. Bristed on Natural Philosophy, it enlarges the Ideas & improves the Mind. I read Doctor Parnell's poetical works[83] & a play, *The Citizen turn'd Gentleman*.[84] The letter I wrote to my Smith is to go by the *Dublin*, suppose the worst shou'd happen & he never returns, what then will be the fate of poor Sally? Why, she must resign to her fate without murmuring.

Thursday, 22 February

Go to my cousin Gatlan's at Pilstyle,[85] with Miss Bristed, they press us to stay all night, but we refuse, Philip Gatlan walks to Slaugham with us. We are catch'd in a violent storm, & wet through. He stays all night. We marry him to my sister Bet & are merry upon the occasion. Think there has been so much rain we must stay till Saturday.

Friday, 23 February

Mr. Gatlan goes home, he is to call for us Saturday morning. I work on Miss Seawell's

---

79   John Bristed, M.A., was Rector of Slaugham from 1749 to 1783. He was also the Rector of St. Anne's and St. Michael's in Lewes.

80   Miss Anne or Nany Curtis was the only daughter of Edward Curtis and Anne Griffith, and was thus a first cousin of Henry Smith, on his mother's side. She married the Horsham clockmaker, William Murrell, in May 1762.

81   Cuckfield is the nearest town to Slaugham, where Sarah was staying with the Bristeds.

82   Possibly a reference to one of the Rev. Thomas Hutchinson's books.

83   Dr. Thomas Parnell (1679-1718) was an Irish poet and clergyman who was a friend of Alexander Pope and Jonathan Swift. Sarah may have been reading his *Poems on Several Occasions*, first published in 1721 and including *A Night-piece on Death*, which is thought to have inspired the "graveyard" school. Another collection, the *Posthumous Works of Dr. Parnell, containing Poems Moral and Divine*, was published in 1758.

84   *Mamamouchi, or the Citizen turn'd Gentleman* was a play by Edward Ravenscroft, first published in 1672. It was based on Molière's *Le Bourgeois Gentilhomme*.

85   The exact family connection between the Gatlands and the Hursts has not yet been discovered, but it was almost certainly through the Taskers, who came from Balcombe. Pilstye Farm, where a house was built by the Gatlands in 1647, lay to the south of Balcombe, just off the road to Cuckfield. This branch of the Gatland family were farmers and landowners - Walter Gatland of Pilstye bought the Borde Hill estate, just outside Hayward's Heath, in 1705 and the family owned it for the next century.

handkerchief read *The Biter*, a Comedy,[86] play at cards. Chat on frugality, I from that hint write an advertisement for the sale of frugality & discretion, read it to Mr. & Mrs. Bristed who like it much. Wind high, uneasy on my Dear Smith's account.

Saturday, 24 February

Come from Slaugham. Miss Bristed with us. Mr. Gatlan disappoints us & we walk it alone. Work very hard, reflect on the trifling satisfactions this world produces. Violent headache, expect to find a letter from Miss Pigott but have none, pine to hear from Smith tho' I know it is impossible, foolish girl.

Sunday, 25 February

At Church twice, call on Miss Curtis, go & make the Wedding visit by Mrs. Tasker. A great deal of company but no conversation, this is allways the case in mix't companies, the converse of one dear friend is infinitely preferable. Molly Reynolds tells me she knew I had a letter from Captain Smith, such a day, this surprises me but she accounts[87] ... *(page torn)*

Monday, 26 February

Work all the morning. Drink tea at Mrs. Reynolds'. Tom Brian writes a Note & brings it himself; t'is to desire I'd dance with him, a heap of absurdities, compliments & nonsense. I go to dancing, nine couples. My cousin Gatlan comes & dances with Bett. Tom Brian behaves like a mad fool *[and]* says he is violently in love with me.[88]

Tuesday, 27 February

Reflect on the flatteries bestow'd on me by Tom Brian, strange Sex we are that cannot avoid being pleased with what our reason despises. Drink tea & spend the evening at Doctor Smith's, play at Cards, they are I believe a very unhappy couple. T'is not without some reason that Libertines fear Matrimony, how few there are that behave well in that state. I am inclinable to think all those who disagree in marriage wou'd be equally faulty & unhappy in any other situation, t'is a solemn alteration of circumstances & the consideration that it may be for the worse makes it more so.

Wednesday, 28 February

Ash Wednesday, at Church twice. Miss Bristed & I instead of buying *[?ashes]* give a penny to a poor beggar.[89]

---

86   *The Biter* was an unsuccessful comedy by Nicholas Rowe (1674-1718), who was appointed Poet Laureate in 1715. He also wrote *The Fair Penitent* and *Tamerlane*, both of which Sarah saw performed in Horsham by a company of strolling players, in April 1759 and March 1761 respectively.
87   Molly (Mary) was a daughter of John and Ann Reynolds, born in 1727.
88   Tom Brian was the son of Thomas Brian, the former Governor of Horsham Gaol. He was born in Horsham in 1731.
89   The observation of Ash Wednesday sometimes involves the use of ashes to mark the foreheads of those who attend church, as a sign of repentance. The text is not very clear, but it would seem that a donation was given for the ashes, for charity. It would seem that Sarah and Miss Bristed preferred to give their money directly to a beggar.

MARCH 1759

Thursday, 1 March

Am terrified with an account that Mr. Pigott's doors at Slinfold open every night tho' they take great care to secure them. T'is extremely odd for he is a man whose veracity I can depend upon. Apparitions, if such there are, have no occasion to open doors to gain entrance. I am at a loss but wish to see him, being much concern'd at the fright he must be in. Dine, drink tea & spend the evening at Mrs. Wicker's.

Friday, 2 March

Great uneasiness on my sister Bet's account, Papa surprised her with the fellow she keeps company with,[90] he & Mama are very much provok'd yet know not what method will prevent it, foolish girl she is rushing into Ruin. My brother & sister Molly going to be Inoculated; Mama uneasy at this, nothing but trouble. Dreadfull fears on my Dear Smith's account, I doubt he ever will return, if he does not oh may I soon follow him.

Saturday, 3 March

At home all day, how imperceptibly time passes, we mind it not as it flies, yet often regret the loss of it. Oh, may I never spend mine in wickedness or folly but learn to prize each fleeting moment, as I well know they never can return. Think on my Dear Smith, pray for his safety, wish to hear from Mr. Masterman but cannot expect it.

Sunday, 4 March

Troublesome dreams, fancy I am a Pilgrim in great danger from Wild Beast. Imagine I see my Smith, embrace & part from him, ah where is he now, on the Wide Ocean but there is the same divine power presides by Water as by land, in that I trust. Dine at Mr. Edward Curtis's; how things veer about, some time ago I never enter'd the House on the family dispute about my affair with Smith.[91]

Monday, 5 March

Nany Curtis dines with us, we are very merry. Drink tea at Miss Powell's. Chat with Mrs. Tredcroft, she passes most severe censures on poor Miss Hutchinson in regard to Bill White, see the unhappy consequences of behaving indiscreet, few will pity none redress, but all condemn whether acquainted or not with the real Motives of people's acting.

---

90   Presumably Will James, mentioned on 9 February.
91   Edward Curtis (born 1696) lived in South Street, and had a stationer's business. He was married to Ann Griffith, the sister of Elizabeth Smith (mother of Henry). He served as Churchwarden in 1747-8. His father Edward had been a tailor, and Master of the House of Correction in 1712. His uncle Richard was a mercer who supplied the needs.of the Irwins of Hill's Place and looked after their affairs. Another uncle, Thomas Curtis, became a Quaker and trained as a surgeon, practising in Horsham before moving to Wallingford in Oxfordshire. His grandson, William Curtis (1746-1799), was a famous botanist, who published *Flora Londinensis*, and was the first editor of *The Botanical Magazine*.

Tuesday, 6 March

Nany Curtis finds that the reason of her Aunt Smith's going to London was to prevent the Captain's coming again to Horsham,[92] this seems likely but how can we believe a noted liar? Why are they so inveterate, I have never injur'd them, t'is I suppose my want of fortune is the grievance. Mrs. Doctor Smith[93] drinks tea here & Miss Curtis; we play at cards, Miss Bristed goes home & I am not sorry. Miss Bristed is near thirty,[94] yet she affects the tittering behaviour of a Girl, or else is so gloomy none can gain a word from her, a character in my opinion, I wou'd have people attain an even disposition of Mind.

Wednesday, 7 March

Mrs. Lutman lends me the part of *The History of our Saviour* by Nelson, I read it to Bet Hunt, she concurs with me in thinking it a most excellent performance.

Thursday, 8 March

Headaches — what poor mortals we are, how trifling a disorder discomposes our whole frame & renders us incapable of acting like rational creatures. Write as I intended to Bet Smith in defence of my poetry. Papa tells Mr. Tredcroft that Gibraltar will be taken by the French, how can one person take pleasure in making another uneasy, he knew this would give pain, he has a strange *[?humour]*.[95]

Friday, 9 March

Call on Mrs. Tasker, she says I am graver than usual, the reason is I have lost her company. Agreable chat with Jenny Hunt. A most dreadfull day with high winds, oh where is now my Dear Smith, toss'd on the wide Ocean at the mercy of the ruffling Billows. Read in Pliny's *Letters* fine descriptions of his *[illegible words]* for a Heathen what Christian acts better.[96]

Saturday, 10 March

Am excessively surpris'd that I do not hear from Miss Pigott, sure she is ill. Miss Powell drinks tea here, Doctor Smith comes in & says I thought you was to have a Captain, but Captain Smith is no more, I start & turn pale but recollecting myself tell him I suppose he is made a Major, this he confirms, the "Merchant"'s news, may it be true.

---

92 Ann (Nany) Curtis's *"Aunt Smith"* was Henry Smith's mother.
93 Wife of John Smith the surgeon.
94 Hannah Bristed, daughter of the Rev. John Bristed and his wife Jane, was baptised at St. Michael's, Lewes, on 27 August 1731.
95 Edward Tredcroft held a profitable sinecure connected with Gibraltar, mentioned in a letter from Edward Dickinson, London agent to the Viscounts Irwin, in August 1768 (HM MSS Cat. No. 794.20). He had probably obtained this office as a reward for his political support of the Lords Irwin, because Henry Ingram, then M.P. for Horsham, later 7th Viscount Irwin, was appointed Commissary for Stores in Gibraltar in 1727.
96 Pliny the younger (c. 61-c.112) was a Roman writer and official whose ten books of letters were still widely read.

Sunday, 11 March

Joy is more destructive to repose than Sorrow for this by stupifying the Mind throws it into a sort of Lethargy while that rouses the faculties, sets the spirits in a ferment & renders it incapable of repose. The News of my Dear Smith's promotion hinders me of many hours' repose. I wish it is true, thanks be to the Divine power for this & all his blessings.

Monday, 12 March

Alas, when will my perturbations end, ignorant girl answer thy own foolish question, never but with life, how quick is the transition from joy to sorrow. Last night I was in raptures because my Smith is promoted, tonight I am uneasy at his brother's nonsense. Mr. Pigott here, says he shall break with Miss Godfrey, God forbid all the sex should be thus wavering.

Tuesday, 13 March

A very kind letter from the worthy Mr. Masterman acquainting me that the *Northumberland* had lost her mast & was oblig'd to put in there before she cou'd proceed on her voyage. Mr. Parry, the Chaplain, sends his compliments.[97] I write to Mr. Masterman, my dear Smith, Miss Seawell & Sally Sheppard. Send Miss Seawell's handkerchief.

Wednesday, 14 March

Quite ill with the rheumatism. "Merchant" Smith says the Captain is to be station'd this year in the West Indies but God forbid, for if the dearest thing to me on earth is to be so long absent I shall not wish to live. Begin working a pair of habit ruffles. Wind very high, how fare the poor sailors, Heaven protect them.

Thursday, 15 March

Mr. Maningham & Mr. Piggot call, his house is now very *[illegible word]*, has not heard from his sister. Miss Hutchinson sneers at poetry, poor Girl, I wish she had never done anything which more deserves contempt.[98] Chat with my Aunt Tasker, we determine to act right & then despise all the malicious world can say, read some poetry "*Know Thyself*," a very fine thing wrote by Dr Arbuthnot.[99]

Friday, 16 March

Receive a note from Mr. Piggot acquainting me that he has heard of his sister & she is well & happy with her Dear Jones, makes an apology for not writing to me. Mr. Piggot avers Platonic Love for me, I disapprove of it, but accept & return his

97   Mr. Parry was one of Henry Smith's shipmates with whom Sarah corresponded quite frequently.

98   Catherine Hutchinson, eldest daughter of the Rev. Thomas Hutchinson, D.D., Vicar of Horsham.

99   John Arbuthnot (1667-1735) was physician to Queen Anne, and a friend of Alexander Pope and Dean Swift. He wrote one poem *Know Thyself*, published anonymously in 1734, but he also wrote on mathematics and medical matters, and was described by Dr. Johnson as "*the most universal genius*".

friendship. Violent pain in my side, reflect on the happiness of early Death & the troubles avoided by it, but live we must our appoint'd time, t'is best then to bear misfortune with fortitude & composure.

Saturday, 17 March

Talk to Mrs. Luttman on Molly's affair, persuade her to talk with Drew Michell, as he still dangles after the Girl. Chat with Bet Hunt who says that Captain Smith will not be in England for many years, part envy & malice, I will not regard it.

Sunday, 18 March

My Uncle & Aunt Tasker dine & spend the day with us. I go to Mrs. Luttman's, desire Molly to forbid her lover's coming unless he declares to her mother his intentions are honourable. A great deal of chat about my Smith, say I had rather he die than prove false, but God forbid I shou'd experience either of these shocking evils.

Monday, 19 March

My sister & brother are Inoculated, Mama in tears & grief on the occasion. We complain of Misfortunes, but most of those we feel are imaginary. Molly Luttman tells me she has discarded her lover, villainous fellow. I hope she will soon get the better of her regard for such a worthless wretch.

Tuesday, 20 March

Am excessively surpris'd that I have heard nothing from Miss Gittins. What can be the meaning of her silence, time & patience Girl will reveal all Mysteries. Mrs. Wicker drinks tea here, tells us "Merchant" Smith says the Mud in Tanbridge Lane has supplied the Miss Ellis's with Brain, this shews his disappointment for he wou'd gladly have been ally'd to their Brains, as muddy as they are. [100]

Wednesday, 21 March

Ride with Doctor Smith to his Inoculating house & see my brother & sister. Drink tea & spend the evening at Mrs. Wicker's with the Miss Ellis's, Mr. Tredcroft's family & Seymour Powell,[101] play at quadrille. Mrs. ?[Wicker] says she is determined to tell Doctor Griffith [that] "Merchant" Smith behave[s] in a villainous manner with regard to me & the Captain.[102]

---

100   The Misses Ellis of Tanbridge, Henrietta Anna Maria (b. 1735) and Mary (b. 1738), came from one of the wealthiest families in Horsham at this time. Their father, Henry Ellis, had inherited a considerable amount of property in Shipley and Nuthurst from his great-uncle, and bought the Tanbridge estate in 1731. Sarah records his death in on 9 August 1762. The Misses Ellis held the Red Lion burgage, a substantial property on the corner of West Street and the Carfax, in their own right. They had inherited it in 1756 from their aunt, Anne Pilfold, née Harding, the widow of Dr. James Baker, who had owned it previously.
101   Seymour Powell was the only son of the late Rev. Thomas Powell and his wife Anne (née Seymour - now Mrs. Bridger). He was born in Horsham in 1734.
102   Dr. Griffith was the uncle of Griffith *"Merchant"* Smith.

Thursday, 22 March

Drink tea at a Quaker's.[103] Very well behav'd sociable people & not so much formality as is generally found in the Sect. Can Religion consist in preciseness & a particular set of phrases? No, certainly. Go & see *The King of Prussia in War*.[104] Finish a poem *"Soliloquy by Moonlight"*; read it to Bet Hunt who approves.

Friday, 23 March

A charming fine morning fills the Mind with ineffable pleasure. Chat with Bet Hunt and with Jenny, how friendly does this old hypocrite behave to my face when in her heart she hates & wou'd do me all the Mischief in her power. Drink tea & spend the evening at Mrs. Wicker's, she tells me more of the Merchant's inveteracy.

Saturday, 24 March

I wish the affair was determined one way or the other, for sure suspense is, of all others, the most terrible situation. When we know the worst, the Mind endeavours to fortify itself & stay the torrent of ill fortune, but while fluctuating between hope & fear, now one now t'other is predominant, & the heart on continual rack with the cruel conflict. Read in Mr. Maningham's poems; write to [Mr.] Pigott.

Sunday, 25 March

At Church. Mr. Maningham preaches, a very eloquent discourse on the Pharisee & Publican, against ostentation in Religion's spiritual pride; he did right in not extolling the external part of worship, at least if he thinks his own practices right. Walk with Drew Michell to see my brother & sister. Have a great mind to introduce Molly Luttman's affair, but think it will only tend to make myself enemies, he is a sensible young fellow.

Monday, 26 March

Very busy in the shop, Mrs. Luttman comes down to know if I mention'd any to Drew Michell of Molly's affair. I tell her no & give my reasons for it, persuade her to speak to him, she promises me she will. Miss Tredcroft & Bet Philips drink tea here. I write to Sally Sheppard in verse, send it by Bet Cook.[105]

Tuesday, 27 March

Mrs. Luttman sends for me, tells me she has reveal'd to Drew all that lay on her mind, & positively told him he must desist from coming there or declare what his intentions were. He protests they are honourable & all matters are made up. Walk

---

103 Probably Sarah visited the family of the Quaker, George Holmes, who lived in the Carfax, next door to the *King's Head*. A descendant of this family, George Bax Holmes, was an important collector of dinosaur fossils in the 19th century.

104 It is not at all clear what Sarah means here – she may have been referring to an entertainment, or a painting, celebrating the victories won by King Frederick II of Prussia, generally known as *"Frederick the Great"*.

105 Elizabeth, or Bet, Cook, born in 1737, was the younger daughter of the widowed Mrs. Ann Cook, the landlady of the *King's Head Inn*. She must have been going on a trip to London.

to see my brother & sister, met with a little country girl whose simplicity at once both pains and charms me, how wou'd this girl wonder at the World.

Wednesday, 28 March

Ever wakefull fancy brings my Dear Smith to my sight, delusive dreams, oh that you had been true, but this is a happiness perhaps I may never again enjoy. Mr. Pigott drinks tea here, agreable conversation with this friend, who I believe is really & sincerely such, he brings me *The Man of Pleasure*,[106] which I begin reading to Bet Hunt, some of it very loose but I believe true. Thank Heaven that plac'd me in so humble a position, if these are the vices of High Life. Oh my Almighty Father, grant that I may flee from the vices I have ever been guilty of & resist all the temptations that may hereafter fall in my way.

Thursday, 29 March

A letter from Sally Sheppard, Mr. Pigott & Mr. Maningham here, the former brings me *The Journey through Life* & *Lloyds' Evening Post* to read, an Essay Ironically discommending Mr. Pitt.[107]

Friday, 30 March

Mrs. Wicker tells me she mention'd "Merchant" Smith's behaviour to Doctor Griffith with all the aggravating circumstances she cou'd think on, he partly owns & partly denies the fact. How much uneasiness has their dislike occasion'd me & yet why shou'd it? I think I may be certain the Captain will be just, but if he is not Oh prudence, pride & reason fly to my aid.

Saturday, 31 March

The long expect'd letter from Miss Gittins arrives, she is well, company prevented her writing, she gives me leave to acquaint Mrs. Tasker of her affair with Captain Vaughan. A venerable well looking old man asks charity, said he had been shipwreck'd, lost a wife & family & all his effects, how dreadfull. This is the direct way to my heart, wish it had been in my power to have bestow'd more on him than I did. Oh ye rich, this is all I envy ye for, that power of doing good. What pleasure can equal the relieving [of] our fellow creatures in distress, yet how few exercise this godlike beneficence.

---

106 This was probably Sir Richard Steele's essay on *The Man of Wit and Pleasure*, published in *The Spectator* on 23 August 1711.

107 William Pitt the elder, known as *"The Great Commoner"*, succeeded the Duke of Newcastle as Secretary of State in 1756, but resigned in April 1757, only to be recalled to form a government with Newcastle as Prime Minister, and himself in charge of the conduct of the war, as Paymaster of the Forces. Pitt was a vigorous, wise and successful war leader, and Britain and her allies routed the French on land and sea, during the Seven Years War. Pitt resigned in 1761 when the majority of the Cabinet refused to declare war on Spain. He became Viscount Pitt and Earl of Chatham in 1766, and died in 1778.

APRIL 1759

Sunday, 1 April

Walk to Papa's farm Highland,[108] with Mama, Aunt Waller, Aunt Grace & Aunt Tasker, am told of Miss Gittin's former imprudent conduct. Much concern'd at it, cruel World that will not forget the indiscretions of youth, though amply aton'd for by repentance & amendment.

Monday, 2 April

A letter from Miss Pigott, & another from Parson Parry, one of my dear Smith's old Messmates, to tell me the *Echo* frigate was sailing from Portsmouth to America, if I thought proper of writing to the Captain. Walk to Slinfold, & spend the day with Mr. Pigott who professes the greatest friendship for me, lends me the *[Centaur]* in five letters to a friend says t'is a fine *[illegible word]*.

Tuesday, 3 April

Write to Captain Smith to go by Captain Laforty in the *Echo* frigate, my Heart is full of the tenderest regard for him, which *[in]* spite of myself will flow to my pen. Oh when shall I again be bless'd with the sight of him, I oft gaze on his lifeless Image,[109] but that dear original is wanting. Make a visit at Tanbridge with Mrs. Wicker.

Wednesday, 4 April

Very busy but very cheerfull, my good spirits are occasion'd by the hope that the Supreme Being will enable me so to act as to deserve his divine favour, & that life will by his gracious providence prevent me from deviating from the right. My sister Bet behaves in a monstrous manner to her Papa and Mama, which causes great uneasiness.

Thursday, 5 April

Read in *The Centaur* to Bett Hunt who likes it much. Papa blames me for an oversight of his own, I still my rising passion & convince him of his error, may I allways be enabled to act this. Thyer White[110] runs away again, Mr. Pigott here, who endeavours to excuse her & blame her parents, but we confute him. Walk on the Causeway with my Aunt Tasker.

Friday, 6 April

Am told the Man who pretended he had been shipwreck'd & I reliev'd was an Imposter, am shock'd to find there is so much deceit in Human Nature. Go to

---

108 Highland Farm, rented by Richard Hurst from Guildford Hospital, was on Horsham Common, near the present junction of Comptons Lane with St. Leonards Road. The farm buildings were still there in 1951, but a school was built there in 1977.

109 The miniature or silhouette of Henry Smith, which Sarah possessed. This is almost certainly the silhouette reproduced in this book, though Henry looks a little older than one might expect. But he was thirteen years older than Sarah, and had been on active service for more than four years.

110 See the previous reference to Thyer White on 4 February 1759.

Church, a funeral Sermon preach'd by Doctor Hutchinson, a fine discourse. The afternoon & evening at Mrs. Wicker's, read *The Centaur* to her. Thyer White found again & brought home, unhappy Girl.

Saturday, 7 April

See in the paper, that the *Echo* was to sail Wednesday or Thursday & my letter to my dear Smith cou'd not arrive there till Friday night, how unlucky I am, hush no repining. Write to Miss Pigott, Papa ill, dreadfully uneasy on the occasion, gracious Heaven restore him. The Clock now strikes eleven, the Moon shines in full lustre, how still & serene is the face of Nature, pleasing sight let me indulge it.

Sunday, 8 April

At Church twice, melancholy reflections on seeing Mrs. White,[111] unfortunate Woman has lost one Daughter, that was an ornament to Human Nature,[112] & the eldest of the surviving ones[113] likely to give her more trouble than her death cou'd occasion. Mrs. Wicker dines with us, we are very merry on our Journey to London. I drink tea & spend the evening with her.

Monday, 9 April

Dream that I am shipwreck'd & then made a Slave, but escape after great danger & difficulty. The thoughts of my dear Smith occasions these strange Ideas. He has this day been gone 4 months. Write to Sally Sheppard. Begin reading *The Journey through Life* to Mama, after read in Pliny's *Letters*. Who can look on these remains of Antiquity without reflecting on the Instability of all earthly things, the most memorable persons of old Greece & Rome are swept away, even their tombs are heaps of Ruins. Is it then right to be extremely anxious about anything that can befall us here?

Tuesday, 10 April

Very busy all day, at night finish 1st volume of Pliny's *Letters*.

Wednesday, 11 April

Very restless night, it rains much what a surprising effect has the Weather on most dispositions. Indeed we are poor creatures & are led just as spleen, caprice, folly or Reason guides, but this last is seldom predominant. Play at Picquet with Papa, then begin the 2nd volume of Pliny's *Letters*, some very affectionate ones to his wife.

Thursday, 12 April

Violent headache with sick fits, how terribly am I afflicted with this pain, but I will not repine, for it is much easier to bear than many others I have felt. Take a walk with my Aunt Tasker & then a solitary turn on the Causeway by myself. Finish the

111 Mrs. Bathia White, the wife of the lawyer William White, was the daughter of John Waller, former landlord of the *Anchor Inn*, and a first cousin of Sarah's uncle, Thomas Waller.
112 Mary Shelley née White, whose death was reported on 5 January 1759.
113 Thyer (Bathia) White.

story of Leonora in *The Journey through Life,* a very pretty thing, abounds with excellent moral instructions.

Friday, 13 April

Good Friday, Mr. Pigott comes to breakfast, I go to Church & receive the Sacrament. All day at Mrs. Wicker's. When I come home at night find Papa just returned from a journey & much out of temper, sure ill nature is a vice, none I am sure is productive of greater mischiefs. Oh may I guard against every symptom of it.

Saturday, 14 April

My dear Smith has been gone to Sea two months yesterday, he must be arriv'd in America, sure I might have heard before this, but I will not be impatient. Go to Mrs. Wicker's, Jack Smith there, just come from London, which prevents my going in.[114] Begin some verses on Mrs. Wicker's leaving snuff.

Sunday, 15 April

Meet Jack Smith in the Croft but never look at him, so he had no opportunity of bowing or speaking to me. I sincerely forgive all the injury they have attempted to do me with their brother the Captain, but Christianity does not oblige me to cringe to those that wou'd trample me under their feet. Finish the verses to Mrs. Wicker & give them her. Jack Smith says the King of Prussia is dead, Heaven forbid.[115]

Monday, 16 April

Dine at Mrs. Seyton's with my Aunt Waller, Aunt Tasker & Graham, the Supervisor and his wife, she a very pretty behav'd woman, he by all accounts a vile fellow to her.[116] See in the papers that the *Echo* is not yet sail'd so hope the letter I wrote will reach my dear Smith. Go to Mr. Tredcroft's to eat Easter Cake.

Tuesday, 17 April

Walk to see my brother & sister who are recover'd from the Smallpox, & at the Airing house, they express great joy at seeing me.[117] We have a great deal of company at tea, Mrs. Wicker obliges me to read the verses I made on her leaving snuff. In whatever company I am, the thoughts of where my dear Smith is & how employ'd still intrude.

Wednesday, 18 April

Set out for a walk of 4 mile with my Aunt Tasker & Jenny Hunt, but their thoughts

---

114 John Smith (1727-1800), brother of Henry, who also seems to have been initially opposed to his brother's marriage to Sarah. He was a City of London merchant, with a business in Lad Lane.

115 Frederick II, King of Prussia (1712-1786), whose outstanding military successes during the Seven Years' War earned him the title of *"Frederick the Great"*. The report of his death was clearly false.

116 George Graham, the Supervisor, was mentioned as such in the 1758 and 1763 Land Tax records for Horsham Borough, in a list of salaried officials. He lived in the Carfax. Mr. Seyton was also listed as a salaried official, but not given a title.

117 People who had received a smallpox inoculation were confined in an isolated house on Horsham Common.

alter & they go down to Dales & drink tea. I am angry & turn homeward, recollect myself, go back again, not to be so easy put out of temper again. Hear as I come home from Mrs. Bridger's[118] that the post has a letter for me. I seek him but in vain, am excessively impatient, who can it be from?

Thursday, 19 April

Wake very early, when the Mind is agitated how impossible it is for the Body to have any rest. Nany Thrush[119] told me false, there was no letter for me. Papa receives a letter from Mr. Cox acquainting him that he may make a great interest of his money. He refuses to get any, I tell him he was to blame in mentioning it to the Counsellor.[120]

Friday, 20 April

Some strolling Players come to Town, poor creatures if they expect to live here, they will find themselves miserably disappointed. Mrs. Hunt here in the afternoon, she is a very Loquacious Woman, talks much & little to the purpose.[121] Few women have the gift of taciturnity. Miss Powell & I go & Look for the post, she has 2 letters but alas I have none.

Saturday, 21 April

Papa is extremely angry & uses me very ill, because I do not the moment he bids copy the letter he is to write in answer to Mr. Cox. He says I trifle my time away & neglect things of consequence. How surprisingly then have I been mistaken to fancy myself industrious. I weep excessively about it.

Sunday, 22 April

Excessively uneasy that my Papa & I have had a difference, & uneasy on a trifling disappointment in business, thus we veer about, now with anxiety now without. My brother comes to Mrs. Wicker's & gives me high entertainment with his chat. Receive a letter from the good & kind Mr. Masterman, acquainting me that he shall soon be in London, how happy shall I be if I can see them when I go to town.[122]

Monday, 23 April

Papa & I are reconcil'd, how I hate disputes, yet I am sometimes to blame. Hear "Merchant" Smith says the air of Horsham shall never blow on him again if my

---

118 Mrs. Anne Bridger (née Seymour) was the widow of the Rev. Thomas Powell, and was now the wife of Arthur Bridger. They were married in Slaugham on 10 November 1743. The Bridgers lived in East Street, in a burgage property called "*Ashleys*".

119 Anne Thrush was a daughter of Joseph Thrush and his wife Ann, born in 1731. Joseph Thrush was a former servant of Lord Irwin who was made a burgess of Horsham in 1738, bound to vote in Lord Irwin's interest..

120 Counsellor Cox, the Hurst's London lawyer, was mentioned again during Sarah's visit to London in May.

121 Mrs. (Mary) Hunt was the wife of Charles Hunt, the Usher of Collyer's School, and the mother of Bet, Jenny and Sally.

122 Mr. Masterman and his wife were friends of Henry Smith, living at Plymouth.

Dear Smith marries me, this makes me uneasy, yet why shou'd it, I may be certain of his fidelity. Begin writing to Miss Gittins, read a poem.

Tuesday, 24 April

Go & see my sister Molly at the Airing house. Mr. Cutler, a young fellow I see there, tells me Plymouth is a sad blackguard place, am sorry for it as if I ever have Captain Smith it may perhaps be my destiny to live there. Finish writing to Miss Gittins. Meet "Merchant" Smith, he never bows nor looks at me. Read in Maningham's poems.

Wednesday, 25 April

Vastly pleas'd with the thought of seeing Mr. & Mrs. Masterman when I go to London, impatiently expect to hear they are arriv'd there, hope I shall not be disappointed. Walk to see my sister Molly, when I return am told Mr. & Mrs. Tredcroft say some very unkind things in regard to me & Captain Smith, is this the behaviour of relations? But the malice & envy of a country town is endless.

Thursday, 26 April

Am told & plainly see indeed how much Miss Tredcroft dislikes me, t'is no wonder I told her of her faults, fatal indiscretions that might have been her ruin, this freedom hurt her pride & t'is for this she hates me. How few of us can distinguish between our friends & foes; agreable chat with Jenny Hunt & my Aunt Tasker.

Friday, 27 April

A very gloomy day & my spirits allmost as gloomy, hear my Uncle Waller accus'd my Uncle Grace with stealing his hay, the ill natur'd world gladly propogate the scandal, how cautious must we be in our behaviour, what an Age we live in, eager to hear & industrious to relate our neighbours' faults. Write a prayer or an awfull acknowledgement of the Supreme Being.

Saturday, 28 April

Read my prayer to Bet Hunt who likes it much or pretends she does, a great deal of chat ensues, sure she must be a finish'd hypocrite or she cannot hate me as much as I am told. Begin writing a letter to Mr. Pigott, occasion'd by his saying it was Mr. Maningham's opinion that virtue shou'd be practic'd for its own sake, without hope of reward or fear of punishment.

Sunday, 29 April

I dine with all the family at my Aunt Grace's, go to Church, walk in the Croft, a most delightful day, every bush exhales perfume at this enchanting season of the year. Oh Almighty author of Nature, who can sufficiently admire thy works. At Mrs. Scut's christening,[123] many of my own Sex & much impertinent chat. Receive a very kind

---

123   This was the christening of William Scutt, the second child of William and Jane Scutt, the sister of Amie, Anne and Seymour Powell. Her first child had died in infancy.

letter from my Dear Sally Sheppard, she says I am in the right not to depend on my affair with my Dear Smith, sure it will rend my Heart strings to part.

Monday, 30 April

A letter from my cousin Hurst with a pressing invitation to East Bourn, am oblig'd to her but must not expect to go. Am invited to Mrs. Tredcroft's but make a visit to Nany Curtis. The players act *The Fair Penitent*,[124] have a tolerable house & they say did it pretty well & am glad on't, t'is a sad thing not to succeed.[125]

MAY 1759

Tuesday, 1 May

Walk to see Mr. Nathaniel Tredcroft,[126] with Mrs. Wicker, Miss Powell, Mrs. Tasker & Miss Tredcroft. We play at Matrimony, are excessive merry & then dance. Nat was very drunk, sure nothing is a greater deprivation of human nature than this shocking vice. Finish the letter to Mr. Pigott, read some poems.

Wednesday, 2 May

Sir Charles Eversfield takes some tickets of the Players & bestows them on some young girls. Bet Hunt very much vex'd at it, poor old creature what wou'd she have, past the age of gaiety & folly herself, she is bursting with envy as if she regrets the trifling scenes are past. I hope when I am an old Maid I shall not be such a wretch. Afternoon at Tanbridge.

Thursday, 3 May

Bet Hunt begins relating her intrigue with Sir Charles, to give me I suppose a high Idea of the Virtue that cou'd resist such temptations but the Misfortune is I do not believe he ever had such thoughts, good heavens, to view her & the blooming Nany Cook, wou'd a man hesitate a moment which he shou'd chuse for a Mistress.[127]

Friday, 4 May

Bet Hunt finishes her romantic tale, insufferable creature, first run into dangers & then expect to be applauded for escaping. Oh keep me from Vanity, that poisoner of the Mind. Go to the Play, excessively low spirited occasion'd by remembrance of the

---

124 *The Fair Penitent* was a play by Nicholas Rowe, first performed in 1703 and said to be one of the *"most pleasing"* of English tragedies. It contained the character Lothario, whose name is now used to mean a rake.

125 Companies of strolling players visiting Horsham at this time performed in the arcaded Market House, boarded up for the occasion. Later in the century the town had a theatre in the Carfax.

126 Nathaniel Tredcroft, brother of Edward, was living at North Heath at this time, probably in the farm which had been brought into the family by Mary Michell, heiress to the North Heath estates, on her marriage to Edward Tredcroft in 1735. Nathaniel had previously been a linen-draper.

127 Ann, or Nany, Cook, born in 1736, was the elder sister of Bet Cook.

many tender scenes that pass'd between me & my Dear Smith when the Players us'd to frequent Horsham, busy memory recalls the hours he has waited for the pleasure of conducting me a few paces.[128]

Saturday, 5 May

Papa talks of leaving his business, what then shou'd I do, to live an idle life I shou'd despise myself, well then if my affair with my Dear Smith go off, I shall go out in the World. Mr. Pigott comes to take Leave of me before I go to London, a wet day yet did not prevent him, am oblig'd to the friendship of this Worthy man, give him the letter.

Sunday, 6 May

Walk in the Croft, inclinable to rain yet vastly pleasant, everything is now in bloom, & to see Nature in perfection gives infinite pleasure to a thinking Mind. Make a visit to the Miss Haines, very agreable girls, one a beauty.[129] Take a walk with them. Miss Powell & I seek for the post, meet my Smith's mother who insists on our going in to read the News, she treats us so kindly I am surpris'd. No letter from Mr. Masterman.

Monday, 7 May

Ride to Dorking with Mrs. Wicker, then take the Coach & set forward to London. Two very agreable women in the Coach & a strolling player, much chat about things of no consequence. Arrive in London about five o'clock. Extremely fatigued. My Uncle very angry with Papa, I cannot tell the reason but it makes me uneasy.[130]

Tuesday, 8 May

Go in the Borough,[131] pay some money and buy some goods, dine at Mr. Hales, a hosier, then take water to White Hall, & call on my Dear Sally Sheppard, who is in raptures to see me & goes with me to the Miniature Painter's, I am to sit for my picture Friday. I weep very much at what my Uncle says of my Papa, yet how can I help it.

Wednesday, 9 May

Walk with Mrs. Wicker to Mrs. Laight's in the St. James' Market,[132] leave her there & take Sally Sheppard to Grosvenor Square to see Miss Pigott, but do

128 The Market House, where the players performed, was literally a few paces from Sarah's front door.
129 These were the daughters of Evershed Haynes of Oakwood, Surrey, who was said to have brought them to live in Horsham so that they might find husbands. Ann Haynes married Richard Grinstead, and their sons became partners with John Lanham in the Horsham Bank, which was in business from 1796 to 1815.
130 Robert Hurst, the London tailor, who was in partnership with his brother Richard.
131 The "Borough" was that of Southwark. It had a well-known market, said to be the oldest in London. The Horsham wagons (and later stage coaches) left from inns in Southwark, and many Sussex people went there to shop or do business.
132 Mrs. Laight (1719-1804) came from Horsham and was a friend of Mrs. Wicker. She was Elizabeth Chasemore, daughter of John Chasemore, butcher of East Street, and she married Nathaniel Laight at St. James, Westminster, in 1755.

not find her at home, walk back thro' the Green Park. Go to Ranelaugh with a great party at a great expense which I cannot afford.[133] T'is a giddy round & no diversion.

Thursday, 10 May

Do some business at our Linnen Draper's, then walk with Mrs. Wicker into St Paul's,[134] & see the company at the Rehearsal. Am vastly star'd at, but cannot tell for what reason, it cannot sure be for my Beauty. Call on Mr. Ford, the Tobacconist, he presses me to stay the evening but I refuse, return home & play at cards.

Friday, 11 May

Call on Counsellor Cox for Mr. William Wicker's Will,[135] he receives me very kindly & asks me to go to Ranelaugh, but I excuse myself. Go to Schuler's, the Miniature Painter that drew the picture I have of my Dear Smith, & begin a sitting for mine.[136] Go to the Play, *A New Way to pay Old Debts* & *Tom Thumb the Great*, am much diverted.[137]

Saturday, 12 May

Out again for my picture, carry Sally Sheppard to see it, who says it is a great likeness. Go to Mr. Kendall's, a Stuff Warehouse in Gracechurch Street, he compliments excessively my person & understanding. A gentleman comes in by accident & gives me the same commendations. A letter from Miss Pigott.

Sunday, 13 May

At Church in the morning, then walk up to my Uncle George's, who teases me about Captain Smith, I shew his picture, but afterwards repent it. All my friends blame me for not being married, but in my opinion there was reasons enough to prevent it. I wish I was out of this noise & hurry, the calm still life for me, with the dear converse of a few sociable friends.

Monday, 14 May

My Uncle greatly blames my Papa & says he is selfish & ungratefull, I cry very much, it gives me great concern, yet how can I help it. Wou'd to Heaven their affairs

---

133 Ranelagh Gardens was one of the public pleasure gardens in London, and was at this time considered to be more fashionable than the older Vauxhall Gardens (in 1741, the entrance fee to Ranelagh was two shillings and sixpence, as opposed to one shilling to Vauxhall). The gardens were in the grounds of Ranelagh House in Chelsea, near the Royal Hospital, and contained a Rotunda, where concerts were held, and a *"Chinese Pavilion"*.

134 Sarah probably means St. Paul's Churchyard, where there were shops and public buildings, rather than St. Paul's Cathedral.

135 William Wicker, who died in 1751, was the husband of Mrs. Wicker.

136 These are probably the silhouettes of Sarah and Henry reproduced in this book.

137 *A New Way to pay Old Debts* was a popular comedy by Philip Massinger (first performed c. 1625) and *Tom Thumb the Great* or *The Tragedy of Tragedies* (1731) by Henry Fielding, combined satire and burlesque and was very successful. Fielding wrote *The History of Tom Jones, a Foundling* (1749), generally considered as his masterpiece and the greatest comic novel of the 18th century. He also became London's Chief Magistrate and founded the Bow Street Runners.

was settled. Go to Drury Lane Playhouse, see *Othello* & *The Diversions of the Morning*.[138] Am conducted home by young Seawell, excessively tired.[139]

Tuesday, 15 May

All the morning at the Haberdasher's, do all my business there & stay dinner, vast deal of chat with young Seawell about Matrimony. He expects a good fortune & a clever woman, but he thinks they seldom meet. I put an advertisement in the paper to desire the good Mr. Masterman if he is in Town, to call at the *Woolpack* that I may see him.

Wednesday, 16 May

My Uncle & I have more words. Bet Smith, Sally & I go out in a frolick to have our fortunes told, the Man we go to descants a long time on mine, I have no faith in these things, but the fellow told me many transactions of my past life. Go to Vauxhall with a large party, a vast deal of company, charming fine evening.

Thursday, 17 May

Walk up to my Uncle George's. Mrs. Park & Miss Ellis drink tea here. No letter from home, excessively uneasy, place all full in Dorking Coach, so must be oblig'd to stay till next Wednesday, I most earnestly wish to be at home in my Business. Thus are we ever restless & our minds in continual perturbation.

Friday, 18 May

Mr. Masterman to my inexpressible satisfaction answers my advertisement. I write a note for him & leave *[it]* with young Alsop to whose care & secrecy I am excessively oblig'd.[140] Dine with Mrs. Wicker at Mrs. Laight's in St James' Market. Receive a *[word omitted]* Mr. Masterman that he shou'd be glad to see me, determine to go in the morning.

Saturday, 19 May

Receive an exceeding kind reception from Mr. & Mrs. Masterman. A vast deal of chat about my Dear Smith, they promise to come & drink tea with me on Monday. He is a very sensible agreable Man, she not so amiable but I fancy a worthy Woman. Walk to White Conduit House with Mrs. Wicker & my Cousins Smith, a vast deal of company.[141]

Sunday, 20 May

Am made excessively uneasy by my Aunt's[142] saying a gentleman ask'd her how she cou'd suffer me to go to Vauxhall in a Linnen negligee, for I look'd like a woman of the

---

138 *Othello* by William Shakespeare, first performed in 1604. *The Diversions of the Morning* was a satire on contemporary actors and public figures written by Samuel Foote, first performed by himself on 22 April 1747 in a bid to evade the licensing laws. It led to the closure of the theatre and was later revised in a more acceptable form.

139 "*Young Seawell*" was presumably a brother of Sarah's friend Miss Seawell.

140 "*Young Alsop*" was probably a clerk to one of her uncles, or Counsellor Cox.

141 White Conduit House in Islington was another popular pleasure garden at this time.

142 Probably Aunt Sally, with whom she was staying, or her Aunt Elizabeth Smith.

Town, ungenerous creature to tell me this when it was her perswasions induc'd me to be of the company, for I made objections on account of my dress, but I am conscious of my upright intentions, & will learn to despise ill nature, envy & malice.

Monday, 21 May

Present of a white cloak from Miss Seawell, in return for the Handkerchief I work'd her. Take leave of them & all my acquaintance. Sally Sheppard dines with me. Mrs. Masterman comes to drink tea, he is Ill or wou'd have accompanied her, I leave her with reluctance, but so it is decreed.

Tuesday, 22 May

Come down from London with Mrs. Wicker & Miss Pigott in the Horsham stage for the first time of its travelling,[143] an agreable Journey enough, Miss Pigott expresses great concern at leaving London, I wish she was posses'd of every thing that wou'd be pleasing to her, but ought we to expect this, I think not.

Wednesday, 23 May

Very busy putting my goods to rights, business is very pleasant were it not, like every thing else, full of perplexities. Shew my picture to my Aunt Tasker, she does not think it so great a likeness as Captain Smith's, t'is not so flattering a one I'm sure. I wish the Dear gentleman had it. I fancy it wou'd give him pleasure.

Thursday, 24 May

Mr. Pigott here, I don't think he behaves well to his sister, but his disposition is extremely unsteady, yet his friendship for me seems real. He says the essay I wrote on Virtue deserves to be engrav'd in Marble, but I am sure this propensity to writing creates me more enemies than friends, because from the corruption of our Minds we are more prone to envy than admire, & often endeavour to lessen what we cannot imitate.

Friday, 25 May

Frequently view my Dear Smith's picture, & wish to see the original, what shall I wish for after this, something no doubt as unattainable, but there is no setting bounds to fancy nothing but Death can terminate our hopes & fears, & this event may not be far distant from me. Shall I then be over anxious how my affair with the Captain is decided? It will be at most but a few years spent in disquietude of Mind. Death will lay his Icy hand on this animated clay, & all my perturbations in the grave shall end.

Saturday, 26 May

Write to Bet Smith. Wonder I have not heard from Miss Gittins.

Sunday, 27 May

At Church twice. A delightfull day fills my Mind with that sweet serenity that allways results from these heart enlivening prospects. Make a visit at Tanbridge, but

---

143   The first passenger stage coach from London to Horsham ran from *The Spur* in Southwark on Tuesday and Saturdays, for a fare of 6s.

the Miss Ellis's have so much pride & reserve they are excessive disagreable, but I suppose they think it right to keep people in trade at a distance. Well, let them do it, I will not complain but am sorry I am oblig'd to be in their company.

Monday, 28 May

One of our fair days, busy in the shop.[144] T'is quite diverting to observe the different behaviour of the Country people, uncultivated by education, how are such generally despised & for what, their misfortune not fault. Miss Powell & Miss Hutchinson here, the latter rattles strangely about her being in Love.

Tuesday, 29 May

Mr. Harbroe & young Napper of Rudgwick here, they say the former is a Fop & the latter a clown, how difficult it is to please, in fact it is impossible.

Wednesday, 30 May

Bet Hunt tells me that Doctor Griffith & Captain Smith have both attempted her Virtue. How I despise her insinuations, her Lovers are Chimeras, bred in her own Brain. Her years shou'd now tell her these discourses are highly ridiculous. She now reveals her great love to Doctor Griffith, charges me to be secret, tells me he now courts Mrs. Wicker, & believes it will be a Match, says he is the most execrable of Villains. Most astonishing that a Woman of her understanding shou'd make herself thus ridiculous.

Thursday, 31 May

Walk with my brother to Slynfold. Mr. Maningham & his Fanny there, he appears to be in some confusion. Oh Guilt, Guilt what a fiend art thou, ever these great [?Lovers] (or great Libertines) that seem to despise the censures of the World & yet are afraid it shou'd pry into their actions, but I sincerely pity Poor Fanny, & think her situation truly deplorable, she is excluded from all society, & dependent on the caprice of a man who has ruin'd her.[145]

JUNE 1759

Friday, 1 June

Stay all night at Slynfold, pass our time in agreable chat. Mr. & Miss Pigott make great protestations of friendship which I sincerely return, we part with reluctance.

Saturday, 2 June

Bet Hunt tells me Doctor Griffith is at Mrs. Wicker's every night till eleven or

---

144   This was the Horsham Whitsun Fair (a movable feast) established by a charter granted by King Henry VI in 1449. It was originally held for three days but was now only held on Whitmonday.

145   This suggests that Fanny was living with the Rev. Thomas Manningham as his mistress. This incident seems to have affected Sarah's friendship with Mr. Manningham, as she does not mention him again.

twelve, how shall I act in this affair? I almost think it is my Duty to acquaint her with it, yet how shall I do this without embroiling Bet Hunt, for as much my enemy as she has been I will not do her an injury willfully.

Sunday, 3 June

Jack Smith at Church, I hope I can look on all that family (notwithstanding their inveteracy against me) without malice or revenge. Drink tea at Mrs. Wicker's, relate to her all that Bet Hunt told me, but conceal my author, she protests it is all false. What then ought to be the punishment of those who can invent such notorious falsehoods, & that she shou'd make me her confidant is most surprising. No letter from Gittins.

Monday, 4 June

Miss Powell & Miss Hutchinson promise to dine at Slynfold, then are afraid of the weather & disappoint me. I write to Bet Smith, Sally Sheppard & young Alsop, desiring his acceptance of a chicken, for the trouble he was at in regard to my advertisement concerning Mr. Masterman.[146] Walk in the Park.

Tuesday, 5 June

Go to Slynfold with the above young Ladies, they receive us very kindly, a vast deal of rattling talk with Miss Hutchinson, she wishes for a husband, strange girl, how mad & unaccountable. I at her desire write some verses to young Harbroe expressing her love to him in a strange & ludicrous manner.

Wednesday, 6 June

Stay all night which was a very stormy one, Miss Pigott not satisfied at Slynfold tho' she knows her being there is most convenient, but Matrimony is the Goal she aims at, but it may be long e'er she reaches it. Write some more verses when they were all in a high rattling chat. Walk home in the evening, Pigott with us.

Thursday, 7 June

Words with my sister Bet, put myself in a Passion, which am afterwards sorry for, tho' she deserves it. Mrs. Tasker tells me Bet Hunt rails in a monstrous manner against Mrs. Wicker, envy & jealousy devour quiet, Jealousy of one that never lov'd her and envy of one that never injur'd her. Walk in the Park with my sister Molly who tells me some disagreable things in regard to my sister Bet's behaviour, I have done my endeavour to make her better, but she regards me not.

Friday, 8 June

Mrs. Wicker drinks tea here, Mr. John Shelley here several times, at last gives me the Play George Harnwell acted. Mr. Shelly drunk & rattles strangely, I suppose t'is to forget if possible his amiable wife whose loss hangs heavy on his Mind. This bad

---

146 Horsham chickens were highly regarded and much in demand at this time – the Dowager Lady Irwin had them sent by the dozen from Hill's Place to London or her house in Windsor at Christmastime.

turn in him is I imagine occasion'd by a wrong education which instead of teaching him by strength of Reason to alleviate his sorrow makes him fly to what is only a momentary relief & will in the end double his vexation.[147]

Saturday, 9 June

Walk up [to] the Park[148] in the evening, everything delightfully serene & still, the Moon is full, in full Majesty of her silver beams.

Sunday, 10 June

At Church, Doctor Hutchinson makes an excellent discourse on these words in Job *"He doeth great things which we cannot comprehend"*. He first expatiates on the wonders of the Creation & then exhorts us to believe in the Trinity tho' we cannot comprehend it. Walk in the Croft, hear that Nany Cook is going to have Lord Irwin's Cook. Walk to Highland. A note from Mr. Pigott, he calls me the Sappho or tenth Muse, I answer it & invite them.

Monday, 11 June

Miss Powell's admirer here, a Clergyman, she is they say going to be married & will live beyond Salisbury.[149] I am sorry to lose her but wish her happy more so than she ever has been, for trouble early attack'd her. Mama & Bet go to Dorking for 2 or 3 days. Mrs. Wicker drinks tea with me, read in Baxter upon the Soul.[150]

Tuesday, 12 June

Mrs. Tredcroft calls on me in the Morning, much chat about Miss Powell & her lover, she is surpris'd it was not known, but Miss Powell took the only method in the World to prevent it, she kept her own secret. Mr. & Miss Pigott come to dinner, he goes home but she stays all night & we go to the Play, *Hamlet* & *Lethe*.[151]

Wednesday, 13 June

Miss Pigott regrets the absence of her lover[152] but what is the distance of Wales to that of North America, where my Dear Smith is, & perhaps in imminent danger. Mr. Pigott comes for his sister, we all drink tea at Miss Powell's, like her lover much. Go to Mrs. Bridger's, from thence to supper at Mr. Tredcroft's, thus life flees.

Thursday, 14 June

Work a handkerchief for Mrs. Bridger, [?go] to dine at Mr. Wicker (in) [sic] go up &

---

147 John Shelley was born in America and did not come to England until the age of fourteen. His father was criticised in a Chancery case in 1752 for not ensuring that he had been properly educated for his great *"fortune and circumstances"*, as the eventual heir to all the property owned by his great-uncle, Edward Shelley.
148 *"The Park"* is Denne Park, on the top of Denne Hill.
149 Amie Powell married the Rev. John Townshend on 18 June 1759, in Horsham.
150 Richard Baxter (1615-1691), who wrote *On the Immortality of the Soul* in 1682, was a Puritan divine and military chaplain during the Civil War, but refused a bishopric after the Restoration. He was a prolific and influential writer.
151 *Hamlet* by William Shakespeare was first performed in 1602. No play or entertainment called *Lethe* has been identified.
152 The Rev. John Jones.

see Mrs. Luttman & Molly, am sent for home to Mrs. Wicker, who stays & chats a considerable time. No news yet of Miss Gittins. What can occasion this neglect? Sure my last letter miscarried, this I shou'd be much vex'd at & hope it is otherwise.

Friday, 15 June

Mrs. Wicker dines with us. Mama & Bet returns home, the former acquaints me that Bet has got an admirer at Dorking, I wish it may be true; it may prevent her going on with the fellow she now keeps company with.[153] Mrs. Tredcroft & Miss drink tea here, Miss Upton calls in her Chariot for something in the shop.[154]

Saturday, 16 June

A note from Miss Upton, I answer it, Bet relates to me the whole affair of her new lover & says she refer'd entirely to her father, I commend her prudent behaviour. I call on Miss Powell who wishes me health & happiness [and] enquires after Captain Smith. Mr. Townsend says I am the prettiest girl in the place, I thank him for the compliment, but alas what are the fleeting charms of person, if I really do possess any. They invite me into Dorsetshire, but Heaven knows how I shall be dispos'd of.

Sunday, 17 June

At Church twice, my sister Bet extremely angry at my having a pair of lac'd double ruffles, oh envy, thou balefull vice. Poor Mrs. White here, she pathetically laments the death of Mrs. Shelley, & I sincerely sympathise with her.

Monday, 18 June

Miss Powell married & goes away, I have lost a valuable acquaintance, but console myself with thinking it will be more conducive to her happiness. Miss Orlton[155] here, she tells me how much Doctor Ford, a gentleman in London, admires me. Walk with Mama, meet '"Merchant"' Smith who never speaks. His bad behaviour affects me greatly, yet why shou'd it, suppose it alters the sentiments of my Dear Smith this is the worst that can happen, & shall a creature design'd for immortal happiness make itself miserable about anything can befall it here?

Tuesday, 19 June

Mr., Miss Pigott & her lover dine here. I go to the Play, *Cato*, dreadfully perform'd.[156]

---

153 Presumably Will James, previously mentioned on 9 February and 2 March.

154 Miss Anne Upton lived at Strood Park, the daughter of Captain Richard Upton, of the East India Company and his wife Sarah Cowper, who both died before she was twelve years old. She had inherited the Strood estate from her uncle Edward Cowper, the last of his line. Her grandfather, Henry Cowper, had been M.P. for Horsham, elected in 1701, 1702 and 1705.

155 Miss Orlton was one of the daughters of the late Hugh Orlton, died 1755, who had property on North Heath (Horsham Common). Her sister Lucy married John Michell, the brother of Drew Michell - see the entry for 23 September 1759.

156 *Cato*, a tragedy by Joseph Addison, was first performed in 1713. It was his most famous work of fiction, dealing with such themes as individual liberty v. government tyranny and Republicanism v. Monarchy. It is thought to have been a literary inspiration for the American Revolution, as it was well known to several of its leading figures.

Wednesday, 20 June

Write a note to Miss Gittins enquiring the reason of her long silence. Papa speaks harsh to me, I weep, my temper is surprisingly meek, but I will not discompose myself for every trifle. Walk up in the Park with Molly, begin reading *The Connoisseur* to Bet Hunt. '"Merchant"' Smith & Doctor Griffith come in. I walk home.

Thursday, 21 June

Mr. Powell returns from attending his sister Townsend to London, expressing great concern for her loss. Take a walk with Molly in the Park, delightfully pleasant & serene, how beauteous is the face of Nature after a hot day, how wonderfull are thy works Oh Almighty, & yet how incapable we often are of relishing these enjoyments.

Friday, 22 June

Hear that '"Merchant"' Smith behaves in a vile manner to his brother, how difficult it is to know peoples tempers, & how great a misfortune is a bad one. At the Play, *Othello*.[157] When I return home Mama acquaints me she has receiv'd a letter from Bet's Dorking Lover, desiring permission to come & pay his addresses to her.

Saturday, 23 June

In a high fret about my work, ridiculous & even wicked girl, let me remember this & beware for the future. Miss Bristed here, I tell her of Nan Curtis's being in love with a Player, she blames her much. Bet's admirer comes, an excessive plain Man, & gives himself airs in despising the Country people & diversions. Papa tells me he does not think it will be a proper Match for Bet, I tell him he knows best & must enquire.

Sunday, 24 June

At Church twice. Walk in the Croft, excessive pleasant. Sally Hunt[158] says she's sure Mr. Hill is a lover of Bet's, I laugh it off, take a walk in the Park with Bet Hunt, Jenny, my Aunt Tasker, Bet & Mr. Hill, they ask me about him, I tell them I wish it may be a Match, but can't tell whether it will or not.

Monday, 25 June

Bet's gentleman seems violently in love, we are to enquire into his Character & circumstances. Mr. Tredcroft laughs at her excessively, & says who wou'd stay in Horsham, when going out for two or three days produces a Sweetheart. Write to Mrs. Turner at Dorking & send all the work I had done for her.[159]

Tuesday, 26 June

Mr. Hill goes home, but says he hopes soon to see his Bet again. I write to my Aunt Smith desiring she wou'd enquire about him. Read to Bet Hunt in *The Connoisseur*.

---

157   Sarah would have been able to compare this performance with the one she saw in London on 14 May.
158   Sally Hunt was the sister of Bet and Jenny Hunt, and later went to live in Cowfold.
159   This was presumably needlework for Mrs. Turner, wife of the Vicar of Dorking.

Ride with Mr. Tredcroft's people to their farm at Hauxbone *[Hawkesbourne]*, go & see *The Busy Body*, last time of our players performing.[160]

Wednesday, 27 June

Mrs. James says Bet has jilted her son, how cautious ought young people be of their behaviour, for dreadfull at last are the consequences of indiscretion. Very busy Ironing, at night read in *The Connoisseur* some of it very good, & some trifling, ill plac'd ridicule, allmost too low for the pen.

Thursday, 28 June

Two ships I see in the papers come from the place where my Dear Smith is. His mother very uneasy that they brought no news of him, but I think she has no reason, he might not be appris'd of their sailing or twenty accidents might prevent his writing. I will however think so if possible.

Friday, 29 June

Most people alarm'd with the report that the French intend to invade England. I give not much credit to it, but my Heart burns with ardour in my Country's cause. Why was my aspiring Soul cloath'd in a female body, & plac'd in too low a situation ever to assert itself? How happy are they who die in the service of their fellow creatures but, since this is denied me, let me endeavour to shine in the social Life, & be remarkable for patience & ever humble virtue.

Saturday, 30 June

Doctor Smith decries my poem on *Moonlight* tho' he had never seen it. I write some verses on it, & send them to Miss Pigott. A letter from my Aunt Smith, she says a Turner is a very mean business, & Mr. Hill's shop is the picture of poverty, so fancy my sister Bet's love affair will come to nothing. Walk to Slynfold, vastly pleasant.

JULY 1759

Sunday, 1 July

All day at Slynfold, agreable conversation with Mr. & Miss Pigott, at Church twice, t'is a very dull place, certainly we ought to make ourselves Easy wherever our lot is cast, but I fear as well as I love writing & reading I cou'd not be happy there. Oh society thou dear invaluable blessing yet what a thought of evil dost thou sometimes occasion. Mr. Harbroe drinks tea with us, I walk home, Mama meets me, not well, heaven forbid she shou'd be Ill.

Monday, 2 July

Write an answer as from Mr. Harbroe to Miss Hutchinson, in verse. Doctor Smith

---

160   *The Busy Body*, a play by Susanna Centlivre, was first performed in 1709. It was a great success and was much performed throughout the 18th century– the chief character, Marplot, was one of David Garrick's favourite comic roles.

says I am a fanatick poet, well let him, but I think he has given much greater indications of lunacy. Frame some pictures at Mrs. Wicker's, walk in Mr. Tredcroft's garden, then up in the Park, meet Sir Charles Eversfield, who compliments me on Mrs. Shelley's *Elegy*, then enters into a chat on the deceitfullness of Man. Tell him I never was deceiv'd by the Sex, *"because"*, says he, *"you had the happiness to fix on a Man of sense & honour"*. I hope I have.

Tuesday, 3 July

Go to meet Mrs. Turner, but instead of her a letter from Mr. Turner with an excuse.

Wednesday, 4 July

Very busy, begin a poem on the folly of being conspicuous. Walk in the Park with Molly, then chat with Jenny Hunt, an amiable girl. Send to the Post who brings me three letters, one from Miss Gittins, one from Sally Sheppard, & the last from my Dear Smith, who sends me a Journal of all that has passed in his absence, says nothing but his circumstances shou'd have prevented our union before this. Yet says if I cou'd like any person better, I shou'd make myself happy, & he wou'd endeavour to make himself. Cruel man, it is impossible.

Thursday, 5 July

Walk the Causeway with Miss Tredcroft, her father & mother. Mr. Tredcroft tells me the '"Merchant"' says he will arrest my Dear Smith as soon as we are married. Heaven forbid he shou'd be involved in distress on my account.

Friday, 6 July

A letter from my Cousin Bet Smith who says Mr. Hill will not be a proper Match for my sister. Walk in the Park with Bet, meet Sir Charles, very agreable chat with him. Walk on the Causeway with my Dear Smith's mother.

Saturday, 7 July

Mama talks to me concerning my affair with Captain Smith, & asks me how I think it will terminate, I tell her not in matrimony I believe. Write to young Alsop, to enquire what money is due to Mrs. Luttman[161] on her son's account. Sally Sheppard comes to Horsham, I hope to enjoy great pleasure in her company.

Sunday, 8 July

Walk down to Mrs. Wicker's before Church, see Jack & Charles Smith & attempt to push out in the garden. Charles calls & says nobody wou'd bite me. I step back & look like a fool, he is very civil. At Church twice, make a visit at Mrs. White's, she laments the unhappy loss of Mrs. Shelley, & the more unhappy behaviour of her daughter Thyer. She asks me when I heard from the Captain. I make no scruple of owning I had lately, she pities my situation.

---

161   Mrs. Luttman seems to have been pursuing a claim to an inheritance on her son Philip's account.

Monday, 9 July

Papa goes out, Mama Ill, I behave with all the tenderness my ill-nature will permit. Begin writing a poem, the folly of being conspicuous. Walk in the Park with my Dear Sally Sheppard, are catch'd in an unexpected shower, take shelter under a Tree & moralize on the vicissitudes & uncertainties of human life.

Tuesday, 10 July

Am surpris'd with the sight of Miss Woodhams from Lewes, she dines here, I ask after all my acquaintance, she is a most affected girl, I ask her to make some stay but she refuses.[162] Sup at Mrs. Tredcroft's, talk of Mr. Blunt's being married, wish he had fell in with Miss Gittins, begin writing to my Dear Smith.

Wednesday, 11 July

Very much out of temper all the Morning, such frequent states of Ill humour ought not to be permitted, I blame myself much. Very merry with Sally Sheppard, & Jenny, drink tea at the former's house, with Mrs. Laight from London, then walk in the Park. Write to my Dear Smith till twelve o'clock, 2 sheets full.

Thursday, 12 July

Very busy all the morning. Write to Mr. Masterman; inclose Captain Smith's *[letter]*. Mrs. Laight, Mrs. Wicker & Sally Sheppard drink tea here. We all walk in the Park, then on the Causeway with Mrs. Tredcroft, who says that trade people going to the Assembly at Brighthelmstone[163] has spoilt it, for people of Quality don't chuse to be in company with them.

Friday, 13 July

Certainly when they chuse their private friends it shou'd be those whose education & manners bear the nearest affinity to themselves, but objecting against meeting them in public is full as absurd as disliking to travel the same road or going by the same means to Heaven.

Saturday, 14 July

Sure these sentiments cannot be call'd noble, that word implies a general complacence & diffusive Benevolence, which are the peculiar Priviledges of Quality & a generous education, while on the contrary I shou'd imagine such confin'd notions cou'd only harbour in a Plebeian Soul. Mr. Bridger dies.[164]

Sunday, 15 July

A letter from good Mr. Masterman, & another from young Alsop about Philip Luttman. Answer Mr. Masterman's, & write again to Captain Smith, who is

---

162 Sarah spent a month with Miss Woodhams in Lewes in 1756.
163 Brighton.
164 Arthur Bridger appears to have been a moneylender, as he held a mortgage on the *King's Head Inn* in 1751. This perhaps explains why he was so much disliked in Horsham (see entry for 16 July below). He came from a clothier's family in Godalming, and had inherited property from his mother. In his will, he asked to be buried in a leaden coffin near his parents.

expected home about October. I wish yet dread to see him, how happy shou'd I be to live with this dear Man, but doubt that will never be my lot. Walk in the Park with Sally Sheppard, much agreeable chat, we condole one another.

Monday, 16 July

Excessively busy making mourning for Mrs. Bridger, she (nor indeed any body else) feels no concern for her loss, he liv'd unregarded & dyed unlamented, has lost his fortune to those he never cared for, & disinherited a son who had a natural tho' not a lawfull right to his possessions.[165] The Miss Elliss's here, pretty merry.

Tuesday, 17 July

Think much on the uncertainty of my affair with Captain Smith, allmost dread yet wish for a peace, as then my doom will be decided. Drink tea at Mr. Powell's, with Mrs. Wicker, Mrs. Laight, Mr. Pigott, & Sally Sheppard who sings a great many songs, walk on the Causeway with Miss Tredcroft.

Wednesday, 18 July

Fair day,[166] eternally noisy, with puppet shows & Jack puddings, good heavens how is human Nature debas'd by these creatures. Mr. Butcher from Hurst[167] obliges Miss Tredcroft & me to go & see the Wild beast, he keeps us by force, how disagreeable is this from indifferent people. Perpetual noise & confusion, how shocking to a serious Mind, that is inclinable to moralize on every trifling incident.

Thursday, 19 July

Walk in the Park with Sally Sheppard, then go with a large company to the Puppet show, what are we but puppets, drawn by the wire of every tempestuous passion.

Friday, 20 July

What an insipid life, in my own opinion, do I lead, yet in that of others few are more active indeed. It is not the part allotted us in the great Drama, but our manner of performing it that we must account for. My situation in Life deprives me of the means to be usefull to my fellow creatures, but I may be good & happy.

Saturday, 21 July

The last Fair day, very busy in the Shop. Sally Hunt drinks tea with us. Mr. Hill,

---

165 Sarah's opinion is borne out by Arthur Bridger's will, in which he left an annuity of £80 to an illegitimate son called Richard Bridger, als. Goodjer, but made his nephew, the Rev. Richard Bridger, his chief heir (WSRO Wiston MSS 1485). He left his wife a life interest in his house in East Street, known as Ashleys. She died in 1763, and Ashleys passed to the Rev. Richard Bridger, who still held it in 1782. A Mrs. Elizabeth Bridger was the owner at the time of the enclosure of Horsham Common in 1812.

166 The Horsham July Fair was the oldest and most important fair held during the year, and brought a great deal of business to the town. The Charter for the Fair was granted by King Henry III to William de Braose, Lord of the Manor, in 1233, for an annual fair beginning on St. Thomas's Day, 7 July. It lasted from three to nine days, ending on a Saturday (if it started on a Friday then it lasted until the following Saturday). The change in the calendar in 1752 brought the opening day to 18 July.

167 Hurstpierpoint.

Bet's lover comes again, tho' he has been denied, declares he can keep her extremely well & shall never be happy without her. Papa is at a loss what answer to make him. Walk with Miss Tredcroft, who seems quite fond of me.

Sunday, 22 July

Ride to Cuckfield with Papa pursuant to an invitation from Mr. Chasemore,[168] breakfast at Slaugham, excuse myself to Miss Bristed for not visiting Miss Woodhams while she was there. When I return home the post brings me a letter from Mr. Masterman, I offer to pay for it & to my great surprise find I have lost my pocket Memorandum Book & Captain Smith's picture & my own, am like to faint.

Monday, 23 July

Papa sets out the Cuckfield Road at 4 in the morning, to recover my loss if possible. I am in dreadfull anxiety, fearing what hands this book might fall into, for tho' there is nothing criminal my whole heart is laid open. At 9 he returns, & brings my little treasure, I am thankfull.

Tuesday, 24 July

Very busy all day. Papa goes to London, partly to make further enquiry about Mr. Hill. Mr. Pigott calls, with a young gentleman, his sister is well they say. Miss Hutchinson is raving mad, how dreadfull is this whatever the occasion, she is sent from home, oh Love, can such things be thy doings.

Wednesday, 25 July

Mr. Pigott, his sister & a young gentleman from London come to breakfast with us. They dine at Doctor Hutchinson's. I spend the afternoon at Mrs. Wicker's. They come to me in the evening. Miss Pigott says they talk'd much of me & Captain Smith, & said if I had him I shou'd be very happy.

Thursday, 26 July

Miss Pigott here all night. The gentlemen come again to dinner, with Mr. Powell, Mrs. Wicker & Sally Sheppard. We tell fortunes & are merry, but Mr. Pigott falls asleep, we rally him severely. They go home. I call on Mrs. Luttman & settle the letter of Attorney about her son's money.

Friday, 27 July

Madam Smith says, what shou'd the Captain do with such a wife as me who can only sit with a book in her hand,[169] sure it is impossible I can work more than I do. Direct Mr. Powell[170] about the letter of Attorney, intend sending it to London by Mr. Pigott, who offer'd his services.

---

168 Francis Chasemore (1715-1762) was an attorney who lived in Cuckfield, whose son later went to school with Sarah's brother Robert. His grandfather, Joseph Chasemore, was a Horsham surgeon, whose wife was a great-aunt of Sally Sheppard.
169 This comment by Henry's mother suggests why she opposed his marriage to Sarah.
170 This makes it clear that Seymour Powell was a lawyer or lawyer's clerk. He probably worked with Mr. John Parham.

Saturday, 28 July

Very much employ'd, consequently very little time to think, when I do t'is of my Dear Smith, who is I fear at this time in great danger. Heaven preserve him. Three gentlemen drink coffee here, from Cuckfield. They rally me on the loss of my pocket book, I can bear this now I have it again.

Sunday, 29 July

Mama & all the family out except Bet & me. I spend my day in philosophick meditations, going to Church, & writing to Miss Gittins. Give her a description of Vauxhall, & make some remarks on our passion for amusements. Drink tea with Sally Sheppard, then walk on the Causeway. My Dear Smith's mother calls me in to read the News, I obey, she is vastly civil & I am vastly pleas'd.

Monday, 30 July

Miss Tredcroft calls & desires I wou'd go with her to Tanbridge. I promise. While there our Maid brings me a note from Miss Pigott entreating me to come over to Slynfold for she wanted to ask my advice. I obey, take my leave of the company & set off directly.

Tuesday, 31 July

She tells me her brother said at parting, if she went to Marlow he'd prevent her ever entering his doors again. I advise her not to run the hazard, tho' not out of deference to him, but lest he shou'd misrepresent things to her other relations. I leave her & return home, am excessively concern'd at Mr. Pigott's behaviour, & wish it otherwise.

AUGUST 1759

Wednesday, 1 August

Pay Mrs. Bridger the visit of condolence, as it is call'd, tho she is far from being affected, indeed how can she, for the loss of such a husband, but oh how dreadfull must this separation be, when mutual love cements the Marriage, the parting of Soul & body cannot be so shocking. Oh may it never be my lot to survive my Dear Smith.

Thursday, 2 August

Out of humour in the morning, for no reason. How much pains has it cost me to master this bad temper, & yet far from being accomplish'd. Drink tea at Mrs. Wicker's, then Sally Sheppard calls & we take a walk in the Park. Find Mrs. Tredcroft & Mrs. White here on my return, they rail at the unhappy Miss Hutchinson.

Friday, 3 August

Work very hard till evening, then walk with Sally Sheppard. We look forward to a state of Old Maidenism with a vast deal of pleasure, agree to live together &

fix upon a house on the Terras [?*terrace*] belonging to Sir Charles.[171] Delightfull moonlight evening, take several turns on the Causeway by myself. Wish to see my Dear Smith.

Saturday, 4 August

Resolve not to go to Marlow as my Papa seems rather averse. There is a certain grace in conferring an obligation, which greatly enhances the favour, to bestow with repining or reluctance entirely dissipates the merit. Read Wesalies' poems, *The Battle of the Sexes*, a pretty thing; *The Mastiff*, a fine satire on our proneness to what is forbid. Play at cards at Mrs. Bridger's.

Sunday, 5 August

Stay at home from Church in expectation of writing to London. Read in *Henry & Frankes*, a collection of delicate sensible letters, interspers'd with various moral, humane & religious sentiments, maintains the punishment of the Wicked is not eternal. I am inclinable to think the same, but makes Virtue independent of hope or fear, which I cannot allow, as being contrary to its very essence, believes we shall know each other in another Life, a sentiment that allways gives me the highest joy to think conformable with reason.

Monday, 6 August

Drink tea at my Dear Smith's Mother's. She behaves very civil, we walk in the garden. T'is a sweet house, how supremely blest shou'd I be to live there with my Harry, but Oh I fear so great a happiness I shall never deserve. Excessive low spirited, but endeavour to exert myself & shake it of tho' in vain.

Tuesday, 7 August

Mr. Blunt is married, to a very young lady, which occasions various speculations, well Mrs Blunt is posses'd of a large fortune & a Coach.[172] I have been all day ironing, & to fatigue myself still more, walk for diversion, yet wou'd not I change situations, thus are we ever repining at our own lot, yet cannot find the person who in every respect we think happier.

Wednesday, 8 August

Write to Miss Pigott & desire her to come over. She answers my letter but cannot accept the invitation. Walk with Sally Sheppard. Bet Hunt angry at the Bells ringing for the Wedding,[173] Oh envy may I erase every spark, if any is lurking in me.

---

171 Presumably a cottage on Denne Hill, near the mansion of Denne House.

172 Samuel Blunt came from a family that owned property in Sussex and Hampshire. He built Springfield Place in North Parade for his first wife, Sarah Gale, the daughter and co-heiress of the ironmaster Leonard Gale, from whom he inherited the estate of Crabbet Park, near Worth. Sarah died in July 1758, leaving a daughter Charlotte, then aged six. Samuel had now married Winifred Scawen, whose father owned the Manor of Reigate. Samuel and Winifred had three sons, and the family was mentioned often in John Baker's diaries.

173 The bells were probably rung to celebrate Samuel Blunt's wedding, though it did not take place in Horsham.

Thursday, 9 August

Am surpris'd with the sight of Miss Pigott, she comes in a great ferment to consult me about meeting Mr. Jones, it happens very unlucky as my Papa & brother were to set out for Marlow the same day. However I procure her a Man & horse, but give her strict injunctions to send Mr. Jones back as soon as possible. Pay Mrs. Lampert, Nany Cook that was, a Wedding visit.[174]

Friday, 10 August

Bet Hunt teases me with her nonsense, love to Doctor Griffith & jealousy of Mrs. Wicker, I tantalise her. Great rejoicing for a victory gain'd by Prince Ferdinand of Brunswick over the French in Germany.[175] How inhuman is this, what destroys part of the species makes another part rejoice. A letter from Mrs. Townsend.

Saturday, 11 August

Walk to Slynfold. Have the very great pleasure to see Miss Pigott return'd & hear she had seen Mr. Jones. I hope he got back time enough to see my father, & then all will be well. Mr. Pigott comes back in a tolerable humour, brings me a letter from young Alsop which informs me that Philip Luttman's money cannot be receiv'd in London.

Sunday, 12 August

Miss Pigott tells me she is determin'd to be married. I disswade her from it & mention the consequences, but I pity her situation. Good heavens, who can desire Life, how many thousand heartaches do we experience to one satisfaction. We determine not to tell Mr. Pigott of his denying his sister going to Marlow, he behaves quite civil to us. I return home.

Monday, 13 August

Miss Tredcroft tells me that the company at Mrs. Blunt's were surpris'd at Nany Cook's being call'd a Bride, & making her appearance. How far will pride of Birth & fortune carry people; in short, they hardly think us of the same species. Mrs. Turner from Dorking comes.

Tuesday, 14 August

Mrs. Turner is an excessive merry woman, she chats & laughs all day. Captain Miller, her son, appears to be good natur'd, that's all. Mr. Turner comes & brings Master Miller, a most beautiful child.[176] I take a surprising fancy to it, poor little infant, to what troubles & dangers may he be expos'd in Life.

---

174 The marriage of Ann Cook does not appear in the Horsham or Warnham parish register, so it may have taken place in London.

175 Prince Ferdinand of Brunswick defeated the French at Minden with an Anglo-Hanoverian force. This was a major land victory for Britain and her allies in the Seven Years War, and was one of the reasons that 1759 was later called the *"annus mirabilis"*.

176 Mrs. Turner (née Challen) was previously married to John Miller of Chichester, and had a son by him, Captain Challen Miller, who was the father of this child. She was also the mother of John Miller, who had married Helen Catherine Michell, niece of Timothy Shelley.

Wednesday, 15 August

Work for Mrs. Turner in the morning. Dine at Mrs. Wicker's. The Smiths come from Lewes Races, talk of making a Ball, but I hope the girls will show a proper resentment for the bad characters they have given them, & decline their invitation.[177] No time for reading nor writing, which grieves me much.

Thursday, 16 August

Talk of going to Brighthelmstone but fancy that will be all. Charles Smith speaks to me, I return his compliment. They all go for a walk, I chuse to stay at home & read a little. I see Mrs. Blunt at a distance, she appears to be exceeding genteel, & made like Miss Gittins. Walk & chat with Sally Sheppard.

Friday, 17 August

Dine at Mr. Parham's with Mr. /Captain/ & Mrs. Miller.[178] In this couple we may see the bad consequences of indiscreet marriage. He was a minor, but she much older, he is now in the prime of life, & she is in the decline. They will spend their fortune before they come to it & what then will become of posterity.[179]

Saturday, 18 August

Mr. /Captain/ & Mrs. Miller & Mr. Parham dine with us, the latter takes up Philpot's essay on education & says with an anger, such a fellow pretend to write, better he'd minded his dancing.[180] In general what a confin'd manner of judging is this, for how seldom is a person's genius consulted in the profession they follow, yet if they attempt anything out of their sphere, tho' ever so well executed, they are hooted like an owl by daylight.

Sunday, 19 August

I go to Brighthelmstone with my Uncle & Aunt Tasker, & two gentlemen from Kingston. Papa is very much out of temper about it, we have a smart debate, how unreasonable they are when I am such a slave to the business, yet wou'd deny me the most trifling pleasure. We get there in the evening.

Monday, 20 August

Rise early & walk down to the Sea, how awfull, how tremendous a sight /it/ is, & how insignificant an atom am I in my own Idea when I view these wonders. Go in the evening to Shergold's fine Room & see the company dance.[181] A gentleman

---

177 The Smiths mentioned here are presumably the brothers of Henry Smith, Griffith, John and Charles. The Lewes Races were an important social occasion in the Sussex calendar.

178 Captain Challen Miller and his wife Elizabeth, the sister (or half-sister) of John Parham, the Horsham lawyer. She was ten years older than her husband.

179 Captain Miller had not yet inherited the property of his wealthy grandfather Stephen Challen, of Oving, near Chichester, though he was the presumptive heir.

180 This would appear to be a reference to Stephen Philpot of Lewes, who kept a girls' school at Lewes at St. Anne's Rectory – leased to him by the Rev. John Bristed - from 1733 to 1770. He had studied with the best London dancing masters and published an *Essay* in 1747 on the rôle of dance in women's education. It is possible that Sarah went to his school.

181 Shergold's Coffee House or "grand tavern" was one of the first places in Brighton to have a ballroom.

stands next me & pays me a number of compliments which I very little regard. But soon as the company sets into country dancing Shergold's sister enquires my name of a lad in our company, I hear it & forbid its telling.

Tuesday, 21 August

She assures me there was no harm intended; it was a gentleman who thought he knew me & wou'd be glad to pay his respects, but I seeing nobody there I ever spoke to am fright'd & go home that minute, yet afterwards repent very much I had not presence of mind to ask his name.

Wednesday, 22 August

Find my father in a very good humour, which I am extremely glad of. Go in the afternoon to Mrs. Bridger's with my two London Aunts[182] & Mrs. Wicker. They play at cards seven hours. I slip away & take a walk with my Sally Sheppard. How idly do most people endeavour to spend their time & how unusefull to themselves & fellow creatures.

Thursday, 23 August

Violent headache, but I bear it with the more patience, as I have not been thus afflicted a great while. Walk out with Sally Sheppard, the Bells ring for a victory obtain'd by the King of Prussia, over the Russians.[183] Sure this must be conducive to a peace, how earnestly do I wish it my lot will then be decided.

Friday, 24 August

Dine at Mr. Tredcroft's. My Aunt Smith says my Mama is handsomer than either of her daughters. I am piqued at it, but how ridiculous was it to be so, beauty is a fleeting shadow, if I were possess'd of it in an eminent degree, & I ought to rejoice that my mother looks well as it is an indication of health.

Saturday, 25 August

Very busy about household affairs, pickling, etc. How little time have I had lately for writing & reading, yet it may be all for the best. I shou'd grow quite unsociable if these amusements were too much indulg'd. Walk in the Park with Sally Sheppard, a serene evening, we both enjoy it.

Sunday, 26 August

At Church in the morning, a strange clergyman preaches, on the omnipresence of God, the whole discourse extracts, dislike his delivery. Walk to Dame Reynolds' with Mrs. Tasker & Sally Sheppard, we are like to meet Sir Charles but avoid him. Write to my cousin Bet Smith. Take my leave of my Aunt Sally, who goes tomorrow morning. Her opinion concerning poor Mrs. White's troubles very ungenerous.

---

182 Sarah's *"London aunts"* were her father's sisters, Elizabeth (Mrs. Smith) and Sarah Hurst.

183 Although King Frederick II of Prussia performed many notable feats of arms during the war, he ultimately triumphed because the Russians unexpectedly decided to change sides in 1762, when the new Tsar, Peter III, came to power. This enabled Frederick to secure Silesia at the Peace of Hubertusburg, in 1763, and won for Prussia the status of a great European power.

Monday, 27 August

Papa ill. Extremely concern'd at it, pray most fervently that his disorder may be transfer'd to me. Walk with Sally Sheppard, poor dear girl, she is excessively unhappy, wish it was in my power to relieve her anxiety. Read in Montaigne's essays [*Essais*], he don't approve of Women's having a learned education, are our minds then not worth improving, these Lordly men will have it so.[184]

Tuesday, 28 August

Drink tea at my grandmother's, [185] play at quadrille. Walk with Sally Sheppard on the Causeway, express & congratulate each other on the pleasure our mutual friendship affords.

Wednesday, 29 August

Bet Hunt offended at some little unmeaning gallantry between a Boy & Girl, we rally her & tell her she's past it that provokes her spleen. At Mrs. Bridger's all the evening, play at quadrille, how passionately she loves cards. Gives us an account of her dining at Lord Irwin's, nothing but made dishes. I am difficult & doubt I shou'd be starv'd in such a family. Luxury is I think as little excusable as any vice.

Thursday, 30 August

Read in Montaigne, he blames Pliny the younger for his vanity, yet soon after owns it is inherent in our compositions. He has a fine essay on friendship, only I think rather too confin'd. He says it must be stinted to one, or t'is no friendship, but this I can contradict by experience, for I have four dear friends, that I wou'd die to serve.

Friday, 31 August

Violent headache. How often is this poor machine out of order, yet how many years may it be before t'is quite run down, & laid in the silent grave.

SEPTEMBER 1759

Saturday, 1 September

A note from Miss Pigott, acquainting us my brother is well. She thinks her brother will leave Slynfold. I am concern'd at this, for then she must marry. Walk with Sally Sheppard, poor dear girl, how my heart aches for her, she expects to hear every post that her lover is married, what a situation are we both in, for my Smith may perhaps be dead. But Heaven avert this dreadfull shock, or fortify my mind to endure it.

---

184   Michel Eyquem de Montaigne (1533-1592) was one of the most influential writers of the French Renaissance, who popularised the essay as a literary form. His *Essais* (literally *"attempts"*) merge serious intellectual speculation with anecdotes and autobiography.

185   Mrs. Elizabeth Hurst, widow of the tailor Robert Hurst of Horsham (1670-1729), lived next door to Mrs. Wicker in the Causeway (South Street).

Sunday, 2 September

Make a visit at Mrs. White's with Mrs. & Miss Tredcroft, have now an opportunity of comparing these two beauties, Miss Tredcroft & Miss Bet White.[186] They are both sweet girls, Miss White has the finest face, & Miss Tredcroft the genteelest shape, a pretty face is a great advantage, when not spoil'd, (as is often the case) by affectations.

Monday, 3 September

At my Aunt Waller's with Mrs. Tredcroft's family. Walk on the Causeway with Miss Nany Powell.[187] It is near eleven o' clock, the moon shines in full lustre, ah where is now my beloved Harry, perhaps amid the din of War.

Tuesday, 4 September

Finish my habit, ruffles & frill. Walk in the Park with Miss Nany Powell, no company to me is like my Sally Sheppard. Papa returns from A?deen *(?Arundel or ?Egdean)* Fair, says he saw Miss Gittins, but she took not the least notice of him. Surely this must be pride in the girl, tho' a very false species of it. Wonder I don't hear from her, I shall write very cooly if I find this to be the case. She knew my situation in life before we commenc'd a friendship.

Wednesday, 5 September

Write to my cousin Bet Smith, & to my brother. Papa out of temper, I weep, but think I am a fool, what is so frequent ought to be grown too familiar to give pain.

Thursday, 6 September

Take some salts for my headach. The Post brings a letter for Papa, says he will insure me one next post from my Smith; he means *[?well]*, but I doubt it, what we greatly wish we allways fear. Sure Quebeck must be taken by this time or they have been repuls'd.

Friday, 7 September

Go to dinner at Northeath to see Mr. Nat Tredcroft, with a large company. We have a very polite entertainment, are merry dancing *[in]* the Barn, walk in the fields. Excessively pleasant. How admirable are all thy works Oh Creator, yet how incapable are we of enjoying or being gratefull for thy bounty.

Saturday, 8 September

A letter from my brother, dictated by Mr. Jones. I write to Miss Pigott in a low desponding manner, occasion'd by my illness, & the disputes of my father & mother, oh Matrimony, how much good sense & good nature dost thou require, how shocking wou'd a disagreement in that state be in my opinion, pray Heaven I may never experience it.

---

186 Elizabeth White, born in 1743, was the third daughter of William White, the lawyer. She married the Rev. John Woodward of West Grinstead in 1764.

187 Nany or Anne Powell was the second daughter of the Rev. Thomas Powell and his wife Anne, born in Horsham in 1731. She never married and died in Horsham in 1802.

Sunday, 9 September

Stay from Church, weak & ill in health & spirits, much disturb'd at the animosities of my father & mother. Read the Psalms, lessons, etc. Oh when shall I hear from my dear Harry. Montaigne is of my opinion, that suspense is the greatest of all evils. Begin an epitaph on Mr. Bridger, very severe, but as I can say nothing with justice but what is so, I will never make it publick.

Monday, 10 September

A serene fair and pleasing day. Read the News. Admiral Boscawen has taken 3 French men of War & sunk two.[188] Am surpris'd with the sight of Mr. Trusler, an old sweetheart, pays me many compliments. Read my Elegy on Mrs. Shelley, vastly taken with it or pretends he is, who can resist charm of flattery. Nay none ought, t'is to the virtuous only an incitement to well doing.

Tuesday, 11 September

Montaigne thinks poetry a proper amusement for women, am glad he will allow us to do any thing besides spin & knit. News that Quebeck is taken[189] but no particulars, if so & Smith returns sure my Fate will e'er long be decided, whether I shall be doom'd to celibacy or happy with him.

Wednesday, 12 September

Miss Pigott comes & my Uncle Bob.[190] I have a great friendship for Miss Pigott & like her vastly, but think she talks too much of Mr. Jones to all indiscriminately. Lord Irwin sees my verses on Mrs. Shelley, praises them much, wants to see the Sermon I wrote so long ago, I refuse it.

Thursday, 13 September

A lurking fever every night occasion'd by my anxiety on my Smith's account, but Miss Pigott is much more unhappy than I am with less reason. In short happiness must be seated in the mind, outward objects allways deceive us.

Friday, 14 September

Spend the afternoon at Mrs. Wicker's, my Harry's mother there. She says thought of him makes her very uneasy, but there is no Ship arriv'd yet, so no reason to think he is otherwise than well. Grif *[Griffith]* Smith expects to get 500 a year by the Wine trade, a fine thing if he does, but I wou'd have left another to have said it.

---

188   Edward Boscawen (1711-1761) English naval commander known as *"Old Dreadnought"*, was appointed commander-in-chief of the successful expedition against Cape Breton in 1758. This victory over the French fleet in Lagos Bay crowned his career. Sarah said that he was Henry's *"best friend"* (see entry on 11 January 1761).

189   News of the fall of Quebec was a little premature; it was not until 13 September that General James Wolfe scaled the Heights of Abraham and defeated the French, losing his own life in the final battle.

190   Robert Hurst, from London.

Saturday, 15 September

Walk part of the way with Miss Pigott. Meet Dame Hunt,[191] an old Woman for whom I have a great regard, her honest heart, facetious temper & understanding, far above her situation in life, makes her company extreamly desirable.

Sunday, 16 September

At Church twice, discourse against envy & animosities. Papa & Uncle Bob dispute about dissolving their partnership, a most intricate affair, wou'd to Heaven it was settled. Write some verses on looking at my Dear Smith's picture, no letter from him yet must I still linger in tedious expectation.

Monday, 17 September

Dream I am with my dear Harry, how shocking the disappointment when I wak'd. Begin working a pair of double ruffles. Read *The Adventures of Robert Drury*, if his misfortunes & dreadfull sufferings are true how supreamly blest ought I to esteem myself.[192]

Tuesday, 18 September

Write to Sally Sheppard, to my cousin Bet Smith & a note to Mr. Moore, ironically commending secrecy.[193] Suppose he will be very angry but he is justly serv'd for abusing the confidence I repos'd in him & telling my Uncle & Aunt of my pictures being drawn. Headache much.

Wednesday, 19 September

Begin working a catgut apron.[194] Miss Pigott calls as she goes to dine at Doctor Hutchinson's. Poor girl, her brother will never consent that Mr. Jones shou'd come to Slynfold. Oh these love affairs are endless torments. No letter from Miss Gittins, unkind girl, I am half angry.

Thursday, 20 September

Begin working a catgut apron [sic]. Papa & my Uncle dispute again, good God how disagreeable are these animosities. I wou'd sooner be impos'd on by all the World than quarrel with one half of it. Walk to Highland to take some honey, delightfully pleasant the country is in the summer.

Friday, 21 September

Walk again to Highland, I allmost begin to think that solitude is more to be coveted than Society, except that of a friend we can entirely confide in, & oh how few are

---

191   Dame Hunt was the widow of the previous Usher, Richard Hunt, and grandmother of Bet, Jenny and Sally. "*Dame*" was a courtesy title given to an older woman.

192   *The Pleasant and Surprising Adventures of Mr. Robert Drury, during fifteen years in Madagascar*, by Robert Drury, was published in 1743. Robert Drury was a sailor who was shipwrecked and made a slave, but was eventually released.

193   Will Moore, the journeyman tailor who later married Sarah's aunt Sally (Sarah Hurst).

194   Catgut was a thick corded material normally used for stiffening, but here was the basis for an elaborately worked apron, with a pattern "*fancied*" by Sarah .

these. I have a real one in Sally Sheppard, but she is absent, & Miss Gittin's long silence gives me reason to suspect that she is wavering, but I will wait patiently some time longer, & not censure too hastily.

Saturday, 22 September

One Mr. Lewes calls on me, I was acquainted with him eight years ago at Brighthelmstone,[195] he told me how much Parson Seccombe was in love with me, then expresses many wishes for my Welfare & happiness. I return his compliments, poor man, he looks thin & melancholy, as tho' the world had frown'd since I saw him last.

Sunday, 23 September

Pay Mrs. Michell's wedding visit, every thing in a very elegant manner, all the White family there.[196] Bet White most intolerably affected. My Dear Smith's mother not well, I go to see her which she takes kind.

Monday, 24 September

Walk to Highland to fishing, I grow fond of all rural diversions. This day twelve month I first saw my Dear Smith on his return from North America. Good God, the perturbations I then experienc'd, when will they have an end, my fears hourly increase on his account, my heart dies within me when I think of the dangers he has been expos'd to & the uncertainty whether he has escaped.

Tuesday, 25 September

Walk with Sally Hunt & the two Constables[197] to see Bet Phillips. She will have a good fortune but is totally ignorant of the world, what a blessing is a proper education, yet how few parents are capable of giving it.

Wednesday, 26 September

Work very hard fancying the pattern of my apron, but am often interrupted by people in the shop. Allmost wish I did not love work so well, yet it passes away many hours that I shou'd probably employ by tormenting myself about what hangs like a heavy load at my Heart, the fate of my Dear Harry.

Thursday, 27 September

Very busy in the shop. Some pursuit is absolutely necessary for an active mind. I return at Night to my book with double pleasure after sitting all day close to work. Go with a large posse to a poor Woman that professes fortune telling, I have a despicable notion of these things but it serves for an afternoon's diversions.

---

195 This indicates that Sarah was living in Brighton in 1751, when she was 15 – presumably as part of her education.

196 This must have been the wedding of Lucy Orlton and John Michell, elder brother of Drew, which took place on 13 September in Bramley, Surrey. John Michell had inherited money and property from his great-uncle, John Michell of Billingshurst and Lower Moonhill in Cuckfield.

197 The Constables are not mentioned elsewhere, but a Widow Constable is recorded as living in West Street in the 1758 Land Tax.

Friday, 28 September

Dream that my Dear Smith is married & fancy that I am dreadfully shock'd. How perplexing are these chimeras of the brain, but sleeping or waking he posses my thoughts, I know I am not worthy *[of]* this Dear Man, which makes me fear I shall be depriv'd of him.

Saturday, 29 September

Write to Miss Pigott, desire her to come over to fetch me. She has company but promises to meet me. Compose an Acrostick on Captain Smith, another on Miss Tredcroft, at her desire. Read *The English Hermit*, a volume stuft with absurdities, yet some tolerable good reflections.[198]

Sunday, 30 September

A message from Miss Gittins, desiring my company at Arundel. Walk with Bet Hunt to Nuthurst Lodge, about 3 mile off, a most delightfull situation a prospect of the South Hills, & all the intervening woods & fields.[199] A very kind letter from my beloved Miss Gittins, how pleas'd I am to find her friendship steady, am determin'd to go & see her, if I can possibly contrive it.

OCTOBER 1759

Monday, 1 October

How inseparable are joy & grief, at least how quick they follow one another. My anxiety & suspicion of Miss Gittins is now all vanish'd & smiling peace succeeds. The Woman's fortune telling astonishes me, the circumstance of my letter from Miss Gittins & journey are exactly true.

Tuesday, 2 October

Mrs. Tredcroft here chatting, she gives an account of a grand dinner at Mr. Wicker's.[200] I wou'd not thank Madam Fortune for an estate, with an obligation to live in that manner. Write to Miss Gittins acquainting her with my intentions of going to Arundel, Saturday next.

---

198   *The English Hermit, or the Adventures of Philip Quarles*, was written by Peter Longueville, and published in 1727.

199   Nuthurst Lodge was on the Sedgwick estate, purchased by Joseph Tudor in 1760.

200   This was John Wicker III of Park House, the brother-in-law of Mrs. Wicker. He had married a Kentish heiress and probably spent most of his time in London, in a house he had leased in Cavendish Square. His grandfather, John Wicker I, had married Anne Margesson, from a landed Sussex family. He built the east side of Park House on a burgage plot in North Street called Cockmans, but died in 1720 before he could complete it. John Wicker II (1669-1741), represented Horsham in Parliament and married Katherine Blunt, aunt of Samuel Blunt of Springfield Park. He completed the west or garden front of Park House in Queen Anne style. The diarist John Baker leased Park House in the 1770s, and it became the home of Robert Hurst in 1799.

Wednesday, 3 October

Miss Gittins gives me a description of a young officer, who much admires my letters, I wish he don't alter his opinion when he sees me. An excessive wet day, makes my heart ache for fear I shou'd not go to Arundel. Papa against my going, but so he allways is, very wrong.

Thursday, 4 October

Send Miss Pigott a Melon that Mrs. Tredcroft gave me. Write some verses & send with it. Violent headach, incapable of settling to work, & then I must be bad indeed. Spend the afternoon at Mrs. Wicker's, with Mrs. Bridger, what an easy genteel behav'd woman she is, t'is a pleasure to be with her.

Friday, 5 October

Vastly busy in getting my work done to go my journey. Papa out of humour, well I cannot help it, is it so unreasonable a thing to go out for a week once in three year. A letter from Sally Sheppard informing me she comes home tomorrow, she will be sorry I am out.

Saturday, 6 October

Ride to Arundel with the Post, roads bad. A boy meets us in a Waggon who says he's sure I am a very pretty girl. Then a gentleman exclaims that I am an Angel, who can help being pleas'd with this flattery, tho' the charms of person are not valuable.

Sunday, 7 October

Am receiv'd by Miss Gittins, her Papa & Mama, not only with politeness but kindness. Resolve to keep my Horse, tho' my father said I shou'd not. Go to Church. Walk in the afternoon to Stoke.[201] Drink tea with one Mr. Batsworth, very agreeable conversation with Mr. Gittins.

Monday, 8 October

A Young Cornet of Horse calls on Miss Gittins with a gentleman's compliments, he seems charm'd with our chat, offers to conduct us to Havant, in our road to Portsmouth, we return thanks for his good nature but decline accepting it for prudential reasons.

Tuesday, 9 October

Go to see Goodwood, the Duke of Richmond's seat. View the Hermitage[202] the shell house,[203] & the gardens which are of a prodigious extent, & delightfully situated. The Duke & Duchess knowing Miss Gittins send for us in, & behave very polite.[204]

---

201 Mr. Gittins was the Vicar of South Stoke, near Arundel.
202 *"The Hermitage"* was almost certainly *"the Catacombs"* in Goodwood Park, a rocky dell with a grotto and what Lady Newdigate called a *"hermit's cave"* in 1747.
203 The shell house had been decorated by the 2nd Duchess of Richmond and her daughters with multi-coloured shells from the West Indies.

Wednesday, 10 October

Arrive at Wade near Havant in Hampshire, at Mr. Bold's, an acquaintance of Miss Gittins. We are receiv'd by him & his wife very kindly. Go about two mile & see the Camp on Post Down, a sweet situation, the men were exercising, the Duke & Duchess were there & spoke again with great complaisance.

Thursday, 11 October

Ride to Portsmouth, see a Man of War come in, full sail. View the Dock & all the shipping, am astonish'd at the stupendous sight, to what lengths is human art & industry capable of going. Hear that news is arriv'd of Quebec's being taken, am in raptures with the thoughts of hearing from my Harry, but alas the News proves false.

Friday, 12 October

Give Cornet Wilkinson's love to his sister, who is at Portsmouth. She thinks her brother in danger from the prevalence of our charms, we assure her he is not.

Saturday, 13 October

Write some verses in a pamphlet against Sackville.[205] Return to Arundel, an excessive wet journey. The Cornet waits on us the moment he hears we are return'd, he sighs & looks grave, we conclude he is in love with one of us. The superiority of merit & beauty on the side of Miss Gittins makes me certain it is her, but Cupid is a blind God, & sometimes shoots at random.

Sunday, 14 October

Go to Church. Mr. Gittins gives me to peruse his book against the Quakers. Walk in the Park. Mr. Wilkinson & two more gentlemen join us, the conversation very trifling. Doctor Newhouse spouts some tragedy; I tell him he is very happy in his quotation.

Monday, 15 October

He says my good opinion makes him superlatively so. Cornet Wilkinson says a little matter makes you happy, very true, return'd I, my approbation is a mere trifle. He apologises for his blunder, they extol me for the repartee.

---

204   It is interesting that the Duke and Duchess of Richmond were so friendly and approachable on this occasion, because this was not always the case. A letter from Elizabeth Ingram to her sister-in-law (HM MSS Cat. No. 792.3), said *"I hear that the Duke and Dutchess of Richmond don't please at all in their neighbourhood. Severall Gentlemen and their wives that went there to pay their Complements was hardly asked to sit Down, & not a Single Word spoken to them either by Duke or Dutchess"*. Charles, 3rd Duke of Richmond, had married Lady Mary Bruce in 1757, when he was twenty-two and she was seventeen. They were described by Horace Walpole as *"the prettiest couple in England"*, and their marriage appears to have been happy, though childless. At the time when Sarah met them, the Duke must have only just returned from active service abroad. As Lt. Col. of the 33rd Foot, he was with the British contingent supporting Prince Ferdinand of Brunswick at the battle of Minden in August, and was said to have distinguished himself.

205   Lord George Sackville (1716-1785), youngest son of the 1st Duke of Dorset. He fought in the Battle of Fontenoy in 1745, where he was wounded. He was in charge of all the allied cavalry, under Prince Ferdinand, at the Battle of Minden, but refused to obey his orders to advance, and thus allowed the French to escape complete defeat. He was court-martialled and disgraced, and the verdict that he was *"unfit to serve the King in any capacity"* was read out at the head of every regiment.

Tuesday, 16 October

Ride to Goring about seven mile from Arundel, go over Highdown, a most delightfull prospect of the Sea, & the intervening Country which is beautifully interspers'd with fields & groves. See all the Willes family, like Miss Patty much who is Miss Gittins' favourite.[206]

Wednesday, 17 October

Return home from Arundel, take my leave of all Mr. Gittins' family with great reluctance. Call & dine at Slynfold, see Mr. & Mrs. Walter who are there, don't like her much. A letter, I open it with much emotion, find it is from Parson Parry, my Dear Smith's well, thank God. I go & acquaint his mother with it, who is very much oblig'd to me.

Thursday, 18 October

A violent cold, very much fatigu'd with my journey. Drink tea at Mrs. Tasker's. Go for a walk with my dear Sally Sheppard, she tells me her lover & she have parted, poor girl.

Friday, 19 October

Am agreeably surpris'd with the news of Quebec's being taken.[207] Receive 2 letters, one from my dear, my beloved Harry, who thanks be to thee Father of Mercies is safe & well. I, poor unworthy mortal, cannot deserve thy goodness but may I never be ungratefull for thy favours.

Saturday, 20 October

My other letter was from Parson Parry to whom I am infinitely oblig'd for the kindness & solicitude he has shewn in regard to my Harry. Mrs. Wicker comes & desires to kiss my Harry's letter, I consent, but think it a little odd.

Sunday, 21 October

Griff Smith comes & brings news that Prince has beat the French.[208] Meet him as I go to Church, he takes not the least notice of me, well I cannot help it. Drink tea at Mrs. Wicker's. Give Miss Tredcroft the Acrostick I made upon her. Walk with Sally Sheppard, tell her how much Griff Smith's behaviour affects me, oh when shall these anxieties cease?

Monday, 22 October

Work on my apron. Some trifle or another engrosses our time, & employs our thoughts, sure human creatures were form'd for nobler purposes, things amuse us, but one can give us solid satisfaction, t'is in Thee, oh bright Religion, that lasting peace is founded.

---

206 The Willes of Goring were a large family – eight children and a widowed mother.
207 This shows that it took over a month for the news of the fall of Quebec to be properly confirmed, following earlier conflicting rumours.
208 This presumably refers to the Battle of Minden in August – Griffith Smith's tardiness with the news is perhaps a foretaste of his later lunacy.

Tuesday, 23 October

At Mrs. Wicker's, she repeats a thousand lies of the "Merchant", sure he studies to make himself ridiculous, yet I have the charity to think that his lies are not intended to injure anyone. Read the first number of *The Ladies' Magazine*, don't like it so well as *The Universal*.[209]

Wednesday, 24 October

Very busy in the shop. Chat with old Dame Hunt, very merry to appearance but sad at Heart. Go to Tanbridge with Mrs. Wicker. Tell Miss Ellis we hear "Merchant" Smith has renew'd his addresses to her, she protests t'is false & declares she despises him.

Thursday, 25 October

At Mrs. Tredcroft's to teach Miss her notes on the Spinnet. Am sorry I have forgot [how] to play, but I cannot find time for every thing. They tell me how bad "Merchant" Smith behav'd at Lord Irwin's, am sorry for it on my dear Harry's account. Every body knows I have had letters from Quebeck, perhaps the Captain may be angry, yet why shou'd he be asham'd of his connection with me, but he is afraid of his vile brother.

Friday, 26 October

At Mrs. Bridger's, play at cards. A letter from the good Mr. Masterman to acquaint me he has heard from Quebeck, his wife has been ill which I am much concern'd at, may all my friends be happy, whatever is my own lot.

Saturday, 27 October

Mr. John Ellis[210] calls on me, he says several gentlemen at Chichester protest I am infinitely handsomer than Miss Gittins, pityfull pre-eminence if it is true. If I cannot make my mind equally amiable, what signifies person.

Sunday, 28 October

Write to Mrs. Townsend, to Captain Smith, Mr. Masterman & Parson Parry. At Church twice. Doctor Hutchinson makes an excellent discourse on the care of the soul. Bet Cook tells me the "Merchant" ask'd her if she thought the Captain wrote to me, she told him yes, & wou'd certainly have me, *"why then"* replied he, *"I will never speak to him again"*. Inveterate wretch.

Monday, 29 October

Sally Sheppard work'd with me in the morning. I tell her & Mama how very improbable it is I shou'd ever have Captain Smith. Mrs. Bridger & Miss Pigott here, they ridicule "Merchant", I drink his health out of fun but none of them will pledge me. Play at cards.

---

209   Actually called *"The Lady's Magazine, or Polite Companion for the Fair Sex"*.
210   John Ellis (born 1737) was the son of John Ellis of Stammerham, who had died in 1757, and a first cousin of the Misses Ellis of Tanbridge. He and his sisters were now living in Chichester.

Tuesday, 30 October

Miss Pigott is determined to be married at all events. I disswade her but to no purpose. Sally Sheppard & I walk part of the way home with her. A Junket at Dame Hunt's, with Sally Sheppard & her brother,[211] we are excessively merry, a fine moonlight even, serene.

Wednesday, 31 October

Write out a great many Bills, work on my apron. Walk in the Park with my Sally, remark on the various seasons of the year, now sickly Autumn has stript the trees of all their beauties, or turn'd to a pale yellow their lively green, every bird seems conscious of the change & in languishing notes express their sorrow. Now & then a gleam of sunshine shows that cheerfull Summer unwillingly gives way to dreary Winter.

NOVEMBER 1759

Thursday, 1 November

The "Merchant" says my Dear Harry winters in America, well be it so. I see no likelihood of our union, & his being here only gives us both uneasiness.

Friday, 2 November

Very busy in the shop. Miss Bristed dines with us, invites me to see her, I must go. Chat with Sally Sheppard, in her is all my consolation yet she, poor girl, is unhappy, who is not.

Saturday, 3 November

Miss Tredcroft comes with a pile of work, given her to do by Miss Ingram.[212] She can't perform it, & desires my assistance, which I readily give her, & am pleas'd it was in my power to assist her. Mama & Mrs. Wicker go to Slynfold. Sally Sheppard & I play at Picquet.

Sunday, 4 November

At Church twice. Mr. Osgood[213] makes a very good discourse on the use & abuse of riches, many passages touch "Merchant" Smith nearly, I hope he took them. Write a poem, *The Consolation*. Walk on the Causeway with Sally Sheppard, & think I am now tolerably easy in regard to my affair with Captain Smith, & will endeavour to be so however it terminates.

Monday, 5 November

Write an Elegiac Acrostick, the first letters form these words, Major General James Wolfe, slain at Quebeck. At Mrs. Wicker's, we condone [?*condemn*] Miss Pigott for

211   Stringer Sheppard junior.
212   Miss Elizabeth Ingram, niece of Henry, Lord Irwin.
213   The Rev. Francis Osgood, appointed curate of Horsham and Headmaster of Collyer's School in 1722. He was also appointed Rector of Saltfleetby St. Peter, in Lincolnshire, in the same year, but seems to have preferred to live in Horsham.

intending to marry so imprudently, sure it is not doing Justice to posterity to bring them into the World certain heirs to poverty.

Tuesday, 6 November

Write an Epitaph on General Wolfe, & an Epigram on the French King. Spend the afternoon at Mrs. Wicker's with Miss Ellis, who has heard all the ridiculous lies "Merchant" Smith has told of her. We descant on the pernicious consequences of this hatefull vice.

Wednesday, 7 November

Mama goes down to Tanbridge. Mrs. Ellis[214] tells her "Merchant" Smith said my father was poor, & that several of our London Dealers had been with him to enquire into our circumstances. Villainous fellow, what can he mean? I determine to go to him & ask the meaning of his behaviour.

Thursday, 8 November

A note from Miss Gittins with some poetry, acquainting me she shall be in London today. Go down to the "Merchant", but persuaded by his mother do not speak to him, what the event of all this will be, God knows, sure the Captain will never marry a person this inveterate fellow so much dislikes, but if he prefers such a brother to me, hope I shall have courage enough to despise him.

Friday, 9 November

More of the "Merchant"'s nonsense, but he is gone & now I hope a period to [words omitted] for some time. Very busy in the shop. Work on my apron. Chat with Sally Sheppard.

Saturday, 10 November

Hear that Saunder's fleet from North America is in sight of Portsmouth, which puts my Heart in a violent flutter. Oh love, love, how powerfull is thy sway, & find this report to be false. "Merchant" Smith not gone, how I dread lest he shou'd influence my Harry against me, but sure this is impossible, after so many vows of everlasting fidelity.

Sunday, 11 November

At Church twice, the Doctor preaches a fine Sermon on contentment but when or where shall we find it, t'is not to affluence confin'd nor does it allways dwell with poverty. Oh Almighty Father of the Universe, give me resignation & patience under whatever calamities may befall me.

Monday, 12 November

Dream my dear dear Harry is here. I hear him talk & feel his caresses, sweet delusion, but I wake & it fleets away. Mrs. Reynolds & Nany drink tea with us, Nany sings most charmingly, how fond am I of musick & how seldom an opportunity of indulging this fondness.

---

214   Mrs. Mary Ellis, the wife of Henry Ellis of Tanbridge and mother of the Misses Ellis.

Tuesday, 13 November

Very low spirited, I wonder what I am reserved for, not happiness I doubt, but what an ungratefull I am, who have now such abundant reason to be so & yet am otherwise. Miss Upton calls in her Chariot. I wou'd not step into it & be Miss Upton & not be Sally Hurst, she poor lady has lost the Captain but has got a fortune.[215] My Captain is alive thank God, yet for want of fortune doubt I shall never be his.

Wednesday, 14 November

Spend great part of the day with Sally Sheppard. We talk over past occurrences, some with regret & some with pleasure.

Thursday, 15 November

Mrs. Wicker desires me to be godmother to my Aunt Grace's child. I think it wou'd be ill-natured to refuse, so comply tho' not with any inclination. See in the paper that Admiral Durell & Commodore Holmes are arriv'd at Portsmouth with a fleet from Quebeck & Admiral Saunders is hourly expected. I wonder if the *Orford* will come, I shall soon know.

Friday, 16 November

Spend the afternoon at Tanbridge, t'is now as Shakespeare says the Witching time of night, every thing is silent & all retir'd to rest, but my perturbed Heart is still awake & seems to want it's better half, oh shou'd any accident befall my dearest part, my Harry, the poor sorrowfull remainder wou'd pine itself to death.

Saturday, 17 November

The *Northumberland* stays in North America, poor Parson Parry, but the *Orford* does not, well now my Smith will soon be in England.

Sunday, 18 November

Mama tells me the secret history of Mr. Tudor & family, a gentleman that has bought an estate near Horsham, keeps two Mistresses in the house, one his own, the other his son's.[216] How carefull ought we to be in forming Judgement of Strangers. Drink tea at Harry's mother, she is very civil, not withstanding what I told her of the "Merchant". I wish it is not hypocrisy; doubt she will flame out when Harry comes.

Monday, 19 November

A letter from my dear Gittins, she likes London upon the whole very well but is not passionately fond of its amusements. She says Cornet Wilkinson prov'd to be

---

215 Miss Upton married Colonel John Leland in 1763. He later became a Lt. General and was M.P. for Stamford, in Lincolnshire. He was presumably not Miss Upton's "*Captain*", as Sarah implies that he had died.

216 Joseph Tudor (1692-1774) came from Edinburgh and was one of the Commissioners for Customs in Scotland. He bought the Sedgwick estate from the 3rd Duke of Richmond in about 1760. Sarah's mother seems to be relaying unfounded gossip about the new arrivals. There does not appear to be any reason to think that Joseph Tudor's nephew, William Nelthorpe, was actually his son, as she claimed. His sister Rebecca had married William Nelthorpe, a London banker, and they had four children.

a conceited fop. He appear'd far otherwise. Miss Bet Ingram calls to see my work, bestows most extravagant encomiums on it, a great honour I think.

Tuesday, 20 November

A letter from Mr. Turner at Dorking to invite Mrs. Wicker & self there. This time last year & for a month to come, was my Dear Harry here, we pass'd some of our time agreeably, & some much the reverse, thus life is checquer'd. A faint gleam of joy is generally succeeded by a dark cloud of sorrow.

Wednesday, 21 November

Go over & chat with Sally Sheppard. She, self & Miss Powell stand sponsor for my Aunt Grace's child.[217] We dance & sing at the Christening, every body seems cheerfull, but I have a load at ?[heart].

Thursday, 22 November

Busy in the shop. My apron goes on but slowly. Mrs. Wicker with us. Mr. Shelley comes in & rattles as usual, am sorry to see him so unsteady. Spend the evening at Mr. Tredcroft's, Miss has begun learning on her Spinnet. Wish I had an opportunity to practise, but what signifies it to a person in my situation.

Friday, 23 November

Very busy. Send for Sally Sheppard to chat at Mrs. Wicker's with the Miss Ellis's, they are very merry considering, & stay all the evening. Read *The Fable of the Bees*.[218] Sit up till eleven o' clock, but no post comes in. This solemn time of night suits a love sick Mind & soothes its Melancholy.

Saturday, 24 November

A letter from my Dear Harry, this gives me great pleasure tho' it does not bring the pleasing news of his arrival in England, but that he stays some time longer in America. At tea time I am astonish'd with the sight of my beloved Harry, good God, what unexpected transport, but let me not be too much transport'd.[219]

Sunday, 25 November

At Church twice. Doctor Hutchinson concludes his third excellent discourse on contentment, one of the hardest virtues to practice. Sat up till late with my Harry, he hopes soon to gain preferment, at least thinks he shall not be put of on half pay at the end of the War. Says he shall be oblig'd to live at Plymouth, & thinks next summer must determine our affair.

---

217   Mary Grace was baptised on 21 November, but was buried on 18 December 1759.
218   *The Fable of the Bees, or Private Vices, Publick benefits*, by Bernard de Mandeville, an economist and philosopher, consisted of a poem and an extensive prose commentary. It was published in 1714 and proved controversial, as it was thought to attack Christian values. The poem had originally appeared in 1705 as a commentary on England as Mandeville saw it then. A second volume was published in 1732.
219   Presumably Henry's orders to return to England came after the despatch of his letter, which took longer to reach England than he did.

Monday, 26 November

Write to my cousin Bet Smith, give her an account of my journey to Arundel. Drink tea at my Aunt Tasker's with the Mrs. Michells, Sally Sheppard & my Harry. Sit with him again, I know not if this be right, but his excessive fondness renders it impossible for me to refuse him, especially as he goes away so soon as Friday.

Tuesday, 27 November

Fair day, a great many country people, to hear some of them one can hardly imagine they are of the same species.[220] Mr. Tredcroft & my Harry sup with us & play at cards. They stay late.

Wednesday, 28 November

Mrs. Tredcroft comes & invites us over there with the Captain. We all go, play at cards. My dear Harry is just what I cou'd wish him, neither too talkative nor too silent. T'is now twelve o'clock & I expect him, every pulse beats & every nerve is in a tremble, oh Love, how powerful is thy sway.

Thursday, 29 November

At Church, a solemn thanksgiving for our success in War & our plentifull harvest. Doctor Hutchinson touches on the miscarriages of the late Ministry, to enhance the honour of the present, a circumstance that might in my opinion have been omitted.

Friday, 30 November

Take my leave of Captain Smith, he goes to Portsmouth. Well, Heaven protect him, till I have the happiness of seeing him again. Walk to Dame Reynolds' with Sally Sheppard, very pleasant, tho' at this inclement season of the year. At Mrs. Wicker's, play at cards.

DECEMBER 1759

Saturday, 1 December

News arrives that Admiral Hawke has overtaken the French fleet, sunk & burnt several of them.[221] Sure the War must soon be at an end. Great Illuminations, ringing of Bells, & Bonfires, tho' I think with the Quakers that it is a little inhuman to rejoice at the misfortunes of our fellow creatures, yet self preservation prompts us to it.

Sunday, 2 December

At Church twice. The Doctor adds to his Sermon on thanksgiving & makes a fine discourse. Walk in the Croft with Sally Sheppard. She fears the time is approaching when I shall be married & leave her, but I tell her t'is yet very distant. Write to Miss Gittins.

---

220 The annual "*Teg Fair*" held on 27 November in Horsham was a horse fair.
221 This action by Admiral Sir Edward Hawke (1705-1781) destroyed the French fleet in Quiberon Bay, and prevented an invasion of Britain. He was made First Lord of the Admiralty in 1766, and Admiral of the Fleet in 1768.

Monday, 3 December

Mrs. Wicker & self come in the Stage Coach to Dorking. Find Mr. Turner is going out at which I am much concerned, for his conversation is prodigiously entertaining & improving. Mr. Page comes to see Captain Miller, he is a Dwarf, how thankfull ought I to be that nature has not form'd me thus.

Tuesday, 4 December

Read *The Orphan of China*, a new play, the Language Noble, the distress & sentiments exquisite.[222] Take a walk. Dorking is full as dull as Horsham. See Mr. Page who invites us in, his good sense & good nature amply compensates for the defects of his form, very short-sighted must they be who can see no further than the exterior part.

Wednesday, 5 December

Mrs. Turner says Mr. Turner shall bring Mrs. Wicker a Sweetheart. Play at cards, score with the pocket pieces my Harry gave me, I win 9 games at which they impute my good luck to them & laugh at me heartily.

Thursday, 6 December

Drink tea & spend the evening at Mr. Page's, were entertained in a very elegant manner. Play at cards. He offers to lend me some books, I accept it gladly. Much conversation about beauty.

Friday, 7 December

Walk to Thyers's, a fine situation, commands a delightfull prospect, the Penserose a solemn place, all around verses on Melancholy & retirement with a clock that strikes every minute, a fine Statue of Truth, a picture of an Unbeliever & a Christian in the agonies of Death, their different thoughts so strongly impress'd as one shou'd I imagine, no Art cou'd reach.[223]

Saturday, 8 December

Mr. Turner comes home, we are all excessively merry. Walk out with Mr. Page. Walk again in the afternoon up a Hill, the situation of Dorking is excessively pleasant.[224] Little Master Miller is vastly fond of me. Captain Miller very complaisant.

Sunday, 9 December

At Church, Mr. Turner makes an excellent discourse, the text that we shou'd walk worthy of God. In the afternoon one Mr. Allen preach'd, but such negligence &

---

222 *The Orphan of China*, by Arthur Murphy, was first performed in 1759. Sarah later saw it in Horsham on 2 March 1761. It was probably based on *The Chinese Orphan*, a historical tragedy in verse, by William Hatchett, published in 1741.

223 "*Thyer's*" was a house built by Jonathan Tyers, the proprietor of Vauxhall Gardens, who bought Denbies Farm, on the north side of Dorking, in 1734. Perhaps in compensation for the way in which he made his money, he imparted a peculiarly solemn character to the house and grounds with all the features described by Sarah.

224 The viewpoint from where Sarah could see over Dorking was probably the terrace of Chart Park, on the hill above Deepdene, to the south of the town.

coldness in a Pulpit did I never see. A very agreeable evening, Mr. Turner quite facetious. Mr. Speke who is to court Mrs. Wicker the same.

Monday, 10 December

A conversation on dissenters. Mr. Turner has great charity, says much in praise of Monsieur Pascall's letters which I remember to have read & lik'd.[225] There is a letter from my Harry now at Horsham, t'is painfull to stay for it till Thursday. Play at cards.

Tuesday, 11 December

Clear starch some linnen for Mrs. Turner, after I had made it. Romp with Captain Miller, he washes my face with a knife cloth. Mr. Turner proposes Mr. Speke for a husband to Mrs. Wicker. He appears a good natur'd man, but I have experienc'd that appearances are deceitfull.

Wednesday, 12 December

Go to Church. Mr. Turner reads prayers with a clear distinct & audible voice. Play at picquet with him. Captain Miller & I romp, he pinches my arms black & blue, which puts me to violent pain. Grow a little uneasy as the time draws near that I expect my letters.

Thursday, 13 December

Receive one from my Harry & another from Sally Sheppard to inform me he is at Horsham, surprising. I am sorry at first that I was not at home, but comfort myself with the pleasing hope that I shall see him Saturday.

Friday, 14 December

Think the time long I am now to stay, how fickle is the Human Mind, the least trifle alters its purposes & makes it lose its reason. Mr. Turner reads us the Sermon he preach'd on the Thanksgiving day, a very good one. Captain Miller expresses much concern that he is about to lose us.

Saturday, 15 December

Mr. Turner & all joke with me on my being in a hurry to see my Dear Smith. We take our leave of Dorking & have a tolerable journey home, tho' cold. Find all my friends well. Harry calls to see me, but his brother Griff is down so he makes but a short stay, but gives me the pleasure of saying that he has settled accounts with his Worthless brother, & is not indebted to him.

Sunday, 16 December

At Church twice. Walk in the Croft with my Sally Sheppard. T'is now near eleven at night, the hour I expect my Dear Harry, & my perverse mother is not gone to bed, how great are the torments of expectation.

---

225 Blaise Pascal (1623-1662) was a French mathematician, physicist and moralist, who invented a calculating machine, a syringe and a hydraulic press. By his *"letters"* Sarah probably means *Les Provinciales* (1656-7), which were polemical letters directed against the casuistry of the Jesuits. They were translated into English in 1657.

Monday, 17 December

Sat up till three with my dearest Harry, he is all modesty, love & tenderness. Spend the afternoon at Sally Sheppard's, we are very merry. Harry drinks tea with us. All the evening at Mrs. Tredcroft's, she tells me my lover knew not how to bestow himself till I return'd from Dorking.

Tuesday, 18 December

He makes me a morning visit, we have a dispute, he says none will bear to be told of their faults. I aver that many can, & not only so but will profit by it too. He answers those instances are very rare. Walk to Slynfold with Sally Sheppard.

Wednesday, 19 December

Miss Pigott expects to be married in a fortnight, poor girl. I wish her happy, but fear she is a little too hasty, for marriage without a competency to me is shocking. They fright us with an account of the house being haunted, we return home. Smith meets us.

Thursday, 20 December

Very busy in the shop, must not suffer this love affair to engross all my time & thoughts, but let me pay my gratefull thanks to the Supreme Being for my Harry's constancy & all other blessings. Begin reading *The Brothers*, a trifling novel.

Friday, 21 December

Go to spend the afternoon at Mrs. Wicker's. Harry there, but Mrs. Bridger sends for us. We wait on her, & play at cards. How trifling is this way of spending time, almost below the dignity of a rational creature, but our choice in amusements is as different as our places & indeed, if we reflect on our natural tendency to vice, t'is well if they are only trifling, for alas they are too often criminal.

Saturday, 22 December

Read *Rasselas, Prince of Abyssinia* to Mrs. Wicker, a very pretty thing, shows our general dissatisfaction in true & lively colours, & the impossibility of lasting happiness in this World. Write some verses on reading it.

Sunday, 23 December

At Church twice. Oh may I never swerve from my duty to my Creator. Spend the evening at Mr. Tredcroft's, who was in high good humour. Tells us "Merchant" Smith behav'd worse in London than he had done here, & wou'd if he had not reform'd been ruin'd.

Monday, 24 December

My Harry here in the morning, tells me he had been excessive low spirit'd all night. How we sympathise with each other, my heart was unusually dull. He dines at Doctor Hutchinson's, returns & drinks tea with us, spends the evening at Mr. Tredcroft's. I go to dancing & am allmost surfeited with my partners & compliments.

Tuesday, 25 December

The Birthday of our Blessed Saviour, oh may I never forget, but be ever gratefull for the benefits that were by this event confer'd upon me. Mrs. James comes down, & tells us "Merchant" Smith says, Lord Irwin wou'd never prefer my Harry if he married me. I am sure that it is absolutely false & shall never give me a moment's uneasiness.

Wednesday, 26 December

Harry goes to Portsmouth, takes a tender leave of me. Well, I must support his absence as well as possible, no external signs of discontent however shall appear, I will so far play the hypocrite, for woes of this sort are allways burlesqued. Mr. Tredcroft's family spend the evening with us.

Thursday, 27 December

Work on my apron. Several people come & desire to see it, all agree in extravagantly commending, how fond we all are of being prais'd for our performances. N.B. never to do anything that deserves the contrary. Mrs. Hunt & Sally calls, the latter says she likes Cowfold tolerably well.

Friday, 28 December

Finish reading *The Brothers*, our passion for Novelty is certainly very great, or so many things of this kind wou'd never be encourag'd. Finish reading *Rasselas*, an exceeding good thing, & whoever wrote it knew the inmost recesses of the human Heart.[226] Spend a very agreeable evening at Dame Hunt's with Sally Sheppard & Mrs. Tasker.

Saturday, 29 December

Read *Lucy Weller*, a Novel wrote by the young Lady, author of *The Brothers*.[227] Sure t'is impossible there can exist such villainous Characters as are there. Captain Miller calls & takes me down to Mrs. Wicker's, where is Mr. Speke, her humble Servant. Doubt he will be unsuccessfull, for she seems not inclin'd to marry.

Sunday, 30 December

At Church in the morning. Hear one of the finest discourses the Doctor ever pronounc'd from the Pulpit, he expatiated largely on the certainty of a future state, & that nothing can be so shocking & absurd as the thought of annihilation. Mrs. Wicker, Mr. Speke & Captain Miller dine with us. I hear "Merchant" Smith intends taking his mother to London with him, if so his house will be shut up. I shall see my Harry no more this Winter. Well I will, I must acquiesce, & cheerfully too.

226　*The History of Rasselas, Prince of Abyssinia*, a didactic romance, was written by Dr. Samuel Johnson, and published in 1759. Though Sarah was ignorant of the author, she clearly appreciated the quality of his mind. It is an essay on the *"choice of life"*, a phrase repeated throughout the work, which may have seemed especially relevant to Sarah.

227　The author of these books has not been identified.

Monday, 31 December

Spend the day at Mrs. Wicker's, with Mr. Miller & Mr. Speke. Mr. Jones arrives & brings us the agreeable news of my brother's welfare. Now Miss Pigott will soon be a wife, & I think stands a tolerable chance for happiness if their circumstances were otherwise.

I have now brought this year to a conclusion, & on looking over some of its occurrences, I cannot help laughing, & thinking of Dean Swift's *Memoirs of P.P., Clerk of a Country Church*. Mine are of little more importance to the World, but this method enables me to draw reflections on all that passes, & will I hope tend to the regulation of a conduct not quite blameless, but alas who is without fault, none I believe that now exist, ought we not then to treat with lenity in others, what we are conscious of being in a greater or less degree guilty of ourselves. Learn, oh ye rigid censurers of another's conduct, more narrowly to inspect your own heart, conquer this predominant vice, be no more mole eye'd to imperfections in yourself & Eagle Eye'd to those of [your] (perhaps more innocent) Neighbour.

> Engrave on Sand, that Winds soon drive away,
> Your Neighbours faults, nor, think on them a day,
> But let firm Marble, with your own be stain'd,
> Th' impression keep, till perfect virtues' gain'd.

THE DIARY FOR 1760

[On a loose page]. One year more is flown over my head, or else think, I am exactly situated as I was the last, a dull round of the same transactions is not very agreeable to an active spirit like mine. I shou'd indeed be quite unhappy if it were not for my three favourite amusements, work, writing & reading, with one of these I ever keep my fancy employ'd, for sure it had better be made use of in trifles, than suffer'd quite to stagnate, how necessary it is we shou'd have some pursuit, some … *[?interest]*.

[At the top of the first page is written] Mr. Hutchinson at Maudlin College, Oxford.[228]

JANUARY 1760

Tuesday, 1 January

Old Mr. Shelley here to enquire about Mrs. Wicker's lover, we evade his questions. He abuses Captain Miller in a violent manner, how odious is ill nature & prejudice.[229] Finish the *History of Lucy Weller*, several very amiable & natural characters in it, like it much upon the *[?whole]*.

Wednesday, 2 January

Mr. Chasemore from Cuckfield comes to *[meet]* Mr.?Yonge, this man's character is truly amiable, he is a good natur'd, generous & an honest Attorney. Mr. & Mrs. Jones come to dinner. My friend Miss Pigott is now no more. She makes me a present of a magnet, I laugh & tell her, t'is because she has no further occasion for it now she has gain'd her end in getting a good husband.

Thursday, 3 January

A letter from my Harry, he had apprehensions when he first went to Portsmouth of his Ship's going to the East Indies, but thank Heaven his fears prove false.

---

228 Thomas Hutchinson, son of the Rev. Thomas Hutchinson, Vicar of Horsham, then at Oxford. He matriculated on 28 March 1759 aged 17, at Christ Church, but was at Magdalen College from 1759 to 1762.

229 Captain Challen Miller, brother of John Miller, who was married to Timothy Shelley's niece.

Friday, 4 January

Very busy Ironing. Bet & I have a vast deal of conversation, I tell her she appears to be worse than she really is. Sally Sheppard with us all the afternoon & evening, we play at cards. I shall not I dare say see Captain Smith any more this Winter.

Saturday, 5 January

Write out a great many bills. Papa a little cross & pettish, but I have thank Heaven attain'd such a command over my temper as not to make any reply, this I find is the only method to live quietly with people of indifferent disposition. Write to Captain Smith, am flatter'd very much by a young fellow from Cuckfield, but all this sort of stuff is lost upon me.

Sunday, 6 January

Mr. Tredcroft says a great many ill-natur'd things about my father being Churchwarden, & refuses paying his taxes. Whence can proceed this propensity to be a hindrance to our neighbours, it is surely a diabolical & not a Christian disposition. Oh, may I never be inclin'd to do any person an injury, if it is not in my power to do them good.

Monday, 7 January

Sally Sheppard comes over & chats, I chide her for staying away so long. At Mrs. Wicker's the afternoon & evening, with Mrs. Bridger, the Miss Ellis's & Mrs. Tredcroft, the latter said she heard Miss Pigott was married but very indifferently, for her husband was very Idle.

Tuesday, 8 January

Where, oh where, is the person that can escape the envenom'd tongue of Slander? I vindicate him & say that if he can be call'd Idle who preaches three Sermons every week, and has the care of forty Boys, I don't know who is industrious. Poor Miss Pigott, she cannot hear [?bear] this.

Wednesday, 9 January

Some [?Rhymes] set in my Ladies' Magazine to be fill'd up with verses, I fill them up with three different sorts.[230] Papa & I post all our bills & settle our accounts, take out what cash is due in London etc. Miss Kitty Smith & several of her Boarders with Nany Curtis come to see my Apron.[231]

Thursday, 10 January

Walk out in the Common, with Sally Sheppard & my sister Bet, but the weather was too sharp to be agreeable. Never sure was seen a more wintry prospect, every piece of water is frozen & the ground cover'd with snow, save here & there a

---

230 This is explained better in the entry for 17 January.
231 Miss Kitty Smith does not appear to be related to Henry Smith's family, or to Dr. John Smith. The mention of "boarders" suggests that she and Anne Curtis were running a school or a boarding house.

17. Frontispiece from the 1759 Diary.

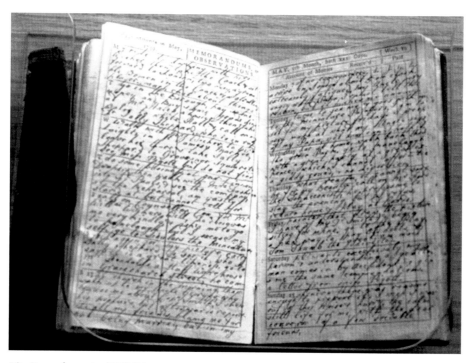

18. Pages from the 1759 Diary.

19. Silhouette of
    Sarah Hurst.

20. Silhouette of
    Henry Smith.

21. Houses in the Causeway.

22. Causeway House, where Sarah lived in her final years.

23. The chancel of St. Mary's Church.

24. Bishop's burgage house where Robert Grace sen. lived.

25. Denne House, the home of Sir Charles Eversfield.

26. "A View of a Bridge near Horsham" - this shows the turnpike road to London with the floodgates of Warnham Mill in the background.

27. Chesworth, where Sarah went nutting.

28. Old cottages by the churchyard.

29. Horsham from Denne Hill.

30. Park House, which Robert Hurst bought in 1799.

31. The old church at Slinfold, where Sarah and Henry were married in 1762.

32. The final page of the 1762 diary.

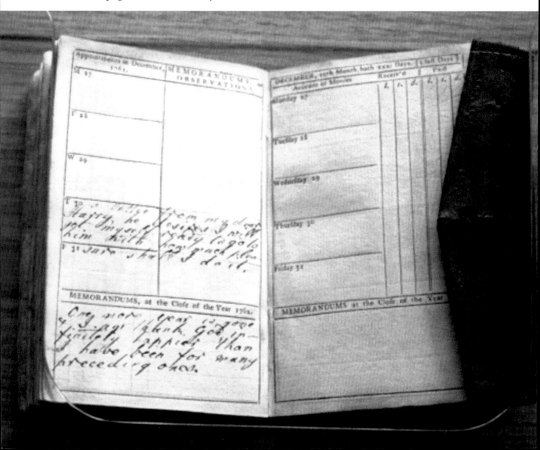

rusty spot of herbage rears its barren head & seems to mock the half starv'd cattle. Thank heaven I am not expos'd to the inclemency of the Season, as thousands of my fellow creatures are.

Friday, 11 January

Finish one side border of my apron; read some of Pope's *Letters*, very good ones to Mr. Wycherly.[232]

Saturday, 12 January

A letter from Mrs. Jones informing me my brother is well, & she thinks herself very happy in her change of situation, I wish she may always continue so. No letter from Captain Smith, what can be the meaning of it? I think he is a little remiss, but my fears are ever awake, something may have happen'd to prevent his writing, impatience however will be no remedy.

Sunday, 13 January

At Church twice. Doctor Hutchinson preaches a most excellent discourse, the text is *"a light to lighten the gentiles"*, he explodes the notion that virtue ought to be practis'd for its own [sake]; this is on the same subject as my letter to Mr. Pigott, & I thought myself vastly happy in hearing it treated with so much greater strength of Reason & force of argument than I was capable of using.

Monday, 14 January

A letter from Captain Smith, he is in London, but can't make Horsham in his road; so desires I wou'd meet him as he is to sail in a few days.

Tuesday, 15 January

Ask leave to go & meet my Harry, it is not approv'd of tho' not peremptorily denied, so I decline going & write him word it is out of my power to do as I cou'd wish. So I shall see him no more till he returns from the Coast of France, where the *Orford* is going to relieve some of the Ships under Sir Edward Hawke.

Wednesday, 16 January

I believe when people grow in years they either forget or are unwilling to own that ever they were actuated by the tender passions. If my father & mother had any sensibility remaining, they wou'd not sure have prevented my seeing my Harry before he goes, but I will bear the disappointment with Christian fortitude.

Thursday, 17 January

Captain Miller calls on me, he is come on a visit to Warnham, I fancy to renew his

---

232 Alexander Pope, the poet (1688-1744) published his early letters between 1735 and 1737, including his correspondence with the elderly dramatist, William Wycherley (c. 1640-1716), who helped to introduce him to the London literary scene. Their friendship cooled after Pope edited Wycherley's verses, and Pope is now considered to have edited his letters to him so as to show off his own precocity.

addresses to his old sweetheart.[233] Write to the proprietors of *The Ladies' Magazine* on Women's learning, send the verses I fill'd up the Rhymes with & a poem entitled *The Consolation.*

Friday, 18 January

Violent headache, oblig'd to go to bed. What a happiness is the company of a person we love in illness, wish for my Harry. Go to Mrs. Bridger's. Win at cards, which I never desire, lest it shou'd make me contract a fondness for this irrational diversion.

Saturday, 19 January

Work all day on my Apron. Mr. Tredcroft & my father tell me I shall spoil my eyes, the latter offers me five guineas not to work it, I refuse the offer. Chat with Mrs. Wicker; see in the Newspaper that Admiral Boscawen is gone to Portsmouth, Captain Smith went to London on purpose to see him, so has lost his Journey, nothing but disappointments. [234]

Sunday, 20 January

At Church in the morning but stay at home in the afternoon. Read *The Universal Magazine,*[235] fine Character of General Wolfe; a distinction made between self love & the love of ourselves, both very prettily defin'd. Chat with Sally Sheppard & Drew Michell. We talk of living together when we are old maids, they desire me to write some verses on it.

Monday, 21 January

Am seis'd with the uttmost astonishment at the Post's bringing back the letter I wrote last Tuesday to Captain Smith, from the general Post Office for me to pay the postage. I send it directly to a friend in London, & write him word of the affair, what surprise has he been under at not hearing from me. What unexpect'd things happen, who cou'd have dreamt of such an affair as this.

Tuesday, 22 January

Call on Mrs. Lampart, Nany Cook that was. She came through Dunstable & says Sally Sheppard's lover will be married very shortly.[236] What a shock was this to me,

---

233 This is rather puzzling. Captain Miller had been married to Elizabeth Parham since 1745, so it is difficult to see how the Captain could *"renew his addresses"* to anyone else, unless his wife had died since 17 August 1759, when Sarah met her at Mr. Parham's. (It may be significant that there was no mention of her during Sarah's visit to Dorking in December 1759, when Captain Miller and his son appeared to be living with his mother, Mrs. Turner). His brother, John Miller, was living in Warnham, so Captain Miller did have connections there.

234 See other entries on Admiral Boscawen on 10 September 1759 and 11 January 1761.

235 The *Universal Magazine* was a monthly magazine which was published in London by John Hinton from the 1740s onwards. It contained the most attractive of all magazine maps, often incorporating decorative title cartouches, and occasionally executed in wash colour. Other magazines of the period increased their number of plates greatly in competitive response to those produced in *The Universal Magazine*. It was still being published by John Hinton in the 1770s, but was then called *The Universal Magazine of Knowledge and Pleasure.*

236 It is likely that Mrs. Lampert and her husband (who was Lord Irwin's cook) had just come down from Lord Irwin's principal seat, at Temple Newsam, near Leeds, where he would have been working during the Christmas season. They would have passed through Dunstable on the way.

& how will it affect my friend. Heaven give the dear girl resolution to sustain it. Excessive low spirited, both for myself & friend.

Wednesday, 23 January

Think Captain Smith shou'd have wrote tho' he did not hear from me, don't suppose I shall have a letter before Monday, good Heaven, what an Age, Oh inspire me ye powers with patience.

Thursday, 24 January

A letter from the amiable Mrs. Townsend. Dame Hunt, Bet & Jenny with Sally Sheppard drink tea & spend the evening here, we are vastly merry, even Sally Sheppard, but how often does the countenance in this respect belye the Heart.

Friday, 25 January

Finish the verses I promis'd to write on Sally Sheppard's & my retirement, she shows them to Drew Michell who prodigiously approves of them. Afternoon & evening at Sally Sheppard's, mixt company, consequently very little conversation but of the insipid or rattling kind.

Saturday, 26 January

A long letter from my ever dear Harry, wondering as well he might at my silence, he expected to sail in six days, so t'is impossible I can see him. I am extreamly thankfull for being reliev'd from the anxiety I have been under. Answer Captain Smith's letter. Receive one from my cousin Bet Smith, she acquaints me she did not deliver the note to Moore,[237] thinking it wou'd do me a prejudice. I write to her & thank her for her prudent behaviour, & send her the verses I wrote last week.

Sunday, 27 January

At Church twice & very good Sermons both from Doctor Hutchinson & Mr. Osgood. Poor Sally Sheppard bears her misfortune with Christian patience.

Monday, 28 January

A letter from my Harry, he was just going to embark from Portsmouth, shou'd pass by Plymouth & desir'd I wou'd write that the letter might meet him there & desires I'd make an excuse to Mr. Masterman, for his not writing to him. I do in every respect as he desires.

Tuesday, 29 January

Spent last night at my Uncle Waller's. A remarkable wager laid between him & my Uncle Tasker that whosoever's wife shou'd have a child first, the other shou'd give them a Plumbcake of a guinea value. Post the shop Books. Excessive low spirited occasion'd perhaps by the blusterous weather & my Dear Smith's being expos'd to it.

237　This is probably Will Moore, who had previously done Sarah a disservice – see the entry for 18 September 1759.

Wednesday, 30 January

Mr. Pigott & Mr. Walter come to Town & dine with us. He tells me he shall send a packet to his sister, I write to her & to my brother. I seem to be quite reinstated in the Parson's good graces, he is, I fancy, perfectly convinc'd that I dissuaded instead of encouraging her to marry.

Thursday, 31 January

Very busy in preparing for company. A letter from my friend, Miss Gittins. She blames me for Jesting with my love affair, & thinks I have not so much regard for Captain Smith as I ought, but a heart rending sigh now convinces me I shall find it too great for my future repose. A good deal of company.

FEBRUARY 1760

Friday, 1 February

See in the Papers there are several Colonels of Marines made. If so, there will be no Majors, & my Smith have no preferment, shou'd he be turn'd on half pay at the expiration of the War, & our union impossible, what heart felt sorrow will be my lot. Avert this, oh gracious Heaven, or give me patience to bear the misfortune.

Saturday, 2 February

A letter from Parson Pigott complaining of indisposition, both of body & mind, but couch'd in the highest terms of friendship, hoping his regard for me wou'd give no offence to Captain Smith. I answer his letter & give him assurance of my real friendship. Begin reading *The Bee*, a periodical composition. Some good letters of Voltaire's, the rest trifling. Nothing of this sort is comparable to *The Spectator*.

Sunday, 3 February

At Church twice. Griff Smith here again, Sir Charles Eversfield at the House of prayer, which he seldom visits. How are we to account for these sensible men's neglect of religion, was it instituted only for the ignorant, & does superior understanding set them above these vulgar notions?

Monday, 4 February

Take a walk with Sally Sheppard, a fine pleasant day for the Season. Commit a great fault thro' the violence of passion, but repent & acknowledge it directly, which I hope will be an expiation. Human nature is frail & liable to err.

Tuesday, 5 February

Finish reading *The Bee*. *The City Night Piece* a very good thing, as affecting as t'is natural, some smart epigrams, a pretty story of conjugal love but several things that I disapprove of particularly & recommending a methodistical way of preaching & moving the passions, rather than convincing the reason of their audience.[238]

Wednesday, 6 February

Papa waits on Mr. Aldridge who is Sheriff, he orders him to make his liveries.[239] Walk out with Sally Sheppard. Write to my Uncle Bob. I can't see nor hear whether the *Orford* sail'd or not, sure Smith wou'd have wrote if he had been still at Portsmouth, at least I think he ought.

Thursday, 7 February

Read the News the *Orford* sail'd from St. Helens last Saturday, so if my Harry writes from Plymouth I may expect a letter next Saturday sennight, how fond we are of anticipating. Mrs. Wicker, Nany Reynolds[240] & Miss Steward spend the evening with us, tolerably merry.

Friday, 8 February

Begin working a handkerchief for Mrs. Turner at Dorking. Mrs. Blunt sends me an apron to draw her some flowers by. Read in *Nature display'd*, a pretty thing, account of Insects in an entertaining manner, by way of dialogue interspers'd with good moral reflections.

Saturday, 9 February

A few lines from Captain Smith, sends me four franks, he is by this time or before at Plymouth, may his guardian Angel be his guide & protector. Am astonished with the news of "Merchant" Smith's being speedily married to Miss Pitt, what surprising things happen, he has been very unsuccessfull, & this seems to be his last resource. Her fortune is indeed considerable, & to this Idol we all pay homage, but what in him can have captivated her is the Wonder.

Sunday, 10 February

At Church twice, a charming fine day. Papa out of temper, we all shed tears, t'is a most astonishing thing there is so little happiness in families, it must be want of care in the choice of a partner for life; but content in short is not to be enjoy'd here.

Monday, 11 February

Hear a great number of ridiculous things that "Merchant" Smith says relating to his matrimony, bespeaks the musick & the Ringers, he says too that the Captain concluded his last letter to him with these words; *"By God I won't have Sal Hurst"*. Ha, ha, ha, a droll conclusion indeed.

Tuesday, 12 February

A letter from my cousin Bet Smith. She returns many thanks & compliments for

---

238 *"The City Night Piece"* was written by Oliver Goldsmith, and first appeared anonymously in the magazine, *The Bee*. It later appeared as Letter cxvii in *The Citizen of the World*. These melancholy, reflective poems, often set in graveyards, became very popular in the 18th century, and marked the beginning of the cult of *"sensibility"*. Thomas Gray's *"Elegy written in a Country Churchyard"* (1751) was the best-known work of these *"graveyard"* poets..

239 Mr. John Aldridge of St. Leonard's Forest.

240 Ann (Nany) Reynolds was the eldest daughter of John and Ann Reynolds, born in 1724.

my poetry. I write to Mrs. Townsend, & send her the acrostick & Epitaph I wrote on General Wolfe. At Mrs. Tasker's afternoon & evening, all our own family, Dame Hunt & Jenny. Very merry, play at cards.

Wednesday, 13 February

Old Mr. Shelley tells me he has heard what Griff Smith said about my Harry's not having me, this has now very little effect upon me. I am perfectly convinc'd it will be Fortune's fault, & not his if we are never united. Mr. Shelley exclaims against the Merchant, who does not.

Thursday, 14 February

A very stormy night. In pain for my Harry, who is at Sea. A letter from him dated Plymouth, he receiv'd mine directed there. Says he has seen Mrs. Masterman, who much approves his choice of me, how pleasing is approbation if we are conscious of deserving it, if not the worst of reproaches.

Friday, 15 February

Mr. Hill calls on me, elder brother to him that courted my sister Bet. He is a conversible man but has the misfortune to be deaf. Gives me an account of *The Desert Island*, a new play, & *The Way to Keep Him*, another. Like his description, & intend to buy them.

Saturday, 16 February

A letter from Mrs. Jones & one from Mr. Pigott with the other 3 volumes of *Nature display'd*. Both of them are full of the highest professions of regard. "Merchant" Smith comes down again. Shows his marriage writings in the Stage Coach & commits a thousand Extra…*[?Extravagances]*

Sunday, 17 February

At Church in the morning. Hear a report that Drew Michell has abandon'd Molly Luttman & courts Sally Sheppard. This last I know to be false, but hurry up to Mrs. Luttman's & enquire about the first, she flies in so violent a passion as surprises, & abuses my friend Sally in a shocking manner. This I cannot bear & vindicate her in the warmest manner, but there is no convincing prejudice.

Monday, 18 February

I am very sorry for Molly Luttman & think Drew a base fellow to entrap a girl so young & innocent. Take a walk with Sally Sheppard, we confer on the affair & join in pitying the girl & blaming him. How happy am I in this respect, who have met with a man truly Just & generous.

Tuesday, 19 February

"Merchant" Smith invites hundreds to his Wedding & commits a thousand extravagances that indicate a disorder'd mind. I am sorry on my dear Harry's account, but alas where is he now, expos'd to the mercy of tempestuous winds & waves.

Wednesday, 20 February

Ash Wednesday, at Church twice. Finish a poem, *Little Cupid turn'd out of his office*. At Mrs. Wicker's, very merry at the poor Merchant's account. Read *The Royal & Grand Magazine*,[241] like them both, part of a fine poem in the latter called *Henriade* wrote by the great Voltaire.[242]

Thursday, 21 February

Read *The Desert Island*, a Dramatic poem, the language is beautifully delicate & descriptive & the moral inculcates this lesson, never to despair whatever evils surround us. Read *The Way to Keep Him*, a comedy.[243] There is not much witt in it, but the moral recommends (what is perfectly Just) the same care of a Woman's person after, as before marriage, being the only method to preserve her Husband's affections.

Friday, 22 February

Take a walk with Sally Sheppard, weather unpleasant & cold, a prodigious stormy night. Low spirited about Captain Smith, oh keep him safe Almighty.

Saturday, 23 February

The inexpressive pleasure of a letter from my Harry, he has thank Heaven escap'd the late storm. Gives me an account of a man of War being lost, about 10 mile from them, & near 750 poor mortals perish'd, how dreadfull is the fate of their friends. Write to my Harry.

Sunday, 24 February

At Church. Doctor Hutchinson makes a fine discourse, the text, *"God is long suffering"*. A fine pleasant day, walk with Sally Sheppard. In the afternoon & evening, a vast deal of conversation on varying subjects. Mrs Smith, the Doctor's wife, drinks tea with us, tells me Miss Hutchinson is married & her friends dislike it, so I fear t'is not advantageous.

Monday, 25 February

See in the papers that the unfortunate Captain of the *Ramillies*[244] has left a wife, poor Lady, how insupportable must be her situation. Oh mercifull Father, grant this may

---

241 *The Royal Magazine* was one of those published by John Coote of Horsham in the 1760s; *The Grand Magazine* was most probably *The Grand Magazine of Magazines, or a Public Register of Literature and Amusement comprehending whatever is worthy of being preserved in all the Magazines and periodical Pamphlets Published either at Home or Abroad...collected and digested by Roger Woodville Esq.*". (A volume containing the 1750 issues can now be viewed online as a Google Book). The title page lists the wide range of material that it collated; *"1. Essays Moral and Entertaining 2. Trade Commerce and Politicks 3. Arts Sciences Natural and Civil History 4. Poetry Novels Tales Letters and Lives 5. Account of Books foreign and domestic 6.Foreign and Domestic Occurrences.* Sarah makes several references to this magazine and her comments confirm that it did indeed cover a very wide range of material.

242 *La Henriade* is an epic poem, in ten cantos, by the poet and philosopher François-Marie Arouet (better known under his pen-name Voltaire). It was written in honour of King Henry IV of France, and was completed in 1723.

243 *The Desert Island* and *The Way to Keep Him* were both written by Arthur Murphy, and first published in 1760 by Paul Vaillant. *The Desert Island*, based on Metastasio's *L'Isola disabitata* was called a "dramatic poem" but was performed at Drury Lane. Sarah saw *The Desert Island* performed in Horsham in October 1762. Arthur Murphy also wrote *The Orphan of China*, which Sarah read and saw performed in Horsham in March 1761.

244 Presumably the man-of-war that was lost — see entry for 23 February.

never be my lot. Walk on the Causeway, a fine moonlight evening, how beauteous, how striking is the scene, erring mortals must adore tho' they cannot comprehend.

Tuesday, 26 February

Very low spirited, reflect on the dangers my Harry may be expos'd to, yet how preferable is my lot (with all this uneasiness) to that of thousands who are now perhaps expos'd to the inclemency of the season, want & wretchedness, while I who am perhaps less deserving enjoy every necessary blessing. Oh may I be every day more worthy of the favours I receive.

Wednesday, 27 February

Drink tea at my Aunt Waller's. Mr. John Shelley there, he behaves very rude & we allmost quarrel.

Thursday, 28 February

Miss Molly Ellis here, desires I wou'd come & see them.[245] Attempt to walk out with Sally Sheppard but t'is so cold we return back. Mr. Pigott dines with us, he has been to Chichester & thinks he shall leave Slynfold.[246] I am sorry for it, I shall lose my friend & my Books. Write to Miss Gittins.

Friday, 29 February

Pigott says Mr. Gittins' disorder is not dangerous, thank Heaven, my friend wou'd be left in a disagreeable situation. Poor girl, she has many enemies at Chichester[247] who hate her for the superior qualities she is possessed of. Walk with Sally Sheppard, a fine moonlight evening.

MARCH 1760

Saturday, 1 March

Mr. Aldridge drinks tea & coffee with us. Write four letters to London, one of them to my cousin Bet Smith. Begin reading the Duke of Buckingham's works, the songs abound in fancy. *Ode to Love*, to Desire wou'd be a more proper name for it, a very loose conclusion. *Essay on Poetry* a very fine thing, as is the *Ode on Brutus*, speaks in the warmest terms of friendship. The *Essay on Satire* but an indifferent composition.[248]

Sunday, 2 March

Hear that "Merchant" Smith is confin'd for a madman, how will this dreadfull news shock my dearest Harry, sure no fool will mention it to him till it cannot be help'd.

---

245 Miss Mary Ellis of Tanbridge, the younger of the two Ellis sisters.

246 Mr. Pigott had presumably gone to Chichester to see the Bishop and tender his resignation as Curate of Slinfold.

247 Probably a slip of the pen for Arundel, where the Gittins lived.

248 George Villiers, 2nd Duke of Buckingham (1628-1687), was a prominent figure in the reign of King Charles II. He was a poet and satirist, who wrote the burlesque, *The Rehearsal*. He appears as Zimri in Dryden's *Absalom and Achitofel*, and figures in a famous passage in Epistle III of Pope's *Moral Essays*.

How greatly must it pain his humane Heart. Drink tea at my grandmother's. Walk with my friend Sally, a most delightfull day, makes everything look cheerfull.

Monday, 3 March

No letter from Captain Smith as I a little expected, but how trifling ought I to think such a disappointment as this. Chat with Bet Hunt, she likes neither *The Desert Island* nor *The Way to Keep Him*. I tell her t'is a proof of judgment to find fault. Spend the evening at Mrs. Bridger's.

Tuesday, 4 March

At Tanbridge. Mrs. White brings a Gazette, with an account that we have taken 3 French men of War, how dreadfull is bloodshed, whoever gains the victory, humanity obliges to be concern'd, & love for our Country glad at this success.[249] T'is now near midnight, the moon shines in full lustre, & all is wrapt in profound silence, Nature seems wearied & at rest. My unhappy heart, in painfull throbings, sighs for my dearest Harry & is a stranger to repose.

Wednesday, 5 March

My father very much out of temper with us all, he is happy in a gainfull business & has a good income, & sure I, by keeping the Books, etc, contribute to his advantage, & yet I fear am thought to be an incumbrance. How painfull is dependence.

Thursday, 6 March

The *Orford* is sail'd before my letter cou'd reach Captain Smith, & he (angry I suppose) hasn't wrote to me again, one incident or another continually gives me uneasiness, but can I presumptuous wretch hope to be exempt from the common lot of mortals.

Friday, 7 March

Am shock'd with the disagreeable news from Sally Sheppard that her lover is married, she is greatly affected, tho' she knew it must happen, & I most sincerely sympathise in her affliction, but suspense is now at an end, & I think absolute despair is preferable. She has, I hope, fortitude enough to sustain her mind & bear this trial heroically.

Saturday, 8 March

Sup at Dame Hunt's with Sally Sheppard, are as merry as our heavy hearts will permit. Read my *Royal Magazine*, like it very well, but intend to change with Drew Michell for his *Grand*.

Sunday, 9 March

Call on my Harry's mother, she is in great affliction on the Merchant's account. I console her, she talks of going to London to be with her unfortunate son. I take a respectfull

---

249 This followed an unsuccessful raid on Carrickfergus, near Belfast, by the French Captain Thurot on 21 February 1760. Captain Elliott, of the *Aeolus* in Admiral Hawke's fleet, gave chase and Thurot's three ships were sunk or captured on 29 February 1760.

leave of her. Walk to Warnham Church. Draw a plan for circulating our magazines, which is very well approv'd of by all the fraternity. Read in Buckingham's works.

Monday, 10 March

Deliver the plans of the magazines to Mr. Vinall, Mr. Michell, Mrs. Wicker & Sally Sheppard.[250] Make a visit to Mrs. Tailor at Lord Irving [Irwin]. See the House which is extreamly neat fitted up, some exceeding fine Prints, which I cou'd spend whole hours in admiring. [251]

Tuesday, 11 March

Go to Slynfold to see Mr. Pigott with Sally Sheppard. A delightfull Day, we have a charming pleasant walk. Write to Mrs. Jones. Read *The Ladies' Magazine*; the verses & prose I sent, subscrib'd Amanda Rustick, are both inserted;[252] some pretty things, well worth perusing.

Wednesday, 12 March

Read Buckingham's works, the story of Herod & Marc Antony, well told. What a Woman was Cleopatra, infamously famous, what crimes has ambition made both sexes guilty of! Read *The Funeral* or *Grief à la mode*, a very witty comedy of Sir Richard Steele, full of satire, mirth & humour.[253]

Thursday, 13 March

The play I read last night made such an impression on my fancy, that soon as Morpheus had clos'd my eyes, I thought my Dear Smith was dead, & I watch'd him three days at the expiration of which time he came to life again. How surprising are dreams, & how badly accounted for by all who have wrote on the subject.

Friday, 14 March

Chat with Drew Michell, mention Molly Luttman's affair. He says he has been a fool, but no knave, I cannot acquit him. A solemn Fast for the War. Observe it very religiously. Oh may there soon be an end of all the disasters occasion'd by it. Go & chat with Mrs. Wicker.

Saturday, 15 March

The unexpected & inexpressive happiness of a letter from my Dear Smith, dated

---

250 This must be the "fraternity" mentioned above, who are to share or circulate their magazines among themselves. Guildford Vinall was a mercer who lived in Market Square.

251 Mrs. Elizabeth Tayleur was the housekeeper at Hill's Place, the Jacobean mansion on the outskirts of the town owned by Lord Irwin. There are a number of her letters to Isabella, Dowager Lady Irwin, giving news of life in Horsham in the Horsham Museum collections. Isabella, Lady Irwin, is known to have bought a complete set of 80 prints of gentlemen's seats by Leonard Knyff, engraved by Jan Kip, in the series *Britannia Illustrata*, first published in 1707. Some of these may have been brought down to Hill's Place - there are 30 prints mentioned in one room in an inventory made in 1766, which are presumably the ones mentioned by Sarah.

252 See Appendix I.

253 *The Funeral, or Grief à la Mode*, was a satirical comedy by Sir Richard Steele, first performed in 1701.

Ireland. His Ship was sent in search of {*?Thurot's*} squadron,[254] am extreamly thankfull to the Supreme *[Being]* for this ineffable satisfaction. Mr. Butcher here,[255] very Jocose he is, Mr. Tudor,[256] Mr. Chasemore here. Read *The British Magazine.*

Sunday, 16 March

At Church twice. Mrs. Tasker desires I wou'd mention to Sally Sheppard her affair with Drew Michell, ask if there is anything in his courting her, & dissuade her from giving him encouragement. I tell her it is a very nice point to interfere in, & I can't presume to give Sally advice. However, I go to her & say as much as is consistent with the very great love I have for her, she tells me she will not engage to him, then is it quite right my friend to give him the least hopes? But alas, such is the vanity of our sex, that we cannot help being pleas'd with a man's liking us, tho' we have not the least inclination for him.

Monday, 17 March

Miss Ellis here, she bespeaks a new silk gown, & I cut her out several things, very chatty.

Tuesday, 18 March

My father in company with Mr. Tredcroft, who tells him the Tradesmen's Daughters dress too much. Poor rancorous mortal, how I pity his disposition, & does the happiness of life consist in such trifling externals. Oh no, with how little regret cou'd I lay aside every gewgaw his envy carps at.

Wednesday, 19 March

I speak to my father in a jocose manner, he returns a very harsh answer. I weep excessively, I am not fit to live in this World, & encounter with the violent spirits in it, my disposition is too meek. Go to Dancing, stay till the Post comes in, but no letter from Miss Gittins.

Thursday, 20 March

Cast up the Cash Book & settle a great many accounts. Mr. Pigott comes to Dine with us, says perhaps he may yet have Miss Godfrey. I exclaim, "*oh how wavering are the Children of men*". Read *The British Magazine*, strange History of Sir Launcelot Gr*[eaves]*,[257] pretty eastern tale etc.

Friday, 21 March

Mama & Bett go to Slaugham for a visit to Mr. Bristed's. I read *The Monthly Review*, they find great faults & very few perfections in most performances; grant

---

254 See the footnote to the entry for 4 March.

255 Mr. Butcher was previously mentioned, on 18 July 1759, as of Hurstpierpoint.

256 This is the first time that Sarah has mentioned meeting Mr. Tudor, though her mother had divulged his "*secret history*" on 18 November 1759.

257 *The Life and Adventures of Sir Launcelot Greaves*, the story of a quixotic Englishman by Tobias Smollett (1721-1771), was published in instalments in his new venture, *The British Magazine*. It was published in book form by John Coote in 1762, but was not a success. Oliver Goldsmith was also a major contributor to *The British Magazine*, which was published until 1767.

all their remarks are just, it only shews, what all must be well acquainted with, that Human Nature is incapable of perfection.

Saturday, 22 March

My cousin Gattlan dines with us, gives me a pressing invitation to Pillsty. Mr. Shelley comes in & behaves as usual very rude. Sally Sheppard tells me Drew Michell has read my verses in *The Ladies' Magazine* & guess'd at the author, he much approves of them.

Sunday, 23 March

Take a morning's walk with Bet Cook. At Church twice. Mrs. Tasker & Sally Sheppard drink tea with me. Sally & I walk on the Causeway, a most delightfull & pleasant evening, much discourse on Religion, we are surpris'd there can be so astonishing a thing in the World as an Atheist. Read the second number of *The Bible*, which must give exquisite pleasure to every sincere Christian.

Monday, 24 March

Reflect on the thousand various perplexities incident to humanity. Mama & Bett come home, Mrs. Bristed with them. Read some of Horace's satires translated into prose by Dunster.[258] Find the World is but little alter'd since Horace's time. We are still proud, envious, covetous & ambitious. Am charm'd with his refin'd notions of friendship. Says we shou'd overlook & excuse to others all our friends' faults, how exactly conformable is this to my own sentiments.

Tuesday, 25 March

Mrs. Bristed relates a story of a very unhappy couple, had she mention'd a happy one, it might have been wonder'd at.

Wednesday, 26 March

From what latent cause can these disagreements in matrimony proceed, is it the aversion we have to confinement, or the perverseness of our natures that will not behave well because we have promis'd so to do? Much chat with Sally Sheppard & Drew Michell.

Thursday, 27 March

Another letter from Captain Smith, he was soon to leave Ireland & join Admiral Boscawen in Quiberon Bay, so probably it will be many months before I shall have the pleasure of seeing him. How kind he is to write *[at]* every opportunity. Spend the afternoon at Doctor Smith's, write to Captain Smith.

Friday, 28 March

Some chat with Sally Sheppard & Drew Michell, he is very assiduous in his visits there, what impression may make on my friend's Heart I cannot say. He is certainly a clever

---

258 Samuel Dunster's translation of Horace's *Satires, Epistles and Art of Poetry* was published in 1729.

young fellow. Walk to Dame Reynolds' with Sally & my Aunt Tasker, but her daughter is dead, & things bear now a very different aspect. Two fine little Boys left motherless.[259]

Saturday, 29 March

Go to Doctor Hutchinson's by my Aunt Smith's desire for a direction to Doctor Crewe, he asks me when I heard from Captain Smith. Did not expect such a question from him, I answer it truly, without hesitation.

Sunday, 30 March

Take a morning's walk with Bett Cook, cold but vastly pleasant. At Church twice. Walk at noon with Sally Sheppard in the Park,[260] *[the]* glorious Sun now sends forth an enlivening & not a scorching ray, everything begins to wear a Spring like appearance. Drink tea at Mrs. Wicker's with Mrs. Tredcroft & much company. A long dissertation on our neighbour's affairs, when oh when will scandal & envy cease.

Monday, 31 March

Walk in the Park after working all the morning. How calm, how sweetly serene is the air & sky. Yet my mind is agitated, fear for my beloved Harry rends my Heart with woes, but that supreme Being who with pitying eye beholds our frailties, will preserve him from all danger, or give me patience to support it.

APRIL 1760

Tuesday, 1 April

Walk with my friend Sally, much discourse on the unsatisfactory nature of Human enjoyments. Impute this partly to the perseverance of our dispositions & partly to its being impossible we shou'd find perfect happiness in this transitory life.

Wednesday, 2 April

Finish reading Dunster's translation of Horace, then read some of Pope's *Imitations*, which last appear to the former as the glorious sun to a little glimmering star, one chears, lights & warms all within its influence, the others twinkling, can only be discern'd when the brighter luminary is absent.

Thursday, 3 April

Some Quakers send word they will come & see us tomorrow, which is Good Friday, tho' their Religion does not enjoin the keeping it, I will not encourage the

---

259 The daughter of Dame Reynolds who died has not been identified, as she does not appear to have been married in Horsham, but it was most likely Elizabeth or Bethia. Their sisters Mary and Anne are both mentioned elsewhere in the diaries as unmarried, and Henrietta Maria, born in 1729, did not marry George Mannooch the grocer until 1762.

260 The "*Park*" was the park of Denne House, as later references to it make clear. It was on the top of Denne Hill, a popular promenade in the 18th century, with a view right over Horsham. There was no other park in Horsham at this time. A park at Hill's Place was laid out by "Capability" Browne, but not until 1768. The present Horsham Park did not exist then – the land attached to Park House was still meadowland and fields, in various ownerships.

profanation.[261] Walk with my Dear Sally Sheppard, old Mr. Shelley enquires after me by the name of Mrs. Smith, I suppose to inform me that my Dear Harry did not sail from Cork till the 20 of last month.

Friday, 4 April

Taken with a violent sore throat, stiff neck & sick fits, how soon is this frail Body put out of order, unable to go to Church. Read my *Grand Magazine*, fine translation of Voltaire's *Henriade*, queer Oriental tale.

Saturday, 5 April

Quite ill all day, the Quakers drink tea here, the company of people I am not intimately acquainted with is by no means agreeable, common topicks of conversation are soon exhausted, & till we know a person's disposition, how can we enter into any other?

Sunday, 6 April

Dream that my Harry is wounded & bleeds much, Heaven forbid an Illusion of this shocking sort shou'd ever be realis'd. Not well enough to go to Church, so have lost two excellent discourses on our Saviour's Death & resurrection, which I very much regret. Walk up to Mrs. Bridger's, but am taken worse with my throat & oblig'd to come home. No letter from Miss Gittins.

Monday, 7 April

In violent pain all day, but think I ought to bear it with patience, as thank Heaven, it is but seldom I am afflicted. Drink tea with Bett Cook, Miss Skinner there, a most beautifull girl, there is something irresistably engaging in a pretty face. I cannot wonder the men are so soon struck with it. External Beauty wou'd certainly be a very great blessing, were it not too often attended by self sufficiency & affectation.

Tuesday, 8 April

Walk over to Dales & drink tea with several girls.[262] We are very chatty till surprised by fighting in the next room, how dreadfull are these scenes of low life, oh may I never be an unfortunate spectator of them.

Wednesday, 9 April

Read my *Grand Magazine*, very pretty essay on the employment of women, droll reflections on the different proposals for a Peace. Mrs. Bridger drinks tea & spends the evening with us. Play at cards.

Thursday, 10 April

Go & help *[with]* Mrs. Tasker's quilt, her Husband rails at my father & affronts

---

261 In the 18th century, Quakers were generally much respected for their integrity and high moral principles, but they were disliked in clerical circles because they refused to pay tithes or other rates for the maintenance of the established Church, and their mode of dress and speech was regarded as quaint. Sarah seems to have shared these prejudices, probably because so many of her close friends were clerics. The Quakers in question were probably the family of George Holmes — see the entry for 22 March 1759.

262 At Warnham Mill.

me. I quit the House in disgust, she sends Mrs. Wicker to me & begs I wou'd return that he may beg my pardon. I forgive without hesitation, indeed I think there is ten thousand times greater pleasure in forgiving than of revenging an injury.

Friday, 11 April

Read *The Ladies' Magazine*, some Just reflections on female education. At Mrs. Wicker's with Mrs. Bridger, play at cards. How is this murdering a fine day & how far superior is the pleasure to walk about & admire the beauties of Nature which at this delightfull Season shine with peculiar Lustre.

Saturday, 12 April

Am vastly surpris'd that I have no letter from Miss Gittins, nor Mrs. Jones. I hope t'is no reason but their Idleness. Begin reading *The Life of Sir Philip Sidney*, wrote about 100 years ago, but so obsolete the stile that I shou'd have thought it had been a thousand.[263] If this is a specimen of the writing in Elizabeth's Reign, how much are we polish'd in this last Century.

Sunday, 13 April

At Church, the Doctor makes an excellent Sermon as usual. Walk in the Park twice, then on the Causeway with Sally Sheppard, Bill White joins us. Cannot say this young gentleman's conversation is very engaging, tho' I don't know that superior understanding is much to be coveted.

Monday, 14 April

Go to help my Aunt Tasker finish her quilt. Mrs. Wicker there, who entertains us with many scandalous things said by Mrs. Tredcroft & Miss Bet Reynolds[264] of their neighbours. Sure it is better to live in a Desert, remote from every human creature, than in society with these worst of savages, these murderers of reputations.

Tuesday, 15 April

Finish reading *The Life of Sir Philip Sidney*, the stile rather better, fine character of Queen Elizabeth, mentions all her virtues but not one of her faults. Drink tea at Mrs. Wicker's with the Miss Ellis's. Walk on the Causeway with Sally Sheppard.

Wednesday, 16 April

Extreamly busy in the shop with various sorts of customers & work, business is certainly the finest thing in the world for depressed spirits. Spend the evening at Mr. Tredcroft's, he out of temper with his wife, oh how disagreeable are these matrimonial bickerings, pray Heaven keep me single if these animosities are unavoidable in a married state.

---

263 This must be *The Life of Sir Philip Sidney*, published in 1652, by his friend Fulke Greville, Lord Brooke (1554-1628). Greville is generally regarded as one of the most extraordinary men of his age, who excelled as poet, courtier, soldier and judge.

264 Probably Miss Elizabeth Reynell – see entry for 18 February 1761.

Thursday, 17 April

Work all day as usual. At night in *The British Magazine* some affecting circumstances relative to General Wolfe. Oh ye powers, protect my dearest Harry amid the dangers the duties of his profession oblige him to encounter.

Friday, 18 April

Mr. Nathaniel Tredcroft dines with us, & Miss[265] drinks tea here. Work all day as usual. Read *The British Magazine*, some fine thoughts on the spring express'd in a very pretty manner, character of the Marquis of Granby. No letters yet, oh suspence, thou racking dreadfull situation.

Saturday, 19 April

Work on my apron, when I wonder will this stupendous piece of work be finish'd. Walk in the Park with my Sally Sheppard, tell her I fancy the poor Merchant's House will be let, if he does not recover. She says it wou'd be a sweet habitation for my Harry & me, but alas I fear such happiness will never be my lot.

Sunday, 20 April

At Church twice. A London tradesman dines with us, he may know his business, but I'm sure he knows nothing else. Walk in the Park. Sir Charles joins us, he utters several very indecent expressions to Bett Cook, whatever opinion he entertains of the Sex, I think he shou'd be a little more reserv'd before those who have at least preserv'd the reputation of modesty.

Monday, 21 April

Extreamly busy all day. Sally Sheppard engag'd which deprives me of my evening's walk, this delightfull weather t'is a great mortification. A letter from Mrs. Jones, my brother is well thank Heaven, but what can be the reason of my dear Gittins' long silence.

Tuesday, 22 April

Read *The Monthly Review*, they commend Langhorne's Poem on Job.[266] Drink tea with Sally Sheppard. We walk in the Park with Bett Cook, a great deal of serious discourse. She is a sensible girl, pity she rattles quite so much. Dispute with Papa, wish his temper was a little more agreeable, or mine a little more abject & submissive.

Wednesday, 23 April

Mama taken very ill, Heaven prevent her being so long, for our loss wou'd be dreadfull indeed. A letter from my amiable friend Miss Gittins, she has been extreamly ill, poor dear girl, but is better & has had a visit from her lover, Mr. Turnpenny, may he be faithfull & deserve her affection. Mr. Gittins too is recover'd.

---

265 Presumably Phoebe Tredcroft, Edward's eldest daughter.
266 William Langhorne (1721-1772) was the author of *Job*, a poem in three books, published in 1760.

Thursday, 24 April

Mama better, thanks to the Supreme Being. Sup at Mrs. Tredcroft's, fall into her way of chat, to animadvert on all our neighbours. All the family are now at rest. Where oh where is my dearest Harry.

Friday, 25 April

Mama continues pretty well. Make a visit at Tanbridge with Mrs. Wicker, Miss Ellis declares Mr. Shelley never courted her. We talk a great deal on poor Miss Hutchinson, that was. I sincerely pity her, without a home & all the comforts a settled situation brings, oh these indiscreet marriages, better sure to pine (if we must pine) in a single state, than make a family unhappy by our imprudence.

Saturday, 26 April

Mr. John Shelley here, rattles strangely. A note from Mr. Pigott. Write to Mrs. Jones, & acquaint her I hope to be at Marlow on the 10th of May, to see her & fetch my brother home.

Sunday, 27 April

A letter from Mr. Chasemore at Cuckfield, with ten guineas to pay for his son's schooling, who I am to bring home with my brother. I write an answer. Drink tea at Mrs. Tredcroft's. A very unpleasant day, wind extreamly high. A great deal of conversation with my father & mother about my affair with Captain Smith. I tell them I will never marry unless he is kept in full pay.

Monday, 28 April

My father seems not to approve entirely of my marrying but why, is it because I carry on all his business & he wou'd find it difficult to do without me? I will if possible perform my duty, but must not regard his interest when it stands in competition with my own happiness, that wou'd be too great a sacrifice.

Tuesday, 29 April

Am told Miss Gittins is shortly to be married to a gentleman, immensely rich, they mean Mr. Turnpenny I suppose, pray Heaven it may be soon, the dear girl will then have some defence from the envenom'd tongue of slander.

Wednesday, 30 April

Very busy preparing for my journey, make a great dependance on my Marlow visit, hope nothing will happen to take of[f] the pleasure. Wish I cou'd hear from my dear Harry before I go. Read the *Gentleman's Magazine*, Lord George Sackville's trial in it, poor unfortunate man. How slippery a path is that of greatness, yet there is few mortals — so enchanting is superiority — but wou'd run the hazard of falling if they cou'd gain the tow'ring heights.[267]

---

267   Lord George Sackville was dismissed from the army for not obeying orders to charge at the Battle of Minden in 1759 (see entry on 13 October 1759), but this was not the end of his career. He was appointed Secretary for the American Colonies and the Board of Trade in 1775, and created Viscount Sackville in 1782.

MAY 1760

Thursday, 1 May

Mr. Pigott here, he gives me a letter of recommendation to a gentleman of Oxford, that he may shew me all its curiosities if I go.[268]

Friday, 2 May

Make a morning visit at Mrs. Cheynell's, what a sweet place is her house & gardens, sure there is nothing fills the mind with so much pleasure as a spot thus elegantly cultivated.[269] Drink tea at Mrs. Bridger's, walk down to Lord Irwin's with Sally Sheppard.

Saturday, 3 May

Very busy all day taking orders & preparing for my journey. Doing business for fathers is attended with very great perplexity, did I carry it on for myself shou'd then be certain what wou'd please, but wisdom consists in being contented with our situation. Miss Bristed comes to bid me farewell.

Sunday, 4 May

Miss Bristed stays all night, she is tolerably merry. Take my leave of my grandmother, then walk in the Park with Sally Sheppard. Sir Charles Eversfield joins us, we enter into a great chat, he makes a joke of our friendship & says t'is all a farce. We endeavour to convince him of its reality, & tell him he has too bad an opinion of the World. He gives us the House on the Hill to live in when we are old maids.[270]

Monday, 5 May

Come to London in the Horsham Stage. Breakfast at Dorking with Mrs. Turner, give her the handkerchief I had worked for her, she highly approves of it. Find all my friends well. My Uncle Bob & my Aunt Sally call to see us at my Aunt Smith's, where I have fix'd my residence.

Tuesday, 6 May

Go & do my business at the Hosier's, dine there. Excessive dirty walking, but these are trifling inconveniences compar'd to what I shou'd suffer if oblig'd to live long in this suffocating place. Go to the Linnen Draper's & do part of my business, call at the Haberdasher's.

Wednesday, 7 May

Do a great deal of business at the Linnen Draper's, dine there. Pay the Haberdasher's,

---

268 This suggests that Mr. Pigott had been a student at Oxford.

269 Mrs. Elizabeth Cheynell was the elder sister of Thomas Waller, who married George Cheynell in Slaugham in 1739. He died in 1747. She occupied a house in North Street, owned by Catherine Lintott, grand-daughter of Bernard Lintott or Lintot, the London printer who published the work of Alexander Pope, and inherited the estates of the Lintotts of Southwater.

270 Presumably the cottage in Denne Park, mentioned earlier.

& buy a black hatt for Miss Bristed. Write a long letter to my father & give an account of all the business I have done, which I hope will prove satisfactory.

Thursday, 8 May

Walk two mile & take our places in the Marlow Stage. Go to the Silk mercer's, pay my Bill & buy myself a gown, cost me £8. Once in 5 year I think a silk gown is not very extravagant. Have the very great pleasure to see in the news that the *Orford*, my Dear Harry's ship, has taken two prizes.

Friday, 9 May

Do my business at the Silk mercer's, & finish at the Haberdasher's, dine there. Jack Smith sends Mrs. Wicker 2 Box tickets for the play, she returns them because I was not at home. I blame her for it.

Saturday, 10 May

Taken extreamly ill, no sleep all night, a violent feaver, yet will not defer my journey to Marlow. Unable to sit upright in the Coach, how uncertain are all the affairs of poor mortals & how wrong it is to [?] dependance as I have done on this journey.

Sunday, 11 May

Find Mr. & Mrs. Jones & my dear brother all well, but cannot take that pleasure I shou'd do in their company if I was well. Keep my Bed till noon, bad cough & sore throat, no possibility of going to Oxford, which is a very great disappointment, but alas we must not call these trifles evils, my disorder is worse, & I shou'd think it much worse if my dear friends knew it.

Monday, 12 May

Continue very ill, send for a Doctor who gives me some medicines, & much advice. Better & take a walk round this sweet place. Marlow is situated in a most delightfull spot, Woods, Water, enamell'd meads, conspire to render it truly beautifull.

Tuesday, 13 May

Much better, take a walk to Byssum Church, & see Sir Thomas Hobey's[271] [monument], has been erected near 200 years, an Epitaph in verse. The Abbey of Byssum was given to King Harry the 8th as a portion to Queen Elizabeth. Ride to Harlifield, a very pretty new-built Seat of Mr. Clayton's, pleasantly situated on the Banks of the Thames.[272]

Wednesday, 14 May

Go to Windsor with Mrs. Wicker & Mrs. Jones in a Post Chariot. See Eaton *(sic)* College, the Castle, the Duke's Lodge & every thing worth notice, but do not daringly attempt to describe the beauties of this magnificent place.

---

271 There are actually two Hoby tombs in Bisham church - the two brothers, Sir Philip (d. 1558) and Sir Thomas (d. 1566) lie side by side, semi-reclining, and their wives are also commemorated by other memorials in the south chapel.

272 Harleyford House, a red-brick 18th century house near Marlow, in a beautiful park.

Thursday, 15 May

Breakfast & dine at Mr. Heather's at the school. Go to Church, walk in the Church Yard which overlooks the Thames & is vastly pleasant. Drink tea at an acquaintance of Mrs. Jones. My cough continues extreamly bad, fear it will settle on my lungs.

Friday, 16 May

Return to London with my brother, whose joy at going home is inexpressive. A most terrible dusty journey, but thank Heavens am better than when I went down. Have the very great pleasure to find on my arrival a letter from my dearest Harry, answer it directly. Captain Smith is afraid he can't see me before the latter end of the Summer, t'is a long long time.

Saturday, 17 May

Go & shew my brother the Waxwork[273] who is highly delighted with it. Finish all my business & I hope shall find a great deal of custom when I get home.

Sunday, 18 May

At Church in the morning. Walk & call on Mrs. Laight who is gone to Horsham. Show my brother Westminster Abbey & St. Margaret's Church, where is a fine painted Window. Walk thro' the Park,[274] very little company, windy unpleasant weather. Drink tea at my Uncle Bob's, a vast deal of chat on various subjects. Wou'd to Heaven I was out of this fatiguing place.

Monday, 19 May

Take my leave of all my acquaintance & prepare to return home with a glad heart. Mrs. Smith knows the family of Mr. Turnpenny, my dear Gittins' lover, very well. She says he has a very large fortune & that Miss Gittins will be lucky.

Tuesday, 20 May

Bid once more adieu to London. A Woman in the Stage Coach talks incessantly, how disagreeable is this loquacious disposition to people who are more inclin'd to think than communicate their thoughts, nay great talkers themselves dislike those of the same turn, considering them as rivals in endeavouring to engross the conversation.

Wednesday, 21 May

My father & mother receive my brother with great joy, indeed how can they look on such a charming child without the utmost pleasure. Extreamly busy in the shop.

Thursday, 22 May

Doctor Smith bleeds me for my cough, says my blood is very much enflam'd. Go & see a box open'd which was left by my grandmother Tasker seven year ago with

273   James Boswell recorded in his *London Journal* that he visited *"Mrs. Salmon's famous waxwork in Fleet Street"* on 4 July 1763, and said it was *"excellent of its kind, and amused me very well for a quarter of an hour"*

274   Probably St. James' Park, which was a fashionable place to walk in London.

orders that it shou'd not be open'd till so long after her death.[275] It contain'd £100 which was given to my Uncle Tasker & Mrs. Grace. My mother & Aunt Waller are dissatisfied & think as she had no right to make a will, it ought to be equally divided. I am of the same opinion, sure it was an odd whim.

Friday, 23 May

The Misses Ellis's here, look over all my goods & buy some.

Saturday, 24 May

Terrible bad still with my cough. Will not write to Captain Smith till I can tell him I am better. Drink tea at Mrs. Wicker's with Mrs. Laight & Sally Sheppard. Walk in the Park, fine weather, how delightfully pleasant does the whole face of Nature appear.

Sunday, 25 May

At Church twice. Walk in the Park with Sally Sheppard, Sir Charles joins *[us]*. We go into Denne House, he lends us the *Trial of Lord Ferrers* & the *History of Tristram Shandy.* Exclaims against matrimony in the bitterest terms, I defend it, he wishes to make a convert of me but Heaven forbid I shou'd adopt such libertine principles, he says no wise man wou'd marry.

Monday, 26 May

Read the trial of the unhappy Earl Ferrers, misled by passion to commit a crime *[that]* shocks humanity.[276] Read the first volume of *Tristram Shandy*, cannot say I understand it but what I do comprehend seems a heap of absurdity & impudence.[277]

Tuesday, 27 May

Very busy at work, far from well. A cloud of melancholy seems to hang over my mind, wish to see my dear Harry, sure he will not prove unfaithfull but a desponding mind fears every thing. Read the second volume of *Tristram Shandy*, a good sermon in it.

---

275 Sarah's late grandmother, Anne Tasker, née Middleton, came from a gentry family who owned Whitesbridge Farm. Sarah's remark that *"she had no right to make a will"* seems strange, but probably most of the property she inherited was settled on her husband, and then on her children, at the time of her marriage. She appears to have shown favouritism towards her only son and youngest daughter in this gift, but it may have been to compensate for the fact that her mother, Susannah Middleton, only left legacies to her three older grandchildren - Ann, Mary and Elizabeth - since Prudence and Ellman were not born when she made her will in 1727.

276 This was probably a pamphlet entitled *The Trial of Lawrence Earl Ferrers, for the murder of John Johnson*, by – Law, which must have been very recently published, as the trial had only taken place in the House of Lords on 16 April 1760 (John Baker, the other Horsham diarist, attended it). It was a sensational case, as Lord Ferrers tried to escape punishment for the murder of his steward by pleading insanity. He was executed on 5 May, in front of a vast crowd. He was the first nobleman in 200 years to be hanged at Tyburn, rather than beheaded.

277 This was also a very new publication. The Rev. Lawrence Sterne (1713-1768), Prebendary of York and Vicar of Sutton in the Forest, published the first two (of an eventual nine) volumes of *The Life and Opinions of Tristram Shandy, Gentleman*, in 1760, a richly comic novel written in very idiosyncratic style. Sterne wrote it while struggling against tuberculosis and an unhappy marriage, but it was an instant success, making him famous and much sought after by London society.

Wednesday, 28 May

Mr. Pigott sends for me, he is very ill. I walk over & spend the Day with him, tho' far from well myself. He is extreamly low spirited. I return home very much fatigued.

Thursday, 29 May

Write to Captain Smith. Taken very ill with a violent feaver.

[No further entries until 11 June, because of Sarah's illness].

JUNE 1760

Wednesday, 11 June

How shall I fill up this Chasm in my Book. The time Heaven knows was spent in excessive pain & misery, it shall then remain Blank to remind me of the Allmighty's mercy in raising me from the Bed of sickness. A letter from my Harry.

Thursday, 12 June

Go down stairs & take an airing in a Post Chaise with my Mama & brother. How agreeable everything appears after such a long & painfull confinement. Walk a little but am soon tir'd, try to work but my Eyes are dim & my head aches. In pain in all my joints, Rheumatism.

Friday, 13 June

Poor "Merchant" Smith is here, quite out of his senses. Mrs. Wicker & I intend taking a Walk. Mrs. Smith calls to us & desire we wou'd go down her garden, we comply, not thinking the "Merchant" was at home, but he soon appears & frights us terribly tho' without any reason, for he behav'd very well, so I fancy he either did not know me or has forgot my connexion with his brother, the Captain, which us'd to agitate him so violently. Heaven restore his senses.

Saturday, 14 June

Ride out on horseback, exercise the Doctor says is the only thing for me.

Sunday, 15 June

At Church twice, but very ill & full of pain in my joints. Walk up to Abel Marsh, a gardener's, & see a Sun Dial made with greens, a great curiosity.[278] Mrs. Tredcroft sends for me to go out in the Chariot. I accept the invitation & we have a pleasant ride in the Forest.[279] A letter from my friend Miss Gittins, she has heard I was ill. A letter from Mrs. Masterman.

Monday, 16 June

Something better but cannot recover my looks, extreamly pale & thin. I hope the

278   Abel Marsh lived in East Street, in a property called Grey's.
279   St. Leonard's Forest, on the east side of Horsham.

alteration in my person if I shou'd not recover my bloom will not estrange my Harry's affections, then indeed I shou'd be miserable. Ride out.

Tuesday, 17 June

Doctor Smith bleeds me for the fourth time, says my blood is not quite so bad as it was, thank Heavens. Hope the Allmighty will hear my prayers & deliver me from my pain. Walk out a little way. Unable to hold it far. Write to Miss Gittins.

Wednesday, 18 June

Dream of my Dear Smith, how I wish yet fear to see him for I dread the shock he must feel on his unhappy brother's account. Purpose going to Slaugham but prevented by the weather, these are trifling disappointments & cannot affect me.

Thursday, 19 June

Wett weather, cannot ride out, tolerably well, thank God, for what I have been. Papa proposes a journey to East Bourn when I am perfectly recovered but fancy t'is only talk. I can never be gratefull enough for the care & tenderness of my friends during my illness.

Friday, 20 June

Papa & brother go to Cuckfield. I am sent for but cannot go because t'is bad weather. Call at Mrs. Luttman's for the first time since my illness. Hear she still behaves in a very ridiculous manner to Drew Michell, foolish Woman.

Saturday, 21 June

Thank God, am much better. Work all day. Walk down to Mrs. Wicker's, who is very busy fitting up her house which she has bought of my Uncle Tasker.[280] Mr. & Miss Bristed come & drink tea. I intend going home with them but Doctor Smith says t'is not proper I shou'd be out in the evening, till the East is dryer & ceases to exhale such noxious vapours.

Sunday, 22 June

Bad weather, cannot go to Church, read *The Monthly Review*, the/y/ condemn *Tristram Shandy* which please/s/ me extreamly as it entirely corresponds with my own sentiments. They commend Sterne's *Sermons* but condemn the method of publication.[281]

---

280 This house (now 17, The Causeway) was bought by Mrs. Wicker's father, William Tasker, and inherited by her brother Ellman, who probably preferred to live in Market Square, where he had his tallow-chandler's business. The Land Tax records show that Ellman retained the orchard behind the house for his own use.

281 By *"condemn the method of publication"* Sarah is presumably referring to the fact that two volumes of the Rev. Lawrence Sterne's sermons were published in 1760, under the title *The Sermons of Yorick*, (a character from *Tristram Shandy*), although a second title-page gave the real name of the author. Sterne said in the preface *"the first will serve the bookseller's purpose as Yorick's name is possibly of the two the more known; — and the second will ease the minds of those who see a jest, and the danger which lurks under it, where no jest was meant"*. Sterne thus cashed in on the success of *Tristram Shandy*, but in fact the sermons, which were quite conventional, in both style and substance, actually sold better during his lifetime than the novel for which he is now chiefly remembered.

Monday, 23 June

Very busy at work, yet quite ill. When oh when thou supream disposer of all things shall I recover my health, but let me not be impatient. Go to Mrs. Bridger's, drink tea & spend the evening. Play at cards. How we trifle away that precious thing call'd time, tho' t'is better spent in trifles than in vice.

Tuesday, 24 June

Read Lord Orrery's *Remarks on the Life & Writings of Dean Swift*.[282] Exceeding smart & sensible observations. A violent pain in my Breast, sure my little feeble Body can never conquer all this illness.

Wednesday, 25 June

Doctor Smith says Lord Orrery wrote in too studied a manner, but I think when a person chuses a subject & confines himself to that in his letters, t'is quite different from the common *epistolata* writing. Ride out. A most affectionate letter from my Dear Harry, in answer to that I wrote him from London. He expresses great concern for my illness.

Thursday, 26 June

Am bleeded again, my blood continues very bad. Terrible bad weather, cannot ride out & nothing else will, they say, recover my health. Work a little on my Apron.

Friday, 27 June

Begin taking the Bark.[283] Doctor Smith thinks nothing else will carry of[f] my feaver. Mrs. James sees my Apron & prodigiously admires it. Ride out a little way. Read some more of Lord Orrery's remarks, like them better the more I peruse of them. There is a Character of all the Authors that flourish'd in Swift's time.

Saturday, 28 June

Much better. Work all day on my apron. Take a walk in the evening with my friend Sally Sheppard, read Captain Smith's letter to her. Write to him with the greatest affection, tell him I am not quite recover'd. Read *The Royal Magazine*, pretty tale on the incapacity of riches to procure happiness.

Sunday, 29 June

Bad weather, talk of riding out only am disappointed. Write to Mrs. Jones, make my illness an excuse for not writing before. Mr. Chasemore brings his son to go to school again with my brother. Bob feigns himself ill because he dislikes going, oh the art of these little creatures.

---

282   John Boyle, 5th Earl of Orrery (1707-1762) was an intimate friend of Alexander Pope, Swift and Dr. Johnson. His *Remarks on the Life and Writings of Dr. Jonathan Swift* were written in a series of letters to his son, and published in 1751.

283   The bark to which Sarah refers was quinine, derived from the bark of the cinchona tree and used as a febrifuge and tonic in the 18th century, for many types of fever. It was sometimes called Peruvian or Jesuits' bark, because it had been brought back to Europe by Jesuit missionaries from Latin America, and found to be the most efficacious remedy for fever then known.

Monday, 30 June

Ride out in the Forest, most delightfully pleasant. Hope my health will soon be reestablish'd that I may apply myself closer to business than I have lately done. Mrs. Bridger here, we play at cards.

JULY 1760

Tuesday, 1 July

Ride to Mrs. Bristed's at Slaugham. They are very glad to see me, & desire I wou'd stay some days. Tell them t'is inconvenient at present, but promise to go again in a short time. A charming pleasant ride home, they accompany me.

Wednesday, 2 July

Very busy in the shop all the morning. Ride to the Hammer Pond[284] in the afternoon, with Sally Sheppard & her brother Stringer. We drink tea there & then ramble about the Forest, such excursions as these are vastly agreeable at this delightfull season.

Thursday, 3 July

Talk of going to meet my father but cannot get a horse for the Day. Sally Sheppard & I go down to Mrs. Wicker's, stay there all the evening. Walk in the garden, vastly pleasant. Finish reading Lord Orrery's remarks on the *Life & Writings of Dean Swift*.

Friday, 4 July

It will be more than 2 long months before I shall see my Dear Harry, but I must, I must & will be patient. Walk up in the Park with Sally Sheppard. Meet Sir Charles who invites us into the garden to eat some cherries. We accept his invitation.

Saturday, 5 July

Sir Charles says there is no such thing as sincere love or real friendship in the World. For a man who has reach'd the age of fifty to say this is shocking, how deprav'd must he think Human nature, since disinterested love & friendship are certainly the two greatest virtues we can boast.

Sunday, 6 July

Our maid, who is gone away ill, I hear is like to die, poor creature. My loss in this truly affectionate girl will be great, happiness I hope will be her lot, here she is friendless & destitute of a home, but when admitted into the blissfull mansions, she

---

284   The Hammer Ponds are a feature of St. Leonard's Forest, and were originally created by the iron-works, which existed there in the 16th and 17th century. The large hammer-forges required water to provide energy, so the ponds were generally sited by a stream, which was then dug out to provide sufficient power to turn the wheel that worked the great hammer. The ironworks were sited in woodland because it provided charcoal to heat the furnaces. When the forges closed down, the ponds remained, and now add much to the beauty of the landscape.

will no doubt be assign'd a place equal to those who now have Palaces to reside in & the World are *[illegible]*.

Monday, 7 July

Read *The Happy Orphan*, a very pretty elegant Novel wrote with the uttmost decency & delicacy, inculcating a fine moral, but by some National strokes I cannot think it was translated from the French as the letter page mentions, I wou'd upon the whole recommend it to the perusal of both sexes, tho' I must confess the expressions of the lovers are rather too enthusiastic.

Tuesday, 8 July

Ride to meet my Aunt Sally & cousin Bett Smith who come to make some stay at Horsham. I drink tea with them, afterwards walk in the Park.

Wednesday, 9 July

Very busy at work, but interrupted by my cousin Bett. She & my Aunt drink tea with us. The conversation turns, I can't tell how, upon thieving, my Aunt Sally said some people cannot help it. Ha ha ha, was ever any Body born of a thievish constitution, how absurd are such notions.

Thursday, 10 July

Drink tea at my grandmother's with my Aunt & cousin. Walk in the Park, a most delightfull evening. Write a letter full of tenderness to my Harry, how I wish to see him out of danger from murderous Cannon & the inconstant Sea.

Friday, 11 July

Work all the morning. Drink tea at Mrs. Wicker's. Walk out, drink a Sillibub[285] at Mrs. Tasker's. Walk on the Causeway with Sally Sheppard, a vast deal of serious chat respecting our future lot.

Saturday, 12 July

No letters, neither from Captain Smith nor Miss Gittins. Excessive low spirited & ill, the mind & Body naturally affect each other, so I am doubly unhappy in having a bad constitution & a dull phlegmatic disposition, for they are seldom both right.

Sunday, 13 July

At Church twice, I wou'd if possible attend my duty, but alas my thoughts are too often wander'd, Heaven forgive me. Dine at Mrs. Wicker's. Go with Bett Cook & Sally Sheppard to drink a Sillibub at Den, how delightfully pleasant is the Park, I allmost wish I was possess'd of enough to satisfie the wants of Nature (which are but very few). I wou'd then bid adieu to the World & all its tiresome bustle.

Monday, 14 July

A letter from my dear Harry. Ride out a little way, my Aunt Sally & cousin dine with us. Walk with Sally Sheppard in the evening.

---

285   A syllabub was generally made from fresh milk and wine whisked together.

Tuesday, 15 July

Work on my Apron. Busy putting goods to rights in the shop. Drink tea at my Aunt Sally's with Mrs. Bridger. Play at cards, how little does the heart enter into those parties, & how insipid is the company of those we have little regard for.

Wednesday, 16 July

Read *The British Magazine*, among several good things a description of the ?Sinian [?*Sheldonian*] with a beautiful copper plate view of it. Drink tea at Miss Orlton's, walk in the evening with Bett Cook & Sally Sheppard.

Thursday, 17 July

Write some long Bills. Walk over to see Mr. Nathaniel Tredcroft with Mrs. Wicker, my Aunt Sally & cousin Bett Smith. Write to Mrs. Jones & my brother, read the latter to Mr. Tredcroft who laughingly approves.

Friday, 18 July

Fair day, quite sick with the fatiguing noise & hurry of it. Much company at Dinner. Mr., Mrs. & Miss Bristed come to Horsham. I return with them to Slaugham in hope the Forest air will recover my Health. We are in danger of being thrown from our Horses, they are more frighted than I who I thank Heaven have rather more courage than my Whimsical Sex.

Saturday, 19 July

Ride to see a young gentleman at two miles distance, his name Grainger, the son of a Pawn broker in London, had been very wild in his earlier days, & been sent to Sea, seems perfectly good natur'd & perfectly ignorant, a character far from guilt & ought [*not*] (as it too frequently is) to be treated with contempt, for t'is certain possible that a person may have a good Heart & an indifferent understanding.

Sunday, 20 July

Dine at Mr. Chasemore's at Cuckfield, drink Sillibub with Mr. Grainger.

Monday, 21 July

Walk out with Miss Bristed, extreamly pleasant. Every thing in Nature wears an agreeable aspect. Mr. Grainger goes to Horsham & brings me a letter from Miss Gittins, she disapproves of the obscene *Tristram Shandy*, how pleased I am. Sends me a very pretty poem entitled *Edwin & Emma*.

Tuesday, 22 July

Ride out with Mr. Bristed, how obliging is this truly good man. Meet my father, Aunt Sally & cousin Bett Smith with Mrs. Wicker, who all come over to see me. They stay & drink tea.

Wednesday, 23 July

Mrs. Chasemore of Cuckfield calls me to attend her to Horsham, take my leave of Mr. Bristed's family with the most gratefull thanks for their kind hospitable behaviour. A very cold ride over the Forest, find all my friends well. Go to the Puppet Show.[286]

Thursday, 24 July

Do some work for Mrs. Chasemore. Spend the day with a very large company at North Heath with Mr. Natt Tredcroft. He gives us a most elegant dinner, play at cards & dance, return home in Mr. Tredcroft's Chariot, laugh heartily at our seeing the Puppet show, (what a trifle diverts when the mind is at ease, but alas when in pain no amusement can please).

Friday, 25 July

Dine at Mr. Tredcroft's, talk of riding out in the Forest, but it was a wet afternoon so we play at cards all the afternoon.

Saturday, 26 July

Another disagreeable noisy fair day, quite ill with a violent pain in my breast, low spirited to the last degree. Mr. Grainger calls, I chat to him a little, but alas, my efforts are in vain. The two Miss Ellis's here. Mrs. Chasemore returns home.

Sunday, 27 July

At Church twice, a fine Sermon by Doctor Hutchinson. Walk in the Croft with Sally Sheppard, & Sally Hunt. Mama, Aunt Sally & Mrs. Wicker all ride in the Forest with Mr. Tredcroft's family. I go with Sally Sheppard to Bet Cook to drink a Sillibub, then walk in the Park. Meet Sir Charles who treats us with Apricocks, & chat on various subjects.

Monday, 28 July

Ride with my cousin Bett Smith & my two sisters in the Stage Coach [with] my Aunt Sally going as far as Warnham. Breakfast at Mrs. Parr's, who treats us with great good nature & hospitality.[287] Walk home about noon.

Tuesday, 29 July

Quite lame & in violent pain. Mr Tudor, Mr. Tredcroft & Doctor Smith dines with us & stay all afternoon. Old Mr. Shelley makes me a present of some Apricocks, as he does to Sally Sheppard, this shows good nature in distributing them to people who have no gardens.

Wednesday, 30 July

Very ill all day, yet work very hard. Walk out in the evening. Sally Sheppard & Bett Cook sup with us. A letter from Captain Smith who is arrived at Plymouth, very

286   The puppet show was probably staged in the Market House, like the plays put on by the strolling players. These occasional shows were likely to be well supported as they provided some entertainment for the townsfolk.

287   Though in the text this is written as *"Mrs Pary"*, it seems certain from the context that this reference is to Mrs. Anne Parr, the sister of *"old"* Mr. (Timothy) Shelley and mother of John Miller's wife. Little is known of her second husband, John Parr, except that he was a widower, but it has been suggested that he was related to Ellen Parr of Kempes in Ireland, who married Roger Bysshe of Fen Place, and was the grandmother of Timothy and Anne Shelley.

much concerned that it was not Portsmouth as then I shou'd have met him.

Thursday, 31 July

Work all day in good spirits, whether occasion'd by my better health or hearing from my Harry I cannot tell. Write to him & desire he wou'd not come to Horsham, alas what a piece of self denial is this, for I excessively wish to see him, but alas what uneasiness must he feel to see his poor unhappy brother, in such a deplorable way, I wou'd not for any gratification to myself give him so much to bear *[last word crossed out]*.

AUGUST 1760

Friday, 1 August

Dine & drink tea with my cousin Bet Smith, sup & play at cards at Mrs. Wicker's.

Saturday, 2 August

Tell Sally Sheppard I have wrote word to Captain Smith he shou'd not come to Horsham, they approve my conduct. There is certainly a very great satisfaction in being applauded for what we *[do]* by those whose judgements we have a good opinion of, it adds to the pleasure which we feel in the approbation of our own minds.

Sunday, 3 August

My Uncle Bob comes down, says my Aunt Sally talks of my meeting her in Surrey. At Church twice, receive the Sacrament. Drink tea at Mrs. Wicker's. Walk in the Park with my cousin Bett, Sally Sheppard, Bett Cook & Sir Charles. He is very complaisant & agreeable.

Monday, 4 August

Work all day tho' we are in a hurry & bustle. The Assizes beginning, two Sea Turtles are sent by the Duke of Newcastle for the Sheriff & Judge, go & see them.[288] How stupendous are thy works, oh Allmighty, in all thy manifest works.

Tuesday, 5 August

Mr. Cox & another young Counsellor lodge with us, go to Church. Doctor Hutchinson preaches. A Ball at night. Sir Cecil Bishop[289] compliments me with being

---

288 Holles Pelham, Duke of Newcastle, was First Lord of the Treasury (Prime Minister) in 1760. He had his political base in Sussex and needed the support of the Sussex gentry who had the right to vote in Parliamentary elections. Presumably the turtles were sent for a *"turtle dinner"*, for the Sheriff and Judges, and all the Sussex gentlemen who attended the Assizes. William Verrall of the *White Hart* at Lewes (formerly the town house of the Duke of Newcastle's family and at this time housing a club which served his interests) published a cookery book in 1759 which gave detailed instructions for dissecting, preparing and dressing a turtle with three different sauces.

289 Sir Cecil Bishopp, 6th Bt. of Parham, M.P. for Boroughbridge, was said to be the father of *"an endless hoard of beauty daughters"*. He had four sons and six daughters by his wife, Anne Boscawen.

the best dancer, but I yield the preference to my sister Bett, who is full as much admir'd for her excelling in this agreeable diversion.

Wednesday, 6 August

Sir Cecil Bishop breakfasts with us & invites us to his seat at Parham. Our gentlemen set off. My partner, Counsellor Stemp of Lewes, calls to pay his respects, Lord Gage too calls on us.[290] Certainly being taken so much notice of by people so far our superior is enough to elate us. But vanity, thou bane to all perfection, Heaven defend me from thy pernicious influence.

Thursday, 7 August

A very wet day, Sally Sheppard here. We play at cards.

Friday, 8 August

Dine with my cousin Bett, talk much of our late agreeable dance, & scheme another. Captain Smith has my letter by this time & I hope has answer'd it. Drink tea & spend the evening at Mrs. Bridger's, play at cards.

Saturday, 9 August

Am told that Mr. Tudor thinks me a very fine woman, short, oh how short is the duration of Beauty. Oh may I acquire qualifications that will be valuable when time has destroy'd my bloom & furrow'd my skin. Drink tea at Tom Dale's.[291]

Sunday, 10 August

Go to Church. Doctor Hutchinson gives us a fine discourse on these words, *"the fool hath said in his Heart there is no God"*. Company to drink tea. Begin teaching our little Prentice Boy to read. All our family are now in Bed, t'is a most dreadfull tempestuous night, all the elements seem in an uproar. How happy am I in knowing that my Harry is not on the wide Ocean.

Monday, 11 August

Work all the morning. Go down to Chisworth[292] in the afternoon & get some of Sir Charles' filberds with Sally Sheppard & Bett Cook.[293] Drink tea at the boarding school with Miss Skinner.[294] Dance afterwards & have a very pleasant evening.

Tuesday, 12 August

Sally Sheppard & Bett Cook desire me to write a note for the Cryer, to prevent anybody but ourselves going to steal Sir Charles' fruit, how he will laugh when he is told of this scheme. Miss Tredcroft drinks tea with us, walk the Causeway.

---

290   The Gages of Firle Place, near Lewes, were one of the leading Sussex Catholic families.

291   Tom Dale was the miller at Warnham Mill, and lived in the nearby miller's house.

292   Chesworth had been a large Tudor mansion, belonging to the Duke of Norfolk, but was now just a farm on the Eversfield estates.

293   Filberds or filberts were hazelnuts, called after St. Phillibert, whose saint's day was 22 August, at which time they were generally thought to be ripe for picking.

294   Probably the boarding school run by Kitty Smith and Ann Curtis, or *"Mr. Vanhome's school"*, mentioned on 18 December 1760; maybe these were the same school. Miss Skinner was previously mentioned on 7 April as a *"very beautiful"* girl.

Wednesday, 13 August

Breakfast at Mrs. Cheynell's. Drink tea at Mrs. Wicker's with the Miss Ellis's. Enquire for the post, but alas, he has no letter from my Smith, What oh what can be the reason, sure my last did not miscarry, allmighty patience fly to my aid & enable me to bear this disappointment. How slowly do the hours pass when weighed down with the lead of tedious expectation. Sure next post will bring me a letter from my Smith.

Thursday, 14 August

Walk out in the evening, tolerably cheerfull, fine pleasant & serene.

Friday, 15 August

Go with my cousin Bett down to Chisworth & get some filberd. Drink tea at Dales. A few lines from my lov'd Harry, he had just heard of his poor brother's unhappy disorder, which gave him as I thought it wou'd the greatest concern.

Saturday, 16 August

Work very hard all day, quite easy & happy now I know my Harry is well, he will write again soon, next to seeing him is that of hearing from him. Write to my Uncle Bob. Walk on the Causeway with Sally Sheppard & Mrs. Lampard, Nany Cook that was.

Sunday, 17 August

At Church twice. Doctor Hutchinson preaches on the Pharisee & Publican. Mr. Osgood on evil speaking. Drink tea with Mrs. Lampard. Walk in the Park. Sir Charles flies when he hears her name, very odd.[295] Walk with Mr. William White before our own door, he gives me an account of the Races.[296] No letter from Captain Smith. Make an Acrostick on my cousin Bett Smith.

Monday, 18 August

A little uneasy at not hearing from Captain Smith, how wrong is this yet for my Life I cannot help the folly. Drink tea with my cousin Bett, the two Miss Whites there, the eldest talks a great deal of nonsense,[297] oh Woman, Woman when wilt thou be discreet, but let me not partially blame my own Sex alone, the men in general shew as many instances of folly.

Tuesday, 19 August

Am call'd up by five o' clock, a most heavenly Joy inspiring morning. I walk out with Sally Sheppard & Bett Cook, divert ourselves with chat/t/ing & nutting.

Wednesday, 20 August

Work on my apron, in anxious expectation of hearing from my Harry. Write a Song on Bett Cook, to the tune of Kitty Field. Drink tea & spend the evening a/t/ Mrs.

---

295 Sarah seems to have forgotten that she had implied that Sir Charles had had an affair with Nany Cook before her marriage — see the entry for 3 May 1759.
296 Presumably the Lewes Races, which were an important social event at this time.
297 The eldest Miss White was Bathia (Thyer) White, whose escapades Sarah had mentioned previously. The other Miss White would have been Elizabeth (Bet). The youngest sister, Charlotte White, was still only a child of eleven.

Wicker's. Receive a very kind letter from Captain Smith, he praises my writing in the warmest terms, expects soon to go to Sea again.

Thursday, 21 August

Shew my Song to Sally Sheppard who likes it. Write to Captain Smith. My father is gone to bed very much out of temper for no reason. I wish I was no longer a slave to his ill humour — Heaven forbid I shou'd have a husband of such a disposition.

Friday, 22 August

Drink tea with a large posse at Drew Michell's & eat Plumb Cake. Sally Sheppard sings the song I made on Bett Cook, who says if true it wou'd be very pretty.

Saturday, 23 August

Walk in the Park, I talk to Sally Sheppard on the prospect of my living at Plymouth. She says going such a distance will break my mother's Heart, but perhaps I may never be join'd to my Harry, ten thousand accidents may happen to prevent it, alas how unhappy must I be to linger out a Life without him.

Sunday, 24 August

At Church, one Doctor Hunt, a visitor at Doctor Hutchinson's, preaches, a tolerable plain sensible discourse, but a very bad delivery. Drink tea a[t] Mrs. Michell, a sweet little neat habitation they have got, how happy shou'd I be in such a one with my Harry, but what signifies looking forward, let me enjoy the present.[298]

Monday, 25 August

A dreary wet day, & cold as Winter, how I dread the approach of that uncomfortable season. Hope my Smith will be here to make the solitary hours gay & sprightly. Work on my Apron, read *The Review*,[299] commends four Elegies. I think them very pretty.

Tuesday, 26 August

Write to Mr[s]. Townsend for the first time since I was ill. Mrs. Bridger drinks tea & spends the evening with us, play at cards. I must soon write to Miss Gittins.

Wednesday, 27 August

Work extreamly hard on my Apron, in hopes of finishing one half but cannot quite accomplish it. Walk on the Causeway, most delightfull & pleasant. The moon shone in full lustre & all nature put[s] on her silent solemn face.

Thursday, 28 August

Walk up to Mr. Tudor's with my sisters & cousin Bett, who are charm'd with the situation of this sweet place.[300] Meet Sir Charles on our return home, busy with his harvest. He desires us to go to Den & ask for the key of his garden to eat some fruits. We accept his offer.

---

298 Probably Mrs. John Michell, the sister-in-law of Drew Michell.
299 Probably *The Monthly Review.*
300 Mr. Tudor lived at Nuthurst Lodge in Sedgwick Park, about three miles to the south of Horsham. The house was well situated with fine views to the South Downs.

Friday, 29 August

A wet gloomy day, but thank Heavens it has no effect on my spirits. Several people call to see the finish'd half of my Apron & much admire it. Write some bills & begin the other part of my Apron.

Saturday, 30 August

Rise very early, a fine sunshine morning after the rain. Such is human Life, one day misfortunes o'ercloud the mind & all is dark & comfortless, the next, hope that sunshine of the soul darts in & causes black discontent to vanish.

Sunday, 31 August

At Church twice. A young clergyman preaches, nephew to Mr. White,[301] makes two excellent discourses. Walk in the Park, go into Sir Charles' garden. Begin writing to Miss Gittins, while I am thus employ'd receive a letter from the dear girl upbraiding my long silence. A letter from my lov'd Harry full of tenderness, wish, but alas t'is in vain, that I cou'd see him.

SEPTEMBER 1760

Monday, 1 September

Ride with my father to Mr. Bristed's at Slaugham, they are vastly civil. A fine pleasant day. Walk about the Forest & observe on the beautifull scenes around & admire the bountifull goodness of our all wise Creator, who has plac'd us here in a Paradise, as our little Island may be justly term'd,

Tuesday, 2 September

Free from the severe cold of the North Pole, nor yet fainting under the excessive heat of the torrid zone, were our passions as moderate as our climate we might be term'd the happiest of nations, but alas we are made miserable by our own bad conduct.

Wednesday, 3 September

Write to Miss Gittins & to Captain Smith. Mr. Tudor dines with us, invites us there next Sunday, he is a sensible old gentleman & seems to like young company. T'is now near midnight, every living creature silent as the grave, how awfull.

Thursday, 4 September

Work on the other part of my Apron. Go down to Chisworth for some filberds. Walk over the Common with Mrs. Wicker, Sally Sheppard, Bet Cook & my cousin Bet. Have a woman to tell our fortunes for diversion, she assures me I shall be married in a month, she cou'd not have told me anything so improbable.

Friday, 5 September

Sit very close to my work all day. Walk on the Causeway in the evening, then read

---

301   This was probably the Rev. John Heathfield, the son of William White's sister Mary.

one of my old *Grand Magazines*. Very pretty account of Ireland & some good Elegies wrote from Italy. No letters from Mrs. Jones or anybody.

Saturday, 6 September

A mountebank comes to exhibit his nostrums & his nonsense.[302] One cannot help looking & laughing at these fooleries, tho' rigid reason condemns the indulgence. A dispute with my father, I am to blame, & how miserable does the consciousness of being so make me, I ought as he is my Parent to submit to his impatient temper without retorting.

Sunday, 7 September

Dine at Mr. Tudor's, a most delightfull day. Consequently we have an agreeable walk. How happy shou'd I be in such a House with my Harry & a competent fortune. A letter from him, praises my writing again, tells me how he passes his time.

Monday, 8 September

Breakfast at Mrs. Cheynell's. Show her my Apron, she applauds it in wonderfull manner, t'is allmost enough to make one vain to have a performance so generally admir'd. Drink tea with Sir Charles, who accompanies us home.

Tuesday, 9 September

Write a long letter to my Smith. Mrs. Child of Dorking drinks tea with us, the Miss Elliss's & their two cousins from Chichester call on me. Walk with Sally Sheppard, she tells me her former lover's wife is ill & like to die, cannot help being pleas'd at this news, in hope the dear girl will be happy at last.

Wednesday, 10 September

Dine at Mr. Tredcroft's with my cousin Bett. Miss Bett Ingram[303] comes in the afternoon, she is extreamly good natur'd, affable & agreeable. Plays on the Spinnet & sings, she admires my work. Mrs. Tredcroft tells her t'is a Wedding apron, she says that is too delicate an affair to touch upon. I am not sorry Lord Irwin's family are acquainted with Captain Smith's attachment to me.

Thursday, 11 September

How truly amiable is humility & good nature, the person who possesses these rare qualities must be regarded with love & complacence.

Friday, 12 September

The two Miss Ellis's of Chichester call on me, the eldest is a joyous girl & seems to have a heart devoid of care, alas this frightfull Demon found early entrance into my Breast. Drink tea at Mrs. Bridger's, Mrs. Blunt comes, she desires to see my Apron, & much admires it.

---

302 A mountebank was an itinerant quack doctor who appealed to his audience by means of stories, tricks and juggling, sometimes with the assistance of a professional clown. Sarah seems to have been fascinated by him, as she went to see him several times.

303 Miss Elizabeth Ingram was the niece of Lord and Lady Irwin, and was brought up by them in Yorkshire after her mother's death in 1739, with her sister Isabella, later Mrs. Ramsden.

Saturday, 13 September

Go to my Aunt Waller's to see the mountebank exhibit. Mr. John Shelley there, he behaves rude to my cousin Bet & sister Bett. I reprimand him, he is angry, but afterwards desires to be reconciled, we exchange forgiveness. Read my *Grand Magazine*, a pretty poem from Abelard to Eloise.

Sunday, 14 September

At Church in the morning. Seiz'd with a violent sick fit & oblig'd to come out, the Air soon recovers me. Drink tea with Mrs. Laight. Walk in the park with Bet Cook & Sally Sheppard, carry Sir Charles a present of a new teapot. A letter from Captain Smith, says he has a very great regard for me, but it does not give him such violent emotions as formerly, before I confess'd mine for him.

Monday, 15 September

What a capricious thing is love, I am angry with Captain Smith for not being unhappy, & if he was so shou'd be extreamly concern'd. My Aunt Smith says I was the Belle at the Assizes, Jack Ellis tells me the same. Dance at the School.[304]

Tuesday, 16 September

Captain Smith wrote me word their Chaplain had been in London. Din'd with Jack Smith & Doctor Griffith, saw a ticket lay on the table for Miss Hurst my aunt to see the museum,[305] he exclaim'd on beholding it, "*God, I have drank more to a Lady of that name than wou'd drown a Dozen Dutchmen*". "*Oh*", reply'd Doctor Griffith, "*what a damn'd thing is Love*".

Wednesday, 17 September

Write to Captain Smith. Sally Sheppard shows my poem on Bett Cook to Sir Charles, he highly applauds it, & says t'is thousand pities a woman with such a genius shou'd be buried in such an obscure place as Horsham, but I doubt little advantage wou'd accrue if I was known in the World.

Thursday, 18 September

Drink tea at Tom Dale's with a large company. Read the first volume of *The Marriage Act*, a novel. Some good characters, affecting story of a Clergyman's distress.[306]

Friday, 19 September

Write a midnight Soliloquy in Blank verse, the first I ever attempted. A very wett day, quite ill with a pain in my breast occasion'd I suppose by the alteration of the Weather. Jack Ellis calls to see me two or three times, flatters me sufficiently & kisses me enough.[307]

---

304 Probably Mr. Vanhome's school, where there was a "*ball*" on 18 December 1760.
305 Almost certainly the British Museum, which was founded in 1753 and established at its present site (then Montagu House) in 1754. Members of the public were admitted by ticket, obtained beforehand from the Porter, from 15 January 1759.
306 *The Marriage Act*, a novel by John Shebbeare, was published in 1754.
307 John Ellis of Chichester, a cousin of the Ellis's of Tanbridge, was probably studying law in London at this time and passing through Horsham.

Saturday, 20 September

Mama expresses some concern about our business decreasing, nothing of that sort shall trouble me, I hope providence will bless our honest industry, & grant us food & raiment, pomp I wish not for. Read the second volume of *The Marriage Act*.

Sunday, 21 September

At Church twice. In the morning walk in the Croft with Bett Cook. After dinner walk up the Park with my cousin Bet Smith, most delightfully pleasant. A letter from my Dear Smith, thinks he shall soon go to Sea, Heaven send him a safe & speedy return. Walk on the Causeway with Doctor Read, he praises my song on Bet Cook.[308]

Monday, 22 September

A very wet day, Winter that dreary Season will soon creep upon us, farewell good roads & sunshine; adieu ye flowing meads & shady once, now leafless groves. Spend the evening at Mrs. Bridger's, play at cards.

Tuesday, 23 September

Work on my apron. Drink tea with Bet Cook. Begin teaching her quadrille.[309] Write to Captain Smith, he sent me the numbers of the Lottery tickets he has a share in. I give them to my cousin Bet Smith to register when she goes to Town. I wish but make no dependance on their coming up prizes.

Wednesday, 24 September

Mr. Tudor dines with us, & stays all [night], to look on a man of his years & then to reflect, that he has not yet quitted the follies of Life is really a melancholy reflection. Read *The British Magazine*. Some very entertaining & instructive stories.

Thursday, 25 September

Begin reading *The Review*. A very wet day, work on my apron. I wonder what will be my future lot in life, how natural is the desire of prying into futurity yet how happy it is hid from us. See the *Orford* is in Plymouth Sound, so my Harry will soon sail.

Friday, 26 September

Set the shop to rights. My father is certainly a very odd man, one day nobody so happy & rich, the next none so poor & miserable. How few there are whose actions are guided by reason instead of caprice. Begin writing to Miss Gittins. Write some verses, a droll petition for a Peace.

Saturday, 27 September

Go to my Aunt Waller's to see the mountebank. Jack Shelley tumbles me on the Bed, I am angry with him. Finish writing to Miss Gittins, send her my *Midnight Soliloquy* & desire her remarks on it. Finish reading *The Review*.

---

308   Dr. Read was the doctor who later cared for Sarah's brother, in January 1762.
309   Quadrille was a card game, and also a dance.

Sunday, 28 September

At Church twice, my Aunt Smith & cousin Bett & Uncle Bob all dine with us. Go with Sally Sheppard & Bet Cook to Mr. Parham's for some grapes, he lends me a Sermon preach'd at the visitation at Lent, a very good one. Go down & take my leave of my cousin Bet.[310] My Uncle Bob sneers at my writing poetry. I defend myself with all the warmth I am capable of.

Monday, 29 September

A letter from Captain Smith, their Ship has had some damage in the late storm, so will not yet go to Sea, how happy shou'd I be if I cou'd see him, but alas it may be long first. Mr. Pigott calls, he was going to Lewes, but the bad weather prevents, so he stays all day.

Tuesday, 30 September

Spend the afternoon with Sally Sheppard at Mrs. Tasker's, who is ill. Write to Captain Smith, send him *The Wish*,[311] in this Dear man is all my consolation amidst the troubles & disasters the World abounds with. Finish reading *The Dialogues of the Dead*, approve of them very much.[312]

OCTOBER 1760

Wednesday, 1 October

My father & Uncle Bob dispute about settling their affairs, how dreadfull is the thought that their business is so intricate. We may perhaps at my father's death be left quite destitute, or at best our fortunes in his power, but in that supreme Being I trust, who never abandons virtuous innocence.

Thursday, 2 October

Hope to see my Dear Harry about December, cannot expect it before. Drink tea at Mrs. Tasker's who continues ill. Sally Sheppard spends the evening with us, we play at cards to beguile the hours, are very merry.

Friday, 3 October

A fine still serene day which is extreamly agreeable after the tempestuous weather we have had so long. Poor Mrs. Tasker continues very ill. Read *The Christian's Magazine*, *Life of Lord Cromwell the Blacksmith's son*, oh ambition what dangers attend the pursuit of thy bewitching charms.

---

310 Bet Smith, her mother and *"Uncle Bob"* were presumably all staying with Sarah's grandmother, Mrs. Elizabeth Hurst, at her house in South Street.
311 It seems likely that *"The Wish"* was the poem Sarah had just written, which she described as *"a droll petition for a Peace"*.
312 *"The Dialogues of the Dead"* mentioned here were most probably those by George, Lord Lyttelton and Elizabeth Montagu, published in 1760, though there were existing works with the same title by Lucian, Thomas Browne, Fénelon and Fontenelle.

Saturday, 4 October

Busy cutting out work in the shop. Go & have a stare at the mountebank. Receive a letter from my cousin Bet Smith, she is safe arriv'd at home, sends me word that the ring my Aunt Waller gave me some time ago is Rubies, I determine to have it set fashionably.

Sunday, 5 October

At Church in the morning. Write to my cousin Bet Smith, give her a droll account how the whole face of Nature is alter'd since her departure. Drink tea & Sillibub with Sally Sheppard & Bet Cook. Write to Mrs. Jones & Mr. Jones. Sally Sheppard spends the evening with us, her lover's wife is recover'd, so I fear she will never be united to the man she most loves.

Monday, 6 October

The Post made it late before he brought me my Dear Harry's letter, & I grew a little impatient; he repents not coming to Horsham. It still continues terrible weather. Write out a great many bills, play at cards with my father & mother.

Tuesday, 7 October

Walk down to Chisworth in the morning, with Bet Cook, extreamly dirty yet pleasant. The Sun that has so long been obscur'd by watery clouds shone forth with gladdening lustre, but this pleasing scene is soon dispell'd & it rains. Write to Captain Smith.

Wednesday, 8 October

Write to my brother. Write out Mr. Tudor's Bill. Miss Tredcroft comes over to desire I wou'd show her how to do her work, a handkerchief very pretty. Read part of my *Grand Magazine*, very just Essay on the luxury of Women, prevent[ing] their marriage.

Thursday, 9 October

Uneasiness about some disappointments in business, alas this Life I think is replete with little else, but hush repining for trifles, think on the misery thy fellow creatures suffer who inhabit Countries now laid waste by horrid Wars, destructive ravages, these are Woes. But I feel the effects of War, tho' remov'd from its seat, fears for my dearest Harry tortures my anxious Heart.

Friday, 10 October

Walk to a little farm house & drink tea with Sally Sheppard & Bet Cook, very pleasant but dirty. Call at Mrs. Wicker's, Doctor Griffith comes in.

Saturday, 11 October

Mrs. James tells me she has heard of my song on Bet Cook. What cou'd I say on such a subject, she cries, oh malice when wilt thou find perfections in thy Neighbours. Finish reading my *Grand Magazine*, some very pretty verses on a Wedding day.

Sunday, 12 October

At Church twice. We were to have din'd at Mr. Tudor's (the) *(sic)* t'is excessive bad weather & prevents us. Mama seems vext at it, how can people make such trifleing things disappointments. Drink tea & sup at Mr. Tredcroft's, he tells Miss she grows excessive fat & eats too much, how disagreeable is this, very few indeed know how to make a right use of power.

Monday, 13 October

A letter from my Dear Smith, he tells me he had very great pleasure in perusing the verses I sent him, & says his friends gave them due praise. This perhaps they might do without *[illegible]* any. I desire him to explain this ambiguous expression.

Tuesday, 14 October

Captain Smith is apprehensive there will be a Spanish War. Heaven forbid. Write to him. Mr. Tudor sends two Turkey Polts *[poults]* & comes to dinner. We converse on *The Dialogues of the Dead*, he pays me several very polite compliments, invites us all up tomorrow. Read *The Ladies' Magazine*.

Wednesday, 15 October

Go to dinner at Mr. Tudor's, a very fine day & we have a most delightfull pleasant walk to this charming place. Write to my cousin Bett Smith, chide her for the shortness of her epistle. Wish for the company of my dear Harry.

Thursday, 16 October

Papa & Mr. Tudor goes to London, how extreamly fond this man is of my father, I doubt the intimacy is too great to subsist long, for nothing violent is lasting. Mr. Tredcroft's family & Mrs. Bridger drink tea & spend the evening with us, he cannot keep his temper at cards.

Friday, 17 October

My Aunt Grace brought to bed of a girl,[313] her Husband affronts me, but I impute it to his ignorance & go to see her, being above resenting his ill manners. Drink tea at Tanbridge. Sup at Mrs. Tasker's with Sally Sheppard & Bet Cook.

Saturday, 18 October

A letter from Mr. Jones informing me that his wife is safely deliver'd of a daughter. I am extreamly glad the poor Lady is out of danger. A letter from my dear little brother, but of his master's dictating. Write to Mr. Pigott, acquaint him his sister is brought to bed.

Sunday, 19 October

To Church twice, very much indispos'd. Drink tea at my Aunt Waller's. Walk with Sally Sheppard & Bet Cook to the Turnpike Gate, a charming pleasant evening.[314] Meet Doctor Burry, he invites us home with him & treats us with meed, we chat

---

313   This was Priscilla Grace, who died two months later and was buried on 17 December 1760. She was the second daughter of Robert and Priscilla Grace to die in infancy.

314   The turnpike gate mentioned here was probably the one at the bottom of Pict's Hill, on the road to the south.

an hour.[315] A letter from my Harry, dated Monday morning, he expected to sail in a few hours.

Monday, 20 October

Extreamly uneasy at my father's staying so much longer than he intended, fear some accident has befallen him, but am reliev'd from this anxiety by his arriving with Mr. Tudor for whom he staid. Walk to the Turnpike Gate.

Tuesday, 21 October

Walk to Warnham to see Miss Michell[316] with Bet Cook, a fine day. Mrs. Parr asks me after Captain Smith, I tell her he is gone to Sea again. A letter from my cousin Bet Smith, very well wrote for such a girl. Spend the evening at Mrs. Wicker's, play at cards.

Wednesday, 22 October

Mr. Tudor tells my father that by what he has seen of me, I am exceeding sensible & clever. I thank the Old Dear for his compliment, & will — nature permitting — endeavour to deserve it. Drink tea at Mrs. Tasker's with Sally Sheppard & Mrs. Wicker. Read *The British Magazine*.

Thursday, 23 October

Drink tea & spend the evening at Mr. Tredcroft's. He is very cross & gives his wife pettish answers, how disagreeable is ill-nature, but doubly so when shewn to those for whom we ought to have the greatest tenderness, but alas this seldom subsists between a wife & husband.

Friday, 24 October

Mr. Tudor calls on us, I was cutting out round frocks, he tells me I shou'd not do such work but read. I answer him that reading must be only my amusement, not my business. Spend the evening at Mrs. Wicker's.

Saturday, 25 October

A letter from my Dear Miss Gittins, she does not think beauty a misfortune, but an advantage. I differ from her & shall give my reasons in my next. Write to Captain Smith, relate the anxieties I feel lately from my father & Uncle not settling their affairs. Write to Mr. Masterman. Read part of *The Royal Magazine*.

Sunday, 26 October

At Church twice. Doctor Hutchinson makes an excellent Sermon on Hypocrisy. My father talks of buying Mr. Parham's house, which I cannot help thinking a

---

315 Dr. John Burry lived in West Street, opposite the *Swan Inn*. He was a convivial character who later became very friendly with the other Horsham diarist, John Baker, in the 1770s. There is a large collection of documents relating to him in the Horsham Museum archives. (HM MSS Cat. Nos. 370-372 and 1599-1603).

316 Henrietta Michell, daughter of John Michell and Anne Shelley of Warnham (now Mrs. Parr). Her sister Anne had married the Rev. Samuel Shuckford, Vicar of Warnham in 1753, and her other sister Helen Catherine had married John Miller in 1758. Henrietta Michell died unmarried in 1778.

bad scheme.[317] Walk to the Turnpike Gate with Sally Sheppard. Drink tea at Mrs. Tasker's. A report that the King is dead, I hope t'is false, for I fear a young one may be of prejudice to my lov'd country.

Monday, 27 October

The News of his Majesty's Death confirm'd. Oh Royalty, thou canst not fence against the [the] impartial Dart of this gloomy Tyrant. What matters it now that thy fame was spread in distant Realms, & the savage Indians own'd thy potent sway.

Tuesday, 28 October

Extreamly busy all day selling mourning. Miss & Mr. Tredcroft drink tea with us. Sally Sheppard & I sup at the *King's Head*. Write to my cousin Bet Smith & four more letters to London.

Wednesday, 29 October

Miss Upton here all the morning & Miss King[318] buys a great many things, looks at my Apron, says it is the compleatest piece of work they ever saw of the kind. Sally Sheppard & Bett Cook come here to cards. Papa comes home from the Fair very ill.

Thursday, 30 October

My father quite ill all night, good Heaven, sure he has not taken the Smallpox when last in London. Read the News, a man of War lost, hope it is not the *Orford*, but if it shou'd & I have lost my dear Smith, oh grant me patience Allmighty to sustain this heavy trial.

Friday, 31 October

My father extreamly ill. Mama & I are frighted to Death allmost. Oh Providence how unsearchable are thy dispensations & who shall murmur at thy decrees, but Oh Allmighty Father, supreme governor of the Universe, preserve the Life of this dear Parent.

NOVEMBER 1760

Saturday, 1 November

Doctor Smith thinks my father's disorder is the Smallpox. Mama in dreadfull agonies; it is too much for me to bear my own sorrows, how little capable then of

---

317 *"Mr. Parham's house"* is now Causeway House, and houses Horsham Museum. It is amusing that Sarah considered buying it *"a bad scheme"*, as this was the house where she was later very happy to live during her widowhood!

318 Miss King was possibly one of the sisters of Peter King, later 6th Lord King, who married Charlotte Tredcroft, younger daughter of Edward and Mary Tredcroft, in 1774. The Kings lived at Ockham Park, near Ripley, in Surrey. However, as she is always mentioned in Sarah's diaries as being in company with Miss Upton of Strood, it may be that this Miss King was Miss Upton's companion.

comforting her. He sends for Mr. Powell & gives orders for the making his Will, oh what a Heart rending stroke is this.

Sunday, 2 November

Pass a most melancholy day in attendance on my poor father, various consultations about moving him, he desires to go to Mrs. Wicker's. She reluctantly consents, fearing the neighbours will be displeas'd. T'is now near midnight, I am watching with anxious Heart my dear parent, the wind & rain in hollow murmurs seems to sooth my grief.

Monday, 3 November

My father is carried away to Mrs. Wicker's, Bet goes to help attend him. I am dreadfully shock'd at his removal. Pray Heaven he may return safe & get the better of this terrible distemper, my poor mother is allmost inconsolable.

Tuesday, 4 November

A letter from my Uncle Bob expressing his concern at my father's illness. I write to him & my Uncle George desiring they will come down. We are in great perplexity because we cannot have the Nurse my father depended upon, she was to come from Doctor Smith's House but the patients will not part with her.

Wednesday, 5 November

I ride over to the inoculating House, & beseech them to part with their Nurse, they reluctantly consent. I ride home quite rejoic'd & send my Horse back for her. Write again to my Uncle Bob, the Doctor assures us my father is like to do well.

Thursday, 6 November

No letter from my Dear Harry, what can be the reason. Thought of him will intrude amidst all my anxiety. Oh Life, thou surely art replete with ills, one evil to another still succeeds & still our course to happiness impedes.

Friday, 7 November

A letter from my Uncle Bob promising he & my Uncle George will come down & assuring me that, if my father does otherwise than well, he will be a father to us. I hope providence will raise us friends shou'd we want them, but God will I trust restore my Parent.

Saturday, 8 November

Hear that Mrs. Bysshe Shelley is dead, poor young Lady.[319] I am concern'd for her, she was my earliest acquaintance & I have still a regard for her, tho' time & absence has lessen'd our intimacy. See the effects of girlish imprudence, had not she so soon rush'd into matrimony she might not have fell such an untimely sacrifice.

---

319 Mrs. Bysshe Shelley was Mary Catherine Michell, the heiress to the Stammerham estates. She had married Bysshe Shelley secretly in 1752, at the age of sixteen. Edward Tredcroft, who was her uncle and guardian, brought her up after the early death of both her parents, and is known to have objected to the marriage. He had probably hoped that she would marry John Shelley, the elder brother, who was heir to all the Shelley estates, rather than Bysshe, who was a younger son.

Sunday, 9 November

My two Uncles arriv'd last night, the Doctor George[320] thinks there is no danger in my father, so they set off again this morning. Go down Mrs. Wicker's garden & enquire how my father does. Doctor Smith calls to me & says he is tolerably well. Read my *Grand Magazine*, a droll poem exposing the superstition of the Romish Church, in a dialogue between the French King & Mas *[?Monsignor]* Brogli.

Monday, 10 November

No letter from my dear Harry. What oh what can be the meaning of it, so many ships as have come from Quiberon Bay since he went. The Doctor pronounces my father out of danger, I thank thee Allmighty for this blessing. Oh give me a gratefull Heart.

Tuesday, 11 November

Quite ill all day, in violent pain, the gravel they tell me, to how many disorders is this poor machine liable? How much pain of both Body & mind have I suffer'd & yet so young, sure my shattered frame can never sustain these continual conflicts. Play at Piquet with Sally Sheppard.

Wednesday, 12 November

Sleep badly, extreamly restless, my mind foreboded my father's illness, sure this portends no new misfortune, but let me not anticipate, I already experience evils enough without dreading those to come. Drink tea at Mrs. Tasker's, a Country man talks a great deal, one really wou'd think without being convinc'd by our senses that nothing Human cou'd be so ignorant.

Thursday, 13 November

Work all day extreamly hard. Doctor Smith calls in the evening & chats with me two hours on history, politicks & War. Quite ill again at night, oh health when wilt thou restore me thy long lost valued blessing.

Friday, 14 November

Sit very close to work all day. Am told that my sister Bett behaves very ill to one of the Nurses that is in with my father, mean girl, she cannot help shewing her insolent temper wherever she is which makes herself unhappy & all who are so unfortunate as to be concern'd with her.

Saturday, 15 November

The inexpressive satisfaction of a letter from my Harry, wrote in the tenderest, politest terms, 2 sheets full. Read it to Mrs. Tasker & Sally Sheppard, who both very much commend it, write to him. Poor Mrs. Shelley brought to be buried.[321] I cannot help shedding tears at the sight of her Hearse.

---

320 George Hurst was an apothecary, so this was presumably why Sarah called him "*Doctor George*".

321 At the time of her death, Mrs. Shelley was living in Steyning, at Chantry Green House. Bysshe Shelley was building a mansion at Warnham Place where they intended to live. This was abandoned after her death, but Bysshe used the materials to build Castle Goring near Worthing in 1793.

Sunday, 16 November

At Church twice. Walk in the Croft with Sally Sheppard. Go & see my father through the windows, he is a most shocking figure, sure the Smallpox is the most dreadfull distemper that ever Human nature was afflicted with. Walk at the Turnpike with Sally Sheppard & Bet Cook. Read over again my Dear Smith's letter with infinite pleasure.

Monday, 17 November

Very busy all day. Make a Bonnet for Mrs. Bristed. Mrs. Wicker throws herself into hysterick fits for fear any of her neighbours shou'd take the Smallpox of my father, sure it wou'd be time enough to give herself so much uneasiness when such an event has happen'd but, as tho' present evils were not sufficient, we are generally fond of anticipating future ones.

Tuesday, 18 November

Make a cloak for Sally Chasemore.[322] Papa goes to Doctor Smith's House in Mr. Tredcroft's Chariot.[323] I hope he will soon come home again to his business. Quite ill, oh pain sure thou art an evil.

Wednesday, 19 November

Wish most ardently to see my Dear Smith, but alas what signifies a transient view & then to be snatch'd from me again. Wou'd to Heaven we were united forever. The lottery has begun drawing now, if my Dear Smith is lucky. Hitherto he has not been so, but we know not what to [illegible].

Thursday, 20 November

Very busy all day in the shop. When I wonder shall I finish my Apron, I shall set about it again with reluctance. The Wind excessive high, oh how my Heart aches for my dearest Harry, sure these perturbations must injure my health. Ride over to Home Bush to see my father who is quite well.

Friday, 21 November

Hear Mr. Alldridge[324] dyed suddenly this morning, poor man. The poor have lost an excellent master & benefactor, see how fickle are the scenes of Human Life, about six months ago he gave us a Ball, now he has quitted this transitory stage & rests, I hope, [free] from care & pain.

---

322   Sally (Sarah Ann) Chasemore, born in 1750, was the eldest daughter of Francis Chasemore, the Cuckfield attorney.

323   Dr. Smith lived in the Carfax, according to the Land Tax records, but it is clear from subsequent entries in Sarah's diary that Richard Hurst was moved to Holmbush (*Home Bush*), which Doctor Smith seems to have used as a suitable place for isolating a patient with smallpox. There was a farm of this name on the road from Horsham to Crawley, which was probably where Richard Hurst was taken, but there was also another place with the same name in St. Leonard's Forest.

324   Mr. John Aldridge of St. Leonard's Forest.

Saturday, 22 November

A letter from my Uncle Bob acquainting me the stocks are now very low if my father designs to buy in. Receive a muff & tippit from London made of the marten skins my Dear Harry gave me; the person who dress'd them writes me word they are worth six guineas.

Sunday, 23 November

Mr. Alldridge[325] sends here for some patterns of cloths, I rise in a great hurry & send them. At Church in the morning, wear my new muff & tippit. Walk in the Croft. Mr. Blunt congratulates me on my father's recovery. [A] Welchman comes to take our grass,[326] how much are these things out of a Woman's latitude, yet why are they so, only from our being unaccustom'd to intermeddle with them.

Monday, 24 November

A letter from Captain Smith dated Basque Road,[327] a very pretty letter & it gives me great pleasure, but when shall I have the superlative one of seeing him. Write to Mrs. Jones, congratulate her on the Birth of her Daughter. Play at Picquet with Sally Sheppard.

Tuesday, 25 November

Ride over to Home Bush to see my father. We have a vast deal of conversation, he is quite hearty. His having the Smallpox will I hope be a future advantage to him, at present am certain it has been a great prejudice in his business, but who shall prescribe [illegible word] to thee, oh Omnipotence, & say this or that is right or wrong.

Wednesday, 26 November

Ill all night with a fever & violent headach, continue bad all day. Oh health, when wilt thou smile on my cheek & chase the livid paleness. Write to Mrs. Jones, Miss Gittins & my brother. Acquaint them with my father's disorder.

Thursday, 27 November

Fair Day, a great many people in the shop, am fatigu'd with waiting on them. Captain Miles [?Miller] calls on me, asks after my Dear Smith. Mr. Grainger calls, he desires I wou'd enquire out a maid servant for him. A prodigious kind friendly letter from Mr. Pigott, answer it.

Friday, 28 November

Mr. Pigott has certainly a very great friendship for me. I have experienc'd his attachment in a thousand instances, however fickle he may be with respect to

---

325   This is probably Abel Aldridge, the brother and heir of John Aldridge who had just died.

326   St. Leonard's Fair on 17 November was the one at which the Welsh cattle drovers traditionally sold their beasts, which they had driven from Wales. They usually arrived a few days early to rest and feed the cattle. This Welshman was presumably arranging to feed his animals at the Hurst's Highland Farm — he had arrived too late for the fair on 17 November, but may have been hoping to sell his stock at the horse fair on 27 November.

327   The Basque Roads were off the French coast, near La Rochelle.

others. None of my Harry's lottery tickets are drawn yet, I wish kind fortune wou'd bestow us two or three thousand, it will be of infinite Service, but vain are wishes, we must after all be content with what is allotted. [328]

Saturday, 29 November

A great many country people in the shop, it is an amusement to see the honest simplicity of some & the affected rustick archness of others, oh Nature how variable are thy productions.

Sunday, 30 November

Ride over to Holmbush with my sister Molly to dine with my father. Walk out to see the beautifull Hollys that grow in abundance on that farm, oh Nature, or more properly thou God of Nature, how wonderfull are thy productions, the mind looks up with awfull reverence to the great first cause. Wet in coming home.

DECEMBER 1760

Monday, 1 December

A letter from the Lottery office acquainting me one of my Harry's tickets is drawn a blank, oh Fortune, Fortune, thou blind deity, fear we shall never experience thy favours. However it is one satisfaction to reflect that t'is not in the power of these disappointments to give me one moment's uneasiness.

Tuesday, 2 December

Work all day extreamly hard. Begin writing the history of Sally Sheppard which I promis'd to send Miss Gittins under the name of Celia. My father comes down Town & into the shop, a great many people wellcomed him home.

Wednesday, 3 December

A letter from my cousin Bet Smith, gives me a particular account of the Fashions. Drink tea at Mrs. Wicker's with Sally Sheppard, she relates some of my sister Bet's insolent behaviour to the Nurses while at her house with my father, am sorry the girl makes herself so ridiculous.

Thursday, 4 December

Another lottery letter containing another Blank. Work all day, not well. I am allmost tir'd of complaining, but youth — that time for enjoyments — can afford no pleasure if unattend'd by its chief blessing, health. But cease repining, if pain in this world is my lot, my residence here must be the shorter time, & I shall be earlier introduc'd to that place where disorders & uneasiness are no more.

---

328 The State Lottery was an institution in 18th century England. In 1731, Henry Ingram (later 7th Viscount Irwin), and his mother, Isabella, bought a £10 ticket in the Lottery in the hope of raising enough money to enable Arthur, 6th Viscount Irwin to pay Charles Eversfield of Denne for the burgages they needed to gain political control of Horsham — again without success.

Friday, 5 December

Sally Sheppard here all the evening, some very agreeable conversation. Play at Picquet, how dreary wou'd many of my hours pass if not enlivened by this dear girl.

Saturday, 6 December

A letter from my amiable friend Miss Gittins, commiserating the anxiety I must have felt during my father's illness, & congratulating me on his recovery. Finish Sally Sheppard's history, play at picquet with Sally Sheppard. Read her history to her, she says I bestow more praises than she deserves.

Sunday, 7 December

Write some verses on Sally Sheppard not being any longer my bedfellow. My dear father returns home, I receive him with inexpressible joy. Dine at Mr. Curtis's on Venison. Mr. & Mrs. Tasker drink tea & sup with us. What a happy event is my father's returning safe, can I be too gratefull.

Monday, 8 December

Very busy in the shop. Doctor Smith calls & desires I wou'd draw up an address to the King, which the Balliffs & Burgesses intend to send. *"No Sir"*, I reply, *"I will not interfere with the business that belongs to men of Learning & genius"*.

Tuesday, 9 December

Doctor Smith & Mr. White quarrel about the address which was compos'd by the latter, & neither English nor grammar. Work a little on my apron. Cut out a Dozen frocks etc, to go to Steyning. Begin writing to Miss Gittins. Mrs. Wicker dines with us.

Wednesday, 10 December

Read my *Grand Magazine*, a collection of epithets on all the English Kings. Go on with my letter to Miss Gittins. Work a little on my Apron. Not well, oh Allmighty Father of the Universe, grant that for all my faults these bodily disorders may be a sufficient atonement.

Thursday, 11 December

Dine at Mr. Powell's with Sally Sheppard, Bet Cook & Will White. What a stupid young fellow this is, nothing lively, nothing sensible but quite a sheepish Dolt. Play at cards & are tolerably merry. Mr. Tredcroft at our House when I return home. Write to my brother to let him know he is to break up at Christmas. Poor little fellow, how he will rejoice.

Friday, 12 December

Write again to Miss Gittins. My father not in a good humour. He does not love to see me thus employed, which I am concern'd at. I wou'd not disoblige him, yet cannot quit this favourite amusement.

Saturday, 13 December

Work on my Apron, busy in the shop. A letter from the lottery office with the last number of my Harry's drawn a Blank, poor Harry, thou art quite unfortunate, but the fickle goddess seldom bestows her favours on any so deserving.

Sunday, 14 December

At Church twice. Doctor Hutchinson preaches on this text, *"There is no respect of persons with God"*. Walk in the Croft with Sally Sheppard & Bet Cook. Write to my Uncle Bob & my cousin Bet Smith. Taken extreamly ill with the Headach & oblig'd to go to Bed.

Monday, 15 December

Doctor Smith tells me the sailing of a large fleet is countermanded, which he thinks has the appearance of an approaching Peace. Alas, I fear this conjecture is ill founded. Papa taken ill, oh health, thou dearest best enjoyment, may my Parent soon have thee restor'd.

Tuesday, 16 December

Dry rub the Hall in hopes exercise will do me good, but it proves too violent & makes me worse. Violent headache, work on my Apron. Oh thou Allmighty supream, governor of the Universe, restore me to health if it be thy blessed will, or give me strength & patience to endure the disorders thou for wise purposes art pleased to inflict.

Wednesday, 17 December

Doctor Smith sends me some medicines to strengthen me. Something better & in great spirits. Begin writing to Captain Smith, I wonder when I shall have the pleasure of seeing him.

Thursday, 18 December

Work on my Apron. Go to Mr. Vanhome's school Ball, dance with Miss Bet White, who behaves very free & is good company. Miss Tredcroft dances with Tom White,[329] who appears very fond of her, he is I think one of the most beautifull youths I ever saw, I am allmost ready to envy everybody that has such a glow of health in their countenance which poor I am depriv'd of, but I will not repine.

Friday, 19 December

The longest life is but short & passeth away like a dream, oh may I when translated to another attain that felicity which cannot be found below.

Saturday, 20 December

Mr. Grainger here from Cuckfield. Come out all over in a violent rash, when will my bodily sufferings be at an end. Write to Captain Smith & to Mr. Masterman. My Dear brother comes from school. We are all extreamly glad to see him, & he diverts us very much with his agreeable chat.

Sunday, 21 December

Very ill all day, cannot go to Church. T'is not the pain I suffer that gives me the greatest uneasiness, it is (such unaccountable mortals we are) lest my disorders

---

329 Tom White was the younger son of William White the lawyer — he later became the Rev. Thomas White, Rector of Faccombe and Tangley in Hampshire (1745-1788). He has a *"poetical epitaph"* in St. Mary's Church, Horsham, which may have been written by Sarah.

shou'd alter my person & deprive me of my dear Smith's regard, oh how miserable must I be shou'd this be my fate.

Monday, 22 December

Taken extreamly ill with a violent Rash & fever.[330]

[No more entries until 27 December]

Saturday, 27 December

Got up vastly weak after being confin'd to my Bed ever since Monday. Receive a letter from my amiable friend Miss Gittins lamenting my ill health. Sends me a poem on the King's death, very pretty, a vision, the descriptive part of which is most delightfull.

Sunday, 28 December

She sends me too a burlesque song on an officer entitled *St. Lammaria*. I write an answer to it, reprimanding her for ridiculing personal imperfections. My Dear little brother is continually with me & has been a very great consolation during my illness. Am much better thanks to the Allmighty.

Monday, 29 December

Very ill again, oh Allmighty Universal Father, look down with pitying eyes on a poor mortal labouring under thy displeasure. Write some verses for my brother, who is vastly diverted with them. Mrs. Wicker & Sally Sheppard come to see me.

Tuesday, 30 December

Work a little but am very unable, excessive low spirited. No letter from my Harry, how I wish to see him, but have very little expectation of enjoying that satisfaction this winter. My fever returns & I am quite ill again, oh give me patience great God, & support my spirits amidst these pains thou art pleased to inflict.

Wednesday, 31 December

My brother diverts me very much with telling stories of his schoolfellows & the manner they pass'd their time. Read the Account of that once magnificent place Palmyra in a magazine.[331]

---

330 Possibly Sarah had scarlet fever or chickenpox.
331 Two Englishmen, Robert Wood and James Dawkins, visited the site of the great city of Palmyra in the Syrian desert in 1751, with an Italian architect, Giovanni Battista Borra. Borra drew a magnificent panorama of the ruins of Palmyra on three sheets, which was published in Wood and Dawkins' book, *The Ruins of Palmyra*, in 1753. The highly decorative Palmyran style became very influential on architects and designers in England, notably Robert Adams, who created a famous "Palmyra ceiling" at Osterley Park. Borra's panorama was reproduced in contracted form with an article in *The Grand Magazine*. Sarah made several references to articles that she read in *The Grand Magazine* at this time.

Memorandums at the Close of the Year 1760

This is the last day of the Old Year. I am now in a very weak state of health & little prospect of amendment, my sufferings are great, but I trust that the Supreme Being will soon cure, or enable me to bear them, with the resignation becoming a Christian. May Heaven preserve me ever in as good a situation as I am at present, & may I never close a Year more unhappy. I am bless'd with competence & plenty, tho' dependant on my friends, but their kindness prevents this dependance being the least irksome. May I deserve their goodness by perfect filial duty. If I should be united to my Harry, (pleasing hope but dash'd with fear) may I meet with that affection he has allways profess'd for me, & may we be patterns of conjugal happiness.

33. London Bridge as Sarah would have known it – the houses were not pulled down until after 1760.

34. Whitehall, where Sarah went to meet Sally Sheppard and have her miniature painted.

LAURENCE STERNE AM
Prebendary of York &c.&c.

35. The Rev. Lawrence Sterne, whose *Life and Opinions of Tristram Shandy, Gentleman* Sarah disliked, but whose sermons she admired.

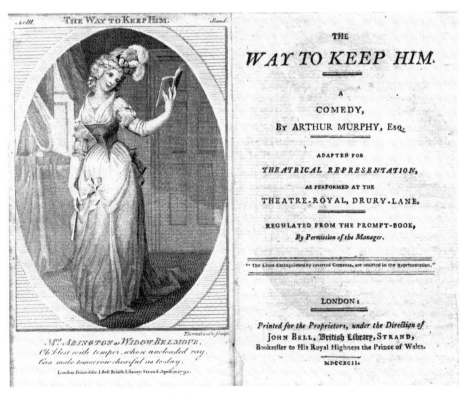

36. *The Way to Keep Him* — a play that Sarah read twice.

37. Tamerlane, by Nicholas Rowe, which Sarah saw performed in Horsham — *"never sure was a more wretched performance — it was a severe punishment rather than a diversion"*

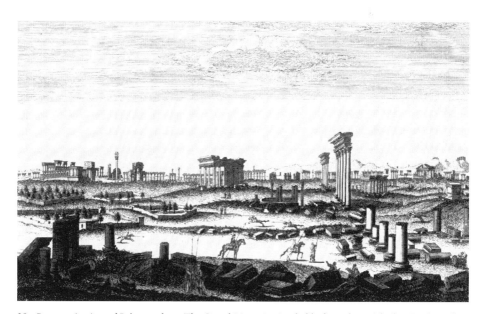

38. Panoramic view of Palmyra, from *The Grand Magazine* (probably from the article that Sarah read on 31 December 1760).

39. View of Eastbourne.

40. The village of Upperton, where Sarah's cousins lived.

41. Hastings, which Sarah visited while staying at Eastbourne.

42. Winchelsea, where Sarah saw the cambric manufactory.

43. Chichester, where Sarah lived in her later years before returning to Horsham.

44. Chichester Cathedral.

45. Robert Hurst in later life.

46. Bysshe Shelley, who relied on Robert Hurst to look after his affairs.

47. The memorial to Henry Smith in the chancel, as it was before the restoration of St. Mary's Church in 1864.

48. The nave before restoration, showing the pews and central pulpit that Sarah would have known.

THE DIARY FOR 1761

Expences of my Arundel Journey;	
On the road	1.0
To the Man	2.6
Going in the Sea at Goring	0.9
Seeing Arundel Castle	1.0
A Man & Horse to go to Hampton *[Littlehampton]*	1.9
A D(itt)o	2.0
Washing in the Sea	0.9
Carriage of a riding Hat	0.6
A flannel Jacket	1.10
To the Servants at Goring	3.0
Lost at Cards	1.0
Shoeing my Horse	1.0
Washing my Habbit	0.9
Going to Bourn	7.0
At Bourn, Brighthelmstone, Lewes, Goring	1.15.0
Horse hire	1.7.0
Washing	1.6
For being bleeded	2.6
(illegible)	5.0
Coming home	<u>4.0</u>
	£4.19.10

JANUARY 1761

Thursday, 1 January

Come down stairs after my painfull confinement very weak and ill, but extreamly gratefull that I am once more permitted to recover from the Bed of sickness. Play at shuttle cock with my brother to exercise myself & divert him.

Friday, 2 January

Mrs. Tredcroft & Mrs. Bridger call to see me, the former tells me I am grown fat instead of thin with my illness, she sometimes talks at random. Sally Hunt drinks tea with me. I have a great respect for this honest, prudent, well behav'd girl.

Saturday, 3 January

Mr. Chasemore & his son here, from Cuckfield. No letter from Captain Smith, what can be the reason, but hush, let me have no repining. Probably he has had no opportunity, for I think him true & hope he is safe. Read the first volume of *The Female [?Quixote]*[332] intended to ridicule our fondness for Romances, but alas we are, I think, run into the opposite extream, & instead of keeping our lovers at such an awfull distance, treat them with a disgusting familiarity.

Sunday, 4 January

Not well enough to go to Church. Mr. Tredcroft, Miss & Mrs. Wicker drink tea with us.

Monday, 5 January

Spend the afternoon & evening at Mr. Tredcroft's, Doctor Smith there, who tells me all my troubles will soon be at an end, for he thinks a Peace is very near, I wish his prognostications may prove true. Mrs. Tredcroft admires my sable Tippit.

Tuesday, 6 January

Very busy in the shop posting Books, & writing out bills. Cut out a Dozen of Sailors' Jackets to go to Shoreham. I wonder what will at last be my situation in life. At present my employments are various as the Weather; one moment poetical Ideas raises me above the World & all its trifling concerns. The next my thoughts are employ'd on the meanest domestic occurrences. I cannot check my risibility at the striking contrast.

Wednesday, 7 January

My father goes to an entertainment given by our Members of Parliament, Sir Lionel Pilkington & Mr. Ingram.[333] At Mrs. Bridger's.

Thursday, 8 January

No letter yet from my Harry, what oh what can be the reason, sure he is safe. Walk out in the Town. Agreeable chat with Jenny Hunt. Sally Hunt with us, we play at cards. Bob goes my halves & interests himself very *[word omitted]* in my success.

---

332 *The Female Quixote* by Charlotte Lennox was a successful novel published in 1752.
333 Charles Ingram was the son of Colonel Charles Ingram, M.P. for Horsham from 1737 to 1748, and the nephew of Henry Ingram, 7th Lord Irwin. Charles was first elected to represent Horsham while still under age, in 1747, (an illegality which was overlooked), and was re-elected in 1754 and 1761. Sir Lionel Pilkington was elected in a by-election in 1748, after the death of Colonel Ingram, and was re-elected with Charles in 1754 and 1761. He came from Wakefield in Yorkshire, near the principal seat of the Ingram family, at Temple Newsam, just outside Leeds.

Friday, 9 January

Mr. Tudor here, we have a great deal of conversation on Peace, War & various subjects, he thinks there is now a probability of a Peace; the King seems *[illegible]* inclinable. Walk out in the Common, the Sun shines & it was extreamly pleasant. Read my *Grand Magazine*, which is now discontinued publishing, I am sorry for it as the performance had great merit.

Saturday, 10 January

A quarrel with my sister Bet. She is a most insolent girl & I cannot see any obligation I am under to submit to her ill behaviour, nor will I do it. Mamma blames her much but to no purpose.

Sunday, 11 January

At Church in the morning. Walk in the Croft with Sally Sheppard who tells me my song on Bett Cook was very much commended by Mr. John Parham & Mr. Ashburnham, & disapprov'd by Mr. Mills; those who envy cannot like. Hear of Admiral Boscawen's death, am very much concern'd; he was my Harry's best friend, and is besides a National loss. [334]

Monday, 12 January

No letter from Captain Smith, sure there must be something extraordinary in his long silence. A great may Ships have arriv'd from Queberon Bay, yet none brings me any tidings. An elegant entertainment at Mr. Tredcroft's, we play at cards.

Tuesday, 13 January

Read *The Monthly Review*, some very pretty portraits from various prospects of Mankind, Nature & Providence. Drink tea & spend the evening at Sally Sheppard's. Bett behaves very ill, won't play at cards & goes away. I acquaint her mother who blames her & tells Papa.

Wednesday, 14 January

He does the same upon which she defies him with unparalleled insolence, he very much exasperated pushes her, she runs to grandmother & tells a long story of ill usage, but not a word that her ill behaviour is the cause.

Thursday, 15 January

Mrs. Wicker, Mrs. Waller & Mrs. Tasker interferes, I tell the latter how much cause I have to dislike her, indeed I would not bear to live with her were it not for my parents with whom & for whom I will endure all sorts of inconveniences. Read *The British Magazine*.

Friday, 16 January

Very busy in the shop. Mrs. James comes down & drinks tea with us, tells Papa he

---

334 Admiral Edward Boscawen had just been given the post of General of the Marines (in December 1760), but his death on 10 January 1761 cut short a brilliant career. Sarah seems to have heard this news remarkably quickly, as he had only died the previous day.

is under great obligations to my sister Bet for attending him in the Smallpox. Write to Mrs. Jones; we shall lose soon my beloved brother who must return to school.

Saturday, 17 January

The inexpressible pleasure of a letter from my dear Smith, wrote Christmas Day. He is well thank Heaven, & hopes to see Horsham about the latter end of March. But alas there is no satisfaction without alloy, my Joy at this news is considerably damp'd by a letter from my fair friend Miss Gittins who informs me she has not heard from her lover Mr. Turnpenny a great while, which gives her much uneasiness. I hope he is not false, poor dear girl, how I pity her anxiety & wish I could relieve it.

Sunday, 18 January

At Church twice. Walk in the Croft & in the Common.

Monday, 19 January

Write to Miss Gittins a very long letter to console her for Mr. Turnpenny's silence, & assign probable reasons for it. Miss Michell of Warnham drinks tea with [word omitted]. An officer calls whose name is Parker on a sleeveless errand. I believe his motive was curiosity.

Tuesday, 20 January

We have a great deal of company to drink tea & spend the evening, Miss Tredcroft here full dress'd, she is a most charming girl in person & I think shap'd like my Dear Miss Gittins, but how infinitely short falls the intellectual part. Play at cards very late, some conversation about *The Minor*, a Comedy wrote by Foote, a Player, in ridicule of the Methodists.[335]

Wednesday, 21 January

Keep my Bed all day with a violent pain in my Breast & head. Rise in the evening, & being at home alone, employ myself in writing a *Vision to the Memory of the late Brave Admiral Boscawen*.

Thursday, 22 January

A letter from my Cousin Bet Smith, desiring some poetry. Write to my Dear Harry, send him the verses on Admiral Boscawen. Work a little on my Apron. Mr. Bysshe Shelley calls, he is grown extreamly thin.[336] Sally Sheppard spends the evening with us, play at cards.

---

335   Samuel Foote's satirical play, *The Minor*, was censored by the Lord Chamberlain because of its depiction of George Whitehead, one of the founders of the Methodist Church, as "*Mr. Squintum*". Methodism was becoming a controversial issue at this time, due to the enthusiastic response it was evoking among common people. William Hogarth produced a print, called *Enthusiam Delineated*, which he addressed to the Archbishop of Canterbury. It was later extensively reworked and published under the title *Credulity, Superstition and Fanaticism*, in 1762.

336   This followed the death of Bysshe's wife, Mary Catherine, in November 1760.

Friday, 23 January

Quite ill all day, work on my Apron, a little. I wish this everlasting piece of work was finish'd, I wou'd not then live such a sedentary life. Drink tea & spend the evening at Mrs. Wicker's. A dispute with Sally Sheppard about the pronunciation of Venice, return home very ill.

Saturday, 24 January

Both my hands swell'd in such a manner as to take away the use of them, am allmost in despair & think I shall never recover my health.[337] But that Allmighty Power who depriv'd me of this blessing can in his own good time restore it to me, & will I hope, or else take me from this scene of trouble & folly to a place of endless happiness. The Lord gave & the Lord taketh away, bless'd be the name of the Lord.

Sunday, 25 January

Take Physick, am visited by Mrs. Wicker & Sally Sheppard. Read in *Nature Display'd*.

Monday, 26 January

Very ill, oh when will my sufferings be at an end. Presumptious question, foolish girl, endure patiently present evils & humbly wait their removal. Read *The Royal Magazine*, some very indifferent verses on the late King.

Tuesday, 27 January

An exceeding fine day, walk out, which I think is of great service to me. Call at Mrs. Wicker's, who accompanies me & Sally Sheppard. Tell them I do not think I shall live long, they hope my apprehensions are too gloomy & endeavour to raise my spirits.

Wednesday, 28 January

Something better, wish earnestly for my dear Harry when his enlivening conversation wou'd, I hope, perfect my cure. Walk out with Sally Sheppard, call on Bet Cook who we find in tears - who is alas without their troubles? Mr. Tredcroft asks me when I last heard from my Harry.

Thursday, 29 January

No letter from Miss Gittins as I a little expected. Poor dear girl, I am extreamly solicitous for her welfare, & hope her lover will prove just. Begin writing to Mrs. Townshend. Very ill all night, no sleep, quite low spirited, fear I shall never get the better of this obstinate disorder.

Friday, 30 January

The Martyrdom of King Charles the First. At Church twice. Walk up in the Park with Mrs. Wicker, a very hard frost but fair & clear, and I think there cannot be a

---

337 It seems very likely that Sarah suffered from rheumatoid arthritis. She complained about rheumatism in her later letters, but the swelling of which she complains here suggests arthritis.

more beautifull sight than the ground covered with a white frost, when Sol's bright beams sparkles on the surface.

Saturday, 31 January

Better thank God than I have been some time. Finish writing to Mrs. Townshend, send her my *Vision on Admiral Boscawen*. Work on my apron, hope to finish it *[by]* Easter if sickness & accidents do not prevent. Sally Sheppard here, we play at cards.

FEBRUARY 1761

Sunday, 1 February

At Church in the afternoon. Doctor Hutchinson preach'd. His are allways excellent discourses, let the subject be what it will, but I thought he greatly wander'd from his text & drew conclusions no way deducible from it. Drink tea at Mrs. Tasker's with Mrs. Wicker, some chat about Sally Sheppard & Drew.

Monday, 2 February

Work on my Apron, begin writing to my cousin Bet Smith, make some verses on the strolling Players we have in Town. Sally Sheppard, Bet Cook, Nancy Reynolds drink tea & spend the evening with me, they tell me I look pretty well recover'd from my late illness, thank God, I am much better.

Tuesday, 3 February

An exceeding fine *[day]*, it quite enlivens my spirits. Walk out, how agreeable does the Sun's genial ray appear at this dreary Season. Spend all the evening alone, wish for the company of my Dear Harry.

Wednesday, 4 February

Ash Wednesday, at Church in the morning. Now is approaching a Season which ought to inspire every Xtian *[Christian]* with the most serious reflections, may I look on this transitory life as nothing more than the road to a better & wean if possible my regard from these dear objects that rivet me to Earth. Oh my dear Harry, we must one day part, Heart rending thought, were it not for the joy & full hope that we shall meet again I could not bear the agonising reflection.

Thursday, 5 February

My Father ill, oh nature, nature how severe thy pangs.

Friday, 6 February

Work all day on my Apron. A message from Mr. Pigott acquainting me that he is very ill, & desires me to go & see him, promise him a visit on Sunday if my health permits. My father is excessively low spirited, which depresses mine, seeing him unhappy instantly makes me so.

Saturday, 7 February

Read my *Vision on Admiral Boscawen* to Mrs. Wicker & lend it her. No letter from

Miss Gittins, poor dear girl, I am in the utmost concern for her. Shou'd her lover be false I tremble to think on the pangs it will cost her, heaven avert this evil.

Sunday, 8 February

At Church twice. Doctor Hutchinson preaches on self denial. Mr. Pigott comes here to lay intending to go up to London in the Coach, he makes me ten thousand professions of regard & friendship. Poor man, he is very ill & goes for advice.

Monday, 9 February

Mr. Pigott told me he heard Captain Smith was married. Good Heaven, if this kind of News had been true. What if it had, hope I shou'd have found fortitude enough to support me & pride enough to despise a man who cou'd act so meanly.

Tuesday, 10 February

Sir Charles Eversfield sends Sally Sheppard, Bet Cook & me each a ticket for the play & the pleasing assurance that there is a fine prospect for *[illegible word]*. Spend the evening at Sally Sheppard's with Bett Cook, some very agreeable chat.

Wednesday, 11 February

My father in a very ill humour, without a cause, but parents I suppose have their privilege, & we must bear it without murmuring. Doctor Smith asks me when I heard from my Harry, & if I don't expect him soon. Read *The Ladies' Magazine*.

Thursday, 12 February

Very busy ironing. An excessive cold & snowing. My poor constitution can hardly bear this rigorous season. Intend going to the Play, but there is not company enough for them to act, poor Mortals, they'll starve.

Friday, 13 February

A solemn Fast for the War. At Church twice. Doctor Hutchinson makes a fine discourse, & well adapted to the occasion he takes notice of the advantages, & expatiates on the miseries of War. Bett Cook tells me Doctor Griffith says I am not a proper Mate for Captain Smith, my family is not good enough, sure t'is equal to his, oh ye vain empty things.

> By education & by birth obscure,
> Ten thousand pound would these great failings cure.
> My Wit wou'd lively be, my face divine,
> And nameless graces in each action shine.

Saturday, 14 February

A letter from my dear Miss Gittins, she is at Mr. Bold's at Havant. Has heard nothing from Turnpenny, faithless Man, am afraid he now deserves that epithet. She sends me another song, which I answer, proposes our being together in the Summer at Little Hampton, wish such an event may happen.

Sunday, 15 February

At Church twice.

Monday, 16 February

Work all day on my Apron. Begin writing some verses, *Little Reason Triumphant*. Go to the Play, *Cleone*, a tragedy,[338] but very ill perform'd, there is one, & but one, good Player, to see the rest is rather a mortification than a diversion.

Tuesday, 17 February

Mamma & I make a morning visit at Mrs. Cheynell's, she pays a Bill. Mrs. James was ill & out of temper,[339] I wonder how she wou'd behave was she in my bad state of health. Spend the afternoon & evening at Mrs. Bridger's, who gives us a very genteel supper.

Wednesday, 18 February

Mr. Osgood & his sister Miss Reynolds [*Reynell*] spend the evening with us, what a droll creature she is, her look is a comedy.[340]   Mr. Osgood tells me March is very near, alluding to the report of my Harry coming in that month, pray Heav'n he may.

Thursday, 19 February

Spend the afternoon & evening at my Aunt Waller's with a vast deal of company. Mr. John Shelley there, he behaves tolerably well, which is something extraordinary. Play at cards. I sincerely hope the season for this diversion will soon be at an end.

Friday, 20 February

Sally Sheppard & I make a visit to Mrs. Wicker. We tell her how ill Doctor Griffith has us'd me, with respect to my affair with Captain Smith, & how many disrespectfull things he has said. She can hardly credit it, but is determin'd to tell him of it.

Saturday, 21 February

Work on my apron. Finish *Reason Triumphant*. Send Sally Sheppard the verses on Admiral Boscawen, she shews it Drew Michell, who approves, several more hear it & guess the Author, which will I suppose excite Malice & envy, whose keen fangs I have so often experienc'd.

Sunday, 22 February

At Church twice. Begin writing to Miss Gittins. Everybody but me is now retir'd to rest, for never sure was a more tempestuous Night, the howling winds are let loose

---

338 *Cleone*, a tragedy by Robert Dodsley, was first performed in 1758; it was an immediate success and had a long run at Covent Garden. Robert Dodsley was a bookseller and publisher as well as a writer; he published many of Dr. Johnson's works and suggested and helped to finance Johnson's *English Dictionary*. He also published Thomas Gray's masterpiece, the *Elegy written in a Country Churchyard*, in 1751.

339 This suggests that Mrs. James was living with Mrs. Cheynell — perhaps she was a relative or a housekeeper.

340 Elizabeth Reynell was actually Francis Osgood's sister-in-law — he had married Katherine Reynell, daughter of the late Canon John Reynell, Vicar of Horsham and Master of Collyer's School, in 1723, but she had died in 1738.

from their Caverns. My Heart dies within me when I reflect that my dear Harry is expos'd to this dreadfull storm, oh preserve him Heav'n.

Monday, 23 February

Work all day & write several bits [*?bills*] out. At the play with a vast deal of company, *The Mourning Bride*, they perform the two first Acts tolerably well but close very indifferently, making some very laughable Blunders.[341]

Tuesday, 24 February

My father goes out to see one Mr. Payne, who lives near Turners Hill, stays all night.[342] Finish writing to Miss Gittins. Send her *Reason Triumphant*. Sup at Sally Sheppard's with Bet Cook & Drew Michell. Read *The Monthly Review*.

Wednesday, 25 February

My father returns home, is in a good humour but on my mother saying one wry word is all storm & rage. Oh liberty, the choicest gift of Heav'n, if I enjoy'd thee, the smallest pittance wou'd be an Empire. How evident it is we know not what to wish, I thought if he recovered from the Smallpox I shou'd never know another trouble, but alas, I find a sad reverse.

Thursday, 26 February

Mamma goes to the play, *The Beggar's Opera*, very indifferently perform'd.[343] Work on my apron till eleven o clock.

Friday, 27 February

Copy a letter for my father to Mr. Tudor, who is in Scotland. Spend the afternoon & evening at Mr. Osgood's, with Mr. & Mrs. Tredcroft.

Saturday, 28 February

Good Heaven, how fast the latter talks & what she says how trifling, which indeed is generally the case of those who are incessantly cackling, yet she is reckon'd among women of sense, but understanding does not consist in a flow of words, but in a certain rectitude of behaviour, which may be observ'd but is difficult to define.

---

341 *The Mourning Bride* by William Congreve, first performed in 1697, was the only tragedy that he wrote.

342 Mr. Payne was probably related to John Payne of Ligg's Heath, who married Margaret Shelley, sister of Timothy Shelley, and was High Sheriff of Sussex in 1738. He died before 1743, so this man may have been his son.

343 *The Beggar's Opera*, by John Gay (1685-1732), a poet and dramatist closely associated with Alexander Pope and Jonathan Swift, was first produced in 1728, using well-known tunes and ballads as a burlesque of Italian opera. It was an immediate success and the characters of Captain Macheath and Polly Peachum soon became household names. It was also seen as a satire on the government of Sir Robert Walpole and the corruption of the governing class. Sarah had probably seen a much better production in London, where it was frequently revived.

MARCH 1761

Sunday, 1 March

At Church twice, a most delightful pleasant day. Walk up in the Park with Bett Cook, the birds all tun'd their little throats & seem'd to hail approaching spring. Drink tea at Mrs. Wicker's with a vast deal of company, they talk of one of the Players, his name Harding, give him very great praises, which indeed he merits. I write some verses on him.

Monday, 2 March

A young girl dines with me, to whom I made a visit about fourteen years ago. Her name Hughes, she lives at Storrington.[344] Harding's Benefit, go to the Play tolerably well perfom'd, it was *The Orphan of China*, an exceeding good play.[345]

Tuesday, 3 March

My father excessively out of temper, which makes me as much so; oh my dear Harry, why don't you come & rescue me from this worse than Turkish slavery.

Wednesday, 4 March

Finish the other half of my Apron & now have only about a week's work to join it. What can be the meaning I hear nothing of Captain Smith, but I will hope he is well.

Thursday, 5 March

Work all day on my Apron. At night at the Play *Tamerlane*, or rather a Burlesque upon Tamerlane, for never sure was a more wretched performance,[346] it was a severe punishment instead of a diversion, fancy they must soon quit this place & exhibit elsewhere.

Friday, 6 March

Sally Hunt calls on me; & Nany Hughes to take her leave of me. Very busy all day. Sitting so much certainly impairs my health, I must use more exercise when the weather will permit or I shall utterly destroy it. Read in *The Old Woman's Magazine*, a very smart performance.

Saturday, 7 March

No letter from Captain Smith, I thought e'er this he wou'd have been in England, but I am inur'd to disappointments of this, when I wonder will my suspenses &

---

344 Presumably Nany (Anne) Hughes, mentioned again on 6 March. The Hughes were well-known in Storrington, as tanners, fell-mongers and glovers.
345 Sarah had previously read this play, by Arthur Murphy, on 4 December 1759.
346 *Tamerlane* was an original play by Nicholas Rowe, first performed in 1702. Tamerlane was meant to represent King William III and the villain Bajazet, King Louis XIV. For many years it was regularly acted on the anniversary of William's landing at Torbay in 1688, to celebrate the *"Glorious Revolution"* which ensured Protestant supremacy in England.

uneasiness have an end. Alas how painfully pleasing are these conections, we are desirous of loving & being lov'd yet ever anxious concerning the beloved objects wellfare, which poisons all our joys.

Sunday, 8 March

At Church in the morning. Walk to Warnham Church in the afternoon, with Sally Sheppard, Bet Cook & my sister, an excessive pleasant day & we are very merry. My Uncle Bob comes from London.

Monday, 9 March

Work all day on my Apron. Expect a letter from my Harry, but alas am disappointed, sure his next will bring me the news of his Arrival in England. Bett & I go in to see the two last Acts of the Play & the entertainment, which last was *The Stage Coach*, intolerably bad performance & an excessive low thing.[347] They intend playing but twice more, believe I shall go the last time.

Tuesday, 10 March

My Uncle Bob & Papa spend their evening at Mr. Osgood's. Sally comes over & we play at cards. Doctor Smith comes in & we have a great deal of chat, he says he thinks my Harry is gone a long time, t'is now indeed fifteen months, an age to be absent from what we love.

Wednesday, 11 March

Read my *Universal Magazine*. Make an addition to the Song on Harding & make another on Lain, an excessive bad Player.

Thursday, 12 March

Finish my Apron to my inexpressive satisfaction, such another piece of work I will never more undertake. Write out several bills & deliver them. Read *The Ladies' Magazine*. Very little worth notice except Voltaire's life begun, it gives me vast satisfaction to read the Memoirs of eminent Men, especially those who have excell'd in literary performances.

Friday, 13 March

Very busy putting the Shop goods in order. Shew my Apron to Mr. Tredcroft who wishes me health to wear it.

Saturday, 14 March

Rise very early & when I had given it over, the Post brings me a letter from my dear Harry, wrote in a very splenetick state, being excessively tir'd of being so long at Sea. They have taken a prize or two, which was in the Papers & I was several times wish'd joy.[348]   Captain Smith told me he did not write to his mother so I

---

347   *The Stage Coach* was a farce translated from the French by George Farquhar and P.A.Motteux, first performed in 1704.

348   At this time prize money - realised from the sale of a ship captured in war - was divided among the captors, so Henry could expect to benefit financially from this action.

thought it was best to call & let her know he was well, she did not express much gratitude for the favour.

Sunday, 15 March

A delightfull fine day, walk twice up in the Park, & go twice to Church.

Monday, 16 March

The happiness of another letter from Captain Smith, he was going on a six weeks cruise, five of which is now expir'd, so I hope he will soon be in England. A letter from Mrs. Jones, acquainting me that they intend coming to Slynfold & keeping a school, of which I am extreamly glad, as well on their accounts as that my brother will be so near us.

Tuesday, 17 March

Mrs. Wicker tells Doctor Griffith what he said concerning me & Captain Smith, he denies it with ten thousand imprecations. Write to Captain Smith & Mrs. Jones. Not well.

Wednesday, 18 March

[The] Miss Ellis's here in the morning for a new hatt & Cloak, I thought they had quite forsaken us, I wou'd not be of such a fickle disposition for the Universe. Walk up in the Park with Sally Sheppard, meet Sir Charles, who obliges us to go to Den & drink tea.

Thursday, 19 March

Read *The Monthly Review*, the Authors maul the 3rd & fourth volumes of *Tristram Shandy* in a most unmercifull manner, but no more than it deserves, by their account of it. Sally Sheppard comes over & we play at cards. Quite ill with a violent pain in my breast.

Friday, 20 March

Good Friday, at Church twice. Very few people there, sure all Christians ought at least to keep this day holy. Call at Mrs. Wicker's & see her new Room, which she has fitted up very smart. Hope to hear from Miss Gittins tomorrow.

Saturday, 21 March

Write out all the Ellis's Bills, which engages me all the morning. A pain in my breast all day, Doctor Smith says I must beware of taking Cold.   Mr. Tredcroft here, I lay him a Pot of Coffee that Mr. Medley is chosen for Seaford.[349]   He asks me if Captain Smith is arriv'd in England.

---

349 Seaford was an important Sussex port in the Middle Ages, at the mouth of the Ouse, but its population was decimated by the Black Death. It was a *"rotten"* Parliamentary Borough, which still retained the right to send two members to Parliament, like Horsham, despite its decline in importance. Sarah's conversation with Mr. Tredcroft on this subject raises the possibility that he may have had ambitions to become an M.P. Since the Irwin family had appropriated both the seats in Horsham for their family and friends, he would have had to look elsewhere for the opportunity to stand for election.

Sunday, 22 March

At Church twice, a fine day but cold. Walk in the Croft. After dinner walk to Dales with Bet Cook & my sister Bet, meet Seymour Powell who gives us sixpence to spend, which occasions a great deal of mirth. Drink tea at Mr. Tredcroft's & eat Easter Cake.[350]

Monday, 23 March

Mrs. Childs from Dorking calls on me, with several gentlemen & ladies, walk down to the Church with them, they criticise on the poetical epitaphs.[351] Go down to Tanbridge, they pay me all their Bills & are tolerably cheerfull tho' Miss Ellis was not well.

Tuesday, 24 March

Walk up in the Park with Mrs. Wicker & Mrs. Tasker, Sir Charles comes out & joins us, & intreats us to go in & drink tea, but we plead a prior engagement. Spend the evening at my Aunt Grace's, Seymour Powell comes in & by his droll behaviour makes us very merry.

Wednesday, 25 March

Work all the morning, go in the afternoon to Dales with a large Posse, to drink tea & eat Easter Cake; we are vastly merry, but alas my Heart mixes not in these diversion[s]. I sigh amidst a peal of laughter, sigh for the absence of him that I wish to have forever with me, fifteen months, tedious lingering months, since last I saw [him], & when I have again that pleasure, it will I fear be of very short duration.

Thursday, 26 March

Breakfast at Mrs. Cheynell's, shew her my Apron which she prodigiously admires, spend the afternoon at Mrs. Curtis's.

Friday, 27 March

Sally Sheppard & Bet Cook drink tea with me. Take a walk in the Park, see Sir Charles at a distance but avoid him, go all round Den House, he calls to us on our return, obliges us to go in & upbraids us for running away from him; he accompanies us very near home.

Saturday, 28 March

Very busy taking an account of what goods is wanting when I go to London. Sure I shall now hear that Harry Smith is arriv'd in England, wou'd to Heaven I cou'd see a period to this state of hopes & fears. Read in *The Old Woman's Magazine*, a very smart letter to the College of Physicians.

---

350 *"Easter Cake"* in this instance was probably a large plum cake, commonly provided on special occasions, but small Easter cakes were baked in some parts of the country. These appear to have been little curd tarts, sometimes called *"Maids of Honour"*.

351 There is now only one *"poetical epitaph"* in St. Mary's Church, in honour of the Rev. Thomas White, who died in 1788, but it is interesting that there seem to have been others there in 1761. This suggests that Thomas's epitaph, which may well have been composed by Sarah herself, was written in line with an existing tradition.

Sunday, 29 March

At Church twice, walk in the Park. Sir Charles calls to Bett, Sally Sheppard & I walk away. We are determin'd not to go to Den any more, fearing it may prejudice our Characters, in the opinion of those who cannot or will not see the purity of our intentions. Drink tea at Mrs. Wicker's.

Monday, 30 March

Ill all night with a violent fever, & cold. No letter from my friend Miss Gittins, what can be the meaning of it, sure no accident has befallen her. Sally Sheppard spends the evening with [word omitted] play at cards. Read in *The Old Woman's Magazine*.

Tuesday, 31 March

Work all the morning. Drink tea at Mrs. Wicker's with Molly Reynolds & Jenny Hunt, the latter is very ill & looks dejected, she cannot yet recover the loss of her lover. Read *The Christian Magazine*. The stile of it is low & trifling.

APRIL 1761

Wednesday, 1 April

The Election of Members to represent the Borough in Parliament,[352] this brings to my remembrances the Ball we had seven year ago, on the same occasion; how different is my situation now, my dear Smith then liv'd at Horsham & I had the satisfaction of seeing him every day; but let me ask my Heart one question; was I happier then?

Thursday, 2 April

Certainly no, I saw him at least by stealth, consequently with anxiety, our meetings were imbitter'd; sufficient then to the day is the evil thereof, I then mourn'd his presence, and now his absence; if perfect serenity is ever attainable in this world it must be after we are past this state of hopes, fears & wishes.

Friday, 3 April

Ride out with my father. Walk out in the afternoon, to a Country House & drink Tea.

Saturday, 4 April

A letter from my amiable friend Miss Gittins, she likes *Reason Triumphant*, is return'd from Mr. Bold's at Havant. Says her passion for Fame is equal to mine. My father repines at our business not being so good as usual, it certainly

---

352 This election was not contested and so was a mere formality, with Sir Leonard Pilkington and Charles Ingram (nephew of Henry, 7th Viscount Irwin), being re-elected as the two members of Parliament for Horsham. Henry, Lord Irwin, died three days later, at Hill's Place, on 4 April; but Sarah makes no mention of this important event. Lord Irwin was well known in Horsham, as he had lived there for several years before succeeding to the title, and visited the town quite often after handing over his principal seat, Temple Newsam, to his nephew Charles on his marriage to a rich heiress, Frances Shepheard, in 1758.

is not, everything in this World is mutable, our own dispositions partake of this inconstancy, it may then be [a] matter of concern but not of wonder.

Sunday, 5 April

At Church twice, & walk twice, go into Den at Sir Charles's intreaty, he entertains us with madeira & Apples. Drink tea at Mrs. Wicker's with Mrs. Laight from London.

Monday, 6 April

Very ill with a pain in my breast. Walk up in the Park by myself, a great many melancholy & some pleasing reflections. Think if my Dear Harry shou'd prove inconstant my fate will be deplorable, then consider that the Supream Power can supply me with fortitude to endure this & every other misfortune he thinks proper to inflict.

Tuesday, 7 April

Walk out & return home wet. Read in *The Royal Magazine*, go to Bed not well at nine o' clock.

Wednesday, 8 April

Very busy all day washing & ironing, out of temper because it is wet weather, oh how absurd & ridiculous is this, & what is still worse angry with Mamma for not contriving it better, NB to beware of such behaviour for the future.

Thursday, 9 April

Iron all day, Mamma & I dispute, we are both in the wrong, both rash in our expressions & tenacious of our province, but t'is my place to concede, which my obstinate temper finds very difficult. I must endeavour to rectify this disposition.

Friday, 10 April

Sally Sheppard, Bet Cook & I go to Church with Nany Baker to see her married.[353] Breakfast at Mr. Curtis's, break some Cake over the Bride's Head & are very merry. Help pick & chop Raisins for Wine till I am exceedingly tir'd, t'is with reluctance I assist in any of these domestick affairs, but since my situation in Life renders it necessary am determin'd to overcome this reluctance

Saturday, 11 April.

Read *The Jealous Wife*, a new Comedy, wrote by one Colman, but does not merit the [?commendation] & applause it has met with.[354] No letter yet from Captain Smith. Sally Sheppard & Bet Cook & myself intend going a long walk, but wet weather prevents us.

---

353 Anne Baker married Richard Smart, a wheelwright from Billingshurst. Sarah and Sally Sheppard were listed as witnesses. Anne Baker has not been mentioned previously; and the name Baker does not appear in the Horsham Land Tax for this period. Possibly she was a relation or servant of the Curtis family, as the wedding breakfast was held at their house.

354 *The Jealous Wife*, by George Colman the elder (1732-1794), first performed in 1761, is now considered to be one of the best plays of the mid 18th century — of very high quality and extremely funny. It was based in part on Henry Fielding's *Tom Jones*, and the main character was one of David Garrick's most famous roles.

Sunday, 12 April

At Church, Doctor Hutchinson preaches an excellent Sermon on the government of the passions, alas how difficult to practice his lessons. Drink tea & spend the evening at Mr. Tredcroft's.

Monday, 13 April

Accompany Bet Cook a little way in the Stage Coach, she is gone down to see her sister. Meet my old acquaintance, Nat Bristed[355] with his Wife, we chat over a great many of our former transactions. No letter from Captain Smith, at which I cannot help being excessively uneasy.

Tuesday, 14 April

Sally Sheppard tells me a very ill-natur'd speech of Doctor [?Griffith], relating to her & me. I wish the poor man wou'd apply himself to some business, which might probably prevent his impudent remarks on his innocent neighbours.

Wednesday, 15 April

Work all day but very ill with a violent cold. An excessive dull wet day & my spirits not very good, read *The British Magazine*.

Thursday, 16 April

The long expected letter from my Dear Harry, he is arriv'd at Plymouth, & has wrote to the Admiralty for leave to come to Horsham, which I hope they will grant & let me enjoy his dear conversation. Take a walk with Mrs. Wicker & Sally Sheppard. Write to Captain Smith.

Friday, 17 April

Go down to the Milk fields by six in the morning, to drink milk which I am advis'd to for the recovery of my health. Not well, this ugly pain in my breast again. Drink tea & spend the evening at Mrs. Wicker's with Jenny Hunt, we are vastly merry.

Saturday, 18 April

Another letter from my dearest Harry, he hopes to come soon, a violent pain in my breast all day. Mr. Gatlan & Mr. Chasemore from Cuckfield here, the latter gives me half a Dozen Franks.[356] Go to Bed very ill.

Sunday, 19 April

Keep my Bed all day with a fever, pray Heaven I may get better before my Harry comes, else what satisfaction can I have in his company. Oh pain & sickness, how severe have been thy attacks on my poor frame within this last year.

---

355   Nathaniel Bristed was the son of the Rev. John Bristed of Slaugham, baptised on 16 February 1733 at St. Anne's, Lewes. The reference to their *"former transactions"* further suggests that Sarah might have been at school in Lewes.

356   Franks were free postage, and most welcome when postage was very expensive. M.P.s, government officials and lawyers had the privilege of franking a letter by signing their name on the wrapper.

Monday, 20 April

Something better & walk out with Sally Sheppard, who is in a very indifferent state of health, which greatly adds to my concern.[357] Mr. Tredcroft's family drink tea & spend the evening with us. Mr. John Shelley comes, t'is rumour'd he intends to Court Miss Tredcroft & his behaviour has the appearance of it.

Tuesday, 21 April

Walk out with Sally Sheppard, a most delightfull fine morning, but I am too ill to enjoy it. Ride out, & am caught in a shower, read the *Review,* they don't approve *The Jealous Wife.*

Wednesday, 22 April

[No entry]

Thursday, 23 April

A letter from Mrs. Townshend, she wishes me better health & commends my Poetry.

Friday, 24 April

[No entry]

Saturday, 25 April

[No entry]

Sunday, 26 April

Continue very ill till this morning when I am thank God something better. Walk up in the Park, a serene pleasant day. My father, mother, sisters & self drink tea with my grandmother, the Old Lady tells me I have an excellent character.

Monday, 27 April

Intend to ride out but it is a very cold unpleasant day. No letter from Captain Smith, I fear he cannot get leave of absence; yet I hope my fears are groundless. Write to my cousin Bet Smith.

Tuesday, 28 April

Walk out with Sally Sheppard, poor dear Girl, she is quite ill, & I am far very far from well. We drink tea at Mrs. Wicker's. She has a fine Head of Brockles[358] which she intends to save for Captain Smith. Mrs. Humphrey[359] comes from London & says she met him there, & he desir'd her to acquaint his mother he shou'd be at Horsham this week, sure I shall have a letter from him tonight.

Wednesday, 29 April

Drink tea & spend the evening at Mrs. Bridger's. Enquire at the Post Office but no letter for me, dreadfull what can this mean, sure my Harry after so long

---

357 It is possible that both Sally and Sarah were suffering from a seasonal illness or virus which was often prevalent at this time of year (literally, spring fever).

358 Presumably broccoli.

359 Mrs Judith Humphrey, wife of Philip Humphrey and widow of Thomas Vinall, was the mother of Guildford Vinall, the mercer. She lived in part of the old Talbot and Wonder, a former inn, in Market Square.

a perseverance cannot forget or disregard his Sally. If he does, but let me not encourage this shocking conjecture!

Thursday, 30 April

Write a very long letter to Miss Gittins. Mamma is ill. Acquaint Sally Sheppard that I have not heard from Captain Smith, she pities my situation & thinks it strange.

MAY 1761

Friday, 1 May

Lord bless me, how shall I support this dreadfull suspence. No letter tonight, cruel Man, sure this neglect cannot be design'd, oh supream power give me patience to bear this anxiety.

Saturday, 2 May

Work as well as my Head & Heart will permit. The Coaches come in & no Captain Smith, they were full & he cou'd get no place. He sent word to his mother he will come next Tuesday, three more nights & days of cruel suspence, how, how, shall I bear it.

Sunday, 3 May

Lament my situation to Mrs. Wicker, she blames me for being uneasy, & says no doubt he will excuse himself, he may, but oh I fear it. Ride out with my father. Captain Smith arrives & soon after him a letter which I shou'd have had last Wednesday, away ye unjust suspicions.

Monday, 4 May

A fever all night & no sleep, occasion'd by my Joy, which has on me a more violent effect than grief. Captain Smith tells me of several presents he has brought me. Sup with him at Mrs. Wicker's, he laughs & tells me his love is worn out, only in jest sure, how miserable shou'd I be were it true. Very little sleep again, how shall I live thus.

Tuesday, 5 May

Drink tea at Mrs. Tredcroft's, Captain Smith cou'd not accompany me, how insipid is every hour not pass'd with those we love.

Wednesday, 6 May

Quite ill all the morning, walk in Mrs. Wicker's garden. Captain Smith spends an hour with me in the shop, Seymour Powell engages him in chat. Ride to Mr. Bristed's at Slaugham, meet Miss Michell, her sisters & several gentlemen in the Forest.[360]

Thursday, 7 May

Sit up late with Captain Smith, talk much of our future settlement in Life, but ah, I fear it will never be my lot to live with him. Oh Father supream, give me

---

360 Probably Henrietta Michell of Warnham and her sisters, Mrs. Shuckford and Mrs. Miller — see entry for 19 January 1761.

strength of mind to think all thy dispensations are for the best whether it is in the disappointment or success of our wishes.

Friday, 8 May

A letter from my Dear Miss Gittins, she desires me to call on Miss Bates, an acquaintance of hers in London, & to call at her false lover's lodgings. Captain Smith dines with us, then he, Mrs. Wicker, Sally Sheppard & myself ride over to the Hammer pond & spend a most agreeable afternoon.

Saturday, 9 May

My Harry calls in the morning, he expects his brothers down, tolerably well & easy thank God. Mr. Pigott, Mr. Shelley & Captain Smith drink tea with me. A vast deal of chat, read in *Sir Charles Grandison*.[361] Ill all day.

Sunday, 10 May

At Church twice, Doctor Hutchinson makes an excellent discourse. Sir Charles tells my sister I must surely now be happy. Ride out in the Afternoon. Sit up till twelve with Captain Smith, he promises never to marry if I shou'd die, which assurance has made me much happier than I was, I cou'd not bear the thought that any person shou'd succeed me in his affections. He makes me a present of a piece of India Muslin for a Negligee & petticoat, & another for aprons & ruffles.[362]

Monday, 11 May

Dine at the Farm house with Sally Sheppard, Bet Cook, Drew Michell & my sister Bet, we are vastly well entertain'd & very merry.

Tuesday, 12 May

At home all day & work very close, Captain Smith here several times, he has certainly a great regard for me, but I fear not so great as mine for him. Hush hush, busy imagination, ever studious to torment thyself, can'st not thou enjoy the present minute that blesses thee with his presence & leave Futurity to his all wise direction who will certainly dispose every thing for the best.

Wednesday, 13 May

Walk out in the Country & drink tea with Sally Sheppard & Bet Cook, extreamly pleasant.

Thursday, 14 May

All the morning with my Harry, wash & Iron him a Pair of ruffles that I work'd for him a great while ago. I hope I hope he will continue his regard for me else how wretched must I be. Drink tea & spend the evening at Mrs. Wicker's with Mrs. Bridger.

361 *Sir Charles Grandison* was written by Samuel Richardson, who also wrote *Pamela* and *Clarissa*, both successful novels in the *"familiar letters"* form. He was also a printer who became the Master of the Stationers' Company.

362 Muslin was a delicately woven cotton fabric, which took its name from the town of Mosul, in what is now Iraq. It was much sought after at this time.

Friday, 15 May

Write out several Bills, on Sunday I must go to London & leave my Harry, cruel business, thou foe to love. Hear the dreadfull news of Mr. Gittins' death, alas my dear friend, how great must be your distress & how violent is my concern for you. I had thoughts of writing, but what words can I find to address you in, all all must fall short of your loss & my sensibility of it.

Saturday, 16 May

Mr. Grainger calls, & makes me a great many compliments. Write to poor dear unfortunate friend Miss Gittins.

Sunday, 17 May

Very busy preparing for my London Journey which I must go tomorrow, & leave my Harry, patience lend thy aid, for now indeed I want thee. Go to Mrs Cheynell's between Church & walk in her garden. Drink tea at the *King's Head*, where is my Harry that he comes not?

Monday, 18 May

Captain Smith rises by five in the morning to see me set off for London, I part from him in tolerable spirits, I hope he will not be oblig'd to leave Horsham before I can return. Arrive safe in Town, go to the Play to hear Miss Brent sing, but are disappointed.

Tuesday, 19 May

My father & I do our business at the Linnen Draper's, dine there, go to the Stuff Warehouse. Mrs. Wicker, my father & self go to the Play to see *The Jealous Wife*. I thought it but an indifferent thing when I read it, & very little better in the representation.[363]

Wednesday, 20 May

Am much better in health, thank Heaven, than I was at home. Go to the Hosier, in the afternoon to an auction Room in Spring Gardens to see a collection of Pictures. A letter from my dear friend Miss Gittins. She bears her father's death with the resignation becoming a Christian.

Thursday, 21 May

Busy all day at the Haberdashers, I am quite tir'd of the dirty place, & sincerely wish I was return'd to Horsham & my Harry. Jack Smith, my Harry's brother, takes Mrs. Wicker & me to the Play, *The Conscious Lovers* & *Polly Honeycombe*.[364]

Friday, 22 May

Call on Mrs. & Miss Seawell, shew them my Apron which they prodigiously admire. Papa goes out *[words missing]* Town. Quite ill, alas I cannot continue well any time.

---

363 See Sarah's previous remarks on *The Jealous Wife* by George Colman on 11 April 1761.

364 *The Conscious Lovers* was a sentimental comedy by Sir Richard Steele, first performed in 1722, and admired for its high moral tone, while *Polly Honeycombe*, George Colman's first play, produced in 1760, was an amusing satire on the sentimental novel, and novel readers.

Drink tea at my Uncle George's, call on Miss Bates but she was not at home.

Saturday, 23 May

Mrs Wicker, my cousin Bet & self walk out, but it was wet & unpleasant. Drink tea at my Uncle Bob's with Mrs. Parke. Write to Captain Smith but have no letter from him as I a little expect'd. Go to find Mr. Turnpenny's Lodgings, my Gittin's false lover, but without success.

Sunday, 24 May

At Church in the morning. Dine with Mrs. Wicker & my Aunt Sally at Mrs. Laight's. When I return home am surpris'd with the News of Captain Smith's being in Town, he sups with us & perswades me not to go on Tuesday, as I intended, alas how can I? He might go to Plymouth next Friday.

Monday, 25 May

Captain Smith calls in the morning & desires we wou'd accompany him to Kensington Gardens which we promise. Dine at my Uncle Bob's, my Harry calls us at four, we take a Coach to Kensington, drink coffee & then Walk in the Gardens, which are indeed most delightfully pleasant, my Harry is all love & kindness.

Tuesday, 26 May

Captain Smith spends an hour or two with us in the morning, I live but in his company; alas what shall I do when Friday comes, that day must separate us, perhaps for years. He drinks tea with us. Mr. Ellis[365] calls after supper, we shew him the Prussian exercise,[366] & are quite merry.

Wednesday, 27 May

Go with my cousin Bet to see Mrs. Holmes, an acquaintance of hers, who desir'd to see my Apron. Then go again to enquire after Turnpenny, but can hear nothing of him. Captain Smith here all the afternoon, we go into the Back Parlour, which excites the mirth of Mrs Wicker & my cousin Bet.

Thursday, 28 May

Captain Smith shews me a letter from the Chaplain of the *Orford*, his name Grant, he has lately lost his sweetheart, Sally Forward, the most affecting epistle I ever read. Captain Smith gives it me at my desire. Go to the Play, & see his Majesty there; Garrick plays *King Lear*.[367]

Friday, 29 May

Go out in the Morning; my Harry & I meet at the door, we are both excessively affected at parting, he stays with me three hours, which seem'd so many Minutes.

---

365 Probably John Ellis of Chichester.
366 Possibly a dance based on the military exercise.
367 It is surprising that Sarah does not sound more excited about this experience — seeing the great David Garrick playing Shakespeare's *King Lear* in front of the young King George III! But she was probably too distressed by the thought of having to part from Henry next day to appreciate it fully.

Was to set out for Plymouth at four in the afternoon; Oh protect him, thou Power Supreme, & comfort my despairing Mind.

Saturday, 30 May

Set out for Horsham. Very disagreeable company in the Coach, so I divert myself with reading two Pamphlets my Harry gave me, *The Rosciad*, wrote on the Players & *The Apology (addressed) to the Critical Reviewers*.[368] Begin writing to Captain Smith at the *Red Lion*, Dorking. Arrive safe at Horsham but seem to have lost something & cannot find it, alas it is my Harry.

Sunday, 31 May

Not very well all day, Oh Love thou destroyer of my health & repose when wilt thou recompence me for all the evils thou hast made me suffer. At Church in the Afternoon, drink tea at Mrs. Bridger's.

JUNE 1761

Monday, 1 June

Extreamly busy all day in the shop, putting up the goods I bought in London & serving my customers. Mrs. Tredcroft here all the afternoon. How incessantly does she talk & upon nothing of any consequence to herself or hearers.

Tuesday, 2 June

Busied in the Shop all the morning. Spend the afternoon at Mrs. Wicker's. My letter that I wrote to Captain Smith from London did not arrive here till he was gone, & I have great reason to think that his mother open'd it instead of sending it after, this vexes me tho' there was nothing of any consequence, yet it was very impertinent in her; letters ought allways to be sacred.

Wednesday, 3 June

Work all day, a little chat with my Sally Sheppard in the evening. Read *The Royal Magazine*.

Thursday, 4 June

Taken extreamly ill with a violent fever.

Friday, 5 June

[No entry]

Saturday, 6 June

[No entry]

---

368 *The Rosciad* was a satirical pamphlet written about the London stage by Charles Churchill, which caused controversy. It was followed by *The Apology addressed to the Critical Reviewers*, in which Churchill answered his critics. Later he supported John Wilkes and attacked the artist William Hogarth. Hogarth replied by lampooning Churchill as *"The Bruiser"* in an engraving that depicted him as a bear, published in 1763.

Sunday, 7 June

A letter from Captain Smith.

Monday, 8 June

[No entry]

Tuesday, 9 June

Write to Captain Smith but am so ill am hardly capable.

Wednesday, 10 June

[No entry]

Thursday, 11 June

[No entry]

Friday, 12 June

[No entry]

Saturday, 13 June

Write to Miss Gittins to know if they will take me at Arundel for a Boarder, to recover my health. What a large Blank is my Book, which cou'd be filled up with nothing but pain & Misery.

Sunday, 14 June

Thank God I am much better, & Doctor Smith gives me great hopes that I shall quite recover. Sally Sheppard & Bet Cook drink tea with me, I am thank God much better. A letter from my dear Harry full of the tenderest sentiments.

Monday, 15 June

A little return of my fever in the Night. Ride out in the Forest hold it tolerably well. Work a little on my return but am taken with a violent headache. Mrs. James comes down, she tells me I am not fit for an inhabitant of this World, indeed I think so too for I am incapable at present of both business & pleasure.

Tuesday, 16 June

Write to my dear Harry in the morning, give him an account of my illness, & weep over the letter. Spend the afternoon & evening at Mrs. Tredcroft's Miss's Birthday.[369]

Wednesday, 17 June

Ride out, but t'is cold wet bad weather & hardly fit for such flimsy constitutions to stir abroad. A letter from Miss Gittins desiring I wou'd come to Arundel & one from my Dear Smith acquainting me they expected to Sail as last Sunday, Heaven protect him from all dangers. He says he never shall be happy till my name is chang'd to his, I wonder when that will be.

Thursday, 18 June

My father gives me his leave to go to Arundel in a fortnight. Ride out in the afternoon but t'is cold & unpleasant & I am gloomy as the Weather.

---

369   This was Phoebe Tredcroft's 18th birthday.

Friday, 19 June

Ride to Mr. Miller's at Warnham in the morning, they have a charming pleasant Garden, & seem to live in a sweet & snug Manner, how happy shou'd my Harry & I be in such a situation.[370] Mrs. Tredcroft take me out in the Forest in her Chariot, & allmost talks me to Death.

Saturday, 20 June

Write to Mrs. Jones & my brother with several letters of business to London. Walk up in the Park with Sally Sheppard. Sir Charles desires us to walk into Den, we comply & chat half an hour. He express'd great pleasure in seeing me abroad, but told me I am in love, most true, but that's not the cause of my present illness.

Sunday, 21 June

At Church in the morning, ride into the Forest in the afternoon. Then walk in the Park & now am at home quite alone at liberty to pursue my own reflections. What a surprising, what a various World we live in, some pass away Life in silent obscurity, others on the World's busy stage are in continual action, but who can determine which is the happiest? The Good may be content in either, but I believe happiness is reserv'd for our future Lot.

Monday, 22 June

Walk up in the Park, but the Dew had made it too wet for me to walk. Ill when I come home.

Tuesday, 23 June

Work all the morning. Ride with my father in the afternoon to his farm at Nuthurst, walk all over the ground, a vast deal of fine growing Timber on it, how agreeable is a rural life, with a companion we love, tho' with them any place is so, alas Harry.

Wednesday, 24 June

Ride to Slaugham to see Mr. Bristed's family, with my father, Mr. Miller & Mr. Powell. When we return home am agreeably surpis'd with a letter from my Dear Harry dated off Brest, relates the sudden Death of one of his friends, a Marine Officer, who has left a disconsolate Young Lady his sweetheart behind him, she lives at Plymouth where he drop'd down dead; good God, what a shock she must have received.

Thursday, 25 June

[She is] a very fine girl, I saw her at the Turnpike when we went to Kensington just setting off with her father to Plymouth.

Friday, 26 June

A violent thunder storm in the Night, very ill, no sleep. Oh Power Supream how awfull, how wonderfull are all they works, look down with pity on me thy poor

---

370   John Miller, son of Mrs. Turner of Dorking, and his wife, Helen Catherine Michell.

weak sinfull infirm creature, & restore me to health, I beseech thee. Spend the afternoon at Mrs. Wicker's with the Miss Ellis's, who are as grave & silent as ever.

Saturday, 27 June

Ride out in the morning to Highland, walk about the Garden, a letter from my cousin Bet Smith, she thinks my illness is occasion'd by Captain Smith's absence. Write to Miss Gittins to acquaint her I shall be at Arundel on Thursday next.

Sunday, 28 June

At Church twice, Doctor Hutchinson tells us we shou'd patiently bear & profit by reproof, let who will be the reprover. A very hard lesson, & but little practis'd I believe. Wear a new Gown made of the India Muslin Captain Smith gave me, which is prodigiously admir'd. Mr. Tudor drinks tea with us.

Monday, 29 June

Work all day. Doctor Smith tells me they concluded at Lady Irwin's where he din'd yesterday that I was in a consumption, but he assur'd them to the contrary & then Mrs. Tredcroft supposed I was to be married when the Captain return'd. He answer'd he did not believe it, for he thought we were both fools to be married till we can be settled, most true, but t'is hard for prudence so far to overcome inclination.

Tuesday, 30 June

At Mrs. Wicker's with Sally Sheppard cutting out a flower Pot for a Chimney Board, a very difficult piece of Work.[371]

JULY 1761

Wednesday, 1 July

Busy all the morning packing my Cloaths for my Journey. Afternoon at Mrs. Wicker's again, finishing the Chimney Board, which is prodigiously admir'd by all who see it. Take my leave of all my acquaintances.

Thursday, 2 July

Go to Arundel, a very pleasant Journey. A Master Coomber is my guide, he desires I will be of good courage, my father desires I wou'd not stay long. Miss Gittins meets me about half a mile from the Town, & receives me with great joy. See Arundel Castle, a fine prospect from it.

Friday, 3 July

Ride to Little Hampton to wash in the Sea with Miss Gittins, an exceeding fine day the Ocean quite serene & calm, What an awfull sight. When we return find Mrs. Willes & Miss Patty [Willes], relations of Miss Gittins. Very ill after going in the Sea.

---

371 A chimney-board was used to shut up a fireplace in the summer. Presumably the flower pot (or vase) was attached to it, as an ornament.

Saturday, 4 July

Work all the morning & walk in the Garden; Miss Gittins reads a Poem of ?[Mur]phy's to us, a good thing. Then several Papers in the *Spectator*, she reads extreamly well. Ride again to Hampton [*Littlehampton*] to wash, agrees quite well with me. Write to my cousin at East Bourn to let them know that I intend making them a visit, accompanied by Miss Gittins.

Sunday, 5 July

Go to Goring with Mrs. Willes & Miss Patty, Miss Gittins & self are at their House, & Mrs. Gittins at Mrs. Dautry's. We are very politely receiv'd by Mr. Willes & his brother the Captain. Mr. Foreman is there, a gentlemen who thinks he is extreamly merry when he is obscene.

Monday, 6 July

Bathe in the Sea; vastly merry with the Miss Willes, who are all sensible girls, the youngest son is excessively like my brother, which naturally attracts my notice.[372] Mr. Willes shews great fondness for me, laments my being engag'd, asks me many questions concerning Captain Smith, which I answer without prudish reserve.

Tuesday, 7 July

Bathe in the Sea again. I think t'is of great service to me. Write to my father, desire to stay a month. Mr. Willes plagues me all the time I am so employ'd, bestowing the most extravagant encomiums on my person & mind, I rally him with all the spirit I am mistress of.

Wednesday, 8 July

Ride several mile on the Sea sand with Captain Willes, how delightfull is the prospect of the Ocean, yet terrible. Drink tea with an old Maid and have our fortunes told, what idle stuff.

Thursday, 9 July

Ride to Tarring to put a letter in the Post, receive one from Mr. Masterman acquainting me that my letters were forwarded to Captain Smith. Call on Mrs. Vallence, Miss Hutchinson that was, who expresses great joy to see me.[373] Bathe in the Sea again.

Friday, 10 July

Am surpris'd at the assiduity of Mr. Willes, he is ever restless when I am out of his sight, he certainly has a transient liking for me. Leave Goring with regret, Mr. Willes accompanies us part of the way, desires me to correspond with him, I consent if he will begin, but he desires I will, which I refuse; so how it will be I know not.

---

372 Younge Willes Esq. (born in 1731) had three sisters, Margaret, Martha (Patty) and Christian, and four brothers. The youngest boy, Charles, born in 1750, was exactly the same age as Sarah's brother Bob.

373 Catherine Hutchinson married William Vallance of Southwick in 1760, from a family of brewers; he died at the age of 28 in 1767, leaving her with two daughters, Anne and Catherine.

Saturday, 11 July

He calls on us in his road to Mr. Luxford's,[374] presses me to go to the Assembly.[375] I tell him am afraid it will be dislik'd, as I am the daughter of a person in trade. A letter from Mrs. Hurst, informing me she shall be glad to see us. Write & let her know we will be there next Wednesday. Write to Sally Sheppard & Bet Cook.

Sunday, 12 July

At Church in the morning, a letter from my father with one inclos'd from Captain Smith, acquainting me with great concern that a junior officer is prefer'd to the rank of Major. A most unfortunate accident.

Monday, 13 July

Write to my father. Walk with Miss Gittins to Walburton about four mile to see a Miss Phipps, her cousin. She is an intimate acquaintance of Miss Charles, a young Lady who is to be married to a friend of Captain Smith's; hear several of her letters & admire them greatly.

Tuesday, 14 July

Write to Captain Smith a tender complaisant letter. Mr. Willes calls & insists on my going to the Assembly but I refuse. He comes again & swears I go, I comply, he dances with me & we spend the afternoon very agreeably. Mrs. Luxford carries me home in her Chariot. Mr. Willes kept me up till 12 o' clock, tormenting me with his love & his extravagant compliments.

Wednesday, 15 July

Set out for East Bourn, breakfast at Brighthelmstone, Mr. Hurst meets us as Newhaven, & we have a pleasant Journey of forty mile, a fall from my Horse, no hurt.

Thursday, 16 July

Miss Gittins & myself are both extreamly fatigued after our Journey, receive a very kind reception from my cousins. Write to my father. Young Gilberd calls on us.[376] Walk to see Lord Northampton's Gardens, pleasant but formal, except a fine grove which is delightfull.[377]

---

374 The Luxfords probably lived in Arundel, as Mrs. Luxford gave Sarah a lift home after the Assembly there on 14 July. They may have been related to Alexander Luxford, who was a glover in Horsham.

375 In Arundel, since Sarah had now returned to the Gittins' house there.

376 The Gilberds, or Gilberts, owned one of the four manors of Eastbourne, formerly in the possession of the Gildredge family, who were related to the Eversfields of Denne. The Gilberts lived in the old Manor House, and retained possession of the property into the 19th century.

377 Sir Spencer Compton, second son of the 3rd Earl of Northampton, bought Eastbourne Place from the Wilson family in 1723, and renamed it Compton Place. He remodelled the house, which had a beautiful setting, and laid out the gardens. At the time that Sarah was there, the current *"Lord Northampton"* would have been the 7th Earl, grandson of Spencer Compton's nephew.

Friday, 17 July

Very bad weather, the wind extreamly high. Stay within all day & work for Mrs. Hurst which is charity indeed, she poor Woman having lost the use of one Arm. The Miss Gilberds call & invite us to breakfast tomorrow morning, but we are to ride to Beachy Head.

Saturday, 18 July

Ride to Beachy Head, am amaz'd at the stupendous height of those Cliffs, above five hundred feet from the surface of the Water. My cousin Hurst is exceeding good natur'd & obliging. Work in the afternoon for Mrs. Hurst, a young gentleman nam'd Mortimer calls to see us.[378]

Sunday, 19 July

At Church twice. Call on the Miss Gilberds, who tell Miss Gittins & me there are several gentlemen goes to Church on purpose to see us, a fine motive indeed. Go to Sea in my cousin's Boat, go on board a small Ship, the Captain is extreamly civil to us. I am vastly sick & right glad to set on Shore again.

Monday, 20 July

Young Mortimer tells Miss Gittins & me, we are to be taken up, for we ran about seeking whom we may devour. Write a very long letter to Mrs. Wicker giving her an account of all my journey. Write to Captain Smith by a little Sea Captain who was going to Bellisle, & offer'd to carry it in the politest manner.[379]

Tuesday, 21 July

Young Mortimer is very particular in his behaviour to Miss Gittins, believe he likes her much. Drink tea at Mr. Lushington's a Clergyman; his daughter is a very agreeable young Lady & extreamly civil to us.[380] Go into the Sea.

Wednesday, 22 July

A Clergyman, his name Williams, calls to see us, how much curiosity does a new face excite, especially if they are reported pretty. Ride to see Hurstmonceux Castle, a vast Pile of Building, & the most entire of that kind now remaining in England. Parson Williams, Mr. Gilberd & Mortimer Sup with us & keep us up fooling till two in the Morning.

Thursday, 23 July

Take an unwilling Leave of my Bourn relations & ride to Lewes, find the Lady

---

378   It is probable that *"young Mortimer"* was John Hamilton Mortimer, the artist, who was born at Eastbourne in 1740. He was made a Royal Academician in 1779, but died before he could receive his diploma. His father, Thomas Mortimer, was a collector of Customs, but claimed descent from the Earls of March. His brother Roger was an artist of some renown, and young John was said to have got his artistic talent from his uncle. There is a later reference to Mr. John Mortimer on 5 September 1762.

379   Belle Isle was an island off the Brittany coast, where British troops landed in April 1761. The stronghold of Palais surrendered on 8 June. Henry was presumably now stationed there.

380   The Rev. Henry Lushington was the Vicar of Eastbourne from 1742 to 1779.

we intended being with gone out so are oblig'd to lay at the Inn. Write to my mother a long letter.

Friday, 24 July

Ride to Brighthelmstone & breakfast there, more company than when we pass'd thro' it last. Wash in the Sea here, set out for Goring, the road over Shoreham ferry excessive bad, a very pleasant road afterwards. Are wellcom'd at Goring by my lover Mr. Willes who is certainly very fond of me.

Saturday, 25 July

Miss Gittins goes home & leaves me at Goring. Mr. Willes certainly likes me but I dare say the transient flame will soon decay. Ride to Broad Water to a Cricket Match where I saw the most beautifull girl my eyes ever beheld, a farmer's daughter, her name Hersy. Mr. Willes offends us & we send him to Coventry, that is all the company agree not to speak to him, but he severely punishes me for my silence by sitting in the same chair & hugging me all the evening.

Sunday, 26 July

Go to Church, a very neat one, but the most shocking humdrum old Parson I ever heard. Walk to Highdown Hill, a most delightfull prospect.[381]

Monday 27 July

Mr. Willes goes from home. Captain Willes & I have a most violent game of romps. Begin writing to Sally Sheppard, bathe in the Sea. Miss Gittins not in a very good humour, am sorry to find her temper is not extraordinary. Spend the afternoon at Mrs. Dautry's, play at cards.

Tuesday, 28 July

Bathe in the Sea, a vast deal of chat with the Misses Willes, they talk of going into business & not live dependant on their brother. Take my leave of them with a vast deal of concern. Arrival at Arundel. Write to Sally Sheppard & Bet Cook. Take a walk, meet Captain Bellenden & Mr. Howard.

Wednesday, 29 July

Go into a cold Bath but I think it don't agree with me. Make a visit at Arundel Castle to Mr. Howard, he treats us most elegantly with fruit, Sillibub & flowers, go up to the top of the round Tower, old Howard gives me a luscious kiss, how disagreeable is age when they mimic the follies of youth.[382]

---

381 Highdown Hill is the site of the well-known *"Miller's Tomb"*, where the miller of Highdown Mill, John Olliver, was buried at the age of 84 in 1793. It bears lines that he is said to have composed himself. He built the tomb in 1766, and at the same time had his coffin made, which was henceforth kept under the bed in his cottage nearby.

382 Mr. Howard was presumably a relative of Edward Howard, 9th Duke of Norfolk, who inherited the dukedom in 1732, and died in 1777. He spent little time at Arundel, since he was far more concerned with remodelling Norfolk House in St. James Square in London. Some improvements were made at Arundel Castle in the 1760s, but it was not until Charles, 11th Duke, succeeded in 1787 that the building was restored and became the Duke's principal seat.

Thursday, 30 July

Go to Chichester. Call on the Miss Ellis's but they were not at home, call on Dr. Frances. Dine at Mr. Smith's[383] but he was not at home, sup at Walburton's[384] & find him with his Son, says he shou'd not have known me.

Friday, 31 July

Mr. Willes calls to take us to Angmering Fair, he shews excessive fondness for me. Dine at Mr. Foreman's, a rich Farmer, with the Miss Willes & a vast deal of Company.[385] Mr. Willes very particular in his behaviour, Miss Phipps very civil.

AUGUST 1761

Saturday, 1 August

Young Foreman attends me home, which was an excess of complaisance, as he left so many pretty girls behind him; but he expresses so much admiration for me as astonishes me, sure there cannot be in my person anything so very attracting, to be thus notic'd.

Sunday, 2 August

At Church twice, bleeded in the Morning, think it necessary before I go for a constancy in the cold Bath. Miss Willes & Charles come from Goring, drink tea at Mrs. Moore's, a grocer's. Take a walk & are catch'd in the rain. Miss Gittins is very much afraid I shall be sent for home tomorrow, & seems excessive unwilling to part.

Monday, 3 August

Am sent for home, pack up all my cloaths, & prepare to return to my friends & old Horsham. Take an affectionate leave of Mrs. & Miss Gittins. A very pleasant ride home, find all my friends well; but Sally Sheppard gone to London, which gives me some concern.

Tuesday, 4 August

Am congratulated by Mrs. Hutchinson & every body for looking so much better after my journey. Call on Betsy Cook who says I am ten times handsomer. Write to Captain Smith, a very tender letter, which perhaps may never reach his hands. Take a Walk with Mrs. Wicker.

Wednesday, 5 August

Work all day. My brother comes home, poor little fellow. I am delighted to see him. Take a walk in the afternoon, vastly pleasant, I think home is now very agreeable after

---

383   It is possible that the Mr. Smith mentioned here was one of the Smith brothers — William, George and John — who were all well-known painters in Chichester in the 1760s.

384   A Richard Walberton lived at Chichester *"without South Gate"* in 1785.

385   A John Foreman was the occupier of Egelsdean Farm in Angmering in 1785. It seems likely that this was the place where Sarah dined.

my long absence. Bob gives my father & me a very diverting account of the election at Marlow, what bribery & corruption, oh Britain, such are thy Patriots.[386]

Thursday, 6 August.

Take a walk out in the country to drink a Sillibub. Meet Sir Charles, he is surpris'd to see me look so damn'd handsome, as he expresses himself, brings us quite home.

Friday, 7 August

Continue going into the cold Bath every Morning, which I think is of infinite service to me. Drink coffee, tea & sillibub with Sir Charles. Miss Ingram, Mrs. Tredcroft & Mrs Wicker passes, he burst into a forc'd laugh which offends them much. Presents me with a brace of partridges.

Saturday, 8 August

Eat Sir Charles Eversfield's Partridges which prov'd extreamly good. Mr. Tudor here, invites me to dine with him on Monday with .... Miss Tredcroft. Write to Mrs. Hurst at East Bourne, send an Acrostick, compos'd on that place. She desir'd some of my performances.

Sunday, 9 August

At Church in the morning, very wet & unpleasant, an excellent discourse by Doctor Hutchinson. Write a long letter to Miss Gittins. Make two Acrosticks on Mr. Willes & send them to him inclos'd to Miss Gittins. Expect a letter from Captain Smith but am disappointed.

Monday, 10 August

Dine at Mr. Tudor's; ride up, a pretty dinner & a hearty wellcome, but we cou'd not enjoy his fine prospect, as usual, the bad weather prevented. Mr. Osgood behaved remarkably civil to me the whole day, & riding home in the evening. Doctor Smith tells us the names of the Stars & expatiates on the pleasure found in studying Astronomy.

Tuesday, 11 August

Walk to Slynfold to see Mr. & Mrs. Jones who are extreamly glad to see us, they have got a sweet little Girl. Read *Caractacus*, a Dramatic Poem which gives an account of the ceremonies of the old Druids & English Bards.[387]

Wednesday, 12 August

Mr. & Mrs. Jones dines with us. Take a walk & meet Sir Charles who chats with

---

386   In view of Sarah's views expressed here, it is amusing that Robert Hurst was later very much involved in rigging the 1790 election in Horsham in favour of the Duke of Norfolk's candidates!

387   *Caractacus* was a dramatic poem by William Mason, first published in 1759. It was used as the libretto for an opera of the same name. Mason also wrote a long poem on gardening and was himself a garden designer. In 1785, he refused an offer to become Poet Laureate.

Betsy Cook & me. No letter from Captain Smith. Read the *Review* for .... June, they approve *[illegible]* & *Hamel*, an Oriental tale.[388]

Thursday, 13 August.

Work on my Stays all the morning, the Miss Elliss's here they admire the neatness of my work. Drink tea at my Aunt Waller's with Mrs. Cheynell & company. Walk down to Chisworth with Betsy Cook, gather some of Sir Charles's filberds.

Friday, 14 August

Go down to Chisworth with Betsy Cook for some of Sir Charles's filberds, a fine warm morning. Drink tea at Mrs. Wicker's, she tells me Charles Smith enquir'd very kindly after my health, I shou'd be oblig'd to him if I thought him sincere. Read to Mamma.

Saturday, 15 August

A kind letter from my friend Miss Gittins, she applauds my last letter highly & sends me a pretty Tale she wrote on our being disappointed at Lewes. Work all day. My father seems out of temper with me, I have done nothing. Write to Bet Smith.

Sunday, 16 August

At Church twice, a very good Sermon by Doctor Hutchinson. Write to Mrs. Townshend give her an account of my Journey & company. I am not so fond of writing as formerly, nor indeed of any sedentary employment, exercise suits my constitution better, as well as my disposition. Go to Tanbridge with Mrs. Wicker. Walk on the Causeway.

Monday, 17 August

Work a little in the morning. A letter from Mrs. Hurst express'd in very kind terms, desires me to come & spend the winter with her, but I fear my father will not consent. Dine at Mr. Tredcroft's with Mr. Tudor, Mr. Osgood, & several more, a very elegant Dinner.

Tuesday, 18 August

Go down to Chisworth get some Apples, Plumbs & filberds. Betsy Cook & I are vastly merry, work in the afternoon. Betsy Cook drinks tea with us, walk up in the Park, vastly pleasant. Meet Sir Charles & Mr. John Parham with a gentleman who plays most sweetly on the French Horn.

---

388 Hendrick Hamel was the book-keeper on the Dutch "jaght" *Sperwer*, which was wrecked on the coast of Korea in 1653. He and his surviving companions were imprisoned, because the Koreans wanted the existence of their country to be kept secret, but eventually a few of them escaped and reached Japan in 1666. The ship's journal caused a sensation when it was published in Rotterdam in 1668, because Hamel was the first Westerner to reveal the existence of this hitherto unknown country to Europeans. The book was translated into French, German and English. An English transcription of the original journal by Henny Savenije is now available online.

Wednesday, 19 August

Very busy all the morning posting the Shop Books, a disagreeable but a necessary piece of work. Drink tea with Mrs. Laight, with my friend Sally Sheppard who is thank Heaven return'd.

Thursday, 20 August

A letter from my dearest Harry, expressing great concern for my sickness, & joy at my recovery, & informs me the Captain who he thought was put over his head, is not advanc'd in the Marines & Lord Anson[389] has assur'd him nobody shall in preference to him, am glad of this but great men's promises are precarious. Walk out with Sally Sheppard. She tells me a deplorable *[word omitted]* of poor Mrs. Lamport's unhappy circumstances.

Friday, 21 August

Go to Cuckfield with my father, sister & Mr. Jones. Dine at Mr. Chasemore's, who makes us very wellcome. Bett's Horse falls down as we return home, & frights me excessively.

Saturday, 22 August

Not well all night, go in the Cold Bathe, which makes me worse, a very bad sore throat & pain in my limbs. Young Gatlan calls here, & romps with Bett; my Uncle Bob & Billy Smith comes down from London. Oblig'd to go to bed quite ill.

Sunday, 23 August

Ill all day not able to go to Church. Employ myself in reading some of my dear Harry's letters, & wishing for his company, alas in vain, wou'd to Heaven this frightfull War was ended, of which at present I see but little probability. Mr. Chasemore from Cuckfield calls on us.

Monday, 24 August

Ride down to Billingshurst with Drew Michell & Sally Sheppard, very much disappointed at Betsy Cook not going, she is allways the Life of the Company. A very fine Day, the roads but indifferent. Find myself much better when I get home.

Tuesday, 25 August

Go down to Chisworth with Betsy Cook, get some plumbs & filberds. Dine at North Heath with a very large posse; a very genteel dinner, vastly merry.[390] As we return home Miss Tredcroft & I go into Doctor Smith's to hear his blind daughter play on the Spinnett.[391]

---

389 George, Baron Anson (1697-1762) was made First Lord of the Admiralty in 1751, after defeating the French off Cape Finisterre in 1747. He was appointed Admiral of the Fleet in 1761. He wrote *Voyage round the World* (1748) which described his three-year circumnavigation of the globe when he captured £500,000 of Spanish treasure.

390 The dinner was presumably given by Nathaniel Tredcroft, who was previously said to be living at North Heath. He gave a similar dinner on 7 September 1759.

391 This is the first reference to his daughter's blindness, but maybe it helps to explain Doctor Smith's tendency to criticise others.

Wednesday, 26 August

Work all morning on my stays. Sally Sheppard is ill with a sore throat, poor girl, her health is now as bad as mine was. Drink tea with Mrs. *[illegible]*, an old acquaintance, how many have I lost since she was married. Betsy Cook talks of going to Storrington to keep her brother's house, the absence of this good natur'd lively girl will affect me much.[392]

Thursday, 27 August

Very busy all day at work, & writing to Captain Smith, a very long letter. Miss Upton here in the evening, & Miss King. Take a little walk. Play at cards.

Friday, 28 August

Work all day, a bad afternoon, cannot walk. I dread winter excessively, hope my Harry will come, or else that I shall go to East Bourne. Read in *The Library* for June, *The Life of Christ*; they endeavour to prove what I have no inclination to deny.

Saturday, 29 August

Work, write & busy in the Shop all the morning. Drink tea at Miss Curtis's & eat plumb Cake. Walk in the Park with Betsy Cook, meet Sir Charles, go home with him. He treats us with Tea, Sillibub & Peaches, asks me when I heard from Captain Smith. I answer him truly, if Smith is displeas'd at my frankness he does not deserve my regard, for that wou'd indicate he is asham'd of his regard for me.

Sunday, 30 August

Walk with Mamma & all our family to dine with Mr. Tudor at Sedgwick, a pleasant walk there but wet home. A letter from my cousin Bet Smith.

Monday, 31 August

Work in the morning & read *The Review*, some of it very entertaining & improving. Go down to Chisworth with Betsy Cook, get some of Sir Charles' filberds, walk round the Park. Vastly pleasant but summer's grace serene must soon give place to gloomy Winter & all its dreary train of cold dark days & long nights.

SEPTEMBER 1761

Tuesday, 1 September

Walk out with Sally Sheppard & Bet Cook to drink a sillibub, go a nutting round the fields with great success.

Wednesday, 2 September

Very busy all day ironing, low Work for a person of my genius, ha ha ha, hence arises all the vanities & absurdities in Life. We fancy we ought to move in a higher sphere, & so despise the employments of our station; how truly laughable is this;

392　John Cook, Bet's brother, was a mercer in Storrington.

Thursday, 3 September

The highest wisdom consists in performing contentedly the duties of our situation, self is a very dangerous thing & ought never to engross our attention for as often as it does so often do we overrate our abilities, & imagine Fortune has been extreamly remiss in not rewarding them,

Friday, 4 September

The hardest lesson in the World is humility, the voluptuous shall become temperate, the miser generous, & the fickle constant before the proud are humble. I have more than the seeds of this fault in my disposition, & often think my rank in Life far below my merit, when most certainly t'is far above them.

Saturday, 5 September

A letter from Captain Smith, he thinks of staying at Sea till November unless call'd home by a Peace, which he [*word omitted*] will not be, what a lingering has ours been, I wish t'was terminated one way or the other, I am heartily weary of the frightfull suspence it has caus'd me to spend at my prime of life in fruitless expectation without forming a connexion that wou'd have been my support to the end of it.

Sunday, 6 September

At Church in the morning. Walk out with Sally Sheppard, express my fears that I shall soon lose her by matrimony. A very unpleasant wet afternoon.

Monday, 7 September

Very busy all the morning pickling & baking. Work on my stays in the afternoon. Read the News, a very large St. Domingo Man taken by one of our men of War.[393] I wish it had been the *Orford's* good fortune. Walk on the Causeway with Mamma & Mrs. Wicker.

Tuesday, 8 September

Walk over to Mrs. Miller's at Warnham, to enquire the Character of a Maid for Mrs. Wicker, my brother & Bill Smith[394] went with me, excessively hot. Spend the afternoon at Mrs. Wicker's. Sup at my grandmother's, play at cards. The poor old Lady declines very much.

Wednesday, 9 September

Work on my stays in the morning, walk out in the afternoon with Sally Sheppard. Vastly pleasant, we lament the loss of Betsy Cook which must happen soon. Will White drunk, comes & makes choice of me for a Wife; we laugh excessively at him & tell him he is engag'd, he says I am the same, but hopes if an accident happens to Captain Smith that he shall have the forsaking of me.

---

393 The British had seized Roseau in San Domingo, in June 1761, and the power of the French in the West Indies was finally broken by the capture of Martinique in February 1762. The capture of this San Domingan warship was an incident in this naval campaign.

394 This Bill Smith was probably a son of Dr. Smith, rather than Sarah's cousin from London.

Thursday, 10 September

Go out a whole day to Nutting with Sally Sheppard & Jenny Hunt, vastly merry & come home vastly tir'd.

Friday, 11 September

Finish my stays, which fit me extreamly well. Read *The Ladies' Magazine*, Voltaire's life continued. Affecting story of a prostitute. Walk on the Causeway with Billy Smith & my brother, they entertain me highly by their harmless sensible prattle.

Saturday, 12 September

Work all the morning, walk in the afternoon to Dales with Mrs. Wicker & Sally Sheppard. Bet Cook & her sister Lamport arrive, what an unhappy poor mortal must this latter be, if she had any sense of feeling, but her Mind is not the most delicate; if it had she cou'd never have acted so imprudently. Thank God I am not so unfortunate, may I be ever gratefull, & endeavour to deserve the blessings I dayly receive.

Sunday, 13 September

At Church twice. Walk to Abel March's garden to see the Egg plant,[395] a very great curiosity.

Monday, 14 September

My father receives a letter from Mr. Hurst at Bourne desiring he will let me spend some time with them; but my two sisters behave so extreamly ill that it wou'd be cruel in me to leave them so believe shall give over all thoughts of it.

Tuesday, 15 September

Bet behaves extreamly ill, telling about that she is not us'd well when it is certainly her own fault. My father & mother in a great passion with her, she goes to my Aunt Grace's, & declares she will never return, alas what can be done with such an obstinate temper.

Wednesday, 16 September

Work all the morning. Go in the afternoon to see Sir Charles with Bet Cook & Sally Sheppard, he entertains us very elegantly with fruit, tea & sillibub. It rains extreamly fast, he furnishes us all with great Coats & we have a most terrible walk home.

Thursday, 17 September

Go to Dine at Mr. Tudor's, carry my work, a wet afternoon & evening. We are oblig'd to stay all night, the old Man seems quite glad of our company, & insists on my father's & brother's staying with me.

---

395   The egg plant was almost certainly an aubergine, which was not common in England at this time.

Friday, 18 September

An exceeding fine morning; look over with Mr. Tudor the maps of Surrey & Sussex,[396] he walks home with us. Find my mother quite ill, occasion'd by fretting at my sister's behaviour, who will not return home. A letter from my friend Miss Gittins complaining of my late long silence; & a letter, a very polite one, from Mr. Willes in answer to the Acrosticks I sent him.

Saturday, 19 September

Bet returns home, I condescend to ask her, but I dare say her behaviour will be very little amended; a return of my fever attended with a most violent cough.

Sunday, 20 September

At Church twice, the Doctor makes an excellent sermon on the danger of keeping bad company. Write some verses by my brother's desire; on my father's losing an old Mare, he is vastly pleas'd with them. Hope I shall hear from Captain Smith to night, disappointed none from my Harry but one from Mrs. Townshend acquainting me that she believes her Mother[397] will stay all the Winter with her, I am concern'd at it & a letter from Miss Willes desiring I will go with her to London to assist her in furnishing her Shop, shou'd be very ungratefull if I did not comply.

Monday, 21 September

Go to Slynfold to have my Brother to school.

Tuesday, 22 September

Very busy in the Shop, tire myself excessively. Mamma makes some objections to my accompanying Miss Willes, but I write to let her know I will, sure duty does not require we shou'd be ill natur'd & ungratefull. The Coronation[398] & Bonfire &c &c very *[word omitted]*.

Wednesday, 23 September

All the morning setting the Shop in order against my father's return from London. Spend the afternoon at Mrs. Wicker's, Jack Shelley comes in excessive drunk, follows Miss Tredcroft to Church, what a beastly vice is drunkenness, how it debases a human creature.

---

396 Sarah would probably not have had much opportunity to see good maps of the county, and so would have been interested to see those which had been acquired by Mr. Tudor. Richard Budgen produced the first large-scale map of Sussex in 1724, and many subsequent maps were based on this in the next thirty years, including those of Emanuel Bowen, who produced a series for *The large English Atlas*, beginning with Sussex in 1749. John Rocque, who drew the first large-scale plan of London in 1746 and 1747, in 16 and 24 sheets, also produced a topographical map of Surrey in 9 sheets and a map of Sussex in 1761.
397 Mrs. Bridger, formerly Mrs. Powell.
398 The Coronation of King George III took place on 22 September 1761 - the young King George III was considered to have given a unique demonstration of his piety by removing his crown before he took the sacrament.

Thursday, 24 September

A very long letter from my dear Harry, all hopes of a peace & our being united are vanish'd, quite fear I shall never be so happy.[399] Write to Captain Smith, take a walk with Sally Sheppard. My father returns from London, saw the Coronation of which he gives us an account.

Friday, 25 September

Busy all the morning putting the goods in order my father bought in London. Have a new gown which every body says is the ugliest thing in the World. Go for a walk with Mrs. Wicker, immensely pleasant. Play at cards.

Saturday, 26 September

Hurry about all the morn which I find agrees infinitely best with my constitution. Take a walk with Mrs. Wicker, read Captain Smith's letter to her, she says it is a very kind one. Read the history of Sir Launcelot Greaves, affecting story of some prisoners in the Kings' Bench.[400]

Sunday, 27 September

At Church twice, a very good Sermon preach'd by Doctor Hutchinson on the parable of the Tares & Wheat. Walk up in the Park with Sally Sheppard, fine warm pleasant weather. Drink tea at Mrs. Wicker's with the Miss Ellis's & their cousin Jack.

Monday, 28 September

A letter of thanks from Miss Willes for my promising to go with her to London. Mr. Tudor dines here & invites us up to his house tomorrow. Walk on the Causeway with Mrs. Wicker, tell her I shall go to London next Monday.

Tuesday, 29 September

Walk with Mamma & Doctor Smith, up to Mr. Tudor's to dinner, charming fine weather. The old gentleman comes to meet us & gives us as usual a most sincere wellcome, if he wou'd leave off swearing at his servants I shou'd be right glad.

Wednesday, 30 September

Cut out a great number of round frocks, my father is in high good humour. Walk with Sally Sheppard to drink tea at a Country house. Drink tea, am vastly pleased with their hospitable simplicity & rustic entertainment.

---

399   Negotiations for a peace had been going on between the British and French governments, but William Pitt, the British Minister, had become convinced that the French were intriguing to bring Spain into the war as an ally, and urged a pre-emptive attack on the Spanish treasure fleet, together with an offensive in Europe. In this he was opposed by his arch-rivals, the Duke of Newcastle and Lord Bute, and eventually resigned on 5 October 1761 *"in disgust"*. Henry had probably been following the course of this power struggle and become depressed at the prospect of a continuing war.

400   Sarah has already mentioned reading this serialised novel by Tobias Smollett on 20 March 1760. Part of it takes place in a debtor's prison. The *"Kings Bench"*, named after the Court of King' Bench, was a prison in Borough High Street, Southwark, used mainly for debtors at this time. It was much hated as it was filthy and overcrowded, and subject to outbreaks of typhus fever.

OCTOBER 1761

Thursday, 1 October

My father blames me for promising to go with Miss Willes & buy her goods, how cou'd I be guilty of such mechanic selfishness & refuse her, oh forbid it gratitude, forbid it humanity, wou'd to heaven I was in a situation to be of greater service to them.

Friday, 2 October

Expect Miss Willes but am disappointed. Very busy all day in the Shop; getting ready to go to London. Mrs. James here in the afternoon, a curious dispute whether short or tall Women are the finest.

Saturday, 3 October

Vastly busy, Miss Willes arrives about eleven o' clock, talks to me about her business, I put down some things for her to buy, she is very much dispirited, & fears she shall not meet with success, I give her all the encouragement in my power.

Sunday, 4 October

At Church in the morning, rains in the afternoon. Am afraid we shall have bad weather for our Journey. Walk down to see Mr. Burry, who is a relation of Miss Willes, but he was not at home, I sincerely wish this poor girl success in her business. My Uncle Bob comes down.

Monday, 5 October

An exceeding fine morning. Set off for London in the Stage Coach. Call on Mr. Foreman, an acquaintance of Miss Willes at Epsom, they oblige us to stay [for] dinner. Miss Foreman tells Miss Willes I am a prodigious fine girl.

Tuesday, 6 October

Call at Mrs. Wales in the Borough; see the finest young fellow I ever beheld. Go with Miss Willes to Bright's the haberdashers, they promise to use her extreamly well. Go to my cousin Smiths', they are exceeding glad to see me. Spend the evening there with my cousin Bet.

Wednesday, 7 October

Go to the haberdasher's & do my business for Miss Willes. Dine at my Uncle Bob's, my Aunt goes with us to Westminster Abbey & Westminster Hall to see the manner of the coronation. The Hall &c [etc.] makes a most magnificent appearance.

Thursday, 8 October

Walk up to my Uncle George's, he tells me my cousin his son is going very soon to the East Indies, I cannot see the poor lad first which gives me great concern.[401] Endeavour to get in to Covent Garden playhouse to see the King & Queen but give

---

401   George Hurst junior died at Fort William in Bengal in 1780.

over the attempt after being allmost press'd to death in the mob, then go to Drury Lane & see *King Henry the Eighth*[402] with *The coronation of Anna Bullen.*

Friday, 9 October

An excessive wet day. Dine at my Aunt Smith's, play at cards, take my leave of her & the girls.

Saturday, 10 October

Set out for Horsham in the Coach, take up Mrs. Smith, wife to one of my Harry's brothers, a most agreeable sensible Woman.[403] Breakfast at Mrs. Foreman's, Epsom. Dine at Dorking, walk about the Town with Mrs. Smith; a letter consisting of a few lines from my Harry.

Sunday, 11 October

An excessive wet unpleasant day. Miss Willes don't chuse to go to Church, which keeps me at home, not very well. Sally Sheppard drinks tea with us, Miss Willes likes her much, thinks her very sensible & agreeable, indeed I think she must meet with every body's approbation.

Monday, 12 October

Miss Willes goes home, walk with her through the Park to avoid the bar road,[404] take my leave of her & sincerely wish her success in her business; poor girl, she was born to the prospect of a good fortune independant on the caprice of the merciless World, but the extravagances of her father crush'd these pleasing hopes & left them a prey to penury.

Tuesday, 13 October

Write to Captain Smith. Mamma & I make a visit to his brother Adam's Wife, am charm'd with the engaging behaviour of her sweet little girl.[405]

Wednesday, 14 October

Go down to my grandmother's & settle her accounts with her tenants, the poor old Lady can see but very imperfectly; grant oh most Mercifull father that I may never outlive this nor any of my senses.

Thursday, 15 October

Write to Miss Gittins a very long letter & a short one to Miss Willes. Drink tea at Mrs. Wicker's with Sally Sheppard, stay the evening & play at cards. Write by my father's order to Mr. Heath's;[406] give him a draft on my Uncle for my Brother's board.

---

402 *King Henry VIII* by William Shakespeare, first performed in 1613.
403 Mrs. Maria Smith, wife of Adam.
404 By the *"bar–road"*, Sarah means the turnpike. There was a toll-gate at the foot of Denne Hill, where a fee had to be paid. Miss Willes presumably boarded the coach beyond that, to avoid paying the toll.
405 Her daughter Maria, later to become the wife of Sarah's brother Robert Hurst.
406 Probably Mr. Heather, mentioned on 15 May 1760, at the school in Marlowe.

Friday, 16 October

Work all day. Mr. Tudor invites us to dine with him on Sunday. I do not expect Captain Smith will come into Port before Christmas & then probably will not come to Horsham. How cruel is this separation, oh peace when wilt thou spread thy halcyon wings over Britain's Isle.

Saturday, 17 October

A letter from poor Mrs. Hurst of East Bourne, she earnestly desires me to come & be with her; has had another fall & hurt her leg; wish my father wou'd permit me to go, but he wants me at home, how am I divided.

Sunday, 18 October

At Church in the morning, a very fine discourse by Doctor Hutchinson on this text; *My son, if sinners entice thee, consent thou not.* Dine at Mr. Tudor's with my father & mother & Will White, eat some of the old gentleman's fine grapes. A very dirty walk home.

Monday, 19 October

Work all day very closely, beg my father to let me go to East Bourne, but he raises a thousand objections, which is worse than absolutely refusing. Drink tea at Mrs. Tasker's, they praise my sister Molly as a very fine girl, & /say/ she should be dressed & take notice of herself, amazing is not Youth prone enough to Vanity without having it instill'd into them.

Tuesday, 20 October

Maria Smith comes to see me, sweet little creature, how I love her. Write to Mrs. Hurst, tell her with great concern I can't come to Bourne.

Wednesday, 21 October

Rub several Rooms in the morning, which exercise is of infinite service to my health. Mr. Tudor here, a vast deal of chat with him, then home for Pitt's letter[407] which I transcribe for him out of the Newspaper. Walk with Mrs. Wicker up to Abel Marsh's Garden, to pay him a bill & look at his shrubs, she buys several.

Thursday, 22 October

Walk over to Highland, a fine frosty pleasant morning. Walk with Mrs. Wicker up to the Brick-kiln,[408] call at Mrs. Cheynell's, who is ill or fancies so, which is full as bad. Read in one of my *Grand Magazines*, an account of Asia, how humbling is the reading of history, how small a part of the globe is it we inhabit & how insignificant an inhabitant am I of that part.

---

407 William Pitt the elder, who had just resigned from the government over the question of war with Spain, which he felt to be necessary.
408 There were several brick-kilns on Horsham Common by the end of the century, one owned by the Griffiths brothers, Thomas and Edward, who built the "new" model Gaol in East Street in 1775.

Friday, 23 October

Mr. Tudor dines with us, Doctor Smith, Mr. Bristed here in the afternoon, how I love to hear the conversation of learned Men, what poor ignorant insignificant creatures are we Women but as we have no business but with domestic concerns t'is thought of no consequence, yet I cannot help repining that I know no more.

Saturday, 24 October

See in the news that a Captain Smith of the Marines is dead at Plymouth, good God, but it cannot sure be my Harry, I expected to hear from him about this time & shall be excessive miserable if I have not that satisfaction tomorrow.

Sunday, 25 October

Read several of my *Grand Magazines*, Voltaire's *Candide* is therein intended to ridicule this rule in Morality, that all which providence ordains is for the best; I cannot approve it.

Monday, 26 October

No letter from Captain Smith, be hush'd my tumultuous fears, yet how can they be quieted, oh Reason lend thy sovereign aid & teach me to bear whatever may happen with resignation. Yet, oh Allmighty Power, avert the worst & preserve me from the pangs I must suffer if depriv'd of my dearest Harry.

Tuesday, 27 October

Walk out with Sally Sheppard, a fine pleasant day. Bet Hunt is involv'd in a sad affair, she is threaten'd to be sued for abusing Mrs. Harffey,[409] poor wretch nobody pities her, but thinks she will be justly punish'd for scandalizing all her neighbours so many years.

Wednesday, 28 October

Not well in the morning, fear I am going to have my old feverish disorder, but heaven avert it. Drink tea & spend the evening at Mr. Tredcroft; a very elegant supper, but he was angry because my father would not go. Play at cards.

Thursday, 29 October

A letter from my dear dear Harry, he is alive & well at Plymouth where the *Orford* arriv'd last Wednesday. I wonder whether he will come to Horsham, I wish it yet wish it not, long to see him, yet know his coming will let loose the tongues of nonsense & scandal.

Friday, 30 October

Wrote to Captain Smith last night, told him in a jocular manner that I was going to London & intended making a visit to my friend Mrs. Townshend at Salisbury, what will he say in answer. Mrs. Tasker delivered of a sweet girl.[410]

---

409   The wife of Mr. Harffey, an apothecary of West Street.
410   The little girl was Elizabeth Tasker, who was baptised on 25 November 1761, and married the
      Rev. Thomas Hutchinson, (son of the present Vicar) in September 1788.

Saturday, 31 October

Bleeded in the morning & find myself much better after, go up to Mrs. Cheynell, they ask me when I shall be married, which question it is impossible for me to resolve; Harry I believe intends me the honour of being his wife, when everything is perfectly convenient.

NOVEMBER 1761

Sunday, 1 November

T'is now ten year since Captain Smith singled me out from the multitude as the object of his affections, & ten thousand heart aches has this preference given me, when I wonder will they terminate. It wou'd greatly conduce to my tranquillity if I cou'd think of him with more indifference, but that is impossible.

Monday, 2 November

A letter from my dearest Harry containing a number of kind expressions with an account of Mr. & Mrs. Marriot's commendation of me, which they heard from Miss Phipps, am much oblig'd to that young Lady for her eulogies.

Tuesday, 3 November

Write to Captain Smith, wish he wou'd come to London while I am there, but t'is a long journey from Plymouth & I must not flatter myself with having that pleasure. Mrs. Wicker concludes to go to London with me.

Wednesday, 4 November

Very busy all the morning getting my things ready to go to London, at Mrs. Tasker's in the afternoon. Put several hundred pound of my father's in my stays to buy in the Stocks, am afraid I shall find it a great weight.

Thursday, 5 November

Mrs. Wicker & I set out for London *[and]* meet with very agreeable company in the Coach, a Clergyman's wife from Steyning, a most agreeable sensible Woman; upon the whole a very pleasant journey. Am oblig'd to lodge at my Aunt Smith's, my Aunt Sally having company.

Friday, 6 November

Walk into the Park to see the King go to the Parliament House; the Queen shews herself to the Mob from the Palace Window, she is a very little plain Woman, nor can I think her agreeable.

Saturday, 7 November

Walk with Mrs. Wicker to see Mrs. Laight, lose my way coming back but don't own it to her. Go to the Play, *Romeo & Juliet*. Romeo by Mr. Garrick & Juliet by Mrs.

Cibber, they are both inimitable in the Characters.[411] What a Man was Shakespeare. The entertainment was *The Shepherds' Wedding* intended as a compliment to the King on his Marriage.[412]

Sunday, 8 November

My cousin Bob Smith tells Mr. Tredcroft my father has bought a considerable sum in the Stocks, which grieves his envious rancorous heart. At Church in the morning.

Monday, 9 November

Go to my Aunt Smith's in Fleet Street to see Lord Mayor's shew, & the whole Royal family go to dine at Guild Hall, a fine sight to be sure, but I cannot say it answer'd my expectations; the Duke of York & Prince William Henry[413] look'd much at our window where was Miss Tredcroft & Miss Rushton, a young Lady that boards at my Uncle George's & is indeed a most amiable girl.

Tuesday, 10 November

Get [a] letter from Captain Smith, tells me in a cool manner that if I go to Salisbury he will meet me there.

Wednesday, 11 November

Think he might have come to Horsham, as the Ship stays six weeks at Plymouth, sure he is not withdrawing his regard from [word omitted], patience & calm resignation assist me if it shou'd be so. Buy Shakespeare's *Plays* & *The History of Russia*, with Wesley's poems.[414]

Thursday, 12 November

Go with Mrs. Wicker & Bet & Sally Smith to spend the day at my Uncle George's, go to the Museum[415] but cou'd not be admitted, sat down in a Room where there

411 *Romeo & Juliet* was one of Shakespeare's earliest and most popular plays, first performed in about 1595. David Garrick (1717-1779) did much to bring Shakespeare to contemporary audiences, though both he and Mrs. Cibber (1714-1766) might now be considered a little too old to play the young lovers, as they were both in their late forties. In contemporary terms, this was a great occasion - Garrick was the most highly regarded actor of his age, playing both comic and tragic rôles with equal success; Mrs. Cibber, who had a beautiful voice, was the leading dramatic actress of the 18th century (and the most highly paid).
412 *The Shepherds' Wedding* may have been a song by J.Worgan, sung at Vauxhall.
413 Prince Edward, Duke of York and Albany, and Prince William Henry were younger brothers of King George III. Prince Edward was created Duke of York in 1760 and served under Sir Edward Hawke in 1762, when he was stationed off the Portuguese coast. Henry Smith was presented to him in November 1762 in Plymouth. He died at the age of twenty-eight in 1767.
414 Probably the *Hymns and Sacred Poems* of Charles Wesley (1707-1788), published in two volumes in 1756, by E. Farley. Wesley wrote over 9,000 poems in his lifetime, many of which were set to music, including "*Hark the Herald Angels Sing*" and "*Love Divine, all loves excelling*". It has been said that people learned more about Methodist beliefs from Charles Wesley's poems and hymns than from his brother John's sermons. Methodists became known for their "*sweet singing*".
415 The British Museum, which was opened to the public in 1759 — see footnote for 16 September 1760. The "*room with the echo*" was probably the turret behind the gatehouse of Montagu House, which is shown in an early print. Admission was only by a ticket which had to be obtained in advance.

was a fine echo, Miss Rushton sings, which she repeats when we return home &
plays on the Guitar, in the most agreeable engaging manner;

Friday, 13 November

What a happy girl she is, has an independant fortune of eight thousand pound, if
I was a man & Captain Smith's friend I wou'd wish such a Woman might fall to
his lot & why should not I wish it now, alas there is little probability that he will
ever have me.

Saturday, 14 November

We might certainly have been united long e'er this, but then our family — what
must be done with a helpless family if he had been turn'd off on half pay, 'tis
prudence then, let me not think it want of Love.

Sunday, 15 November

Leave London not in the best spirits because returning home carries me forty miles
further from my dear Harry. Find all my friends well. Go & see Mrs. Tasker & her
sweet little girl. Father hears of the Smug Mare that was stole & whose elegy I wrote
at my brother's desire.[416]

Monday, 16 November

A letter from Miss Willes acquainting me that her business is like to make out
extreamly well. A letter from my Gittins which tells me the pleasing news of her
lover Turnpenny having renew'd his addresses, & sends me a Copy of verses wrote
to her by a young Lady who lives in London, her name Stanley. They are extreamly
pretty, as is Miss Gittin's answer, my poetry is nothing when compar'd with these
two elegant writers.

Tuesday, 17 November.

Spend the afternoon & evening at Mrs. Wicker's.

Wednesday, 18 November

Work all the morning, begin composing a poem address'd to Miss Gittins &
Miss Stanley. Read in *The New Eloisa*, the tenderness of these letters pierces my
very soul, but none who have not experienc'd the enthusiasm of love can relish
their beauties. [417]

Thursday, 19 November

No letter from Captain Smith. I am unable to bear these dreadfull suspences, would
to heaven all my hopes & fears on this score were at an end. How many thousand
anxious hours have I had on his account, & how many more I may experience
Heaven only knows.

---

416 This was presumably the poem that Sarah wrote for her brother on 20 September.
417 *The New Eloisa* was an English translation of *Julie, ou la Nouvelle Héloise*, by Jean-Jacques
     Rousseau, published in France in 1761. It was one of the most widely read novels of the 18th
     century, and very important in the development of romanticism.

Friday, 20 November

Work all day, read *Eloisa* in the evening, am more charm'd with their letters as I proceed, the language is elegant & the descriptions picturesque. Read Miss Gittins & Miss Stanley's poems to Sally Sheppard who is greatly pleas'd with them.

Saturday, 21 November

A kind letter from my Dear Harry, answer it directly. Finish a poem address'd to Laura, Miss Gittins & Miss Stanley whose poetical name is Cynthia & mine is Amanda. My brother comes home for a day or two, sweet Boy, he's vastly grown.

Sunday, 22 November

At Church twice, Doctor Hutchinson *[word omitted]* on this text, "*reverence my sanctuary*". Mr. Chasemore from Cuckfield comes to dine & lay here in readiness for the Coach. Write to my cousin Bet Smith, Mr. Chasemore makes a present of six franks.

Monday, 23 November

Walk to Slynfold with my brother & Master Chasemore.[418] Vastly dirty but I little regard it; there is nothing like a good resolution to conquer difficulties. Find Mr. & Mrs. Jones both well, play at cards in the evening, but her little girl was very troublesome.

Tuesday, 24 November

Work for Mrs. Jones all the morning. Walk home in the afternoon she accompanies me part of the way. I don't know how it is but I feel a peculiar kind of happiness at Slinfold tho' such a dull place. I have never anywhere else such a serenity of Mind.

Wednesday, 25 November

Write to Mrs. Townshend. Mrs. Tasker's child christen'd.[419] My father won't go, tho' invited, which occasions great disputes between my mother & him. Oh the animosities, how dreadfully disagreeable. We are very merry. Mr. Osgood told me I have never look'd so well in my life.

Thursday, 26 November

A letter from Captain Smith & another from his friend Parson Grant, begging I will forgive Captain Smith for saying he would give me up if my happiness requir'd it. I answer them both. My father very much out of temper, he makes us all unhappy.

Friday, 27 November

Fair day, tir'd with the fatigue, noise & nonsense of it. Master Miller comes to see us, he is very much improv'd in stature & understanding, but rather too pert & forward; t'is indeed extreamly diverting in Children, but then one cannot help trembling for the consequences.

---

418   Master Charles Chasemore was the eldest son of Francis Chasemore, the attorney from Cuckfield. He was born in 1748, the first of six children.

419   The child was Elizabeth Tasker, who married the Rev. Thomas Hutchinson, son of Dr. Hutchinson, the Vicar, in 1788.

Saturday, 28 November

Finish reading *Eloisa*, a novel in which much ought to be imitated & much avoided; one sees in Eloisa a hapless victim to youthfull folly called love & the false step it caus'd her to make, she could not help reproaching herself with, when every thing else concur'd to make her happy.

Sunday, 29 November

At Church in the morning, an excellent Sermon preach'd by Doctor Hutchinson. Drink tea & spend the evening at Mrs. Wicker's; read Doctor Trap's poem on Death & Judgement to her, some of the thoughts are good & just & some of the rhymes execrable.[420]

Monday, 30 November

Bustle about House in the morning for the sake of my health. Mary Hoo[?] [*?Howes*] here & speaks disrespectfully of Sally Sheppard. She is an ungratefull Creature, for this good girl has been a great benefactor to her, but alas, where shall we meet gratitude?

DECEMBER 1761

Tuesday, 1 December

Buy a Blank Book at Mr. Curtis's to write my Poems in.[421] My father very angry with me for nothing, oh independance, thou greatest blessing this world affords when shall I enjoy thee, liberty the choicest gift of Heaven, how I sigh for thee.

Wednesday, 2 December

Rub a Room in the morning for exercise. The two little Smiths dine with me. The eldest Maria is a sweet engaging Child; her person extreamly engaging, her conversation surprising for a girl not five years old; I have a very great fondness for her.

Thursday, 3 December

No letter from Captain Smith, a little expected, sure shall have one on Saturday. Begin writing to Miss Gittins, but Mrs. Wicker sends for me which obliges me to leave off. Read *The Monthly Review*, they find but few faults & bestow a great many commendations on *Eloisa*.

Friday, 4 December

Work in the morning, write out my *Road to Fame* for Miss Gittins & Miss Stanley. Read again *The Monthly Review*, *The Christian's Common Prayer Book*

---

420 This poem has not been traced.
421 Edward Curtis was probably the only stationer in Horsham at this time, so it seems likely that Sarah also bought the pocketbooks which she used for her diaries from him. A similar pocketbook for 1760 was also used as a diary by Elizabeth Smart, wife of John Smart, the miller at the Town Mill, which suggests that they were available in Horsham.

recommended, & they think the *Sermon of the Death of Yorick* an excellent piece of humour & are inclinable to think he wrote it himself.[422]

Saturday, 5 December

No letter from my Harry, What can be the meaning, perhaps he stays till he can tell me when he comes or to answer both my last together but neither of these are sufficient excuses. At Mrs. Wicker's in the afternoon & evening, play at cards with Mr. Nat Tredcroft & Sally Sheppard.

Sunday, 6 December

At Church twice, Mr. Osgood makes a very odd sermon & the Doctor a very good one on our duty to our Neighbour. Walk in the Croft with Miss Tredcroft. Spend the afternoon & evening at Mr. Tredcroft's. Mr. Shelley puts on mourning because Miss & he had quarrel'd, we make ourselves very merry by saying that if all who were out of humour were to do the same a great number of us would wear sable.

Monday, 7 December

A letter from Captain Smith at last, he laments our want of fortune which prevents our union, but our desires are boundless, some years ago he would have thought himself extreamly *[word omitted]* in his present situation;

Tuesday, 8 December

But as poor Grainger says there is so many impediments why these two persons shall not be join'd together, that I firmly believe we shall allways remain asunder; write to Captain Smith begging him to be contented & not think about me.

Wednesday, 9 December

Mr. Grainger breakfasts with us, he appears very low spirited, & complains of his dependant situation, thus all the World have troubles. Read Lucian's *Life* wrote about 78 year ago but in such an uncouth obsolete stile that I should have thought it 200.[423]

Thursday, 10 December

Work all day, there is certainly very little variety in my Life, a round of the same occurrences succeed to each other. I can only diversify them by the strength of imagination & thank Heaven mine is tolerably lively.

Friday, 11 December

Mr. John Shelley here all the afternoon quite steady & good company, offer'd to lend me Books, sure I am coming into favour again. Take a walk horribly dirty, yet pleasant & mild weather. I wonder if Captain Smith will come to Horsham before he sails, I don't dare to expect him lest I shou'd be disappointed.

---

422 Parson Yorick was a character in Lawrence Sterne's *Tristram Shandy*, who is generally thought to represent the author himself.

423 Lucian of Samosata was actually a Greek writer of prose satires who lived from c. 125 to 200. He wrote a book called *The True History* which Sarah may have thought was the story of his life, if she was reading a translation. This would explain why she found his style to be obsolete - see also entry on 28 December 1761.

Saturday, 12 December

No letter from Harry, avaunt expectation I am tir'd of thee. Mr. John Shelley brings me some Books, *Chrysal & The Adventures of a Guinea*.[424] Begin making a Song on my Good Neighbours saying Captain Smith's attachment to me is not sincere, the burden of it is; he will never have her, I know.

Sunday, 13 December

At Church twice. Walk in the Croft with Sally Sheppard, read my song to her, she approves & desires a copy, chat with her & her sweetheart Drew. Read in Lucian's dialogues.

Monday, 14 December

A letter from my dearest Harry, he intends coming to Horsham the beginning of January, how glad shall I be to see him. But, but what, hang all buts, I will not lose the enjoyment of present good by anticipating future evil. Make a visit at Tanbridge.

Tuesday, 15 December

Work all day which was a dark dismal one, how disagreeable is the confinement it occasions. Write to Captain Smith & desire if he comes by Portsmouth, to call on Miss Gittins who wants to see him excessively.

Wednesday, 16 December

Begin teaching Hannah Wilder[425] to write, not well all day, but work as usual. In the evening write out my Song for Sally Sheppard, Jack Shelley comes in takes it from me & I have the greatest difficulty in the World to get it again.

Thursday, 17 December

Begin reading *The Adventures of a Guinea*, trite stuff. Work the afternoon. Drink tea at my Aunt Waller's, read in my French Grammar. Sup at my Aunt Waller's, read in *The Ladies' Magazine* to them, they approve my performance.

Friday, 18 December

Walk over to Mr. Jones's at Slynfold to fetch my Brother from School, excessive dirty walking. Mrs. Jones & Bob are very glad to see me. Master Chasemore is out of temper. I shew Mr. Jones a letter which my father found some time ago at our Hall Window, wrote in figures & cyphers, he discovers what it is.

Saturday, 19 December

It was directed to *"Miss Sally the Priest"* meaning Priest I suppose because of the Sermon I wrote, but the inside contain'd a declaration of Love from one of Griffiths' Prentices, his name Rowzier.[426] Strange I'm sure.

---

424 *Chrysal and the Adventures of a Golden Guinea* by Charles Johnstone was an amusing but caustic satire on Britain's allies in the Seven Years' War which met with immediate success when first published in 1760.

425 Hannah Wilder or Walder was probably the Hurst's maid.

426 Rowzier was probably an apprentice to Thomas Griffith the carpenter, who lived on the west side of Market Square in a house called Mallyn Aperyes.

Sunday, 20 December

Master Chasemore, Bob & I come home, are oblig'd to ride over the Flood. Find a letter from Mr. Grant, Captain Smith's friend, he bestows a great many compliments on me & laments his own unhappiness; occasion'd by the loss of his dear Sally. Very much fatigued after my walk.

Monday, 21 December

Write to my Uncle George & send my cousin George an Acrostick on his Name. No letter from Captain Smith which I a little expected. My brother reads to me; sweet fellow, his fondness for me constitutes a great part of my happiness, for the satisfaction we feel in being belov'd by those we love is certainly inexpressible.

Tuesday, 22 December

Very busy all day, my brother reads the News to me. Find Mr. Grant has quitted the *Orford* & is appointed to the *Blenheim*, so those honest Messmates are now all separated.

Wednesday, 23 December

Hear Hannah Walder read which she performs quite well & spells tolerably. Sally Sheppard here in the evening. I shew her Rowzier's fine letter, she is in a consternation about it, & is determin'd to enquire if it was his own composing.

Thursday, 24 December

A letter from Captain Smith, he tells me he supposes I have added Mr. Grant to the number of my correspondents. On this hint I write again to Grant which I did not intend, rally him on his saying I was possess'd of more real honesty than nine tenths of my Sex, & endeavour to console him on the loss of his love.

Friday, 25 December

I should like to commence a correspondence with him, if my Harry approves, for certainly the friendship of a Man of worth & understanding like him is extreamly desirable. I really think the friendship of that Sex is preferable to their love.

Saturday, 26 December

Work all the morning. Finish reading *The Adventures of a Guinea*, fine Character of the King of Prussia, Pitt's Prince Ferdinand, detestable one of Maurert, author of the *Brussels Gazette*. A letter from my cousin Bet Smith, she acknowledges a secret passion for a very amiable young fellow, prentice to a Linnen Draper, but seems doubtfull of a return, poor girl, now she will begin to know sorrow.

Sunday, 27 December

At Church twice. Read some of my poetry to my brother who is very fond of it. Spend the afternoon & evening at Mr. Tredcroft's to chat with Miss about *The Adventures of a Guinea* .

Monday, 28 December

Work all the morning, a most charming fine day. Take a little walk & think if I had company a longer would be agreeable. Read in Lucian's works, his *Voyage to the Moon* very odd stuff, intended I suppose as a ridicule on the astronomers & philosophers.[427]

Tuesday, 29 December

Work all the morning, Very little variety in my life yet some few circumstances excepted I pass it as I like. Mr. Tredcroft's family drink tea & spend the evening with *[word omitted]* we play at cards, Miss Tredcroft will never be mistress of Quadrille, t'is pity but everybody should be perfect in *[word omitted]* they attempt, but this can never be, we are too apt to overrate out abilities, & fancy we are capable of performing any thing. But how do we fall short on trial.

Wednesday, 30 December

Betsy Cook, my dear lively Betsey Cook comes to stay a fortnight; she insists on Sally Sheppard's, my sister Bet & self accompanying her back to Storrington,

Thursday, 31 December

I would willingly but my Harry if he comes will be here at that time, a letter from him, he has not yet *[words omitted]* release. Spend the evening at Mrs. Curtis's.

I am now arriv'd at the period of this year, much in the same situation as I was the last, in every respect but Health on which thank Heaven I now enjoy a better share, may I be gratefull for the inestimable blessing, & oh grant supreme power that before the next year ends I may be happy with my dearest Harry.

---

427 Lucian of Samosata (c. 125-200), claimed to describe a voyage to the moon in *The True History* — see footnote to 9 December 1761. This is thought to have inspired Dean Swift's *Gulliver's Travels*.

THE DIARY FOR 1762

JANUARY 1762

Friday, 1 January

Began the New Year with writing a very long letter to my cousin Bet Smith, send her a copy of *The Certainty*.[428] Desire her to let prudence guide her young passion. Spend the evening at the *King's Head* with Betsy Cook, Sally Sheppard & Seymour Powell, who I believe was drunk & did not behave very delicately.

Saturday, 2 January

Go to keep Jemmy Waller's Birthday with the whole family.[429] Mr. Tredcroft & Mr. Shelley comes in & do not add to the mirth for it puts Mrs. Wicker out of temper. What mortals are we that it should be in the power of such trifles to discompose us.

Sunday, 3 January

At Church twice. The Headache prodigious. Read in *The Review* for November.

Monday, 4 January

Expect Captain Smith every day, but hear that War against the Spaniards will be declar'd today, & for this reason fear he will not come, alas how much I wish to see him. Mr. & Mrs. Jones & Miss comes to stay with us a week. I am oblig'd to spend the evening at Sally Sheppard's.

Tuesday, 5 January

A Ball at the *Anchor*, I dance with my brother who performs extreamly well & seems very fond of it, we had a dozen couple, some very good & some intolerable bad dancers.[430]

Wednesday, 6 January

Mr. & Mrs. Jones & all of us dine at Mrs. Wicker's & spend the afternoon & evening; my Aunt Waller affronts me about the cards, she is an ill behav'd Woman & I am above taking notice of it, being only sorry when people forfeit my good opinion.

---

428   *The Certainty* was probably a poem written by Sarah, not mentioned previously.

429   Jemmy (James) Waller was Sarah's cousin, the son of Thomas and Anne Waller. He was born in 1758, so it was his fourth birthday. He was apprenticed to Dr. Burry in 1777 and later set up his own surgical practice on Horsham Common. He married Elizabeth Smith, daughter of Henry's brother Adam, but she died in 1807. He had an illegitimate son (by Elizabeth Groombridge) to whom he left the bulk of his estate after his death in 1808.

430   The *Anchor Inn* was where Horsham's first Assembly Room was situated in the 1770s.

Thursday, 7 January

A letter from my dear Harry, my fears were indeed prophetick, he cannot come to Horsham, oh grant me fortitude Heaven to support the disappointment. Betsy Cook & Sally Sheppard spend the evening with us, we have a very agreeable dance.

Friday, 8 January

We are all invited to spend the afternoon & evening at Mr. Tredcroft's, my sister Bet is going dress'd in a ridiculous manner, I tell her she is to blame & so she will not go at all, an elegant supper. Mrs. Jones tells Miss Tredcroft's & the two Miss Whites' fortunes, which occasions a great deal of mirth.

Saturday, 9 January

My dear Harry's mother sends for me to know where to direct to him, I inform her & offer my service but she says I should write what she has to say in my next letter. I am astonish'd at this behaviour of hers, poor Woman, she laments as much as I do the Captain not coming to Horsham & laments his going abroad again; I join my fervent prayers to hers for his safety.

Sunday, 10 January

At Church twice, a charming fine day. Walk in the Croft with Bet Cook & Sally Sheppard.

Monday, 11 January

Work all day, a letter from my cousin Bet Smith, she acquaints me that she spent Twelfth Night[431] at Mr. John Smith's, my dear Harry's brother, with the Miss Hannahs,[432] where they danc'd & passed a very agreeable evening.

Tuesday, 12 January

Read my *Review*. Very sensible account of all the Books & pamphlets. Spend the afternoon & evening at my Aunt Waller's with a great deal of company, Mr. Shelley & Mr. Tredcroft quarrel at cards, one is domineering, the other peevish; wonder how they will agree when related.

Wednesday, 13 January

Read in Pope's *Dunciad*, some of it very droll & ludicrous.[433] Some chat with Sally Sheppard about our going to Storrington, which we conclude to defer.

Thursday, 14 January

A letter from my dear Harry, in which he laments his not coming to Horsham. I

---

431 Twelfth Night was celebrated on January 6, the last day of the Feast of Christmas.
432 Henry Smith's sister Elizabeth had married a Mr. Hannah, so the *"Miss Hannahs"* were his nieces and were remembered in his will.
433 *The Dunciad* of Alexander Pope was a mock-heroic literary satire, published in three versions. It was first published anonymously in 1728. The second version, in which Pope confirmed his authorship of the work, appeared in the *Dunciad Variorum* in 1735. The *New Dunciad*, in four books and with a different hero, appeared in 1743. A London edition of Pope's poems was published in 1760. Sarah could have read any of these versions.

answer his letter & acquaint him with all his mother order'd me to say, advise him tho' against my inclination [*not*] to come.

Friday, 15 January

At home all day, saw wood in the morning for exercise, which is certainly a very healthy one. My Heart sinks within me when I reflect on this Spanish War, & how long it may last, perhaps seven or ten years & must be more dangerous to my Harry because the Spaniards' Fleet is so much superior to the French, consequently there will be dreadfull Naval engagements, Heaven preserve my Harry, else how truly miserable must I be.[434]

Saturday, 16 January

Read Pope's *Dunciad*, a truly poetical but excessively severe [?*work*].

Sunday, 17 January

Not well & can't go to Church. Drink tea with Sally Hunt. Am surpris'd in the evening with the sight of Jack Willes the officer, he tells me his Brother Younge cannot get over his regard for me, and allways laments my being engag'd.[435] I am very sorry if it be true, for what is worse than hopeless love. He tells me my friend Miss Gittins had not time to write to me, he is going to London in hopes of getting into the Marine Service.

Monday, 18 January

Go to the *King's Head* to see Bet Cook, we dance 9 couple, my partner a very good one, stay till four in the morning.

Tuesday, 19 January

I was excessively fatigued, & not well all this day. Finish Pope's *Dunciad*, an excellent thing; what a man was he, read some of his miscellanies & epitaphs, how easy how manly do his verses flow, wish I could equal this great master of Numbers.

Wednesday, 20 January

Write a proclamation for a new Tax on kissing, in verse, at the desire of Bett Cook & Sally Hunt, they laugh very much when I read it to them. A terrible dream - fancy I am on the Brink of a frightful precipice, & am sent for to some man very ill.

Thursday, 21 January

A letter from Captain Smith, he is not well. Oh when will the measure of my woes be full. Write to him. Mr. Grainger here; makes me a present of half a Dozen franks, go for a walk with Sally Sheppard & Bet Cook.

Friday, 22 January

A fine pleasant frosty day which is extreamly agreeable after so much Wet. Walk up in the Park with Betsy Cook. Meet Doctor Griffith who says Sir Charles wants

434   War was declared between Spain and Britain on 4 January 1762, but concern about it had already led to William Pitt's resignation in October 1761. The main action was the capture of Havana in Cuba by the British after a campaign from June to August 1762.

to see us. What would I give to know how my dear Smith does, how terrible is suspence, how much more I experienc'd of that dreadfull situation.

Saturday, 23 January

Write a long letter to my brother. Walk in the Park with Betsy Cook, vastly pleasant, a letter from my brother, & one enclos'd for Master Nat Tredcroft,[436] we open & read it which affords us great diversion.

Sunday, 24 January

At Church in the morning, walk in the Croft. Sally Hunt tells me she will not carry my Proclamation against kissing to Cowfold. Am sent for to Slynfold. My brother is very ill with a fever, walk over with my father, mother & Doctor Read, find the poor Child quite bad.

Monday, 25 January

Write to my father to acquaint him my brother is better, he goes downstairs & is pretty well. A long letter from my friend Miss Gittins begging my pardon that she cannot yet tell me all the particulars of her affair with Turnpenny, she has her reasons, I dare say, & I will be content.

Tuesday, 26 January

She sends me a Poem on the game of Lottery Tickets, vastly pretty, a song in imitation of *Arnos Vale*; elegant & a burlesque song on Terry Mason, a gentleman she danc'd with lately, excessive droll, & incloses a Poem from Miss Stanley, in answer to mine. Don't like it so well as her last.

Wednesday, 27 January

My brother is much better thank God, I hope he will soon recover. Read *The Dragon of Wantly*, a Burlesque Opera, a very droll thing.[437] Play at quadrille in my brother's Room. Doctor Read comes over to see him & brings some Bark, tells us Betsy Cook is gone, but with a heavy heart.

Thursday, 28 January

A letter from my dearest Harry, he is vastly concern'd that I am so much griev'd at his not coming to Horsham, wishes I would often visit his mother, is determin'd to see me before he goes abroad, talks of a private marriage. What pleasure would it give me to be his for ever, but I am afraid of consequences.

Friday, 29 January

Write to him & tell him tho' with difficulties that I wish to call him mine. Consult

---

435 Younge Willes fell in love with Sarah when she stayed with his family in July 1761.
436 "*Master Nat*" was Nathaniel Tredcroft, who was still a schoolboy at this time, like Robert Hurst. He was born in 1747 and went to Eton.
437 *The Dragon of Wantley* was a burlesque opera with a libretto by Henry Carey, based on a 17th century poem, which satirised operatic conventions and the taxation policies of Sir Robert Walpole. It was a great success when it was first produced in 1737, but relied much on lavish staging.

Mrs. Jones who says she will not advise but imagines Mr. Jones will join our hands if we desire it. Oh, prudence & Reason direct me for the best.

Saturday, 30 January

Drink tea & spend the evening at Mrs. Knight's with Mr. & Mrs. Jones, my brother & Master Chasemore, play at Whist.[438] One of Mrs. Knight's sons my partner, but sure such a Burlesque upon the game was never before seen; some country people came in & are extreamly vulgar in their behaviour, good God, who can imagine we were all of the same species, what an amazing difference does education make.

Sunday, 31 January

At Church, never heard Mr. Jones preach before, he makes an excellent discourse on the incomprehensible Nature of God & our incapacity to understand his perfections, & manner of acting.

FEBRUARY 1762

Monday, 1 February

A very hard frost & exceedingly pleasant day, begin working a Cap. Talk with Mrs. Jones on my intended wedding, express some fears in regard to consequences & think we shall meet with many difficulties in the accomplishment of this affair.

Tuesday, 2 February

Thursday I shall return home, & then expect a letter from Captain Smith, suppose he will not mention anything of our union because he has not yet had my sentiments on this proposal. If this affair does not answer my expectation I will if possible make a resolution & keep it too; not to give myself the least uneasiness about any future event.

Wednesday, 3 February

Our Boy comes over to Slynfold with some Fish Papa sent Mr. & Mrs. Jones. Read *The Persian Letters*, wrote in a very easy flowing stile, one most affecting story of a Task.[439]

Thursday, 4 February

Take my leave of the good folks at Slynfold at seven in the morning, a hard frost, fine walk home. Receive a letter from my dear Harry containing the strongest assurance of regard. Call upon his mother. Write to him. Play at cards with Sally Sheppard.

Friday, 5 February

Mamma tells me she is vastly uneasy at my sister Bet's keeping company with Will James, I am determin'd not to interfere. Spend the afternoon at Mrs. Wicker's, see

---

438 A Mrs. Knight was mentioned as owning her own house in Slinfold in the 1785 Land Tax.
439 *The Persian Letters* was probably *Letters from a Persian in England to his friend in Isfahan*, by Lord George Lyttelton (1709-1773). A sixth edition was published in 1761.

in the Newspapers that Captain Spry in the *Mars* is come in to Plymouth; now my Harry will know whether he can get on Board her & I shall soon expect the pleasure of seeing him.

Saturday, 6 February

T'is full four days before I shall have an answer to the letter I wrote & half consented to a private wedding, oh how terrible is this suspence, the old saying that use makes every thing easy is a palpable falsity, for I detest & repine at suspence, tho' in my whole life I have scarcely past a day without feeling some degree of it.

Sunday, 7 February

Drink tea & spend the evening at the *King's Head* with Sally Sheppard & a clever young gentleman from Storrington.

Monday, 8 February

Work in the morning. My sister Bet works for me too, a most extraordinary thing. Dine & spend the Day at Mr. Powell's with Mrs. Wicker & Sally Sheppard, Seymour behaves very genteelly & is certainly a good natur'd young fellow.

Tuesday, 9 February

Work all the morning. Spend the afternoon & evening at Mr. Tredcroft's who tells me there is a promotion of twenty five majors in the Marines, if this be true surely my Harry is of the Number. Miss Tredcroft has discarded Jack Shelley & is blam'd by her father for so doing.[440]

Wednesday, 10 February

How much perplexity attends love affairs of all kinds whether the Heart is engag'd or not, it takes away all the pleasure of that part of Life most capable of happiness, when health glows on the cheek & the spirits move in a brisk circulation.

Thursday, 11 February

A letter *[from]* Captain Smith in which he tells me we should long e'er this have join'd Hands if his fortune had been sufficient to support his expenses & maintain a family. The Captain of Marines in the *Mars* will not quit her for him as he promis'd.

Friday, 12 February

Write to Smith tell him I should chuse to be married privately. I wonder what will be his answer & whether this affair will be accomplish'd or not. I should be infinitely happier if it was, but fear its accomplishment will be attended with a great many difficulties.

Saturday, 13 February

Work all day. A Note in the evening from Mrs. Jones desiring me to come over, my poor little brother being ill again. I am very much surpris'd & concern'd & set of for Slynfold directly, an excessive bad dirty walk. Find him better at my arrival, spend an agreeable evening with Mr. & Mrs. Jones.

---

440 This was quite a brave thing for Phoebe Tredcroft to do, since it is clear that her father wished for the wedding.

Sunday, 14 February

Bob's fever returns, write to Mamma to let her know it. Stay at home with him all day & can't go to Church, he grows better in the evening. Read *The Adventures of Philip Quarl*, who liv'd fifty years on a Desart Island on the coast of Mexico.[441] Romantick lies & wrote in a low stile.

Monday, 15 February

My brother is much better thank God, they send him some Bark from Horsham but could not procure me the Newspaper which is the only thing that makes my stay here disagreeable, for tho' I desire little concerns with the busy World yet do I wish to know how they go on.

Tuesday, 16 February

What can be the cause I know not but I find a serenity in my mind when here at Slynfold which I am a stranger to at Horsham, & yet the same reasons for anxiety subsists;

Wednesday, 17 February

I am at the same distance from my dear Harry, & the fears of being united to him ought to be as great as when at Horsham & yet those things affect me not half so severely, sure the distance of four miles cannot make such a difference in the Air as to have this extraordinary effect on my disposition.

Thursday, 18 February

A letter brought me from my dear Harry, he expresses great pleasure at my being intimate with his mother & hopes I will improve her regard for me, he may be certain I shall endeavour it. Our maid is oblig'd to return home directly so cannot answer his letter, which vexes me very much.

Friday, 19 February

Work all day. Mrs. Jones tells me I shall soon be married but I am certain it will not be so, & will endeavour to prepare myself for the disappointment to my Harry. I see no probability of ever being united, & I shall never entertain an opinion good enough of any other man to entrust my happiness with him.

Saturday, 20 February

Leave Slynfold; my Brother (who is pretty well again) & Master Chasemore come home with me. Mr. Grainger here makes me a present of a fine Italian Greyhound with which I am vastly pleas'd & hope he will stay. Write to my cousin Bet Smith.

Sunday, 21 February

At Church twice. Doctor Hutchinson makes an excellent Sermon on this text; *"if we say we have no sin we deceive ourselves"*. As I come up from Church a man who

---

441   Sarah had already read this book, whose full title is *The English Hermit or the Adventures of Philip Quarles*, on 29 September 1759.

lives at Doctor Smith's speaks to me, I answer him civilly but am surpris'd. Am told since that he greatly admires me & my poetry.

Monday, 22 February

Read Suckling's *Poems* & *Letters*, the first are chiefly on love & trivial subjects as are the letters, he appears in my opinion to have been a man of more wit & gallantry than solid judgement. Read his Play of *Aglaura* & *The Goblins*, not many good lines in either. Read his Tragedy of *Brennerall*, & *The Sad One*, both odd things.[442]

Tuesday, 23 February

Begin casting up the Shop by Papa's order who tells me my Uncle Bob & he intended to settle, but I fear I shall not be so happy as to see it done. Play at cards at Mrs. Tasker's.

Wednesday, 24 February

Go on casting up the Shop, receive an odd letter from a young fellow at Cowfold desiring me to write to him either in verse or prose, very badly spelt, & most improper hard words forc'd together, without meaning.

Thursday, 25 February

No letter from Captain Smith. Good Heavens, what can be the meaning of it? Sure he is ill or some accident has befallen him, how dreadfull is this disappointment, how unexpected. Go down to his mother but she has not heard. Oh, when shall I be reliev'd from this state of suspence?

Friday, 26 February

Very busy all day in the Shop, which is a great relief to my depres'd spirits. Write a Poem in vindication of playing cards in Lent & send it to Mrs. Wicker. I would not be without my muse on any consideration, in spite of the envy it has caus'd me.

Saturday, 27 February

A letter from my dear Harry, it had been detain'd on the Road, & was no neglect of his; he is determin'd to be married as soon as he comes into Sussex if I approve, I certainly shall not disapprove of what will make me quite happy.

Sunday, 28 February

At Church twice, I think the coldest day I ever felt. Tell Sally Sheppard that I expect to be married privately when Captain Smith comes, she is amaz'd but approves very

---

442 Sarah was probably reading *Fragmenta Aurea* by Sir John Suckling (1609-1641), a collection of his plays, poems and letters, published in 1646. He was generally considered to be one of the most elegant, witty and brilliant of the Cavalier poets. Suckling's play *Aglaura* had two fifth acts, one tragic and the other not. It was lavishly staged and printed in 1638 at his own expense. *The Goblins* was a romantic drama about outlaws who disguise themselves as devils. *Brennoralt* was a tragedy, in which the melancholy colonel is thought to shed light on Suckling himself.

much, fears he will find great difficulty in getting a License.[443] I hope not, for if I am disappointed shall be very unhappy.

MARCH 1762

Monday, 1 March

Hear the shocking news of poor Mrs. Ramsden's dying in Childbirth, she was eldest niece to Lord Irvin, had been married about a Year. [444] Alas, how uncertain are all sublunary thing[s]. Drink tea & spend the evening at Mrs. Tasker's, talk of little else but Mrs. Ramsden's untimely fate.

Tuesday, 2 March

Work all day. In the evening write a very long letter to Miss Gittins, on various subjects, tell her friendship without constancy is a glittering Bubble, & Love without constancy is a dreadfull Precipice.

Wednesday, 3 March

Mrs. Ramsden brought here to be buried, she died they say about half an hour after her son saw the light who is living; every Body is greatly concern'd for this amiable Lady, & to see her servants' grief would melt the most obdurate Heart. What a dreadfull thing is the loss of our friends.

Thursday, 4 March

A letter from my dear Harry, he is greatly surpris'd & concern'd at my silence when the flood prevented my writing from Slynfold, he has a feeling heart. Write to him, give an account of Mrs. Ramsden's death & burial & compare her former circumstances before she was married to the Colonel with my own, in which there was certainly a great similitude.

Friday, 5 March

Send for my *Review*; an account of some Poems lately publish'd by Mrs. Carter, a Kentish Lady. The extracts from them given by the Reviewers are admirable, & they liberally bestow the praises her uncommon merit deserves. Have wrote to my cousin Bet Smith to send me her Poems & hope to have them by Mrs. Tredcroft.

---

443   Lord Hardwicke's Marriage Act of 1763 *"for the better preventing of Clandestine Marriages"* was designed to end the scandal of secret marriages without parental permission (like that of Bysshe Shelley and Mary Catherine Michell in 1752) performed by unscrupulous clergy who became rich on the proceeds. The new Act brought marriage far more under state control than it had been hitherto, since it required the couple to be married in a parish church where at least one of them was resident, after the calling of banns on three successive Sundays. But there was a way round this for those who could afford it; couples who were of age could marry by special licence, which could be purchased from the Diocesan authorities.

444   Isabella Ramsden was the elder sister of Miss Elizabeth Ingram, and daughter of Col. Charles Ingram. She was married to Lt. Col. Fretchville Ramsden, who came from Yorkshire, where she had spent most of her childhood with her uncle and aunt, Lord and Lady Irwin, following the death of both her parents.

Saturday, 6 March

Think I had better burn all my essays in the poetical way since they certainly bear no greater resemblance to this admirable woman's than dreary December to blooming May, or a small River to the Boundless Ocean.

Sunday, 7 March

Not very [*word omitted*] stay at home from Church, read the ninth volume of Pope's *Letters*, what an easy sprightly manner he wrote in.[445] Drink tea at my Aunt Waller's, spend an hour at Mr. Curtis's.

Monday, 8 March

Cast up my father's Cash Book, & allmost stupify myself with Accounts; a very fine morning, but rains in the afternoon, emblem of Life's uncertainty. Mrs. Wicker tells me the man of Doctor Smith's has paid his addresses to her at which she is very much provok'd; desires I would keep it a profound secret. I tell her frankly I think she was too much in his company which authoris'd his boldness.[446]

Tuesday, 9 March

Spend the afternoon & evening at Mrs. Wicker's with the Miss Elliss's & Mrs. Tredcroft, who rails against poor Seymour Powell in such a manner that I am not able to bear it with common patience.

Wednesday, 10 March

A messenger comes from Mrs. Chasemore of Cuckfield to inform my father her Husband is dead. Good Heaven, how uncertain is every thing in this World, what pangs do I feel for his six helpless children left I fear unprovided for.[447]

Thursday, 11 March

A letter from my dear Harry and another from my friend Miss Gittins acquainting me that she & her mother are going to live at Norwich, this news affects me much. I shall hardly ever see this amiable friend again. Write to her & desire she will [*illegible*]. Write to Captain Smith.

Friday, 12 March

A general Fast for the War. At Church in the morning, Doctor Hutchinson makes an excellent Sermon on the occasion. Walk in the Croft with Sally Sheppard. The expedition Fleet pass'd by Plymouth last Sunday, sure Captain Smith will come now if at all, wonder whether we shall be married or not.

---

445   Sarah read some of Pope's *Letters* previously on 11 January 1760.
446   Probably the same man who was said to have expressed his admiration for Sarah on 21 February.
447   With the exception of Charles Chasemore, the eldest son, who was at school with Robert Hurst but appears to have died young, the Chasemore children did survive the tragedy of their father's early death, and became successful tradesmen in Guildford, Shoreditch and Epsom, from the evidence of their surviving wills. Their mother Jane was able to leave them money and good pieces of furniture and silver when she died in 1782.

Saturday, 13 March

A fine day, walk out with Mrs. Wicker. A letter by Mr. Tredcroft from my cousin Bet Smith, she gives the poor Justice[448] a very bad character. Tells me the Nobleman who is gone abroad with a young Lady & left his wife is the Earl of Pembroke, the Lady's name is Hunter, I wonder is she is the same Miss Gittins gave a very amiable description of some time ago. Alas how fickle a thing is Human Nature, Lord Pembroke married for love not many years ago.[449]

Sunday, 14 March

At Church twice. Walk up in the Park with my brother, a fine morning but cold & wet in the afternoon, which we spend at Mr. Tredcroft.

Monday, 15 March

Write a copy of a letter to the authors of the *Monthly Review* desiring their opinion of my poetry, transcribe & send them my Poem to Mrs. Tasker on her marriage, the *Midnight Soliloquy*, the *Vision on the Death of Admiral Boscawen* & *Cupid's Ramble*; I am afraid they will rank me among the Grub Street writers, or say as they lately did to a poor Poet, *"Silence young Sternold"*. Well let them, Censure or praise, the packet shall go & I shall impatiently expect their answer.

Tuesday, 16 March

Play at cards with my father & mother.

Wednesday, 17 March

Very busy all day Ironing. Sally Sheppard is with me all the afternoon, we talk of our Journey to Storrington which is fix'd for the first of April, if nothing happens to prevent us. Read in Pope's *Letters*, he is an Author I am very fond of on any subject.

Thursday, 18 March

A letter from Captain Smith but good God — instead of bringing news of his coming, it informs me he has applied for leave to go to Sea! Is this treating me delicately after what has pass'd? Write to him & send an *Ode to Patience*, just compos'd. What can I think of his behaviour?

Friday, 19 March

The reason he gives for desiring to embark now is he can go in a good Ship, & with Parson Parry, one of his old messmates, both which advantage[s] he must lose if he stays longer. Well, he may be right, now all my hopes of being soon united to him are over, perhaps his mind in that respect is alter'd which is the reason he won't come; well I can't help it, & won't perplex myself with conjectures.

---

448   Mr. Edward Tredcroft.
449   Henry Herbert, 10th Earl of Pembroke, was born in 1734, and joined the army in 1752. In 1759 he was made lieutenant-colonel of Elliot's light horse and went with his regiment to Germany. In 1760 and 1761 he commanded the cavalry brigade under Lord Granby, and was promoted major-general. In 1762 he scandalised society by eloping with Miss Hunter. He later returned and was restored to favour. He died at Wilton in 1794.

Saturday, 20 March

Very low spirited & my mind greatly discompos'd about Captain Smith, wish to God I lov'd him less; I should then be happier.

Sunday, 21 March

At Church twice. Walk in the Croft with Sally Sheppard, tell her my scruples about Smith's behaviour, she blames me excessively, & says he ought not to have acted otherwise than he had. Walk up in the Common with her to see the place where her House is to be built, a sweet pleasant spot, & I hope she will be happily situated.[450]

Monday, 22 March

Work all the morning. Walk to Slynfold in the afternoon with my sister Bet, find Mr. & Mrs. Jones & my brother well, Mrs. Jones is very much surpris'd at Captain Smith's not coming, & thinks him to blame, so she is of a different opinion from Sally Sheppard. This I know; I should have been happier if he had come, & we had been join'd in indissoluble bonds.

Tuesday, 23 March

Walk up to Hill, a farm House in Slynfold, situated on an eminence commanding a fine prospect. [It] was formerly they say a Priory & has indeed a venerable antique look.[451]

Wednesday, 24 March

My brother comes home with us for two days. Ill with a cold, wish for tomorrow because then I shall have a letter from my Harry, but alas, that will bring me nothing but the confirmation of his going to Sea. Play at cards with my father & mother.

Thursday, 25 March

A letter from Captain Smith, he says he believes he shall come to Horsham, & adds that he is sorry the Marriage Act took place for he should not dislike our being made certain of each other without its being publick.

Friday, 26 March

I write to him & tell him I am excessively surpris'd at his mentioning the Marriage Act because I thought he had known as we were both of age we might be married with a Bishop's License, if that cou'd be procur'd.[452] His starting this objection alarms me, sure he cannot repent of his proposal he made & wish to retract it. Oh Power Supream, relieve me soon from this suspence.

---

450 This implies that Sally Sheppard was to marry Drew Michell. He had his tannery on the east side of Horsham Common, along the Brighton Road, outside the town at that time. (Tanneries were usually built on the outskirts of towns because the tanning process produced offensive smells). A later description of the tannery in one of his letters mentions two dwelling houses (HM MSS Cat. No. 200.25).

451 Hill does not appear to have been a Priory; it was a house owned by the Hussey family in the 16th century, which passed to the Churchars at the beginning of the 17th century. Mrs. Tayleur, the housekeeper of Hill's Place, came from the Churchar family.

452 See the footnote to the entry of 28 February 1762.

Saturday, 27 March

Sally Sheppard has a letter from Betsy Cook to inform us that she cannot get her House ready for our reception so soon as she expected, write to Captain Smith & acquaint him with it. Read in the *History of Russia*, am excessively shock'd at the cruelty & horror which former ages abound with.[453]

Sunday, 28 March

At Church twice, walk up in the Park with my sister Molly, the wind high & unpleasant. Drink tea at Mrs. Wicker's, read three of Sterne's *Sermons*, *the Pharisee & Publican*, *A Vindication of Human Nature* & *A Search after Happiness*, all excellent discourse.[454]

Monday, 29 March

Read in the *History of Russia*. Alexis, Father of Peter the Great, was an excellent Prince as was his eldest son Theodore; how dearly do I ....

[2 pages cut out, and six other pages missing; this results in the second half of each day of the next 7 days being lost & the first half of the entry for April 26 being lost also. Sarah usually wrote right across two pages in her pocket-book.]

Tuesday, 30 March

.... have done. Drink tea with my Mamma & Mrs. Wicker at Doctor Smith's where is my Harry's mother & little Maria, who Doctor Smith's ....

Wednesday, 31 March

.... some, I once was so but uneasiness of various sorts has alter'd my pleasing form. Read the *History of Peter the Great*, what an enterpri ....

APRIL 1762

Thursday, 1 April

A letter from Captain Smith, he is determin'd to come to Horsham if possible & would he says long before if in his power, for he abhors the ....

Friday, 2 April

.... me to be married, sure she would not have me so indelicate as to be forwarder than my lover, who does not yet think it prudent. Come ....

Saturday, 3 April

.... genteel & attends me home. Very busy all day in the Shop, in the evening write several letters for my father, what a happy girl might I ....

453   Sarah bought *The History of Russia* when she was in London in November 1761.
454   These are from the first book of sermons published by Lawrence Sterne in 1760, under the title *The Sermons of Mr. Yorick* (see the footnote to the entry on 22 June 1760).

Sunday, 4 April

.... poems I sent them among them, they are excessive cunning.[455] At Church twice, walk in the Croft with Sally Sheppard, a most delightfull pleasant day. Walk on ....

[Six pages missing for the three weeks 5 – 26 April. Only the second half of the entry for April 26 survives]

Monday, 26 April

.... mighty Power give me strength of mind to go through the tremendous ceremony.

Tuesday, 27 April

My dear Harry has now been in Sussex a fortnight, we conclude to be married at Slynfold, as I have resided there long enough.

Wednesday, 28 April

Married to Captain Smith, oh may I allways deserve & possess his love, we conclude to keep it private till the War is over. Mr. & Mrs. Jones, Mr. & Mrs. Gardiner [456] & my Sally Sheppard are the only persons entrusted with the secret.

Thursday, 29 April

Return home from Slynfold & Nobody suspects I am married.

Friday, 30 April

Oh, how I exult in the thought that my dear Harry is mine for life, may I deserve the happiness I now feel which is great indeed, tho' prudential reasons prevents our living together at present.

MAY 1762

Saturday, 1 May

Three or four hours with my Harry.

Sunday, 2 May

Dine at Mr. Tudor's with my father, sister Bet & Captain Smith, a charming pleasant day. I have got a great cold but am yet well in health & possess most excellent Spirits.

---

455   This is possibly a reference to the poems that Sarah sent to *The Monthly Review* on 15 March.

456   Mr. and Mrs. Gardiner presumably acted as witnesses for the marriage. Mr. Gardiner can be identified as John Gardiner of Slinfold, cordwainer, who made a will in 1777 leaving his cottage adjacent to the churchyard to John Piggott Jones, son of the Rev. John Jones, who had died in 1776. Most of the rest of Mr. Gardiner's property was put in trust for John and his sister Mary, and Mrs. Jones was made the executrix. The will was proved in 1788.

Monday, 3 May

At home all day, very busy all day writing. Captain Smith, my ever dear Husband, calls on me twice, how supreamly happy am I in his company & how melancholy is the reflection that I must soon lose it, but my Reason tells me I must exert its uttermost power & calmly now learn to bear Life's hourly changes.

Tuesday, 4 May

Spend the afternoon at Mrs. Wicker's, tell her am married at which she rejoices much, she makes a solemn promise to keep it secret. Captain Smith comes to me there, is foolishly fond before her, which I chide him for, yet cannot in my Heart be angry.

Wednesday, 5 May

Walk after dinner in the Park with Sally Sheppard. Divert ourselves with chatting & gathering Cowslips.[457] She congratulates me on my Wedding & says she will do the same to Captain Smith when she sees him alone, & he will laugh & show his teeth.[458]

Thursday, 6 May

Busy all day writing, Captain Smith is with me some hours, I return thanks to the supream Being for the happiness I now enjoy in being certain of passing my Life with my dearest Harry, how many dreadfull suspences & perturbations have I pass'd throug[h] e'er I arriv'd at this Haven of happiness, henceforth ye unfortunates never despair of attaining your wishes if they are virtuous.

Friday, 7 May

Captain Smith asks my father's consent to have me & settle as soon as we can - droll enough to ask leave after we are married. But this impropriety could not be avoid'd. My father tells him he will do what he can for us, & wishes us happy.

Saturday, 8 May

Walk over to Dales, drink tea & spend a most agreeable afternoon there with Mrs. Wicker & Captain Smith, he comes home with me, & expresses the greatest fondness for me which makes me happy. Read *The Review*.

Sunday, 9 May

At Church twice, violent headache all day. Captain Smith spends but an hour with me, his sister goes away tomorrow, then may I hope to have more of his company. Walk up in the Park with Miss Powell & Miss Steward. Quite ill & oblig'd to go to Bed, what Constitution have poor I.

Monday, 10 May

Captain Smith with me a little while. Ride to Mr. Bristed's at Slaugham with my father, a fine day. Meet there with one Mr. Newcomb, a Clergyman, very well

---

457   Cowslips were used to make a country wine.
458   This is the only physical description of Henry in the diaries.

acquainted with Miss Phipps & her friend Mrs. Marriot, a droll little man. A pleasant ride home.

Tuesday, 11 May

[No entry]

Wednesday, 12 May

[No entry]

Thursday, 13 May

Dine at Slynfold, my sister Bet suspects I am married & threatens to tell my father. Endeavour to silence her but she grows the more outrageous at my mildness. I then storm in my turn at which she appears frighted & is silent, a vile girl to endeavour to ruin me.

Friday, 14 May

Bet abuses Captain Smith; strange creature, she'll make every Body her enemies.

Saturday, 15 May

Spent all this week happily with my dearest Harry. Walk over to Highland with *[word omitted]* he is all that is good & kind oh how blest am I now, but alas, my situation will soon be revers'd, he has not more than a fortnight to stay; grant me resignation & patience Heaven to support his loss.

Sunday, 16 May

[No entry]

Monday, 17 May

[No entries until Wednesday, May 26]

Wednesday, 26 May

Spend the day at the Hammer pond with Mr. & Mrs. & Miss Tredcroft, Mr. Shelley, Mrs. Wicker & Captain Smith. Go on the Water several times but I am not well & incapable of being merry, the thoughts of my dear Husband's departure, which is fix'd for next Monday, sits heavy at my Heart.

Thursday, 27 May

Dine at the *King's Head* with Bet Cook. A letter from Miss Gittins, she blames me for being married without my friends' knowledge, but if she knew all *[the]* circumstances she could not.

Friday, 28 May

My dear Harry dines with us & Betsy Cook. I am excessive low spirited, oh how dreadfull t'is to think on next Monday.

Saturday, 29 May

Captain Smith spends *[a]* great part of the day with me. Tell him if I die before I see him again that I beg he will acquaint my friends we were married & desire him to be buried by me at Horsham, & that he will never marry again till he finds a Woman he loves as well as he does me, & who loves him as well.

Sunday, 30 May

At Church in the morning, my Harry is to dine at Sir Charles's & does not call here before he goes, which makes me excessive uneasy, oh that we liv'd together. My dear Harry concludes to stay till Thursday, what a blessing do I think this little respite.

Monday, 31 May

Read in *The Adventurer* but alas, my mind is too unsettled to attend. Spend the afternoon at Mrs. Wicker's with Mrs. Laight & my Harry. I expatiate to Mrs. Laight on the regard I have for Sally Sheppard & how well she deserves it.

JUNE 1762

Tuesday, 1 June

Work all day. Mrs. Laight drinks tea with us. Go for a walk with Captain Smith, we lament together the necessity of his departure. Oh Reason, if it be true that thou hast any power over human actions, passions & affections, now oh now exert thy influence & teach me to bear this evil with calm resignation.

Wednesday, 2 June

The last day is this that I shall see my dear Harry for months, perhaps for years. He calls on me four or five times with a Heart as heavy as my own; oh Providence divine, protect & shield him from every danger.

Thursday, 3 June

My dear Husband drinks some coffee with me at five in the morning, at six he bids me adieu, oh what a parting, sure the separation of Soul & Body cannot be so dreadfull. Several of my acquaintance calls to know how I do, I put on a chearfull countenance but alas it belies my Heart, but thanks to the supream Being for making my Harry mine for I am infinitely happier than when in a state of suspence; we must now we have sworn to it pass our lives together, oh may they be peaceable & happy & may I deserve the continuance of his love.

Friday, 4 June

Tell my friend Sally Sheppard that if I die she should desire my friends to have a vault made large enough to hold Captain Smith & me, for he has promis'd to be buried by me.

Saturday, 5 June

Walk over to Dales with a large party to drink tea. Sup at Mrs. Bridger's.

Sunday, 6 June

Go to Henfield with my sister Bet on a visit to a farm House, where there is two young ladies about our age, their name Woolvin. We meet with a very kind reception, the eldest sister is very much deform'd & I doubt illnatur'd, the youngest is handsome, sprightly, engaging & agreeable.[459]

Monday, 7 June

Walk up to Henfield Town with my sister & Miss Jenny Woolvin, the people stare at us as much as the wild Indians do at an Englishman. Call at Mr. Briggs' whose wife invites us to drink tea on Tuesday, walk in the evening up the Common, a pleasant place.

Tuesday, 8 June

I wonder how long my dear Harry will stay in London, hope he will write to me tonight. The two Miss Woolvins, Bet & self ride to Shoreham to see the Harbour that is building, a most stupendous piece of work. A fine ride back over the Downs.

Wednesday, 9 June

Try to milk & the maid flatters me I should soon learn. How peacefull how serene is a rural life remote from the giddy World whose pleasures cannot compensate for its various evils, but alas, we are all inclinable to prefer & think best the situation we are not plac'd in.

Thursday, 10 June

Expect to be sent for home, but Mr. Woolvin tells us it won't be till tomorrow, so we all ride to Storrington to see Betsy Cook, who is surpris'd & pleas'd with our company. Her brother too behaved extreamly well & is vastly charm'd with Miss Jenny Woolvin.

Friday, 11 June

Papa & my brother comes to fetch us home; they tell me there is no letter for me. Oh my dear dear Husband, what can you mean by not writing, sure I shall hear from you tonight. Arrive at home about nine o'clock, wait impatiently till the Post comes in & then to my great disappointment have no letter from Captain Smith. Oh Harry, what can occasion your staying so long in London, but let me not be impatient.

Saturday, 12 June

Go down to my Harry's mother. She has not heard from him, what can be the reason, he must surely be ill.

Sunday, 13 June

At Church twice. Maria Smith dines with me. Wait for the Post's coming in with the most anxious impatience but he brings no letters to Mrs. Smith nor me. I perswade her to write by the Coach, but she coolly refuses & says she hopes the best, but good God, how dreadfull is my situation. Write to my cousin Bet Smith & desire her to enquire after the Captain.

459 A Mr. Thomas Woolven lived at Oreham Place, a farm belonging to Samuel Blunt, of Springfield Place, and owned land in Henfield in the 1785 Land Tax. It seems likely that the Misses Woolven were related to him.

Monday, 14 June

A most terrible night in spite of all my efforts to calm my mind. Oh when shall I posses a tranquil one, I vainly thought my suspences & troubles were at an end, but who alas can say. Misfortune & anguish, thou shalt not approach me.

Tuesday, 15 June

Dine & drink tea at Mrs. Wicker's. A letter by the Coach from my cousin Bet Smith who informs me that my dear Husband left London the Monday after he went from here, but so suddenly that he had not time to take leave of any of his relations, which was I suppose the reason he did not write to me. Thank Heaven he is well, hope shall hear from him tonight.

Wednesday, 16 June

Dine at Doctor Hutchinson's. A letter from my ever dear Harry, he has hopes of being made a Major, pray Heaven he may.

Thursday, 17 June

Write to my cousin Bet Smith, & to my dear Husband to whom I cannot be gratefull enough. Mr. Shelley dines with us, Mr. & Mrs. Jones & myself drink tea with him at Field Place in our road to Slynfold. Find Betsy Jones not well, at which her mother is excessively alarm'd. What cares attend the having a family.

Friday, 18 June

Go to a farm House to drink tea, three or four men very drunk, sure of all vices drinking is the most Brutish & unnatural. Return to Slynfold, a great deal of chat with Mr. & Mrs. Jones. Read over my Harry's letter 2 or 3 times.

Saturday, 19 June

Betsy Jones is quite [word omitted] & her [mother] allmost as bad through grief, I have a very dull time of it & tho' I sincerely pity Mrs. Jones, yet I wish to be at home as I cannot be of any service. Walk in the Garden with Mr. Jones, he says a first real affection is never quite eras'd & I firmly believe it. Thank Heaven for Joining me to my dearest Harry, the first & only person I ever lov'd.

Sunday, 20 June

At Church in the morning, Mr. Jones makes an excellent discourse, his little daughter worse. Drink tea at Mrs. Gardiner's. Am sent for home & arrive there just as a fine shower is beginning to refresh the parch'd Earth.

Monday, 21 June

A letter from my cousin at East Bourne desiring my company soon, I will go if possible. Begin reading *The History of Lidia Fair Child*,[460] drink with Betsy Cook. Walk with Mrs. Wicker in her garden, tell her I hope she will pay me the respect due to a Majoress.

---

460   This work and its author have not been identified.

Tuesday, 22 June

Continue reading the *History of Lidia*, some very amiable characters & some tiresome trite stuff. Drink tea at Mrs. Wicker's, she laments the near prospect she thinks there is of losing me, & I sincerely wish that time was arriv'd when I shall live with my dearest Harry.

Wednesday, 23 June

A very large troop of the Cornish Militia comes to Town. They have with them a fine band of musick which I should never be weary of listening to.[461] Write to my friend Miss Gittins tell her my reasons for marrying & beg her not to mention the subject any more for fear of an accident.

Thursday, 24 June

Make me a pair of mock garnet Necklace & earrings, oh dress, thou enchanting thing, how much doth thou engross of most females' time & thoughts. Hear the musick again which belongs to the Militia. Walk in Mr. Parham's garden, eat some fruit with Sally Sheppard.

Friday, 25 June

Write a little in my Book of Poems, which I have not done before these 3 months. Papa taken ill. Heaven grant he may soon be well again. Mrs. Bridger drinks tea here, murder a whole fine afternoon playing at cards. Walk a little before the door. Mr. Kendal joins me, some chat with him.[462]

Saturday, 26 June

Want to hear from my dear Harry, yet know I can't before tomorrow or Wednesday. My father better, I ask him when he intends going to Bourne, he tells me in about a fortnight. Walk in the Park with Mrs. Wicker & Miss Powell.

Sunday, 27 June

At Church in the morning, my father has a fit of an Ague.[463] Sally Sheppard & Bet Cook drink tea with me. We walk in the Park, Sir Charles sends for us into his garden to eat cherries. A letter from my dearest Harry wrote in the fondest terms, he is uneasy at being absent from me. Alas so am I, but where's the remedy?

Monday, 28 June

My Harry has given me leave to go to Bourne & I have fix'd it for next Saturday sennight. Walk to Slynfold with Mrs. Wicker, are catch'd in the rain, & oblig'd to stay four hours at the Mill House. Mrs. Wicker very uneasy about it. I laugh & tell her this

---

461 Horsham did not at this time have a barracks, so regiments passing through would camp on the Common. The band often seems to have acted as an aid to recruitment.

462 Mr. Kendal is not otherwise known in Horsham but, in May 1759, Sarah visited a Mr. Kendall's warehouse in London. Possibly he had come down to Horsham to do business with her father.

463 An *"ague"* was the term used to describe a malarial fever, with paroxysms, consisting of a cold, a hot and a sweating stage.

is a trifling disaster. Mr. Jones brings us great Coats & Boots & in this droll equipage we
[*word omitted*] through the rain to the great diversion of the people at the Mill.[464]

Tuesday, 29 June

Write a very long letter to my dear Harry, drink tea at Field Place, walk on the
Causeway.

Wednesday, 30 June

Very busy all day getting my things ready for my Journey, write out some Bills. Walk
in the Park with Bet Cook. How dull does every thing appear without my Harry,
when oh when, ye contentious unfeeling monarchs, will ye sheath the bloody sword
& bid calm Peace smile on Europe's Sons, for then & not before can I live with my
ever dear Husband.

JULY 1762

Thursday, 1 July

Walk in the Park with Sally Sheppard, afterward on the Causeway with my dear
Harry's sister-in-law Mrs. Smith, hear the Cannon fired.[465]   Imagine there is some
news, a victory I suppose either by Sea or land.

Friday, 2 July

Mrs. Smith calls of [*sic*] me. She is an agreeable sensible Woman, take a long walk
with her. Drink tea at Mrs. Wicker's, walk on the Causeway. Mr. Tredcroft tells me
Prince Ferdinand has beat the French in Germany; well a victory gives me allmost as
much concern as a defeat, for t'is shocking to hear of the destruction of our fellow
creatures.[466]

Saturday, 3 July

Walk with Mrs. Smith & Mrs. Wicker; the former says Captain Smith will make a
good Husband, I sincerely hope he may & I believe she will be a true prophet.

Sunday, 4 July

Write to London unknown to my father for a Silk Negligée & petticoat against I
go to Bourne.[467] I believe this is not quite right, but as I am married & it will some
when be known I was at this time, I think t'is best to appear tolerably well & not
discredit my dearest Harry. At Church twice.

---

464 The watermill at Slinfold was held at this time by Susannah Steer. She employed Henry
     Booker as miller in 1763; he married her daughter Elizabeth in September 1764.
465   Presumably by the militia encamped on the Common.
466 This was one of many battles in the European part of the Seven Years' War, in which Prussia
     took the leading rôle, supported by Britain and Portugal, against an alliance of Austria,
     France, Russia, Sweden and Saxony.
467 A negligée was a loose gown worn on informal occasions - later Sarah refers to it as her "*new
     Sack*".

Monday, 5 July

Very busy all day ironing. Walk in the evening with Sally Sheppard to see the House Drew Michell is building for her reception, it is situated on a dry part of the Common & extreamly pleasant. Read Shakespeare's *Merchant of Venice*.[468]

Tuesday, 6 July

Work in the morning, call on Mrs. Smith who talks as much as ever, drink tea with her at Mrs. Wicker's. Mrs. Pitt extreamly ill, the Doctor thinks she won't live.[469] Walk in the Park & afterwards on the Causeway, very agreeable chat with Mrs. & Miss Tredcroft. Read Shakespeare's *As You Like It*.

Wednesday, 7 July

Mrs. Smith drinks tea with us, shew her my work'd Apron which she prodigiously admires & says it exceeds anything she ever saw. Mr. Tudor here, waits for the Post. I read the Pamphlets against Lord Bute who is the King's great favourite to the no small mortification of many.[470]

Thursday, 8 July

A letter from my cousin Hurst of Bourne, he informs me he will send for me to Lewes on Saturday next. I promise Mr. Shelley I will write to him. Spend the afternoon at Mrs. Bridger's, play at cards, begin reading *The Taming of the Shrew*.[471] Write to Mrs. Townshend.

Friday, 9 July

Begin writing to Captain Smith in expectation of hearing from him tonight. Am disappointed [by] the man who was to conduct me to Lewes. Mr. John Shelley offers me his man, which I thankfully accept of. A letter from my dear Harry & another from Bet Smith.

Saturday, 10 July

Set out to Lewes at six in the morning, arrive there about eleven, my cousin Hurst from Bourne had been there about ten minutes before me, dine at Lewes & call at several places. Arrive at Bourne extreamly tir'd & oblig'd to walk several miles.

Sunday, 11 July

Pretty well considering my yesterday's long journey. Go to Church in the afternoon, am complimented with a visit from Mr. Lushington the Minister, his

---

468 Apparently it was only now that Sarah started reading the copy of William Shakespeare's works which she had bought in London on 11 November 1761.

469 Mrs. Mary Pitt (née Linfield) was the widow of Robert Pitt, Vicar of Horsham from 1722-1729.

470 John Stuart, the 3rd Earl of Bute, who was formerly tutor to George III, was appointed as First Lord of the Treasury and Prime Minister on 7 May 1762. He was disliked for of his Scottish nationality, his position as the King's favourite, and because his peace policy had brought about Pitt's resignation.

471 *The Taming of the Shrew* by William Shakespeare, believed to have been written between 1590 and 1594.

Wife & two daughters, both very agreeable young Ladies, the eldest they [word omitted] is in a bad state of health occasion'd t'is said by a disappointment in Love, poor young Lady.[472]

Monday, 12 July

Do a little work for Mrs. Hurst, write a letter to my father & give him an account of my journey. Call on the two Miss Gilberts, the eldest is a Beauty & very agreeable.[473] Go to the Assembly, play at cards with a Miss Cavaler[?Calverley], Mrs. Filcox & Mr. Lushington.[474]

Tuesday, 13 July

Set out for Winchelsea with Mrs. Hurst, the two Miss Mortimers, Nanny Smith & Mr. Mortimer.[475] Dine at Hastings, a large ill built place situated close by the Sea between two Hills. Arrive at Winchelsea in great pain with one side of my face excessively scorch'd by the Sun. Mr. Mortimer oils it for me, & behaves to me extreamly civil.

Wednesday, 14 July

Go with all our party down to the Sea to see the new Harbour open'd, a great deal of company, many gentlemen enquire who I am & seem to admire me much. I really thought my Beauty was near faded.

Thursday, 15 July

How happy should I have been yesterday if my dear Harry had been there. Walk to see the Cambrick manufactory that is carrying on here at Winchelsea by some French refugees, extreamly curious.[476] Dine at Rye, the last Town in the Eastern part of Sussex.

Friday, 16 July

Rye has a pretty Harbour, & is situated on a Hill overlooking the Sea & part of the Wild;[477] Mr. Mortimer is allways at my elbow which every body takes notice of, sure he can have no design. He knows I am engag'd but not that I am married.

Saturday, 17 July

Take our leave of Winchelsea, dine about four miles from thence with a relation of Mr. Mortimer's, a very pleasant ride to Hastings where we drink tea. Arrive

---

472 The Rev. Henry Lushington and his first wife, Mary Altham, had four sons and three daughters. Their eldest daughter Jane (born 1738) married Thomas Altham in 1763.

473 The Gilberts have previously been mentioned as one of the main families in Eastbourne- see entry of 16 July 1761.

474 In the 1785 Land Tax for Eastbourne, a Miss Calverley owned two houses, one occupied by a George Philcox.

475 This and all other references to "Mr. Mortimer" probably refer to "young Mortimer", whom Sarah first met in July 1761, and who is thought to be John Hamilton Mortimer, the painter.

476 This cambric factory was mentioned by Frederick W.L. Stockdale, in his *Concise Historial and Topoghical Sketch of Hastings, Winchelsea and Rye*, published in 1817, p. 24. He said "*a considerable traffic was also carried on, about fifty years ago, by a company of merchants, who had a cambric manufactory in this town*"

477 The Weald of Sussex – the hilly part which stretched into Kent – was sometimes called "*the Wild*".

safe at Bourne about nine in the evening which I am not sorry for being very dirty & not a little tired.

Sunday, 18 July

At Church in the morning, a good Sermon preach'd by Mr. Lushington, but his voice is too low to make all the congregation hear. Mr. Mortimer calls on me. The two Miss Mortimers, their brother & the two Miss Russels drink tea with us. Walk to the Sea side with Kitty Mortimer, agreeable chat.

Monday, 19 July

Write Mr. John Shelley an account of my journey & the manner I spend my time & write to my father. The two Miss Lushingtons call on me, walk with them. Doctor Russel proposes a party of fishing for tomorrow. Begin to think I pass my time here rather idly, will endeavour to make myself useful to Mrs. Hurst.

Tuesday, 20 July.

I like being here extreamly well, for I am now relieved from the disputes & animosities that so often arise in our own family & are so excessive disagreeable. A young gentlemen drinks tea with us whose name is Mannix, he is very handsome, modest & gentell behav'd.

Wednesday, 21 July

Attempt going with a large party in Doctor Russell's machine to fishing, but one of the Wheels breaks down & we are all thrown but without any hurt. Mr. Mortimer tells me I am not so handsome as I am sensible. I know this, & yet the truth did not please me much, so vain is Woman of that foolish thing their persons.

Thursday, 22 July

Drink tea at Mr. Gilberd's & spend the evening with a vast deal of company. They desire a sight of my Apron which, being sent for, is prodigiously admir'd. Play at cards, am a winner.

Friday, 23 July

Write by the assistance of Miss Kitty Mortimer a Burlesque poem on the gentlemen of Sussex being so unwilling to serve in the Militia & offer ourselves in their stead; Miss Lushington, Miss Mortimer & I are affronted by an Irishman, his name Mannix coming naked into the Sea while we were Bathing.[478]

Saturday, 24 July

A letter from my father inclosing one from my Gittins which contain'd the whole of Turnpenny's behaviour, alas, it has been vile to the dear girl. She sends me a Poem on my marriage with a frontispiece of her own drawing. A letter from my dear Husband, he wishes he was within two days ride of Bourne; I cannot help concurring in this wish.

---

478   It is not clear whether this was the same Mannix who was described on 20 July as *"very handsome, modest and genteel behaved"*.

Sunday, 25 July

Drink tea at .... At Church in the afternoon, write to Sally Sheppard. Take a walk with Miss Kitty Mortimer in Lord Northampton's Grove, a fine serene pleasant evening. Doctor Russell & Mr. Smith Mortimer sup with us.

Monday 26 July

Write to my ever dear Captain Smith, to my father & to Mrs. Jones. Put on my new Sack[479] & go to the assembly which was a very slender one. Sup at Mr. Mortimer's, who conducts me home & indeed on all occasions behaves with the greatest civility.

Tuesday, 27 July

Am told that I cut all the Bourne ladies out in finery, & was as gay as my Lady Ashburnham,[480] a parcell of fools that can't distinguish being smart from being fine. Ride out with Mr. Hurst, & my head was allmost blown off with the Wind. Mr. Martin from Winchelsea comes.[481]

Wednesday, 28 July

Ride out with Mr. Hurst & Mr. Martin; dine at Mr. Lamb's of Wilmington, drink tea & sup at Mr. Aid's, a farmer,[482] who treats us with much rustick civility. When I reflect on the difference there is between Creatures of the sam[e] species I am all amazement, it seems alltogether occasion'd by their situation.

Thursday, 29 July

Oblig'd by bad weather to stay all night at Wilmington. Drink Sage tea for my breakfast at which Mrs. Lamb is much offend'd & says she hates particular People, this offends me & I tell her am sorry I made so free. Am right glad to return to good Mrs. Hurst.

Friday, 30 July

Think much on my dear worthy Husband, wish to see him but alas I know the wish in vain. Call at Mr. Lushington's & Mr. Mortimer's, young Mortimer drinks tea with us; read some of my Poetry to Mr. Marten & Mr. & Mrs. Hurst.

Saturday, 31 July

Mr. Martin goes home, promises to get me some franks. A letter from my father, he informs me they are all well of which I am extreamly glad, begin making Mrs. Hurst a pair of stays. Go for a walk with Betsy Mortimer & afterward with Mr. Hurst.

---

479 This was probably the *"negligée"* (dress) which she had ordered secretly for her visit to Eastbourne on 4 July.
480 The Earls of Ashburnham were one of the great landowners of East Sussex.
481 A Mr. Marten is listed as the owner of several properties in Winchelsea, including a hop garden and malthouse, in 1785.
482 Richard and William Lambe appear in the 1785 Land Tax for Wilmington, as farmers. Richard Lambe was one of the tax assessors. Mr. Ade was listed as a tenant farmer.

AUGUST 1762

Sunday, 1 August

At Church in the morning, Mr. Lushington makes a good discourse on this text; *"Judge not & ye shall not be judged"*. Mr. & Mrs. Hurst are now both gone to bed & left me to myself, oh that my dear dear Husband was here to bear me company, alas what a cruel distance parts us.

Monday, 2 August

A letter from my dear friend Sally Sheppard, it informs me she is well which affords me a very sensible pleasure. She returns my Song on the Militia & says t'is very clever. Drink tea at Mr. Lushington's with more company.

Tuesday, 3 August

The man brings the Lewes Newspaper,[483] Our Song was too long to be inserted in this week's paper but will in the next. Drink tea down at the Sea side with a vast deal of company. Dance, sing & pass our time excessive agreeable.

Wednesday, 4 August

Bathe in the Sea, go down with Miss Lushington in her mother's Chariot, how amiable is good Nature, & how large a share does this dear girl possess of it. Spend the afternoon & evening at Mr. Lushington's, who are excessively civil to me.

Thursday, 5 August

Walk up in the Town & chat with Kitty Mortimer, who shews me some of her Poetry, which is indeed very droll. Walk out with Mrs. Hurst, go into Lord Northampton's garden & grove, a sweet agreeable retreat.

Friday, 6 August

Begin writing a letter in verse to Mrs. Wicker. A very Wet stormy unpleasant day, stay at home & work for Mrs. Hurst. Imagine my father by this time wants me at home, yet I am not willing to go. Bourne I like extreamly well & its inhabitants.

Saturday, 7 August

Finish my poetical letter, read it to Kitty Mortimer who much approves, as do Mr. Lushington & family. Spend the afternoon & evening with them. No letters from Horsham, nor from my dear Harry, hope to hear from all on Monday.

Sunday, 8 August

Bathe in the Sea with Miss Lushington. At Church in the afternoon. Walk down to the Sea with Mrs. Hurst, a fine evening & we are entertain'd with the agreeable

---

483 The *Lewes Journal* (or *Sussex Weekly Advertiser)* was the first newspaper to be published regularly in Lewes, by William Lee, from 1745 onwards. His son Arthur opened an office in Horsham and married Sally Michell, the daughter of Drew Michell and Sally Sheppard, in 1786.

sight of a large fleet of Ships very near the Shore, how do I wish for my dearest Harry & regret the distance he is at.

Monday, 9 August

A letter from Captain Smith, as usual full of the tenderest expressions, answer it directly. A letter from my brother who tells me poor Mr. Ellis[484] died last Tuesday & that Counsellor Cox was at the Assizes, where he said he would not have been if he had know I was gone out, for he wanted me to go & stay a month with his Wife.

Tuesday, 10 August

My dear Husband wishes we were settled, & says he shall esteem that day the happiest of his Life, so shall I, but alas I see no prospect of that happiness yet.

Wednesday, 11 August

Mr. Smith Mortimer calls on me, just return'd from London.[485] Shews me a burlesque Song made on the Queen's fine Ass that was lately presented to her. Walk out with Miss Kitty Mortimer. Sup at her House. Mr. Willard comes in & taxes us with writing the verses about the Militia that we put in the Lewes Paper, we laugh it off & he swears he'll find it out. [486]

Thursday, 12 August

Dine & spend the Day at Mr. Mortimer's, play at quadrille; bad luck, Betsy Mortimer applauds me for bearing it so patiently. A terrible Night. Thunder & rains excessively.

Friday, 13 August

Finish Mrs. Hurst's stays & she greatly approves of them. Miss Kitty Mortimer comes down to read some of my Poetry which she commends more than it deserves. Wish to see my dear Husband, when oh when shall I have that happiness, he has been gone ten weeks which is an age.

Saturday, 14 August

Work all the morning, which was a very wet unpleasant one, am afraid it will prevent my father's coming to see me. No letter from Horsham & so I think he will certainly come. Walk on the Hill with Miss Kitty Mortimer & look [in] the Wheatear traps but can't find any.[487]

Sunday, 15 August

Am agreeably surpris'd with the sight of my father after I had given over the thoughts of seeing him; all my friends at Horsham are well, my Aunt Smith, Aunt Sally & cousin Bet are there & want me to come home, but my father gives me leave to stay a little longer. Walk down to the Sea side.

484   Henry Ellis of Tanbridge was buried in Horsham on 7 August 1762.
485   Probably Charles Smith Mortimer, who was listed in the 1785 Land Tax for Eastbourne.
486   Thomas Willard (senior) and Thomas Willard (junior) were both listed as living in Eastbourne Town in 1785.
487   Wheat ears, or ortolans, were a great delicacy, much sought after. They were a speciality of Eastbourne.

Monday, 16 August

My father, Mr. Hurst & Mr. Marten walk out & see Lord Northampton's Grove with which Papa is very much pleas'd. He tells me Captain Smith is made a Major, I can't believe it. Go to the Assembly, a vast deal of company, win at cards.

Tuesday, 17 August

My father tells me he has had a dispute with Drew Michell & Sally Sheppard's brother,[488] the consequence of which is that I must relinquish my regard for that dear girl, but I can sooner part with Life. My father & Mr. Hurst goes to Winchelsea.

Wednesday, 18 August

A very wet unpleasant day for the travellers, & indeed for me who don't love to be confin'd a whole day within doors. Read in the *History of Madame Maintenon*. Play at Cribbage with Mrs. Hurst.

Thursday, 19 August

Mr. Smith Mortimer comes down & tells me that my dear Harry is made a Major, he saw it in the News. I doubt this good News at first but he vows t'is true, I am quite happy if it is. Walk to meet my father & Mr. Hurst the Road to Pevensey, they overtake me as I return, they are vastly pleas'd with the journey.

Friday, 20 August

Walk down to the Sea with an intention to wash but am disappointed. Write to my cousin Bet Smith who is at Horsham. My father has given me leave to stay here a fortnight or 3 weeks longer.

Saturday, 21 August

Get up by five to take my leave of my father. Write to Sally Sheppard. A letter from my dear Husband, he expected his Major's commission very soon & kindly hopes this promotion will facilitate our living together. I sincerely wish it may, how blest shall I be when under the same roof with him I profoundly love.

Sunday, 22 August

At Church in the afternoon, drink tea at Mr. Lushington's with two officers of the Surrey Militia, one a good pretty young fellow, the other's name Cross & one of the oddest mortals I ever saw or beheld, said he should not like to live allways with his Wife.[489] God forbid my Husband should be of the same opinion.

Monday, 23 August

Write to my Harry & send him the poetical letter I wrote to Mrs. Wicker. Poor Mrs.

---

488 Stringer Sheppard junior.
489 "*Cross*" has been identified by John Farrant as Francis Grose (1731-91), the artist and antiquarian, who was commissioned as a Lieutenant in the Surrey Militia in November 1759, and was serving as adjutant and paymaster of the 2nd (Western) Battalion which was based in Lewes in late 1762. He is known to have visited Eastbourne, where he made a sketch of Beachy Head in this same week that he met Sarah. He published *The Antiquities of England and Wales* in just over 100 parts between 1772 and 1787.

Hurst is let blood, faints away & frights me excessively. Bathe in the Sea, wish to see my dear dear Husband, alas in vain.

Tuesday, 24 August

All the Lushington, Mortimer & Smith families drink tea & sup with us. Mr. Lushington puts himself very much out of temper at cards. I think people who cannot win or lose with perfect indifference ought never to play, but be only spectators if they must disconcert the whole company by their ungovernable dispositions.

Wednesday, 25 August

Bathe in the Sea, work all the morning, spend the afternoon & evening at Mr. Lushington's, play at cards. An excessive wet night, oblig'd to lay with Miss Kitty Mortimer with whom I have a great deal of chat & am very merry.

Thursday, 26 August

Stay at Mr. Mortimer's all the morning. No letters from Horsham which I a little expected, in particular one from Sally Sheppard, hope that dear girl is not offended with me, I will never give her cause. Work all the afternoon, begin reading *The History of Emily, or a natural Daughter*, a very indifferent Novel.[490]

Friday, 27 August

Bathe in the sea; a most delightfull fine serene & pleasant day, all hands are now employ'd in getting in the Harvest, I shall endeavour to enjoy the remainder of the Summer, oh that my dearest Harry was with me to partake of its beauties.

Saturday, 28 August

Walk down to the Sea & bathe, extreamly pleasant. A letter from my father, he got home safe but wet & a letter from my dear Sheppard, she tells me that neither my Mamma nor sisters will speak to her. Alas, how unhappy will this quarrel make me when I return to Horsham, to be depriv'd of the company of a friend I so dearly love gives me inconceivable concern; there is nothing durable in this World.

Sunday, 29 August

Dine & drink tea at Mr. Mortimer's, walk down to the Seaside, quite serene pleasant weather. Mr. Mortimer treats us with Lobsters.

Monday, 30 August

Help Mrs. Hurst Bake all the morning, Bathe in the Sea. Write to Mamma but am too late for the Post; fix my going home for next Wednesday sennight. Dine at Mr. Turner's, walk in the afternoon. I shall quit East Bourne with reluctance.

Tuesday, 31 August

A great Bustle in the House making preparations for the Harvest Supper. Ride out with Miss Kitty Mortimer behind me which droll sight excessively excites our mirth

---

490 This must be *The History of Emily Willis; or a natural daughter*, the third edition published in 1767. The author seems to have remained anonymous, but also wrote *Memoirs of a Coquet, or the History of Miss Harriet Airey* (1765).

& that of all who meets us. My time passes here pleasantly enough & yet I cannot help repining at the absence of my dearest Harry, whose dear company would well supply the want of every diversion.

SEPTEMBER 1762

Wednesday, 1 September

A great deal of company at the Harvest Supper, the men diverted themselves by smoking, drinking & singing lewd songs, the women rather more decently.

Thursday, 2 September

The Head Ach violently occasion'd by my last night's fatigue; sent the letter to Mamma & acquaint her I shall be at home next Wednesday. A letter from my cousin Bet Smith, she informs me my father is going to the Isle of Wight, & that he desires I would be at home the beginning of next week, so I fix Tuesday.

Friday, 3 September

A very pleasant ride down to West Ham to dinner, a most delightfull serene day which is not very usual here, the Wind I think being generally blusterous. Call at Mr. Lushington's, shew my work'd apron to some Ladies there who admire it excessively.

Saturday, 4 September

No letter from my dear Harry as I a little expected. Call at Mr. Mortimer's, they press me to stay the afternoon with them but I refuse. Walk down to the Sea & Bathe I believe for the last time.

Sunday, 5 September

At Church in the afternoon, drink tea at Mr. Mortimer's with a great deal of company, much chat. Mr. Lushington says a Peace is certain, am extreamly glad of it. Mr. John Mortimer is a sensible agreeable young man,[491] Miss Hirrel is a plain Girl but smart.

Monday, 6 September

A long letter from my dear Harry, he thinks we shall be able to live together about Christmas & desires I would talk to my father about Fortune. I will, but dread this task. Call on all my acquaintance & bid them farewell, write to my Harry.

Tuesday, 7 September

Take leave of good Mrs. Hurst & set out for Lewes with Mr. Hurst, where we arrive about four in the afternoon. Call on Master Ned Tredcroft, & take him to see the slight of hand perform'd in a masterly manner by a German.[492]

---

491 This would appear to confirm that the young Mr. Mortimer was called John and was therefore the artist, John Hamilton Mortimer.

492 Edward Tredcroft, the younger son of Mr. and Mrs. Tredcroft, was presumably at school in Lewes. Many showmen and itinerant entertainers visited Lewes at this time to perform at the Whitsun Fair, the autumn sheep fair, or during the races.

Wednesday, 8 September

A very pleasant ride from Lewes to Horsham, am told as soon as I get home, by my wicked sister Bet, that I am married; she has reported *[it]* all over the Town. Doctor Smith told my dear Harry's mother of it who seem'd very angry.

Thursday, 9 September

Write to my dear Husband & tell him the report, beg he will not come to Horsham till every thing is settled for me to return with him. What a hard task is mine to be oblig'd to perswade him from coming when his being here would give me the greatest pleasure this World can afford.

Friday, 10 September

Write a great many letters of business for my father. Walk out with Mr. Hurst who likes Horsham very well, drink tea at Mrs. Wicker's. Walk on the Causeway with my friend Sally Sheppard but am oblig'd to do it by stealth, cruel restraint.

Saturday, 11 September

Mr. Hurst goes home & my father sets off for the Isle of White*(sic)*; he affects me greatly at his departure by saying there was a hundred pound for me in his drawer, more than he had left me in his will.

Sunday, 12 September

At Church twice, an excellent Sermon by Doctor Hutchinson on this lesson in morality, *"Do as ye would be done unto"*. Miss very much the company of my dear Sally Sheppard with whom I cannot now converse without offending my father; cruel restraint, but I must submit.[493]

Monday, 13 September

Very busy in the Shop all the morning. Work in the afternoon. Mr. John Shelley drinks tea with me. T'is a long time to next Sunday & before that I can't possibly expect to have an answer from my dear Husband to my last letter, the mind has still something to wish for, is still anxious to draw future time nearer & yet we often complain it flies too fast.

Tuesday, 14 September

Walk up in the Park by myself, a charming pleasant evening, meet the Miss Ellis's & return with them.

Wednesday, 15 September

Molly Ellis talks as little as ever she did, t'is sure a surprising thing that she never cloak any of her Ideas in Words; drink tea with them at Mrs. Wicker's, walk afterwards with her.

---

493 Sarah does not explain why she now felt that she had to submit to her father's decree after flouting his wishes only two days previously.

Thursday, 16 September

Am told by several people of my being married. Wish it was once publick & then there would be an end to their nonsense. My father returns safe from the Isle of White very well pleas'd with his journey, which prov'd a pleasant one.

Friday, 17 September

Walk out with Mrs. Wicker, charming pleasant weather but alas, the Sun will soon lose its warmth in our Hemisphere & leave us a prey to Wintry Clouds & storms. This vicissitude is necessary.

Saturday, 18 September

My father asks me what fortune my Harry will expect with me, I tell him I don't know; he says he will give me a present three hundred pound (a small sum) but does not tell me what more he will give at his death.

Sunday, 19 September

At Church twice, an excellent Sermon preach'd by Doctor Hutchinson. Make a visit at Tanbridge, they are all extreamly dull; a letter from my dearest Harry, wrote before he receiv'd my last wherein I acquainted him that our marriage was talk'd of, he is afraid of being put on half pay if there is a peace.

Monday, 20 September

My father bids me tell Major Smith that he will give me three hundred pound down & three more after his death. I hope my Harry will think that sufficient, alas if he is turn'd *[off]* on half pay we shall find it a difficult matter to rub through Life tolerably decent.

Tuesday, 21 September

Poor Mrs. Bridger has very near lost her sight, how sincerely I pity her, what a melancholy thing to be depriv'd of this precious sense. Begin reading letters wrote by a Peruvian Princess, the stile & sentiments are very pretty, but the plan extreamly romantick.[494]

Wednesday, 22 September

Finish Major Smith's frill for his Shirt. My father promises he will do more for me if he can afford it. A letter from my dear Major, wrote in an angry stile, alas how could I help the report & why is he displeas'd with me, he does not approve of my letting my father *[word omitted]* how our affairs stand.

Thursday, 23 September

Write to him & express great concern at his being angry with me; tell him what my father will give me. A smart altercation with my sister Bet, tell her how ill she has us'd me.

494　*Letters written by a Peruvian Princess*, by Françoise Paule Huguet de Grafigny, had been translated into English and a third edition published in 1759.

Friday, 24 September

Tolerably serene & easy, considering the immense distance that parts me from what most I love in this world, oh my dear Harry when shall I behold you again & when shall I have the satisfaction of living with & seeing you every day.

Saturday, 25 September

Alas, our minds are allways fix'd on some future good which we so ardently expect that it takes of the pleasure we might otherwise find in the present. How disagreeable is every place to me where my Harry is not, but let me not complain, for my lot is now infinitely happier than before I was united to him.

Sunday, 26 September

Walk over to Slynfold for the first time since I came from East Bourne, Mrs. Jones is quite big, offer to stand for her little one when it comes. [495]

Monday, 27 September

Papa dines there, says Mr. Tudor told him I was married, his answer was a good thing for me if she is because I can then make my own terms, but I hope he would not be so ungenerous if he knows it as to give me the less for my dear Harry's generosity. I wish it was publick, I detest the artfull part I am oblig'd to act.

Tuesday, 28 September

Begin knitting a caul for a Cap, I have hardly learn'd my business for I can't do it cleverly. Miss Upton, Miss King & Lady Ann Cecil all here for some things in the Shop; it is rather beneath a Major's Lady, as I am, to serve in a Shop, but I must submit to it till my rank is known.

Wednesday, 29 September

Go up to Highland to help divide eight Hives of Honey between us & Dame White, what pity t'is to destroy these industrious insects after all the toil and pains they take; of all Nature's works sure Bees are the most wonderfull.[496]

Thursday, 30 September

Walk to Slynfold. Carry my brother some Honey Comb with which he is vastly pleas'd. Make a visit at a farm House with Mr. & Mrs. Jones & my brother, a most delightfull day, which I enjoy, find that serenity in my mind which I allways feel at Slynfold & hardly any where else.

---

495   Sarah means to stand as godmother.

496   Dame White was presumably the wife of the man whom Richard Hurst employed as a tenant farmer at Highlands Farm. It seems that the Hursts divided the produce of the farm with the Whites.

OCTOBER 1762

Friday, 1 October

Walk home, write an account of the extent & boundaries of Highland Farm. Miss Upton calls in her Chariot, she chats a long time & is very merry. Go to the Play, *The Desert Island*,[497] a little girl plays Silvia extreamly well, but all the rest intolerable.

Saturday, 2 October

Work all day; hope I shall hear from my dear Husband Tomorrow, if not t'is an age to Wednesday, when oh when shall I be blest with his company. Read *The Desert Island* to my mother, & Shakespeare's *Taming of the Shrew*, with the last she is extreamly diverted.

Sunday, 3 October

A very wet day, cannot go to Church. Write to Mrs. Hurst at East Bourne. Mrs. Cook sends for me after dinner, spend the afternoon with her, Doctor Griffith there, a great deal of chat with him about the Players & several subjects. Mrs. Cook, if she pleases, is a very agreeable Woman.[498]

Monday, 4 October

Begin posting my Books & writing out Bills. Spend the afternoon & evening at Mrs. Wicker's. My Harry's mother comes in & is in high Spirits because her granddaughter, Miss Nancy Hannah, is married very advantageously. What chequer work is Life, some Weddings give joy & others sorrow.

Tuesday, 5 October

Impatiently expect a letter from my dear Husband. Read *The Way to keep Him*, a farce.[499] Finish Posting the Shop books Read the historical play of *King Richard the Second*, what a confusion was there in this unhappy Kingdom in those times.[500] Thank Heaven civil wars are now no more.

Wednesday, 6 October

Go into Mrs. Tasker's to meet my dear friend Sally Sheppard. Drink tea there, take a walk in the Common with Mrs Wicker & Miss Powell, very pleasant but cold. A letter from my sister Molly & one from my dear Harry, he tells me he should propose our living together but thinks it best to stay till there is a certainty of War or Peace.

---

497 *The Desert Island* was a play by Arthur Murphy which Sarah read on 21 February 1760.

498 Mrs. Cook seems to have been a very capable woman; she was named as the occupier of the *King's Head Inn* in an indenture of 1751, even before her husband's death in 1756. At that time the *King's Head* was mortgaged to Mr. Bridger, but by 1764, Ann Cook was said (in John Meredew's survey) to own both the inn and the vote attached to it, as a burgage property. She died in 1767, leaving the inn and the vote to her grandson, William Cook.

499 *The Way to Keep Him* was also written by Arthur Murphy, and Sarah had read it previously, on 21 February 1760.

500 *King Richard II* by William Shakespeare, first performed in 1595.

Thursday, 7 October

Mrs. Jones dines with us, Mr. Jones comes in the afternoon. What a happy couple they are, may Harry & I agree as well as they do. Play at cards, win.

Friday, 8 October

Go down to Mrs. Wicker's & find there Doctor Smith's Wife & my Harry's mother, the former wishes me joy & says she hear'd I was married. I answer people will say anything. Captain Smith's mother seem'd greatly agitated & said she knew it was not so, t'is wrong to be too positive, but we too often believe what we wish; poor Woman she will be horridly vex'd when she knows t'is true.

Saturday, 9 October

Read in my *Review* for September; great commendations of a Poem call'd *The Shipwreck* wrote by a Sailor,[501] some account of Rousseau's treatise on education, which was burnt at Paris by the Hangman. [502]

Sunday, 10 October

Mr. Tudor tells my father he wishes Major Smith would take a farm of his & be his neighbour; if he would let it us cheap I wish so too. Spend the afternoon at Mrs. Wicker's, lament to her the loss of my dear Sally Sheppard's company & conversation; a loss which I every day regret.

Monday, 11 October

Work all day, make me a Cloak trim'd with fur, I suppose it will be thought too fine for me. Write to my sister Molly. Read the Play of *As You Like It* to Mamma, I think it is the very best of Shakespear's Comedys.

Tuesday, 12 October

Some London Riders here.[503] Of all trades to get a living I should dislike theirs, such fawning servility I cannot bear. The Miss Ellis's drink tea with us & Mrs. Wicker. Read the *Tragedy of Harry the fourth, the first part,* I am extreamly fond of Shakespear's historical Plays, the character of Sir John Falstaff is truly original &

---

501 *The Shipwreck; a poem* by William Falconer was published in 1762. As a young man, he had been second mate on the *Britannia,* a ship in the Levant trade, which was wrecked near Cape Colonna on the coast of Greece. He dedicated the poem to Prince Edward, Duke of York, who procured him the rank of midshipman in Sir Edward Hawke's ship, the *Royal George.* He wrote other poems and *An Universal Dictionary of the Marine,* which was much used by the Navy.

502 Jean Jacques Rousseau (1712-1778) published in 1762 *Emile, ou Traité de l'éducation,* which so outraged the political and religious establishment that he had to flee to Switzerland. (It is a romance about a child reared apart from other children as an experiment; it greatly influenced educationists like Pestalozzi and Froebel). In the same year he published *Du contrat social (The Social Contract)* which begins *"Man is born free, but is everywhere in chains".* Rousseau came to live and work England in 1766 at the invitation of David Hume, but quarrelled with his British friends and fled back to France, where he completed his *Confessions.* He died insane, in 1778, at Ermenonville, but his books on political philosophy were an important influence on the French Revolution.

503 *"Riders"* is an unusual term , but can be used to mean commercial travellers.

humorous. I saw Quin once in that character & he was surely inimitable.[504]

Wednesday, 13 October

Miss Upton calls in her Chariot & keeps me in chat half an hour. My father praises me excessively & says how kind he will be to me when I am married, little does he think that Job is allready done.

Thursday, 14 October

Very busy all day ironing, Mrs. Wicker here chats with us. Read Shakespear's Play of *Henry the Sixth*, poor weak unfortunate Prince. Wonder I have not heard from Miss Gittins; fear she is angry at my long silence.

Friday, 15 October

Busy all day in the Shop etc. Regret the loss of my dear Sally Sheppard's company, every day takes something from us — friends, fortune, youth or beauty — till at last we drop ourselves into the grave, there closes this scene of trouble & vanity, may I die before my dearest Harry.

Saturday, 16 October

Work all the morning, my father not in an exceeding good humour, surely there must be something constitutional in these fits of ill humour, if so the person who is thus affected ought to be pitied as much as though he labour'd under a distemper, but if he does it only to make people unhappy there is no excuse.

Sunday, 17 October

Dine at Mr. Tudor's, see his Nephew Mr. Nelthorpe for the first time, he is extreamly plain in his person & looks older than his Uncle (alias his father) tho' I suppose he is younger by thirty years; he is sensible & well behav'd, walks with us part of the way home & chats very agreeably.[505]

Monday, 18 October

Walk over to Slinfold. All my pleasure now consists in being here, t'was this dear Place made my dear Harry mine & here I think reigns harmony & tranquillity, for here I am allways better in health of body & mind than any where else. Drink tea at Mrs. Gardiner's.

Tuesday, 19 October

Stick Mrs. Jones' pincushion for her. Poor Woman, she is very near her time & will soon have another infant, I wonder much how I shall behave if I am ever in the same

---

504 James Quin (1693-1766) was an Irish actor who found success at Drury Lane. He was by universal consent the best actor in England, until eclipsed by David Garrick. He retired in 1751, so Sarah presumably saw him before that.

505 William Nelthorpe succeeded his uncle, Joseph Tudor, as owner of Nuthurst Lodge (Sedgwick) in 1774 and died in 1791 aged 74, leaving the estates to his sister Elizabeth (1718-1801). She left them to her great-nephew, James Cowne, on condition that he took the surname Tudor Nelthorpe. There are memorial tablets to Joseph Tudor, Elizabeth Nelthorpe and James Tudor Nelthorpe, and other members of his family, in St. Andrew's Church, Nuthurst. See also footnote to entry on 18 November 1759.

circumstances. A very wet uncomfortable day, cannot walk out. Play at cards.

Wednesday, 20 October

Work all the morning; design'd to go home but detain'd by the Weather. Am sent for about five in the afternoon; my father is ill with an ague, hurry home, am Wet through. My dear Sally Sheppard was married yesterday & is now Mrs. Michell, may she be truly happy, I pray sincerely.[506]

Thursday, 21 October

A letter from my dearest Harry full of the kindest & fondest expressions, he leaves it to my option whether I will go to him or not till Peace or War is determin'd; write him word I chuse to stay till my sister Bet is married & hope that will be soon.

Friday, 22 October

I cannot bear the thoughts of leaving my friends while their trouble about her subsists, & yet how I wish to be with my Husband. Alas, mine is a difficult task, tell him he must not come to Horsham before our marriage is declar'd, another piece of self denial, oh my Heart.

Saturday, 23 October

Mr. Tudor & Mr. Nelthorpe come early in the morning & stay all day with us. Mr. Nelthorpe takes his leave, he goes to Scotland soon. My father tells young James that he will give him with my sister Bet the money his friends demanded, & desires him to take her away very soon for he don't chuse any longer to be troubled with her ill behaviour.

Sunday, 24 October

At Church in the morning, an excellent Sermon preach'd by Doctor Hutchinson against drunkenness, an odious vice indeed & too general. Company in the afternoon; a great deal of insignificant chat.

Monday, 25 October

Work all the morning, I wish oh how much I wish to be with my dearest Harry. I hope the affair of War or Peace will be soon decided that I may enjoy the supream satisfaction of living with the man I love. Drink tea at Mrs. Bridger's.

Tuesday, 26 October

Read Shakespear's Play of *Harry the Sixth*, a poor weak Prince not fit to govern, what turbulent times were those, tis painfull to read the dreadfull havock ambition made. Spend the evening at Mr. Tredcroft's.

Wednesday, 27 October

Work all day, my father very much out of temper, how I detest to see him so. Indeed to me he always behaves well, but it gives me as much pain to hear him

---

506 It rather looks as if Sarah had gone to Slinfold to avoid the embarrassment of not being able to go to Sally Sheppard's wedding. Possibly it was a disagreement about this which provoked Richard Hurst's ill-tempered outburst on 16 October, and Sarah's tart remarks about him.

cross to others as though I was a party concern'd. When shall I live with my Harry, who is good nature itself.

Thursday, 28 October

A letter from Mr. Jones, Mrs. Jones is brought to Bed of another daughter, she sends for me, am sorry I can't go before Saturday or Sunday. Read the second part of *King Henry the Sixth*, his wife Margaret was as turbulent as he was meek.

Friday, 29 October

I long to be over at Slinfold to see how the good Woman does, Mamma tells me she shall be much concern'd when I go away. I shall certainly be sorry too to leave so good a Parent; but that will be overcome by the satisfaction of being with my dearest Husband.

Saturday, 30 October

Go to Slinfold. Mrs. Jones quite well.

[No entries until Thursday, November 4]

NOVEMBER 1762

Thursday, 4 November

Come from Slinfold. A letter from my dearest Harry, very kind as usual. Answer it directly. Can't imagine the reason of Miss Gittin's silence, sure she cannot have receiv'd my last letter.

Friday, 5 November

Work all the morning, begin reading my *Review* some account of a New system of education, translated by the persons who translated *Eloisa* & wrote by the same author.[507] Make a visit at Tanbridge with Mrs. Wicker, am wet through in coming home but luckily take no cold.

Saturday, 6 November

A gentleman comes in & tells my father the preliminaries of Peace are certainly sign'd, if so I shall not see Plymouth but my dearest Harry & I shall settle at Horsham.[508] I hope we shall have enough to live comfortably, that is all I expect. Spend the evening at Mrs. Wicker's.

---

507 This must be an account of the English translation of Jean Jacques Rousseau's *Emile, ou Traité de l'education*, published in May 1762, which Sarah also mentioned on 9 October. Rousseau also wrote the romantic novel *Julie, ou la Nouvelle Héloise*, published in 1761, which Sarah read in translation, and much enjoyed.

508 The Treaty of Paris, which brought the Seven Years' War to an end, was finally signed on 10 February 1763 between Britain and France. It consolidated many of the gains that Britain had made in North America, the West Indies, Africa and India. Five days later, the Treaty of Hubertusberg was concluded between Prussia, Austria and Saxony, which confirmed Prussia in possession of Silesia and made it a major European power.

Sunday, 7 November

At Church in the morning, Mr. Osgood mixes part of the history of England with his Sermon. Doctor Hutchinson preaches against drunkenness, a very good discourse. I hope my dear Major Smith will have half pay for that rank if he is turn'd off, then we shall be able with frugality to provide for a family.

Monday, 8 November

Receive the *St. James' Chronicle* which Mrs. Wicker & I have concluded to take in between us. Peace is certain, I hope it will prove an happy event for my dear Harry & his Sally. Work all the afternoon.

Tuesday, 9 November

Go over to Slinfold, Mrs. Jones, her two Children & my brother all very well. I should not dislike to live in this solitary place with my dear Harry; t'is far from the vices & malice of the World.

Wednesday, 10 November

Come home from Slinfold.

Thursday, 11 November

Am told that my sister Bet has behav'd excessively imprudent, wretched creature.[509]

Friday, 12 November

My father & mother in great trouble about Bet, endeavour to comfort them but want consolation myself.

Saturday, 13 November

A letter from Mrs. Townshend, she gives me a pressing invitation to Salisbury & likewise my dear Harry should have made her a visit if the War had continued & I had gone to Plymouth, I wish I might go.

Sunday, 14 November

Bet Hurst married to young James, I cannot call her my sister; a dismal wedding day, many such I fear would kill me.

Monday, 15 November

Walk to Slinfold, my mind excessively discompos'd about Bet's wretched conduct; oh that I was with my dearest Harry. How shall I tell him her faults & yet I must or he will hear them from others.

Tuesday, 16 November

Return from Slinfold. A hard frost, charming pleasant walking, find my father & mother still unhappy about Bet James; wish her house was ready that she might be gone from ours, I cannot bear to look on her.

---

509   Although Bet's marriage to Will James had already been agreed, it appears that her conduct had brought shame on her family and it was felt necessary to expedite the wedding. Sarah was deeply affected by this.

Wednesday, 17 November

Work all day; Mrs. Wicker perswades me to be reconcil'd to Bet. I cannot, she has done me too many injuries. My Nature recoils & will not own her for a sister, yet will I never do her an injury.

Thursday, 18 November

A letter from my dearest Husband, he tells me the Duke of York makes Plymouth very gay & that he was introduc'd to his Royal Highness & kiss'd his hand.[510]

Friday, 19 November

Write to my dearest Harry, tell him all the affair of Bet & how disagreeable it has made Horsham to me & I had much rather live at Plymouth, which I sincerely wish I may do.

Saturday, 20 November

Expect my sister Molly home but she does not come. Go to meet my brother who comes to stay till Monday.

Sunday, 21 November

At Church, an excellent Sermon preach'd by Doctor Hutchinson on conforming ourselves & being contented in the situation of Life we are plac'd. Drink tea & spend the evening at my Aunt Waller's.

Monday, 22 November

Very busy in the Shop. I wish my dearest Harry would take me out of this employment, how I long to be with him. Fly fast, ye lazy minutes, haste ye tedious ministers of state & conclude the Peace, that I may be blest in the society of him I love.

Tuesday, 23 November

My sister Molly comes home from London.[511] Mr. Jones here from Slinfold, he insists on taking a Ticket for the Play, *The Distress'd Mother*,[512] which they perform tolerably.

Wednesday, 24 November

Write several letters to London. Mrs. Wicker here in the afternoon. Think on & sigh for my dearest Husband, his absence grows every day more insupportable, when oh when shall I be for ever with him.

[No entries until Thursday, 2 December]

---

510 Sarah had seen the Duke of York at the Lord Mayor's Show in London on 9 November 1761.

511 Molly had perhaps been at school in London, or staying with her relations. She was now seventeen years old, so her formal education had probably been completed.

512 *The Distrest Mother*, by Ambrose Phillips, first performed in 1712, was a successful adaptation of Racine's *Andromaque*.

DECEMBER 1762

Thursday, 2 December

A letter from my dearest Harry, answer it directly. A letter from my friend Miss Gittins, she has been ill but is better & going to be married to a Clergyman which News gives me very great satisfaction.

Friday, 3 December

Write a long letter to my cousin Bet Smith; send her my Scheme for a Tax upon kissing. Tell my mother she behaves exactly the same to Bet as tho' her conduct had been ever so good. Spend the afternoon & evening at Mrs. Bridger's.

Saturday, 4 December

Very busy all day, write several letters to London; Bet James is to make her appearance at Church tomorrow, I'll not be there. I must be oblig'd to go & see her, I suppose, well it shall be the first & the last time, how great will be the mortification.

Sunday, 5 December

I wish, oh how much I wish to be with my dearest Harry, far away from all these turbulent folks who wanting Reason for their guide are perpetually driving Headlong down the stream of indiscretion. Go with all the relations to see Bet, am heartily glad this mortification is over.

Monday, 6 December

No account yet in the Newspaper whether the Marines will be kept up.

Tuesday, 7 December

Very busy all day.

Wednesday, 8 December

Write to Mrs. Townshend, tell her how glad I shall be to accept her kind invitation.

[No entries until Thursday December 16]

Thursday, 16 December

A letter from my dear Harry, answer it directly.

Friday, 17 December

Go with Mrs. Wicker to Slinfold, we both stand godmothers for Mrs. Jones' daughter.

Saturday, 18 December

Mr. Hastwell, the Clergyman at Billingshurst, was godfather, he is an agreeable man & his wife an agreeable Woman.

Sunday, 19 December

At Church twice. Drink tea at my Aunt Waller's with Mrs. Wicker & my dear Harry's mother.

Monday, 20 December

Walk out with Mrs. Wicker, she tells me the unhappy situation of Doctor Smith's family occasion'd by his neglecting his Wife & his attachment to Mrs. James,

Tuesday, 21 December

Oh all ye powers that watch o'er virtuous love defend me from the fiend call'd jealousy.

Wednesday, 22 December

Write to Mrs. Hurst & to my amiable friend Miss Gittins. Not very well, pine to see my dearest Husband.

Thursday, 23 December

Very busy all day. Read the Newspaper, eagerly look to see if the Parliament has determin'd how they will dispose of the Marines, but t'is not yet mention'd,

Friday, 24 December

Sure my Harry's next letter will inform me, I wish to know where I shall be settled.

[No entries until December 30]

Thursday, 30 December

A letter from my dear Harry, he desires I will get myself ready to go to him, with how much pleasure shall I do it.

Memorandum: One more year is gone & I am thank God infinitely happier than I have been for many preceding ones.

LETTERS WRITTEN BY SARAH
BETWEEN 1785-1797

Letter from Sarah Smith to her brother Robert, written from (?near) Portsmouth, dated 8 September 1785

Dear Bob,

We left you fast asleep, as at the time I wish'd to do, but before I got to Steyning I remembered the Partridges & was sorry you did not happen to wake. We had a delightful ride over the Downs to Michell Grove,[513] & found Sir John Shelley's road[514] through the woods better than when we travelled it last; at Arundel I missed your garden, for the Town did not produce a Lettuce or Cucumber. We stop'd again at Chichester, & about a Mile on this side that place it began to rain, but not enough to make us put up the Head of the Chaise. We drove into our Stable Yard just as the day clos'd and at that instant it began to blow a hurricane and rain a Deluge, which has continued to this time two o'clock Tuesday afternoon, & no prospect of its ceasing. What few Apples we had are all blown down, the great Elms totter to their Base & have already lost many of their limbs, & I think we shall have good luck if we are not carried off by the Tide, for it is higher than ever I saw before, how fortunate was our choice of yesterday for travelling.

I have wrote to Humphrey to desire he will send the men to you about the Wood next Sunday or Sunday sennight, you will see whether he does or not, the time of cutting is November. I have also told him if he will undertake paying the men, we shall leave the remainder of the Money due for the Coppices in his hands, but if not we shall draw for it directly.

Wednesday: the gale of wind has at last subsided, but has left us & our Neighbours in a ruinous situation, Trees blown down, Barns unroof'd, Ships drove on shore, the Trees & Hedges that are left standing, look scorch 'd as tho' they had been roasted by

---

513   Michelgrove was the home of the Shelleys of Michelgrove, the senior branch of the Shelley family.

514   The Sir John Shelley mentioned by Sarah was probably Sir John Shelley, 5th Bt., who had died in 1783. His son John was only thirteen years old at the time that this letter was written, and had not yet succeeded to the estates and the baronetcy.

a great fire, this they say is caused by the spray of the sea. I think your old Mansion is in the best situation, where no Tides nor Winds can affect it.[515]

Yesterday during the Gale there was a Christening three small fields from our House, the Parson was blown down twice in his road to perform the ceremony, while the dinner was cooking, in rush'd the Sea, put out the fire & a stop to their proceedings till the Tide went off again. I suppose old Neptune was angry that he was not invited to be one of the Guests.[516]

The General has been to Portsmouth this morning and found them all in expectation of Lord Howe.[517]

I will be happy to hear from you very often, but I shall not write (unless I have business) but when I can catch Jervoice to get a frank; as I think such a scroll as this cannot be worth eightpence.

Henry unites in best love to Maria and thanks for her kindness and attention while we were at Horsham, & we hope she is not the worse for the trouble we gave her. As you are fond of visiting we desire you will in person carry our Compliments to all our relations and acquaintance, not forgetting the Czar, who I hope is not quite so despotic but content with a limited monarchy.[518]

I am Your Affectionate Sister,

Sarah Smith

September 8, 1785:

Letter from Sarah Smith to Mrs. Maria Hurst (née Smith) her sister-in-law written from Chichester, 26 March 1795

Dear Sister,

I shall never forgive myself, (if you can) for trusting a letter I thought of so much importance to your peace of mind to Mr. Jervoise; all I can now say to atone for the fault is an assurance that I will never be guilty of the like again.

---

515 It is not quite clear which *"old Mansion"* Sarah means. At the time she wrote this letter, Robert Hurst was living in Causeway House, but it is questionable whether this could be called a *"mansion"*. A couple of years later, Robert lived for a year at Parham House, as Steward, when Sir Cecil Bishopp, 8th Bt., was abroad with the army. He also lived at Penshurst in 1793 as steward for Sir John Shelley Sidney — so it is possible that Sarah may have been referring to one of these great houses.

516 This paragraph suggests that Sarah and Henry were living in a house somewhere outside Portsmouth, close to the sea, surrounded by fields and the odd cottage, rather than in or near the Marine Barracks. This is confirmed by the remark about Henry going *"to Portsmouth"* — had they lived in the city, Sarah would not have made such a comment.

517 Richard, 1st Earl Howe (1726-1799), the commander of the British fleet since 1776. He was appointed First Lord of the Admiralty in 1783.

518 *"The Czar"* is clearly a nickname for someone living in Horsham at this time, but there is no obvious candidate.

On Wednesday the 18th I deliver'd up my dear Wards to Mr. Davis[519] & Mrs.*(Miss)* Russel,[520] in good health & tolerable spirits. Robert[521] came to me again the next day, it being a half-holiday. I sent for Maria[522] on Saturday, but the leave was reluctantly granted, as her governess told me it was contrary to the rules of the school, so I am obliged to be content with having Maria only Sundays. She says she has no objection to School, but wants to see her Mama. Her spoons I bought a week ago with many other articles towels, Books, etc. Writing & Dancing she begun with, French shall be added, her Stays are not yet done. When they are, one frock & one coloured gown is to be made to compleat her Wardrobe, a dancing cap I soon made her out of some of my former finery, and rummaged out a Sash for she told me there was not one young Lady without.

As to Robert, his objections to school are innumerable, some of them I shall mention - His bed is hard, the puddings are too fat, the housekeeper is too lean; the Usher is monstrous ugly, boxes the boys' ears who don't mind their Book, and goes to sleep when they are all at play — Robert carried sixpence to school, some days after he returned me 5½d & said he should not spend any more, because the shop where he dealt sold Gingerbread on Sundays, his weekly allowance of 3d. is also laid up. not so does his sister, her sixpence was nearly gone in two days, but last Sunday, induc'd I suppose by her brother's thrift, she chose to leave some of her allowance, at this rate they will grow rich.

Bob told me all his Schoolfellows flock'd about him and asked, *"which way did you come?"* Another *"where did you come from?"* A third *"does your father keep a Coach?"* I said yes; *"how many horses does he drive?"* *"four said I"*; *"how come you to say so Bob?"* said Aunt; *"because I lik'd to appear grand"*. He is now standing by me chattering so fast I fear I shall not be able to write much more. I did not find my house in so good order as I expected, the first domestic news I heard was, that my female servant was married. I discharg'd her yesterday, & the other comes today. In my Garden I have been wholly employ'd all the fine days, of course I have many things yet unpack'd but I shall be perfectly ready

---

519 David Davis was the master of Chichester Grammar School from 1784 to 1797, which at this time was more like a private boarding school. Latin was taught there, and in a later letter Robert was said to have *"got into the Latin grammar"*.

520 Philadelphia Russell ran a boarding school for girls in Chichester. In 1800, it was said to be a first class school, where the daughters of the county gentry were educated. The house was a large red-brick mansion at the end of South Street., the former home of Sir John Miller. There were about 50 pupils and 10 lady boarders, taught by seven teachers. Miss Russell herself, then a *"venerable, grey-haired lady"*, taught a class of the younger children for an hour in the morning and the afternoon. Her monumental inscription in Chichester Cathedral says that she was for more than half a century *"the kind and patient instructress of Youth"*.

521 Robert Henry Hurst, b. 16 March 1788, eldest son of Robert and Maria Hurst.

522 Isabella Maria Hurst, b. 2 December 1785, eldest daughter of Robert and Maria.

next week, & shall be much disappointed if you do not come with my Brother. I thank him for his news and am

Yours affectionately,

Sarah Smith

Bob sends his love to Papa and Mamma & hopes she did not cry much, we expect to hear from you soon.

Chichester, March 26th, 1795.

Letter from Sarah Smith to her brother Robert, written from Chichester, dated 20 March 1796.

The children are both well, & have escap'd the colds which everybody here has been plagued with, caus'd by the great changes in the weather, from wet to extream cold & frost, & then to heat; no wonder we are all strange creatures, for England is a very odd climate.

I am extreamly concern'd for your's and Maria's great loss in Mr. Adam Smith, but more for her Sisters, who I think it will entirely unsettle, as I fear they will never agree to live with their Mother.[523] Did you bring the worsted and canvas from Penshurst, which I order'd you to steal, if you have not I shall send you on purpose.[524] The bringing of one of your particular friends nearer will not I prophecy add to your happiness,[525] but I shall bear the evils you will suffer with fortitude, as we generally do those which befall others; if that was not the case, you would not have treated with such unpardonable levity Robert's & my sorrow at the prospect of parting; I shall make you no answer but that of Eosop's frogs - What is sport to you is death to us.

The children are to spend the Easter week with me, tho' their parents cannot. I had yesterday the offer of Mrs. Page's House.[526] Mr. Thomas (by his agent Mr. Weller)

523 Adam Smith was the elder brother of Henry Smith and the father of Maria Hurst. This letter suggests that he and his wife Mary (whom Sarah had earlier found charming and sympathetic) were living separately at the time of his death, and his unmarried daughters, Harriet and Sophie, were living with him rather than with their mother. In his will, he left his wife a quarterly annuity of only £50, though he owned six freehold and four leasehold houses in London and property in Horsham.

524 Robert Hurst had been made a trustee of the Shelley estates in Sussex, for Bysshe and Timothy Shelley, in 1792, but when John Sidney, the eldest son of Bysshe Shelley by his second marriage to Elizabeth Perry, came of age in 1793, and into possession of Penshurst Place, Robert also became a trustee of the Sidney and Perry estates.

525 This must be a reference to Bysshe Shelley, who by 1796 had sold Turville Park in Buckinghamshire and moved into the new house he had built, called Castle Goring, near Worthing. A collection of Bysshe Shelley's letters among the Hurst MSS in the West Sussex Record Office shows that he regarded Robert Hurst as a trusted friend and discussed his most private affairs with him.

526 In James Spershott's *Memoirs*, there is a mention of a house belonging to the Page family, which was apparently near to the East Gate. It seems likely that this was the house that Sarah was considering as a new home. John Page stood as a candidate for Parliament in Chichester in 1727.

seems very desirous of my taking it, but I had two objections not to be got over; the first & greatest was, he would only let it for seven years; tho' I do not expect to live half that time. Yet if I do ever remove, I will not stand the smallest chance of ever being displac'd again, by anything but Earthquakes or fire. My other objection was the Rent, 120 Guineas, however I was fool enough to bid £100 per annum for it if I cou'd have a running lease from 7 to 21 years, or one for my life, but neither of these cou'd be complied with, & so ended the negociation: had your talking of wintering at Chichester been anything but a joke, that House wou'd have completely held us all, & when we had chanc'd to quarrel, everyone in the family, including Charlotte Sophia,[527] might have had a separate room, and three left for the Master of the House; I cou'd have had time given me to have wrote to you on the subject, but knowing you as I do, I thought it useless.[528]

I am glad you have found some employment for James,[529] and hope the date of his life may be somewhat longer than you have allotted him. The children are now sitting by me both in a chair; they say they have a great mind not to sign their names, because you took no notice of their doing so in the last letter, but yet they will, & so we are all,

Yours affectionately,

Sarah Smith

Isabella Maria Hurst

Robert Henry Hurst *(signatures between carefully drawn lines)*

Chichester

Sunday, March 20th 1796.

Letter from Sarah Smith to her brother Robert, written from Chichester, dated 20 April 1796.

Dear Brother,

I conclude about once a Month you are not displeas'd to hear the children are well, they are perfectly so, grow tall and fat. My love to Mrs. Hurst tell her I receiv'd the mourning for Maria but not till a day or two after it should have come, by the date of her letter, however I got their mourning done by the following Sunday.[530] Maria

---

527 Charlotte Sophia Hurst, born 2 December 1795, was at this time the youngest of Robert and Maria's family. She married Charles Greenaway, of Little Barrington, Glos., and died in 1875.

528 Despite the jocular tone, this letter reveals something of Sarah's loneliness as a widow, living in Chichester, away from the rest of her family.

529 Probably James James, their nephew - son of their sister Bet and her husband, Will James.

530 Presumably the mourning was for the children's grandfather, Adam Smith, whose death was recorded in the previous letter.

tells me to say that she has done all her plain work, & begun her sampler; my piece is to be set about very soon; and the breaking up is next Monday eight weeks. As to Robert's messages I cannot remember them half, what I can, you shall have; the first is, he shall be very glad to be the head Clerk in the office; the next (which I was not to forget on any account) he is got into the Latin grammar; thirdly he has got in bloom in his garden, three Polyanthus's, two stocks & a crocus; fourthly, the Easter week pass'd off very well, with gardening, walking, eating, music & dancing; the two last amusements are accounted for, by our going to a benefit concert (for which purpose they each produc'd an half crown) and Maria teaching her brother to dance, sometime the Master and scholar agreed tolerably well, but it much ofteener happen's that the scholar danc'd up on all the Tables & Chairs, or threw his Master down and beat her; yet before the eight days adjournment were finish'd, she said he had made great progress. I was very sorry to hear of the little girls' accident, but amongst so many of them it is wonderfull these things do not happen oftener; you have been in that respect, as well as most others, extreamly fortunate. I made my congée to the Card players the 2nd of this month, having had more than enough of being stew'd up in hot rooms, but unfortunately I have not been able to make the use I wish'd of my liberty, having had a severe attack of the Rheumatism. It has made a tour all over me, which you'll say is not much in circumference, however, I hope it is nearly tir'd of the Jaunt; I have got the use of my right hand & leg today, if the other side does not get better tomorrow I shall send for Mr. Street to make me some Bows ----

One of Maria's schoolfellows told her she saw her Papa go into the Court House at Midhurst, but we have all concluded it must be a mistake. My man George & I are quite tir'd of each other; he leaves me on the 29th of May, if you should hear of a young Scrub, between this & that, I shall be oblig'd to you for the intelligence, as I had rather have anything than a Chichester one; I don't recollect that Scrub was a Gardener but mine must *[be]*. No Schoolmaster has yet offer'd his services.
I hope to hear from you soon & am Yours Affectionately, Sarah Smith
April 20th, 1796.

Letters from Isabella Maria Hurst, Robert Henry Hurst and Sarah Smith to Maria Hurst from Chichester, dated 30 and 31 October 1796.

Chichester, October 30 1796
My dear Mamma,
   I am very much disappointed at not seeing you at Michalmas but am very happy to find the time of going home draws near. My cousin Mary is very well after her journey and desires her duty to you and Papa. I must now conclude with love to Papa and sisters. I am your dutiful daughter, Isabella Maria Hurst.

Hon^d Madam,

Your kind letter was very acceptable to me and so was the goose I was at my Aunts when they arrivd & I woud give one to my cross Master. I do assure you I think it has made him better & if you had a nother Goose to send him he woud be quite good. I am a special good boy my Aunt says so. With Duty to papa and love to sisters I have the honor to be your dutifull son Robert Henry Hurst.

Dear Mrs. Hurst,

Maria and Robert are both well and have spoken for themselves, they complain terribly of my pens & in truth not without reason for they are very bad. Mrs Eversfield sent the Goose and desir'd me to drink tea with her, I obey'd the summons and Robert went with me, the old lady was quite well after her journey, & looks as though she wou'd return to Den several years longer.[531]   Your letter was so long in coming I had almost given up both the principal & the substitute, & am sorry it has ended in being disappointed of all my company except Mary Hammond who arriv'd last Thursday.[532] She came to London with Jonathan[533] & his wife & left her Mother but indifferent, & I cannot expect she will permit Mary to stay the Winter as was intended. I am not surpris'd that my Aunt Wicker is not inclin'd to leave her House, as Horsham must be a much alter'd place, and I fear you will find it still worse when your Barracks have got all their inhabitants, these are evils which a peace will lessen if there is one.[534] At this season of the year I shall not insist on my Brother's taking me to Wales. We eat your goose yesterday & thought it the best we had ever tasted. I was going to write a formal complaint against Sir Cecil's tenants for not having sent me any game, I have not seen a partridge this year, but last Thursday farmer Curzen's son brought me a nice young Hare and Woodcock, & told me they had no partridges bred on the estate.[535] With love to my brother & the Children I am

Yours Affectionately,

Sarah Smith

Chichester October 31st 1796

---

531 Miss Olive Eversfield, sister of Sir Charles Eversfield, had been left a life interest in the Denne estate. She was born in 1713 and died in 1803, so Sarah was right about her longevity!

532 Mary Hammond was Sarah's niece — daughter of her sister Molly who had married John Hammond of Great Marlow, Buckinghamshire.

533 Jonathan Hammond, Sarah's nephew, was the Rector of Penshurst, Kent. It seems likely that he obtained the living because his uncle Robert was the trustee of John Shelley Sidney of Penshurst Place.

534 Military barracks were built in Horsham in 1796 as part of the preparations to withstand a possible French invasion.

535 In 1796 Robert Hurst was acting as steward of the Parham estate for Sir Cecil Bishopp, 8th Bt., who was abroad.

Letter from Sarah Smith to her brother Robert, written from Chichester, dated 19 May 1797

Dear Brother,

I have heard Truth resides at the bottom of a Well, & I believe your advice keeps it company, for tho' it is your business to give it, I have always found it plaguey hard to come at ---- Now I never had any of this scrupulosity about me, whenever my opinion has been ask'd I have given it freely , & a thousand times when it has not, for which of course I have neither been paid nor thank'd; & what is worth, been call'd a meddling fool for my pains, & that most likely will be my fate for what follows, but no matter I must go on to the end of the chapter.

When you first inform'd me you were going to that unlucky Castle of Udolpho,[536] I felt griev'd, tho' I cou'd not tell why, but now you say that it is to be <u>Headquarters for a year</u>, I am both concern'd and surpris'd, your servant certainly got his illness by poking about in its damp holes, and your childrens' had the same cause it is very evident, or it wou'd have attack'd the young ones, they have escap'd for no other reason but not being able to rout about as the eldest did; indeed I hope you will give up this romantic scheme, or I fear some of you will be left in the dreary Caverns.

What can poor Horsham have done to you, if you dislike its military populousness, who ever ran away from their defenders: surely those shou'd not who have families and fortunes to protect. Don't you remember what I told you when you gave up the Sessions that you would not know what tricks to begin; the prediction is verified, in this you are not singular, for I never knew a person relinquish their straight line of successfull business (except from ill health or some such necessity) without wandering strangely: I hope something will bring you back to the right path, if not, I must be content with having made the attempt.

I did not take a moment to <u>ponder</u> about your old House. If you purchase Mr. Smith's[537] I will with the greatest pleasure & gratitude accept it, the minute I can get rid of my own, being certain I shall never have such another offer. But if you & Mrs. Hurst (under whose protection I wish to place myself) desert your post, then I am determin'd to stand my ground, buy the first House in Chichester that will come for five or six hundred; & trust to the chapter of accidents for a three or

---

536 The "*Castle of Udolpho*" is possibly Penshurst Place, where Robert Hurst had lived for a year while the heir, John Sidney Shelley, was serving abroad in the army in 1793. Or it may refer to Castle Goring, the newly built house of Bysshe Shelley near Worthing. It is possible that Bysshe asked Robert Hurst to take care of it at this time, if he planned to be away.

537 "*Mr. Smith's*" house was Park House in Horsham, which Robert bought in 1799. Edmund Smith(e) was not related to Henry Smith's family – he was the son of William Smith, who had inherited property in Kingsfold, near Horsham, from his mother before buying Park House in the 1780s. Edmund married Mary Du Cane, the daughter of Phoebe Tredcroft and Peter Du Cane, in 1794.

four Months' summer residence. I think there is no reason to suppose Mr. Smith will sell his House for less than its value, nor can I find any why you shou'd not give it; if you wish for a gentleman's residence, it is one, compleat in every part, & seems to belong to the estate you are in possession of, so Mark, Cassandra says, if you miss it, you will never meet with the like again. I have wrote the above, that you may ponder before we meet on Monday at my old lodgings, Osborne's Hotel Adelphi, where I shall expect you at about five or six in the evening. I shall be in Town before that time but have some business will take me out an hour or two, necessary to have done that day.

Alas poor Dr. Metcalfe, what a superficial observer I am, having always seen every other part of the Doctor's House, family and person in the nicest order, fool that I was, I never look'd into the Garret, taking for granted it was all the same; well I'll certainly take more care another time, & not venture to sport another person's opinion (my own I have long thought good for nothing) till I have taken an exact inventory of the Garret furniture; and yet to say the truth, it is the middle part of the human fabrick has always attracted my attention; for if the heart is right, the head is seldom very wrong. And per contra I have seen what are call'd clear clean Garrets, when my apartment the heart has been in a sad sad litter'd state. What favourites of Nature must you and I be to have them <u>both</u> in excellent order.

Robert's cough is better, and his earache gone, of course Street has not been near enough to assume his bowing attitude;[538] the old gentleman has not given me an invitation for two reasons, the first and chiefest is, that when he has talked of the hollidays, he has been too engag'd in counting the Months weeks or days to think of taking anybody but Maria in his suite; & at those times he looks as tho' he thought my old Aunt is very convenient here, but I'm sure she is not wanted at Horsham; his other reason is, he heard me promise Mary Hammond that if I went more than ten miles from home this summer it shou'd be to Marlow, so I am much oblig'd to you for your invitation, but shall not accept it this summer. Robert breaks up on Saturday June the 17th, Maria not until the Tuesday following, but I can have her bills ready whenever you chuse to fix.

The Lewes paper did not inform me of <u>Mrs. Slater's death</u>, because I never see it, but Charlotte Trower[539] did, I am truly sorry for her, on her children's account who if they were bad before, will not I fear by this event be made much better: poor cousin John too is ill at Bath. I think your old friend Mr. Bysshe must now feel (if he ever can feel) that it wou'd have been right & comfortable to have made friends of <u>some of his children</u>.[540]

---

538 Sarah's obsequious doctor, James Street, was a surgeon and apothecary of Chichester. His wife was the eldest daughter of John and Helen Catherine Miller of Warnham.

539 Charlotte Trower was the daughter of Sarah's cousin, Elizabeth (Bet) Smith, who had married Thomas Trower. Mrs. Slater was Bet's sister, Sarah.

The Sailors' Ropes are a little splic'd together again by the good Seamanship of Lord Howe,[541] the Fleet sail'd on Wednesday morn with the wind right in their teeth, but I suppose it was thought absolutely necessary to go, & make an enemy's Fleet if they can't find one; we may thank your friends the <u>Foxites and Sheridites</u>[542] for all this, and much more I believe. My respects to all friends in Town, farewell, keep your health and spirits; they will be serviceable whether the Consols rise or fall,

Yours,

Sarah Smith

May 19th 1797   The Fleet is return'd, but all quiet.

---

540 There is some evidence that Bysshe Shelley was angered when his son Philip chose to adopt the name of Sidney after his elder brother, John, succeeded to the Sidney estates in 1793 and had to change his name from Shelley to Sidney. Philip died suddenly at the age of 21 in 1799, and it may be that the breach with his father was never healed. His daughter Ariana eloped when Bysshe opposed her marriage to Captain Francis Aicken. His relationship with the eldest son of his first marriage, Timothy Shelley,which was said to be very close in 1791 when the Sussex estates were resettled, also appears to have deteriorated later. Yet it is clear from his letters to Robert Hurst that he took his parental duties very seriously, so Sarah's comment is perhaps not fully justified.

541 Richard, 1st Earl Howe, (1726-1799) was still the Admiral in nominal charge of the Channel Fleet, though his active service ceased in 1794, the year that he won the battle known as *"The Glorious First of June"*. In 1797, he managed to negotiate a settlement with the Spithead mutineers.

542 Charles James Fox (1749-1806) and Richard Brinsley Sheridan (1751-1816) were leaders of the Whig opposition to the government of William Pitt (the younger), now in power. Fox held radical views on the French Revolution and campaigned against slavery. He was a believer in religious tolerance and individual liberty. Sheridan was a successful playwright with liberal views who entered Parliament in 1780 as M.P. for Stafford. Robert Hurst's patron, Charles, 11th Duke of Norfolk, was (rather surprisingly) a prominent supporter of the Whigs, and angered the King and the government by proposing a toast to *"the sovereignty of the people"*.

Appendix I, Sarah's poems

The Lady's Magazine, or Polite Companion for the Fair Sex, Vol. I, page 255.

To the Honourable Mrs. Stanhope.

Madam,

This is the produce of a female, juvenile pen. If you think it worthy a place in your Magazine, it will very much oblige, Your Constant Reader and Most Humble Servant, Amanda Rustic.

Wild of Sussex, Jan. 15, 1760.

The Consolation

When anxious thoughts oppress the mind,
What charm relief affords?
None we in mirth or music find,
Or pompous flow of words.

Broad laughter may, a while, be clad
In Happiness' array;
But soon the heart, that's truly sad,
Sees Folly fleet away.

The charm of soft, harmonious sounds,
May give a transient ease;
But this relief has narrow bounds,
And ceases soon to please.

In crowded rooms, where Slander keeps
Her universal court;
Envy and Discord never sleep;
Each neighbour's woe is sport.

Can heart-felt sorrow here be lost;
And Happiness be found?
No: — on Detraction's whirlpool tost,
Calm, helpless Peace is drown'd.

Since music, mirth with scandal fail,
And all the senses cloy;
Let me, divinest Friendship hail,
Thy source of lasting joy.

Thy steady beams, like Sol's bright rays,
Are permanent and clear;
Not as the lawless meteor's blaze,
That vanishes in air.

A friend sincere, will kindly treat
Each woe that racks the mind;
The sympathetic heart will beat,
Where Friendship's band's[543] conjoin'd,

Dividing thus the load of grief,
Life's ceaseless care is less;
Her soothing converse yields relief;
Her pity can redress.

The flame of Love, too fiercely warms;
His votaries all repine;
Like lightning, his destructive beams
Oft burn as well as shine.

Since then, through life, no greater bliss,
On strictest search we find;
Hear me, ye powers, continue this,
A Friend of Virtuous Mind.

Sarah recorded that she wrote the poem, *The Consolation*, on 4 November 1759, and it seems very likely that it was inspired by her friendship with Sally Sheppard.

543 Possibly this should be "hand", not "band", as printed.

On 17 January 1760 Sarah said in her diary; "*Write to the proprietors of* The Ladies' Magazine, *on Women's learning, send the verses I fill'd up the Rhymes with, & a poem entitled* The Consolation".. The February 1760 issue of *The Lady's Magazine* carried *The Consolation*, and the diary entry for 11 March 1760 reads; "*Read* The Ladies' Magazine; *the verses & prose I sent subscrib'd Amanda Rustick, are both inserted; some pretty things, well worth perusing*". There is a long letter entitled *On Female Education* in the January issue, but this is signed *Deidamia*, not *Amanda Rustic*, so it is not clear whether or not it can be ascribed to Sarah. But the poem can be confidently attributed to her in the light of the diary entries.

The Sussex Weekly Advertiser, or Lewes Journal, No. 841, Monday, August 9 , 1762.

To the Printer,
Sir, By inserting the following Lines in your next week's paper, you will oblige many of your Female Readers.

The SPINSTER'S Address to the BATCHELORS of SUSSEX, who are qualified, but not willing, to serve in the MILITIA.

> Ye Lads of Sussex! Bold and brave,
> Who wou'd your King and Country save,
> But never strike a Blow;
> Attention lend while we advise,
> Tho' you our trifling sex despise,
> It shall our Valour show.
>
> At *Lewes,* on a stated Day,
> Honour call'd loud, but dire Dismay
> Possess'd your Coward Hearts;
> To catch a Pistol, sword or Gun,
> Wou'd not each Lad of spirit fun,
> And bravely act their parts.
>
> But Sussex's poor defenceless Coast
> Her hardy sons no more can boast,
> The're deaf to Honour's call;
> T'is we must now go forth to fight,
> And do our injur'd country right;
> They shine at Rout and Ball.

T'is true, this dreadful Trade of killing
Might make a powder'd beau unwilling
In Scarlet coat to ride;
But we, inflam'd with martial Fire
To humble France wou'd all aspire,
Were we but qualify'd.

Then to avoid those frightful scars,
The Soldier's Lot, from bloody Mars,
In quiet stay at Home,
Supinely spend your harmless Lives,
Do bolder Things, take us for Wives,
We'll prove how we can Roam.

Tho' order'd from fair Britain's isle,
At War's grim Terrors we shall smile,
So high our courage reaches;
Domestick Business you shall mind,
Our Petticoats we'll leave behind
And willing, take the Breeches.

Revers'd the Scene, you must obey,
No more usurp despotic Sway,
Or Worth so vainly boast;
Silence will best become you now,
For since such puny Hearts you show,
T'is we shall rule the Roast.

We are all fond of Pow'r, you know,
Then cannot bear a Thought so low
As Subalterns to chuse;
We Captains, Majors, Colonels claim,
This is your only Road to Fame,
You dare not then refuse.

Pursue this scheme, Applause you'll gain,
And Sussex's Girls will e'er maintain
The Honour of their Station;

Then future Annals sure will say,
We serv'd our Country ev'ry Way,
With gen'ral Approbation.

Then Sirs, if happiness you prize,
And Wisely chuse what we advise;
Your names (t)o *Lewes* send.
Discard your Fears, a third time meet,
Huzzas shall echo through the Street,
To hail the glorious End.

Sarah's first mention of this poem was on 23 July 1762 when she said "*Write by the assistance of Miss Kitty Mortimer a Burlesque poem on the gentlemen of Sussex being so unwilling to serve in the Militia & offer ourselves in their stead.* She sent a copy of the poem for comment with her letter to Sally Sheppard on 25 July, and on 2 August Sarah wrote "*A letter from my dear friend Sally Sheppard…she returns my Song on the Militia and says t'is very clever*". It must have already been sent to the *Sussex Weekly Advertiser and Lewes Journal* for publication, because on 3 August Sarah said that "*The man brings the Lewes Newspaper, our song was too long to be inserted in this week's paper but will in the next*". This was confirmed in the *Sussex Weekly Advertiser* of 2 August 1762; there is a note at the end of the local Lewes news, which says "*The Lines for a Spinster to the Batchellors of Sussex, concerning the Militia, were too long to be inserted in this week, but shall be in our next*". Sarah and Kitty probably gave the poem to the man Sarah mentioned, who delivered the newspaper every week to her friends in Eastbourne. A note at the end of the paper detailed the arrangements for the publication of "*advertisements*", for which they had to pay 3s.6d. Presumably "*advertisements*" could also include poems written by readers. "*Lewes: Printed by W. Lee, where Advertisements of a moderate length are taken in at 3s.6d. each; and Printing in general is performed in the neatest and most correct manner. Advertisements are also taken in by the Men who carry this paper*".

Other poems written by Sarah, as mentioned in the Diaries;

A Ladder to Preferment *(January 1759)*
Elegy on the death of Mrs. Shelley *(January 1759)*
Verses on the death of the Princess of Orange *(January 1759)*
Ode on Miss Pigott's and Mr. Donall's birthday *(January 1759)*
Verses to Betsy Sheppard on her marriage *(January 1759)* *
Soliloquy by Moonlight *(March 1759)* *

Verses on Mrs. Wicker's leaving snuff *(April 1759)*

Verses on Dr. Smith's opinion of her poem on moonlight *(June 1759)*

Answer from Mr. Harbroe to Miss Hutchinson (in verse) *(July 1759)*

Poem on the folly of being conspicuous *(July 1759)*

Epitaph on Mr. Bridger *(September 1759)*

Acrostic on Captain Smith *(September 1759)*

Acrostic on Miss Tredcroft *(October 1759)*

Verses on Lord George Sackville *(October 1759)*

Elegaic Acrostic on General Wolfe *(November 1759)*

Epitaph on General Wolfe *(November 1759)*

Epigram on the French King *(November 1759)*

The Consolation *(November 1759 - see above)*

Verses on reading *Rasselas (December 1759)*

Verses on retirement *(January 1760)*

Little Cupid turn'd out of his office *(February 1760)*

Acrostic on name of cousin Bet Smith *(August 1760)*

Song on Bet Cook *(August 1760)*

A droll Petition for a Peace *(? renamed* The Wish*) (September 1760)*

History of Sally Sheppard *(December 1760)*

Verses on Sally being no longer her bedfellow *(December 1760)*

Vision on the death of the late brave Admiral Boscawen *(January 1761)* *

(Little) Reason Triumphant *(February 1761)*

Verses on the players, Harding and Lain *(March 1761)*

Acrostic on Eastbourne *(August 1761)*

Elegy on the Snug Mare that was stole *(September 1761)*

Poem for Laura (Miss Gittins) and Cynthia (Miss Stanley) *November 1761)*

(probably renamed The Road to Fame*)*

Song on my Good Neighbours *(December 1761)*

Acrostic on name of cousin George Hurst *(December 1761)*

The Certainty *(January 1762)*

Proclamation for a New Tax on Kissing *(January 1762)*

In vindication of playing cards in Lent *(February 1762)*

Cupid's Ramble *(March 1762 - maybe a new name for the poem written in February 1760)* *

An Ode to Patience *(March 1762)*

The Spinster's Address to the Batchelors of Sussex *(July 1762 - see above)*

Letter in verse to Mrs. Wicker *(August 1762)*

*On 15 March 1762, Sarah wrote; "*Write a copy of a letter to the authors of the Monthly Review desiring their opinion of my poetry, transcribe & send them my Poem to Mrs. Tasker on her marriage, the Midnight Soliloquy, the Vision on the Death of Admiral Boscawen & Cupid's Ramble*". There is no indication that these poems were actually published by *The Monthly Review,* though on 4 April there is a mangled reference on one of the pages that were cut out which may be an allusion to them; "*poems I sent them among them, they are excessive cunning*".

Appendix II - the wills of Sarah Hurst, her father and her husband

Will of Sarah Smith, née Hurst, widow, dated 27 March 1802 (HM MSS Cat. No. 2311)

The last will and testament of me Sarah Smith of Horsham widow of Lieutenant General Henry Smith, Col. Commandant of the Marines.

I give to Elizabeth James (sister), Mary Hammond (sister) Captain John James (nephew) James James attorney of Aylesbury (nephew), the Rev. Jonathan Hammond, Rector of Penshurst (nephew), Richard Hammond, attorney (nephew) and to the eight children of Robert Hurst Esq. (brother) £50 each[544]

To Mr. John Smith of Great East Cheap London (cousin) 20 guineas

To Mrs. Elizabeth Trower (cousin) Miss Mary Smith (cousin) Mr. James Waller (cousin) Mrs. Moore (aunt) Miss Sarah Slater (daughter of cousin Sarah Slater née Smith) Miss Grace (eldest daughter of cousin Mr. John Grace) 10 guineas each

To Mrs. Ann Callant[545] (my much esteemed friend) and Mrs. Joanna Elizabeth Bayley[546] (my respected friend) 5 guineas each

To all servants (if they have lived with me 2 years at the time of my death) I give mourning and 5 guineas each, over and above what wages shall be due to them

To Mary Hammond (niece) £500, all my wearing apparel, my Watch, Rings and Trinkets

All above legacies to be paid in one month after my decease in good and lawfull money of Great Britain by my executor hereafter named.

I constitute and appoint the said Robert Hurst of Horsham Park, Sussex, Executor of this my last Will, and I give to him all the Remainder and Residue of my Worldly Possessions. As witness my hand this 27 day of March, One thousand eight hundred and two.

---

544 One child, Mary Hurst, died in 1805, and so did not benefit.
545 Mrs. Ann Callant lived in Rochester, Kent.
546 Mrs. Joanna Elizabeth Bayly was a cousin of Dr. John Bayly (1735-1815), a much respected physician of Chichester.

In this will, Sarah left legacies to both her sisters, all her nephews and nieces and
most of her cousins, with the exception of Elizabeth Hutchinson (née Tasker)
and William Tasker, the children of her uncle Ellman Tasker and Betsy Sheppard.
However, her aunt, Elizabeth Wicker, had left Elizabeth Hutchinson the house she
lived in, so Sarah probably felt that she was already well provided for. But although
the legacies are many and various, the account books reveal that the "remainder"
of Sarah's estate left to her brother, Robert Hurst, was by far the largest of all the
legacies, amounting to more than £10,000.

Will of Richard Hurst, dated 1778 (from a private collection)

This is the last will and testament of me Richard Hurst of Horsham in the county of
Sussex gentleman. First I direct that all my just debts should be paid and I do hereby
charge all my estates real and personal with the payment of the same. I give and
bequeath unto my wife Mary Hurst the sum of £50 and in the case my son Robert
Hurst does not permit her to live in the house now inhabited by myself I devise unto her
12 guineas a year to be paid unto her as long as she shall live. I give unto my daughter
(sic) Sarah Smith and Mary Hammond £20 apiece to buy them mourning and I desire
my son Robert Hurst will give proper mourning unto my daughter Elizabeth James. I
give unto my daughter Sarah Smith her executors or administrators the sum of £10 a
year to be paid unto her by my son Robert after the death of my said wife Mary Hurst
for and during the life of my said daughter Elizabeth James in trust to pay the said
annuity unto my said daughter Elizabeth James for her separate use notwithstanding
her coverture and her receipt only shall be a good discharge for the same. All the rest
of my estate I give unto my son Robert Hurst his heirs and assigns and I appoint him
executor of this my last will written with my own hand this 4th November 1778. Signed
and sealed Richard Hurst. Witnesses John Pilfold, W. Burges, Henry Martin.

This suggests that Mary Hurst did not enjoy a particularly good relationship with
her son Robert in the provision that Richard Hurst made for her support "in the
case my son Robert Hurst does not permit her to live in the house now inhabited
by myself". Despite his promise to leave Sarah £300 in his will, Richard Hurst only
left her and her sister Mary enough money to buy mourning, probably because he
felt that both had married well and did not need further support. He left an annuity
of £10 to his wayward daughter Elizabeth James, probably because her husband
Will James had been declared bankrupt in March 1774. He left the actual payment
of the money as a charge to Sarah. The property that Richard left to his son Robert
included Daniels, Causeway House, Northlands Farm and the lease of Highlands
Farm, plus money invested in the stocks.

Will of Henry Smith dated 12 April 1790 (from a private collection)
(This is a summary of the main legacies, not a complete transcription).

This is the last will and testament of me Henry Smith now residing in the City of Chichester in the county of Sussex Esq.... the capital sum of seven thousand three hundred and fifty pounds in the 3 per cent Consolidated Annuities now vested and standing in my name ...I will and declare such gift and Bequest upon the trusts... John Smith and Robert Hurst trustees ...unto my dear wife Sarah ..and authorise and permit and suffer her to receive the same for her own use and benefit during her life... and after her death the same sum of £7350 in trust to;

1) John Smith (brother) £1,000 - if dead,[547] to be divided among the children of my niece, Maria (Smith), wife of Robert Hurst, as shall be living, equally at the age of 21.
2) Maria Hurst (niece) £1,000
3) Charles Smith (nephew) £500
4) The Rev. William Smith (nephew) £50
5) Elizabeth, wife of James Waller (niece) £500
6) Harriet Smith (niece) £500
7) Ann Smith (niece) £500
8) Sophia Smith (niece) £500 *(all above children of his elder brother, Adam Smith)*
9) Mary Clinton, widow, (niece) £500
10) John Hannah (nephew) £50
11) Sisters of John Hannah (three nieces) whose Christian names I have not in recollection £200 *(children of his sister Elizabeth who married John Hanna(h) of Westminster)*
12) Lt. John James (nephew to my wife Sarah) £150
13) James James (nephew to my wife Sarah) £100
14) (The Rev.) Jonathan Hammond of Great Marlow (nephew to my wife Sarah) £100
15) Richard Hammond attorney of Tunbridge (nephew to my wife Sarah) £100
16) Mary Hammond (niece to my wife Sarah) £150
17) Jane Symonds (niece) Widow and her three children £600 to remain in trust (after the death of my wife) *(Total £6,950).*

Of the residue, £1400 to Trustees to lay out and invest in the purchase of 3 per cent Consols, and to pay my wife the Interest. After her death, half the interest to

547   John Smith died in 1800, before Sarah, so the £1,000 went to Maria Hurst's children.

be used for the benefit of Elizabeth James widow during her life and the other half to Mary Hammond, wife of John Hammond Gent., for her own use and benefit. The Trustees are allowed to make further investments etc. Wife Sarah appointed sole executrix. Witnesses Edward Johnson, William Lee.

It is perhaps remarkable that Henry provided for his wife Sarah's two sisters, who were each to receive half the interest of the £1,400 left for the support of Sarah, after her death. He also left small legacies to their children. But a significant part of his fortune went to Maria Hurst (née Smith), who was both his niece and his sister-in-law, and her children. He also gave substantial legacies to most of his other nieces and nephews — those who received smaller sums had perhaps received financial help previously.

The Hurst family of Horsham

1 Robert Hurst 1670 - 1729 Tailor
. +Elizabeth Osmer 1677 - 1768 Grandmother of Sarah
.. 2 Thomas Hurst 1703 - apprenticed to an apothecary 1718
.. 2 Robert Hurst 1705 - 1763 Tailor of Salisbury Court, Fleet Street, London(also partner of brother Richard)
.. 2 John Hurst 1707 - 1748 Tailor of Salisbury Court, Fleet Street, London
.. 2 George Hurst 1709 - 1783 Apothecary of Devonshire Street, Holborn
...... +Isabella Lee 1714 - 1793
...... 3 George Hurst 1745 - 1780
...... 3 Arabella / Isabella Hurst 1741 - 1772
.. 2 Richard Hurst 1712 - 1780 Tailor, also said to be "mercer and chapman"
...... +Mary Tasker 1718 - 1783
...... 3 Sarah Hurst 1736 - 1808 the diarist
.... +Henry Smith 1723 - 1794 Lt. General, Colonel Commandant of Marines at Portsmouth 1772-1791
...... 3 Elizabeth (Bet) Hurst 1741 - 1802
.... +William James 1738 - 1794 Butcher - declared bankrupt in March 1774
.... 4 John James 1764 - Captain
.... 4 Elizabeth James 1766 -
.... 4 James James 1769 - Attorney of Aylesbury
...... 3 Mary (Molly) Hurst 1745 - 1823
.... +John Hammond 1732 - 1817 of Marlow, Bucks
.... 4 Jonathan Hammond 1767 - 1819 Rector of St. John Baptist, Penshurst, Kent
.... +Anne Chambers 1775 - 1830 daughter of the Rev. William Chambers
.... 4 Richard Hammond Attorney - worked in the office of William Whitton (Timothy Shelley's London lawyer)
.... 4 Mary Hammond
...... 3 Robert Hurst 1750 - 1843 Barrister, Steward of Duke of Norfolk; Trustee of Shelley and Sidney estates
.... +Maria Smith 1757 - 1851
.... 4 Isabella Maria Hurst 1785 - 1873
.... 4 Sarah Hurst 1787 - 1860
.... +John Stileman Bostock 1787 - Lawyer, clerk to Charles Marshall of Steyning
.... 4 Robert Henry Hurst 1788 - 1857
.... +Dorothea Breynton 1794 - 1826
.... 4 Mary Hurst 1789 - 1805
.... 4 Eliza Hurst 1791 - 1875
.... 4 Harriet Hurst 1792 - 1892
.... 4 Charlotte Sophia Hurst 1795 - 1875
.... +Charles Greenaway 1783 - 1859 of Little Barrington, Glos.
.... 4 John Hurst 1797 - 1881 Rector of Thakeham 1834-1881
.... +Catherine Probyn - 1887
.. 2 Elizabeth Hurst 1714 - 1783
...... +William Smith Upholsterer, of London; lived in Fleet Street
...... 3 John Smith of Great East Cheap
...... 3 Elizabeth Smith
.... +Thomas Trower
.... 4 Charlotte Trower 1771 -
...... 3 Mary Smith
...... 3 Robert Smith
...... 3 William Smith
...... 3 Sarah Smith
.... +- Slater
.. 2 William Hurst 1717 -
.. 2 Sarah Hurst 1719 - 1808 Lived in London and kept house for brother Robert; married after his death in 1763
...... +Will Moore

This chart covers most of the Hurst family mentioned in the
diaries, including those who lived in London. It does not
include Sarah's cousins in Eastbourne, who were descended
from Edward Hurst (1675-1760), brother of Robert.

The Middleton and Tasker family

1 Richard Middleton 1654 - 1703 Gentleman, lived at Whitesbridge, east Horsham
. +Susanna Hall 1668 - 1727
.. 2 Ann Middleton 1691 - 1753
...... +William Tasker 1691 - 1756 Gentleman, of Horsham and Balcombe, clerk to John Linfield the attorney
.... 3 Ann Tasker 1716 - 1783
.... +Thomas Waller 1712 - 1799 Butcher
.... 4 Elizabeth Waller 1752 - 1774
.... 4 James Waller 1758 - 1808 Gentleman, surgeon of Horsham Common
.... +Elizabeth Groombridge
.... *1st Wife of James Waller:
.... +Elizabeth Smith - 1807
.... 3 Mary Tasker 1718 - 1783
.... +Richard Hurst 1712 - 1780 Tailor, also said to be "mercer and chapman"
.... 4 Sarah Hurst 1736 - 1808 the diarist
.... +Henry Smith 1723 - 1794 Lt. General, Colonel Commandant of Marines at Portsmouth 1772-1791
.... 4 Elizabeth (Bet) Hurst 1741 - 1802
.... +William James 1738 - 1794 Butcher - declared bankrupt in March 1774
.... 4 Mary (Molly) Hurst 1745 - 1823
.... +John Hammond 1732 - 1817 of Marlow, Bucks
.... 4 Robert Hurst 1750 - 1843 Barrister, Steward of Duke of Norfolk; Trustee of Shelley and Sidney estates
.... +Maria Smith 1757 - 1851
.... 3 John Tasker 1719 -
.... 3 Elizabeth Tasker 1723 - 1802
.... +William Wicker - 1751
.... 3 William Tasker 1725 -
.... 3 Priscilla Tasker 1727 - 1802
.... +Robert Grace 1730 - 1798 "the younger". Tanner and currier
.... 4 Robert Grace 1756 - 1807
.... 4 Elizabeth Grace 1758 - 1827
.... +William Rowland 1758 - Bricklayer
.... 4 Mary Grace 1759 - 1759
.... 4 Priscilla Grace 1760 - 1760
.... 4 Henry Grace 1763 -
.... +Sarah Ansell
.... 4 John Grace 1764 - 1833 Currier
.... +Sarah Colven 1775 - 1821
.... 4 Sarah Grace 1767 - 1799
.... 4 Harriet Grace 1773 -
.... +George Michell
.... 3 Ellman Tasker 1729 - 1772 Tallow chandler
.... +Elizabeth Sheppard 1730 - 1819
.... 4 Elizabeth Tasker 1761 - 1845
.... +Thomas Hutchinson 1741 - 1812 Vicar (or Rector) of Candlesby, Lincs. 1783; Vicar of Beeding 1787
.... 4 William Tasker 1763 - 1807 Yeoman
.. 2 Mary Middleton 1693 - 1725
...... +Henry Michell 1681 - 1717 Gentleman, of North Heath
.... 3 John Michell 1710 - 1711
.... 3 Henry Michell 1711 - 1728
.... 3 Mary Michell 1714 - 1794
.... +Edward Tredcroft
.... 4 Phoebe Phillips Tredcroft 1743 - 1831
.... 4 Nathaniel Tredcroft 1747 - 1825
.... 4 Edward William Tredcroft 1749 - 1822
.... 4 Mary Catherine Tredcroft 1751 - 1835
.... 4 Charlotte Tredcroft 1754 - 1829

This chart shows how the Hursts and Tredcrofts were related

The family of Henry Smith

1 William Griffith - 1719/20 Rector of West Hoathly.
. +Anne Nye 1661 - 1730
.. 2 Elizabeth Griffith 1685 - 1780
...... +John Smith 1683 - 1758 London merchant; appointed quarter-master in the Army by Rich, 5th Viscount Irwin, in 1715
.... 3 Adam Smith 1710 - 1711
.... 3 Elizabeth Smith 1712 -
.... +John Hannah
.... 4 John Hannah
.... 4 Nancy Hannah
.... 3 Adam Smith 1716 - 1796 Linen-draper of Golden Square, and later property owner in London
.... +Mary (Smith) 1729 - 1804
.... 4 Maria Smith 1757 - 1851
.... +Robert Hurst 1750 - 1843 Barrister, Steward of Duke of Norfolk; Trustee of Shelley and Sidney estates
.... 4 Charlotte Smith mentioned on Smith memorial in Horsham Parish Church - died young
.... 4 William Smith 1761 - 1846 Curate of Thakeham for the Rev. Roger Clough 1789-1805
.... 4 Ann Smith - 1828
.... +Edward Roberts
.... 4 Elizabeth Smith - 1807
.... +James Waller 1758 - 1808 Gentleman, surgeon of Horsham Common
.... 4 Charles Smith Linen-draper of King Street, St. James (earlier Golden Square)
.... +Caroline Bakewell - 1842
.... 4 Harriet Smith 1770 - 1800
.... 4 Sophie Smith 1771 - 1851
.... 3 Griffith (Merchant) Smith 1720 - 1763 Merchant, said to be in the wine trade
.... 3 Henry Smith 1723 - 1794 Lt. General, Colonel Commandant of Marines at Portsmouth 1772-1791
.... +Sarah Hurst 1736 - 1808 the diarist
.... 3 Charles Smith 1725 - 1789 Linen-draper of Conduit Street, St.George's, Hanover Square, London
.... 3 John Smith 1727 - 1800 merchant, of Lad Lane, City of London
.. 2 Gainor Griffith 1687 - 1698
.. 2 William Griffith 1690 - 1696
.. 2 Henry Griffith 1692 - 1747 Mercer
...... +Elizabeth Burnell 1693 - 1747
.... 3 Elizabeth Griffith 1720 -
.... 3 Har(r)y Griffith 1722 - Mercer
.... 3 William Griffith 1723 -
.... 3 Charles Griffith 1725 -
.... 3 John Griffith 1728 -
.... 3 Ann Griffith 1730 -
.. 2 Anne Griffith 1693/94 - 1767
...... +Edward Curtis 1696 - 1767 Stationer
.... 3 William Curtis 1730 - 1734
.... 3 Edward Curtis 1732 - 1733
.... 3 Ann Curtis 1736 - 1778
.... +William Murrell - 1795 Clockmaker
.... 4 John Murrell 1762 -
.... 4 William Murrell 1763 -
.... 4 Ann Murrell 1764 - 1768
.... 4 Henry Murrell 1765 -
.... +Elizabeth Griffith 1779 - 1847
.... 4 Ann Murrell 1768 -
.... 4 Fanny Murrell 1770 -
.... 3 John Curtis 1739 -
.. 2 Gainor Griffith 1698 - 1772
...... +Robert Grace 1689 - 1775 "the elder". Tanner.
.. 2 Thomas Griffith 1701 - The " Dr. Griffith" of the diaries, possibly in holy orders
.. 2 Aprincesse Griffith 1707 -
...... +Nathaniel Johnson of Henfield

INDEX OF PEOPLE, PLACES AND PUBLICATIONS
mentioned in Sarah's diaries and letters

People mentioned in Sarah's diaries and letters are shown in normal script; places in capital letters; plays, publications, inns and ships in italics; authors in italics with surname in capital letters. All places mentioned are in Sussex unless otherwise indicated.